EVERY DAY EXCELLENCE

A DAILY GUIDE TO GROWING

DEDICATION

This book is dedicated to those that came before me, and lit the way as the Student Lamp of Pi Kappa Phi Alpha Tau did for me. Hopefully I can spark some light for you so that you can brighten the world.

I have too many people to thank individually, too many influences to say "So and So inspired this."

So I want to, in broad swathes, thank groups, with a couple of specific shout outs.

Marcus Aurelius, Jesus Christ, The Buddha. Stan "The Man" Lee, Einstein, Bruce Lee, The Greatest (Ali). So many others who I never met that have passed and left behind teachings for the future.

With these luminaries I never met, I include my grandparents, parents, aunts and uncles, both blood and by choice that have helped shape me. Family is literally part of my DNA.

To my brothers and sisters and friends and contemporaries that have challenged me, especially those like Rich Kramer and Lauren Taylor (the Snowciopath) and Ant DeGuilio that we have lost. Through challenges we grow stronger, and sometimes when we are not strong enough, we need the help of our peers.

To all the kids, whether it is my own sons or their friends that seem to be my additional children, or the Cub Scouts or the other young ones I can influence over time.

To Damaris for all the work she did on this book and over the years with me, rarely recognized. Same too with Athena.

And most of all to my Muse. You know who you are.

I will always love you A, no matter what.

Joe

FOREWORD

Ryan Holiday will probably never read this, but it was his book *The Everyday Stoic* that directly gave rise to this work. I have followed him on YouTube for a while, and my day begins by grabbing my coffee (a cup always left to prime the day) and reading his words. Then I do a workout of between ten and thirty minutes to awaken my body as my mind and soul (no goose eggs!).

As I was working out (listening to a different Stoic, Jocko Willink, on one device and some Black Sabbath on another) I had my EUREKA moment, put the kettlebell down and came up to type.

Excellence is a habit. Habits need to be acted upon every daily. Every day we have to fight the entropy of age, the creeping chaos of the world. Each day we must make the investment of time and energy, just to maintain where we are relative to inflation, progress, and our own dreams.

And if we invest just a bit more of ourselves than that minimum, we can improve daily. Slowly, inexorably, polishing the jewel that is us. It is the little daily sacrifices and choices that compound over years and decades to make us priceless sparkling multifaceted works of nature and nurture. So today, make the better choices. That's all you have to do. Just do what you should, today.

This work is a guidebook, a daily to do (or not do, or think, or whatever) to help you make the little choices and changes in direction that bend the curve of your career and life. It is simple but not easy, but hopefully in 366 (or 367) days you look back and say "worth it!"

Ben Franklin had his 13 Virtues that he worked on (Temperance, Silence, Order, Resolution, Frugality, Industry, Sincerity, Justice, Moderation, Cleanliness, Tranquility, and Humility) in a rotational basis. With our Scouts we discuss each week a different aspect of the Scout Law (A Scout is Trustworthy, Loyal, Helpful, Friendly, Courteous, Kind, Obedient, Cheerful, Thrifty, Brave, Clean, and Reverent). This book won't be quite as structured, nor have The Daily Stoic's monthly theme of exploration because I've found that by exploring a concept, then another slightly related, then another in a more free-form chain of thought (without going full on James Joyce Ulysses) and cycling back over time will give a more organic growth and development model.

HOW TO USE THIS BOOK

Don't buy it, put it on a coffee table or desk or shelf, and let it collect dust. That's not going to help you.

No matter what version you use (electronic, audial, physical), Every Day Excellence is meant to be consumed like that: every day. Each morning, because that gives you an opportunity to reflect and apply the ideas. If you wait until after dinner, you only have a few hours to take action with the tool of that day before turning in. Better to pick up the new tool early, to play with it for the entire day in different ways so that you are comfortable with it by the end of your day.

Reviewing the page in the evening is not a bad idea. You might even see the exact same words with different eyes based upon experience. The Stoic saying "no man can walk in the same river twice" applies to this book too.

If you have the physical copy of this, mark it up. My old books look old because they have been read and reread, corners bent, writing in the margins. I also tend to have an index card or five handy because very often an idea I get from someone else initiates a cascade of other ideas. Dozens of blog posts have been inspired from something I read or heard or saw, as have countless poems I have composed. Some of them don't even suck!

For the other media, still keep something that you can take notes on. Highlight the electronic copy. Dictate notes on your phone. Whatever will help you to take action and improve today, do it!

Try getting a friend or co-worker to discuss ideas with.

Maybe someone will put together a discussion group online. (Or check out this book's companion website, www.everyday-excellence.com, for our forums!)

Explore the concepts and apply them, because excellence is reflected in your actions, and every day you can exhibit this to the world and yourself.

OPEN DOORS LEAD TO OPEN MINDS

JRRT

01 JANUARY
"Begin with the end in mind."

Stephen Covey

What do you want to achieve this year? I mean really achieve. Not the "Oh, it would be nice to have (or do) X", but the things that are truly going to fire you up? What is going to excite you so that you want to get up early and hit it?

Is it something physical like Run The Year or a Ragnar or a belt promotion in martial arts or a century ride on the bike?

Is it a business goal like "qualify for Million Dollar Round Table", become a member of your Company's exclusive Club, or generate a certain amount of revenue?

Are you studying for the Bar or your Boards, CFP or CPA or CFA exam? Working on finishing your degree?

Spending more time with those you love?

Breaking an addiction?

Taking time for yourself?

What do you want to do?

Write down some goals below, on index cards (or Post It notes), and put them where you will see them frequently. Save your goals on your computer home screen if you really want to be reminded. Share what you want to do with those you spend time with, so they can support you and help you.

Physical Goal:
Work Goal 1:
Learning Goal:
Personal Goal:
Work Goal 2:

02 JANUARY

"Absorb what is useful, discard what is not, add what is uniquely your own."

Bruce Lee

Throw something out today.

Remove something that does not bring you joy.

Clean your desk off.

Throw away that ratty old shirt, or clear your closet and donate stuff to charity.
Get rid of something that bothers you, be it physical or a person that sucks your energy away like a psychic vampire.

Remove something, anything to make your life and business better today. Could be a commitment to something you don't really care about, a couple of contacts in your phone that are filled with negative emotions instead of positive ones, that dating app that tempts you but adds nothing long range to your happiness.

Discard something.

We spend so much time trying to add to what we have, instead of removing the extraneous. Michaelangelo did not build up the David from pieces, but removed the stone from the block to reveal the inner beauty. Remove the stones from around your masterpiece.

Action Item: Look around and get rid of some stuff (physical or virtual) that could be your Albatross.

03 JANUARY
"Honesty is the first chapter in the book of wisdom."

Thomas Jefferson

Being honest with ourselves is critical to helping us remove weaknesses, build strengths, and move towards the future we want.

Great athletes (Ali, Gretzky, Jordan, Brady et al) honestly assess where they (and their teams) were regularly to see where they needed to improve to win and win again. They would watch tape of their worst losses to fire them up, to see their weaknesses, and find things that others were able to exploit so that they could correct them and come back better, more complete, and re-invented if need be to get back to the top of their mountain.

Do you "watch the tape"? Do you debrief after a meeting to uncover what went right or wrong? "After Action Debrief" is SOP (Standard Operating Procedure) in the military, is it SOP in your office? Why not?

Be honest about how you treat your family. We all get tired (especially around the Holidays), and our emotional reserves can dip to critical levels. If you are in this headspace, take a timeout to recharge (even if it is just locking yourself in the bathroom). Honestly assess your current level of stress and tolerance, as it can create a negative feedback loop. Even workaholics spend as much time away from work as at it, and our families are the support network we need at times.

Looking in the mirror unflinchingly is what separates the average from the excellent. I know I suck in certain areas, and tough love is being told I have correctable flaws in certain areas so I can work on my numerous shortcomings. I can also further improve my good aspects to become world class, so the combo of raising my floor in the low points and building up the stronger areas raises my standards and my overall game. Look at how LeBron James or Derek Jeter or Evander Holyfield improved aspects of their performances over time, eliminating weaknesses and becoming more complete competitors. I bet the top performers in your company were not born fully formed superstars, but evolved over time into the models that are held up for emulation.

Action Item: Get a piece of paper (or a white board) and perform a SWOT analysis on yourself. Strengths, Weaknesses, Opportunities, Threats. Be brutally honest.

04 JANUARY
"Do what you can, with what you have, where you are."

Theodore Roosevelt

Don't have all the tools you think that you need to get the job done? "Bully!" old Teddy would say, or "Good" Jocko Willink (US Navy Seal, retired) would tell you. Because it will force you to be more creative and figure out a different way to accomplish your mission.
"Necessity is the mother of invention" is something we have heard since we were kids. Or as my mom would tell me: figure it out.

You don't have all the answers today. You don't have the crystal ball to see what is going to happen in the halls of power or with the stock market or even within your company or home. Doesn't mean you throw up your hands and say "oh well". You do what you can.
Don't have all the info? Make the best decision that you can with what you have.
Don't have all the money to implement that full awesome marketing plan? How can you implement the first steps of it, or create a proxy, or do something that moves you in the right direction?

Do something.

Move in the right direction, because it is better than wasting a day whining, or worse yet giving up at the first sign of difficulty. That's not how greatness operates. That's not how progress works.

Take action, even if it is small and seemingly insignificant in the grand scheme of things. Every blow of the axe on the tree or drop of water on the rock has an effect, even if you can't see it. Do what is within your power, something seemingly as tiny as writing a letter to a Congressman (or Congresswoman), or posting a video online, can be the first stone in an avalanche that changes your world.

Can't run a marathon? Go around the block once.

Study for ten minutes if you can't get an hour to do so.

Don't eat that yummy cupcake, but have a healthy snack instead.

Do the best you can. That's what we are all really trying to do.

Action Item: what is one small thing you can do today towards your big goals for the year? As Nike says: just DO IT!

05 JANUARY

"You don't have to see the full staircase. Just take the first step."

Dr. Martin Luther King Jr.

Zero to One is the title of a book by Peter Thiel (co-founder of Paypal), and represents the infinite difference between nothing and anything. That first sale, that first half mile in a fitness journey, the signing up for a class or investing in your professional development by buying this book and opening it.

Sometimes, we have to operate on faith. Faith that that first meeting for coffee could spark something. Faith that you will have the strength to give up the addiction of cigarettes or gambling or whatever. Faith in your sales cycle or the savings plan or the workout program from a trainer. Have faith that you can finish what you start, and complete that journey even if you can't see every step of the path.

Start.

Then keep going.

David Goggins talks about tricking your mind, of telling yourself "I'll just do a nice easy X (two miles, couple of calls, quick practice session, write one paragraph, insert your own little task here)", and then as you get into it you keep going and can finish the task (long training run, writing this book, earning your designation or hitting that Big Hairy Audacious Goal {BHAG}).

How do you eat an elephant? One bite at a time. Start up that staircase. Take that first step.

Action Item: look at that huge task you want to avoid. Break the start of it into several distinct, tiny steps. Do those.

06 JANUARY
"If you're going through hell, keep going!"

Sir Winston Churchill

Right now might suck.

Typically just under a week into some new endeavor it starts getting to be a drag: you're making the sacrifices and not seeing results. Your muscles hurt from going to the gym and you're tired but haven't lost an ounce (that's why gyms are becoming empty a week after New Year's), you've made the outreach efforts at work but haven't generated any revenue, you crack the book again and it still is all gobbledygook to you.

Don't stop.

This is the Valley of Death, where others give up on their dreams because they realize that it is work. You are going through a "J Curve", getting/feeling worse before becoming better and having a much better trajectory for the year and the future.

"I could just skip this morning." Don't! It takes at least seven days for something to start becoming a habit, you are getting there!

Don't quit.

Survive.

Make it through.

You have a 100% track record of surviving bad days. You can quit, but not today. Just do what you have to, today. Hang on a little longer. One more day of doing it. Quitting is the only final, irrevocable loss.

Get up out of the bed, off of the canvas that you've been knocked down on and fight just a little more.

Action Item: don't quit today. It's that simple, and that hard. Don't quit today.

07 JANUARY

"Music can change the world."

Ludwig Von Beethoven

When the Yankees blared *Enter Sandman*, the opposing team knew the game was basically over because the ONLY unanimous Hall of Famer Mo Rivera was coming in to put them to sleep.

Hulk Hogan, Randy Savage, Ric Flair. The Ultimate Warrior. All great wrestlers basically had a great theme song as their entrance music, where they would hit the ring and it was SHOWTIME!

The opening strains of *Princes of the Universe* by Queen flip my switch and I am ready to GO, be it on stage or for a huge pitch or to hammer out six miles. That song (the theme from Highlander) taps into my primal capabilities and all fear disappears, all doubt is extinguished and I instantly enter a state of Flow.

And when things suck? Might take all of fifteen seconds to shake me out of the funk and engage.

What is your song? What flips your switch, lights you up, makes you hit the ring like you are going to win the title and nothing is standing in your way?

The Rocky Theme with the horns? *Eye of The Tiger*? *Fight Song* by Rachel Patten? Handel's *Allelujah Chorus* from The Messiah? *Lose Yourself* by Eminem? Volbeat's *A Warrior's Call*, or The Dropkick Murphys' *The Warrior's Code*?

Music soothes the savage beast, or can set it free so you can power through the tough days.

Action Item: find your song, and start playing it over and over!

08 JANUARY

"Those who wish to sing will always find a song."

Swedish proverb

Have you played your song yet today?

Do so.

Feel how you get excited, your heart races a little and you actually relax a bit but are ready to perform, be it cranking out some writing or analysis or getting in front of that client or your boss?

Now you have a song in your head and in your heart.

It can often be that easy to change our mood, to improve our outlook.

"You may bind up my leg, but not even Zeus has the power to break my spirit." Epictetus, Stoic philosopher (who was lame from having his leg broken, btw).

"Everything can be taken from a man but one thing: the last of the human freedoms—to choose one's attitude in any given set of circumstances, to choose one's own way." Viktor E. Frankl

Chose to be happy, or chose to be miserable. The former is more fun, more attractive, better for your physical health.

Choosing to be happy takes a little more mental effort sometimes than just falling to the morose wayside and eating a pint of Ben and Jerry's while huddling in a blanket fort and hoping the monsters go away, but it is better in the long term to exert the effort and learn how to be happy inside even in adversity.

Action Item: make a list of five things that make you smile.
OR
Pull up *Always Look on the Bright Side of Life* by Monty Python, and whistle along. Try not to smile - because it's impossible!

09 JANUARY

"Discipline equals Freedom."

Jockok Willink, US Navy SEAL (ret.)

Discipline equals freedom.

If you have the discipline to work hard, you have the freedom to have fun.

If you knuckle down and study, you pass those exams and make more money.

If you have the discipline to workout early, you get an endorphin rush and your pants fit better and you are more productive throughout the day and earn various rewards.

"The successful person has the habit of doing the things failures don't like to do." - EM Gray, from The Common Denominator of Success.

Discipline is a cross functional skill that impacts all dimensions of our work and life. Those who have the discipline to stick with the diet are more likely to have the discipline to do the work in the office. Those that have the discipline to make their bed every morning are more likely to have the attention to detail in other areas. Those who workout regularly are more productive and happier and resilient.

Willpower creates opportunities over time, the stick to it attitude that solves problems and others look to in tough times. The ability to suck it up and do what you have to, not necessarily what you want to, is the difference between champs and chumps.

Discipline equals freedom.

Action Item: look in the mirror. What is ONE tiny thing you can do every day, no matter how seemingly insignificant? Every day, no matter what? Start doing that thing.

10 JANUARY
"Amateurs sit and wait for inspiration, the rest of us just get up and go to work."

Stephen King

One of my Mexican friends told me his father told him at 10: GOYA! Get Off Your Ass! That guy is now incredibly successful and has built I don't know how many successful companies.

Sloth is not a cute cuddly animal but one of the Seven Deadly Sins.

Discipline removes the feeling from getting your work done. It doesn't matter if you FEEL like it, the cows need to be milked and the bread baked and the shop opened and the client served. A crying hungry wet baby isn't going to change themselves or feed themselves if you are tired or sore or sick or just don't feel like it.

I often don't feel like doing what I have to, but I do it. In fact, some core activities I need to do I absolutely HATE! But I do them because they need to be done. Late in any professional athlete's season they are banged up, tired, maybe mentally drained.

They get up and go to work.

Professional writers sit down and crank out words for an hour or a full page every day, even if they are uninspired. They grind it out. Stephen King has written over 80 books, and I bet you he didn't feel like writing many days.

Don't wait for motivation, just get moving and you will move in the right direction towards your goals even if not at full speed.

Action Item: that thing that you are avoiding because you don't feel like it? Do it.

11 JANUARY

"Amateurs do something until they get it right, professionals do it until they can't do it wrong."

Lenny Moore

About five years into my professional career, hall of famer Lenny Moore came and spoke to my office (the Managing Partner was a die-hard JETS fan. Some people are doomed to root for teams that will always break their heart, but they deserve respect because they are true to their beliefs). Moore said the phrase above, and it resonated with me, and forced me to look at how I prepared and changed the curve of my career by forcing me to think like a Hall of Famer and demand my daily focus to become excellent. Professionals can't do it wrong because they have done it perfectly so much they know no other way.

Do you want your heart surgeon to be the doctor that has done it once, in med school a decade plus ago, and got a passing grade? Or would you want someone that has practiced it so much they could literally mend your broken heart with their eyes closed? I hired someone to do some work on my 130 year old house. I was not messing with a slate roof fifty feet off the ground, and anything with water or electricity I would outsource because the downside risk is too great. So when I found the one guy literally sitting there reading *Plumbing for Dummies*, you can understand that I was not happy and fired the amateur immediately. I paid for professionals and expected it.

Now for role reversal. Have you practiced your craft, whatever it is, to the point where it is literally impossible for you to not perform at the highest level?

Why not?

Is what you do, be it financial planning or teaching or law or parenting not that important? Have *Professional Pride*, knowing that your name is going on that work. And that the client has chosen you and your service over others, so you have a moral obligation to do your absolute best for them because if you are doing the work that means some other person is not, and that client is trusting that you will give them your best.

Do it. No matter what you do, if you are collecting a paycheck for it, put your soul into it. Give your best efforts, not just in the moment but in all the moments leading up to it. Prepare for excellence. As Another Hall of Famer Emmitt Smith said: all men are born equal, some just train harder in the offseason. Game time is NOT practice time, it's Show Time.

Action Item: open your calendar. Book out "practice time" to develop your craft, at least 30 minutes at a time, three times a week for the next two months.

12 JANUARY
"Practice? Are we talking about practice?"

Allen Iverson

Allen Iverson had a cavalier attitude about preparation. He made the Basketball Hall of Fame, but never won the championship.

Michael Jordan would practice every moment as if it were Game 7 of the Finals, and heaven help you if you didn't practice like that because he would rip into you and bring you up to that standard or destroy you. Michael Jordan has six rings and is in the debate for the GOAT (Greatest of All Time) in his sport. He knew the value of practice, and imposed it on those around him. The results are in the record books.

Talent will only take you so far. To the verge of greatness, maybe even in to the foothills of the mountains of the elite. But to climb the mountain, to reach the pinnacle of what you do? Practice is what separates the Champions from the good, the Best from the Rest.

Squeeze more out of whatever god given talent you have by sharpening your skills. Reduce the holes in your game; be it confidence in front of clients, technical knowledge, your vocabulary, or some other particular to your development in your field.

Malcom Gladwell is famous for the "10,000 Hour Rule" of practice, that it takes 10,000 hours of focused practice to master something, be it piano or martial arts or selling.

How close are you to this threshold?

Well, get to work working on yourself.

Action Item: look back at your SWOT analysis and see what Weaknesses you can start improving through consistent, mindful practice. Start practicing until it is off the Weakness list.

13 JANUARY

"The victorious General performs many calculations in his castle ere the battle..."

Sun Tzu, *The Art of War*

Ever have that client catch you flat footed by asking "Well, what if we do X instead?" And you are flabbergasted and flustered because you don't know the answer to the question, even though it is only a small change in one of the variables.

What if you were able to say "Great question! I actually ran that scenario, and it changes the need from A to B. So to solve that, we still need to do Steps 1 and 2, but at this level instead of that level."

Hmmm, do you think that client might say internally "Wow, cool they are on top of it! I am definitely doing what this professional suggests because they anticipated variations and changes." They probably wouldn't crystalize their thoughts to that extent, but they would on a gut level feel trust in you because you anticipated potential alternatives and explored them for your client.

Play around with the numbers and do not one calculation but a hundred or more. It's not like you have to use a slide rule or punch cards: your computing power is great enough now to run a thousand simulations before you finish that sip of coffee. Play the "What If" game with the current scenario, and change the parameters multiple times so that not only do you have the output calculations for your client but you develop an intuitive feel and start along the path of wisdom. Know where the dangers are before going to battle. That way you avoid them and don't take an arrow to the knee. Action item: set aside time to play with the numbers, to say "What If?"

Action Item: set time aside to play with the numbers, to say "What If?"

14 JANUARY
"Better to fight for something, than to live for nothing."

General George S. Patton

What do you stand for? What are you willing to fight for?

Is it love? Respect? Your kids to have a better life? The survival of your business, or that promotion? What fortifies your courage so that you can take the actions that make you uncomfortable, because you believe in it more than the pain and heartache and sacrifice needed to achieve it?

Most people say they would die for their kids, but would you LIVE for them? Give up smoking or any other addiction, eat healthy and exercise? Wake up early to study so you can get that degree or designation or knowledge to advance your career? THAT is fighting for them.

Fight for your country? Do you vote? Volunteer to improve the local community? Get involved in the School Board or Planning Board or other way to serve on the local, state, or beyond to not just fight the external enemies but to help improve the lot of your fellow citizens? That is fighting for your country too.

Are you willing to push yourself beyond your comfort zone to help grow your business or improve your career outlook? Are you willing to have that difficult discussion with the coworker or client, even if it scares you and you have to fight your instinct to back away quietly? Or will you stand up and say what they need to hear, not what they want to hear, because it is the right thing for the organization and individual?

Will you tell the person you love that they are screwing up, even if they get pissed at you? Do you love them enough to fight for the best version of them, even willing to fight them for their own good? That is truly living for another.

Action Item: what is that one difficult conversation that you've been avoiding? Go have it. Fight for what you believe, even if you're scared.

15 JANUARY

"Courage is being scared to death and saddling up anyway."

John Wayne

We've all been scared, whether it is of failure, of asking out the pretty girl/handsome guy, or taking that risk in business. We were all terrified in the days following 9/11 or the depths of the Coronavirus pandemic.

Did you curl up and hide? Or did you do what you had to do even if your knees were knocking and your palms sweaty?

When you asked out the good-looking person and they turned you down, did they ridicule you in front of everyone, take out a TV ad and tell the world you are a loser? Probably not.
Will that one risk destroy your career or business? Probably not. But what if it worked out?
Did you fall while learning to ride a bike? Probably, but you kept trying and now you can do so.

Every toddler has ended up on their butt over and over and over again. But did you give up on walking? Thought not.

So why are you afraid now? It's not like whatever you are facing is life or death in almost all situations. Nor is it a 15 foot tall hairy spider with glowing eyes dripping venom that wants to rip out your one eye and eat it while you watch them with the other one. So don't be that scared.

There is an old Stoic exercise that Tim Ferriss (author of *The 4 Hour Work Week, Tools of Titans* and others) adopts: fearcasting. What is the absolute worst thing that can happen? In almost every case it's not fatal, so you can recover. You might lose a few bucks, or have a few moments of embarrassment. Maybe get some scrapes and a great story to tell later.

As Chow says in The Hangover "But did you die?"

Face that fear. Saddle up cowboy.

Action Item: do one thing that scares the poop out of you, every day.

16 JANUARY

"True Cowboys are the ones who aren't afraid to get dirty."

Lane Frost

Do you do the crap jobs?

In many martial arts dojos or dojangs, it is the senior student or assistant Instructors that clean the floor.

First one in office? Make the coffee, even if you occupy the corner office.

No job is beneath you, if it needs to be done and makes things better.

Pick up that piece of litter on the street.

Keanu Reeves was sitting in a café when a lady's car broke down. The superstar jumped up and pushed her vehicle, because that was the right thing. The lady? A young and not yet famous Octavia Spencer, future star of *Hidden Figures* and an Oscar winner for *The Help*. She has adopted his attitude and pays it forward and helps others.

Help that old lady across the street like a Cub Scout would.

Mess in the bathroom? Take 30 seconds and straighten it up.

Take off your coat, roll up your sleeves, and pitch in a bit.

Action Item: do something for someone else today that isn't in your job description and that will help them out or brighten their day.

17 JANUARY
"I can only show you the door. You're the one that has to walk through it."

Morpheus, The Matrix

Will you take the red pill and change your reality, or do you want to be plugged back into The Matrix and forget everything you have been exposed to?

Will you make the choice to be great, or will you choose to fail? Each is the outcome of choices, multiple little choices you get to make constantly.

You have been presented the tools to build a tremendous future. People in your life that will assist you and teach you and believe in you. The entire internet, filled with motivation and information. This book. You.

Will you pick up the tools and build a glorious future? Or will you leave them on the ground to rust and rot?

Pick up the tools, walk through the open door, and go build your empire.

Action Item: choose one tool or technique that you ahve been told about and not put into action yet. Start using it today.

18 JANUARY
"Look on every exit as being an entrance somewhere else."
Tom Stoppard

One door closes, another door opens.

There is a psychological reason why when you walk through an entranceway into another room, you often forget why you went in there. It is your mind purging information and preparing you for the new space, new place, new situation. BTW, if you need to remember why you walked into that room, walk back into the old one and look around. This is an actual technique for memory re-keying, but also applies to leaving a bad situation.

Mathematics teaches us that to any problem there are zero, one, or an infinite number of potential solutions. As an optimist you can refuse to accept the zero or one scenarios simply by expanding the number of dimensions you see the problem in, thinking about them in a higher way. So too with life: there are almost never no alternatives.

Open your doors of perception and the infinite becomes apparent.

There is always a solution, always a way to succeed. Your job is to be mentally ready to find it, to not close off your doors of perception and get stuck, wondering what to do. Step back into the old room for a moment, remember the why, and then walk through the new door and the opportunity within.

Action Item: look around your situation and ask "where could this door go?" Choose one to walk through.

19 JANUARY
"This is the strangest life I have ever known."

Jim Morrison

Or as the Grateful Dead would say "What a long strange trip it's been."

I bet you when you were a kid you never proclaimed "When I grow up, I want to be X", X being what you are and do today. I wanted to be a mad scientist and take over the world, and unfortunately I don't have a death ray and the entire world paying me protection money.

What did you want to be when you grew up? Why?

Do you retain any of that desire? Can you recapture the rapture of childhood innocence and apply it to what you do today for a living?

Look back along your trip, the weird journey of your life. What were some of the key moments that made you better off?

What are some of the ideas or lessons from detours and side quests on the road that have given you experience or skills you can use in your current endeavors?
Steve Jobs as a student would just drop in on all sorts of random classes and see what he could pick up. Some design ideas he was exposed to profoundly impacted the look and feel of Apple. You never know what random experience or meeting can be valuable further down the road.

Action Item: list 3 critical positive experiences from your life.

1.

2.

3.

20 JANUARY
"Burn the past. Turn the page. Move on."

Safura Arsh

Bet you had some pretty bad experiences on your path to today too. We all have our traumas that have impacted us and formed us into the people we are today. But we are not doomed by our past, just influenced by it, potentially tempered like the finest steel into instruments of creation for the future.

We all have scars: some physical, some mental, others emotional. They contribute to our uniqueness, but shouldn't define us. And most scars are the result of us healing from these hurts, be they on our body or in our soul.

For many people, the wounds are deep and still haven't healed. These will take therapy (formal or informal) and time. For those lesser injuries, you have to reflect upon them and should be able to heal thyself.

Action Item: take a piece of paper. Sit down and write one or two really bad things that have happened to you. Brain dump it, cry on the paper. Now take that paper, crumple it up, and throw it out or better yet, burn it. Move on.

21 JANUARY

"With the new day comes new strength and new thoughts."

Eleanor Roosevelt

When dawn comes, the world is born anew. Each day is a separate chapter in your life, and it starts with a blank page.

Learn from the good and bad experiences of yesterday, but do not let them cloud the sunrise today nor shade your vision of the future.

Your body recharges as you sleep, repairs the stresses and prepares for the new day.

Your mind processes the previous day, encoding memories and sorting out the lessons. Sometimes these are reflected in your dreams, as new feelings and experiences are uploaded into your mental core and sometimes don't fit quite right.

But when you awaken, when you get out of that bed, you have the gift of another day. And like in a game, you should have new capabilities, new ideas, and a recharge to commence this part of the adventure.

You can win today, no matter what happened yesterday.

Use your new perceptions and abilities to win the game of today, drawing upon the lessons of the past.

Action Item: what is one way you are better today than yesterday? How are you going to apply it to write a positive chapter for today?

22 JANUARY
"Let your struggle be your strength, not your identity."

Aprilyn Chavez Geissler

April is actually a personal friend of mine for two plus decades, whom I call "The Phoenix" for how she has risen from the ashes multiple times. Every time better and stronger.

Adversity develops our strengths, like resistance when lifting weights builds muscle mass. Like challenges in martial arts or video games develop our skills. Like mental exercise sharpens our reasoning. That which was once impossible is now routine for us.

"Good timber does not grow with ease. The stronger the wind, the stronger the trees." Thomas Munson.

Once you level up, be it a promotion at work, earning a degree, or developing a skill such as cake decorating or archery, do you dwell upon how tough it was or do you enjoy the current level and know that you have an inner core that helped you attain what you have, and will give you the strength to deliver here?

Do you tie your entire perspective (and project it to others) about where you came from and have it negatively anchor you, or do you just draw from it to create your future?
Instead of carrying emotional baggage, have you built the strength to pick up anything that gets in your way? Can you now move mountains because you aren't carrying the weight of the world on your back still?

Action Item: what is the defining struggle of your past? Are you still fighting that battle, or is it a victory in your history book that you can study and learn from?

23 JANUARY

"Still, like air, I rise."

Dr. Maya Angelou

Have you ever watched the mists rise off of a lake in the morning, as the sun starts to warm the air?

Have you ever watched the hawk, soaring high above the fields, its keen eye searching while it rides the thermal current higher and higher, spiraling to heights that would terrify lesser animals?

There is a reason we say that someone "lifts your spirits", or is "always up" as opposed to "down in the dumps". We reach for the stars for a reason.

Lift your chin.

Stand up straight like your grandmother told you to.

Jordan Peterson's *First Rule* is to Stand Up Straight, because of the psychological and neurochemical benefits.

Take a deep breath.

Close your eyes, and picture the lake above. Feel the chill in the damp air and the light of the morning sun on your skin, red through your eyelids. Picture the mist shifting over the surface, and slowly rising, dissipating as the day warms from the east.

You are that calm, that fog lifting.

Stillness, tranquility, peace. These will help you rise above the chaos of the day. The placidity you just experienced is like the air you breath, nurturing your spirit and as critical as the oxygen in the air.

Action Item: set two alarms on your phone, one in late morning and one early afternoon. When the alarms go off, close your eyes and just breathe in the calm for a moment or two.

24 JANUARY

"I believe that visualization is one of the most powerful means of achieveing personal goals."

Harvey Mackay

When we started this year, on the first day you were asked "What do you want to achieve?" And you wrote down your goals. But have you looked at them since? Or are they just sitting there a few dozen pages back, ignored and wasting away like plants in an abandoned office?

How about we really give them some life, make it so they are alive and breathing and viable?

What picture would represent your goals? A round table with a number on it representing the production you want to achieve?

A picture of the resort you will take your family to when you hit certain goals?

That diploma, with your name on it?

That outfit you want to fit into?

The medal from that race you are training for?

Visualize what you want. Feel it. Dr. Julie Bell and numerous other sports and performance psychologists will tell you that the mind can not distinguish from physical action and pre-playing (or replaying) an event in your mind. Visualization of the golf swing, of the free throw, of the kick and victory is the slight edge to achieve and win.

My first major victory in a martial arts tournament came after six months of intense practice. Not just training for over an hour every morning and every evening but mental training. As I awoke or drifted off to sleep each day, I visualized throwing an instant hook kick with my lead left leg to an opponent's head. Hundreds of times I pre-played that exact technique, that exact moment in my mind. Guess how I won the title?

Action Item: find some pictures that represnt your goals and put them up where you can see them ALL THE TIME!

25 JANUARY
"If you aim at nothing, you will hit it every time."

Zig Ziglar

You probably have That Friend. The one that has been aimlessly drifting since school, who seems to have no real purpose in life. They might be surface-happy but they aren't deeply joyful because they don't have anything meaningful to work towards, be it at work or a sport or in their home life.

They don't have anything to focus on, to work towards. They have malaise, an ennui that is dangerous because it can lead them down bad paths in an attempt to find something to fill the voids in their soul. They might have the BMW and nice clothes and fake the smile, but under it they are empty and sad because they aren't committed to something that allows them to organize their life towards something as Nietczshe would say.

Maybe you are That Friend.

Before you step on to a dark path because you don't have a guiding light or a North Star to focus on, something to work towards, let's look for an alternative.

Action item: call your BFF, that person that you can share anything with. Tell them how you are feeling and really talk to them. Have them figure out something you can work together towards, and ask them to be your wing man or woman in it. Be accountable to them, even if it is something small and seemingly insignificant.

Action Item: call your BFF, that person that you can share anything with. Tell them how you are feeling and really talk to them. Have them figure out something you can work together towards, and ask them to be your wing man or woman in it. Be accountable to them, even if it is something small and seemingly insignificant.

26 JANUARY

"Focus and finish."

Master Torres

Young kids are great because they have enthusiasm, but they also often have the attention span of a sugared up squirrel. And that might describe you, because it certainly describes me and the way I get distracted by shiny objects, be it something on my laptop or an email that grabs my attention, or it might be that coworker with the "hey, got a minute?".

Maybe you have that massive project, hundreds of hours of work coding or writing or analysis or fixing something in the house. Something that was started with great attention that fizzled when you realized the magnitude of the task at hand; you get bogged down and frustrated and maybe throw out more than a few choice words.

Or it's studying, writing that paper, or getting through the day with your individual struggle.

Maybe it's your goals for this year.

If an eight-year old autistic kid with ADHD can do what he needs to in a Tae Kwon Do class with all the distractions, I bet you can. Just hold on for a few minutes.

Many people who do a marathon for the first time do "run, walk" where they run for about a mile then walk for a minute or two. Repeat. Repeat. They complete all 26.2 miles, get the same medal as those elite athletes finishing in two and a quarter hours, and for the rest of their lives can say that they did a marathon.

You can do this in your marathons.

Action item: adopt the Pomodoro Method. Set a timer for 25 minutes on your phone, and just plow away on whatever you need to do. Then take a break and repeat.

27 JANUARY

"Great is the art of beginning, but greater is the art of ending."

Henry Wadsworth Longfellow

Leonardo da Vinci created thousands of masterpieces. In his head. He actually abandoned most of his paintings, leaving half done sketches and partial portraits. Imagine what the art world would have been like if he finished even a portion of these.

How many classical works are "unfinished"? Beethoven, Tolkien, and countless others did not complete some of their greatest works.

Einstein spent decades searching for the Theory of Everything, the unifier between spacetime, electromagnetism, and the nuclear forces. We are still looking for it today.

What is unfinished in your work? In your home? In your personal life?

Finish that book. Complete that degree. Get that project done.

Great works like cathedrals used to take hundreds of years to complete, and now take only years.

Even if something in your life is a cathedral, you can still complete your masterpiece.

Action item: finish something.

28 JANUARY

"It does not matter how slowly you go so long as you do not stop."

Andy Warhol

I run really long distances. Like double marathons, because I swore I would never do another marathon (doing two in a day is a double negative, so a positive from a pure mathematics point of view and ok in my convoluted thinking) or 100km in a day or Ragnars (200ish mile team relay races). I am not fast like some of my team members, who seem to be part deer. I am more like a semi-shuffling broken down pirate with a gimp, but I keep going for hours and hours and mile after mile. Because I'm too stubborn to stop, even when my body is like "dude, you just did your third ten km of the day. Chill and have a donut with your feet up."

I don't stop, and that's why I finish.

Building a business is similar. Every day there is a new stack of things that have to be done, plus the normal activities to run the organization and make money. Every. Day. Sometimes I sneak out at 3:00 to spend some extra time with my kids, but after they are in bed I am back at the grind to do what needs to be done because I don't want the business (and the cashflow) to grind to a stop. So I don't stop.

Writing a book is like training for a marathon. Every day sitting down and hitting the keys for at least an hour, even if "not feeling it" at the start. You lace up your running shoes and go even if it is cold or rainy and after the first mile you knock off the cobwebs and the rust and keep going until whatever you are supposed to do that day is done.

Starting is the first part of not stopping.

Those of us who are special needs parents know the feeling of not stopping. Every day, rain or shine, we have to get up and take care of our special kid, whether they are a cancer warrior or autistic or diabetic. They need us because they can't do it on their own, and there are no days off from the battle for them. We might sometimes need to pause and catch our breath (or go into a field and have a primal scream to get it all out). But then we are back fighting for our child. We don't stop.

Earning your degree while working and taking care of your children? You know that it is physically and mentally exhausting, and that sometimes you get frustrated and want to stop. But you won't.

You don't. Why? Because you understand that if you do, inertia will make it that much harder to get going again and you are pushing towards this goal for a reason, for your children and your future and so you keep slogging through it, one assignment after another and one course after another until you achieve what you set out for.

If you don't stop yourself, nothing can stop you.

"Just put one foot in front of the other" echoes in my head when running, taken from the old Christmas special "Santa Claus is Coming to Town". Yes, when it is 88 degrees and I'm dripping and gross twelve miles into my twenty for the day, that song from my childhood plays on loop in my skull.

I don't stop.

"Just keep swimming, just keep swimming..." Dory from *Finding Nemo*. Yeah, sometimes I switch to this mantra for a mile or two. And sometimes when I sit down to write for an hour I quietly say it to myself, especially when I am less than half way through a massive project (like this one) and it seems overwhelmingly huge like the ocean and my efforts are just a little lost fish. But I don't stop, I keep swimming and eventually find P. Sherman in Sydney.

Action item: don't stop. Whatever your marathon, don't stop. Keep putting one foot in front of the other.

29 JANUARY

"The world always seems brighter when you've just made something that wasn't there before."

Neil Gaiman

]When was the last time you made something other than your work product?

Cupcakes (not for a birthday, just because)?

Painted a picture?

Wrote a poem?

Probably been a while if you are like most busy people. Which is everyone.

Creation is not reserved for divine beings, it is our reflection of them.

Make something, even if it sucks, because it probably will. But it is something you made, whether it is that weird Romanian sausage your friend suggested, or a Paint and Sip creation that a toddler would be proud of.

Because you made it, from scratch.

Next time will be better, but this one is still pretty awesome.

How are you going to feel after making, after being an auteur?

Pretty damn good I'll bet.

Action item: go make something!

30 JANUARY
"Every act of creation is first an act of destruction."

Pablo Picasso

Military boot camp is about breaking people down to build them up better.

So is the pledging process.

So is weight lifting, where on a microscopic level you are tearing the muscles so that they can heal and grow, making you stronger for the cellular level abuse.

Businesses often talk about going through a "J Curve", where there is a decline in production while processes and systems are changed, resulting in faster growth and ultimately a better output.

Any athlete that has changed their swing or other technique understands this.

To get better, sometimes you have to get worse first.

To build a new building in a city, they have to tear one down first.

What do you need to blow up to build something better?

Action item: what do you need to break down and build up better in your life? Get out the (symbolic) sledgehammer and get to work.

31 JANUARY

"Balance, Daniel-san! Must have balance!"

Mr. Miyagi, *The Karate Kid*

Yin and Yang.

Hard and Soft.

Emotion and Logic.

Going to extremes may get results in the short term, but it can burn you out.

On your days off, do stuff that allows you to rest from your primary activities. So if you work in an office, make sure you rest your eyes from the computer/TV screens and do a lot of physical activity.

If your work is physical, rest the body and stress your mind with intense thought.

If you are social for work (say sales), seek solitude when off. Especially more so for a stay at home parent, flee from that chaos for a bit and let your partner deal with it so you can recharge.

Understand your dominant tendencies in communication, in interactions, and try to invest time in its opposite.

Hand and foot. Left and right. Male and female. Societies, families, and individuals function best with a balance of the different aspects and attitudes.

Action item: go back to your SWOT analysis and expand it. Now review the Weaknesses and see if there is a theme among them. What can you do to make that theme stronger and bring balance?

FEBRUARY IS THE BORDER BETWEEN

WINTER AND SPRING

Terri Guillemets

01 FEBRUARY
"A wise man will make more opportunities than he finds."

Francis Bacon

In our heads we have a filter that allows us to see the world, called the Reticular Activation System (RAS) that prevents us from being overwhelmed by the sheer volume of information our senses take in. It is part of the reason we notice movement, because it allows us to not get eaten by big nasty animals by diverting attention to the smallest change in the environment.

What you look for, you will find. Positive or negative, it is all there in the world. But if you are subconsciously looking for something you are more likely to find it.

Ask anyone who has had Lasik surgery what the world looks like immediately afterward.

Some of us really do see the world with rose tinted glasses, and it gives us an advantage.

If your RAS is clogged by fear, all you will see is problems and threats, and you might be overwhelmed by anxiety. Negativity will literally cloud your vision.

But if you look for the opportunity, if you program your brain to seek the potential, you will start seeing things you missed before. And the more you work on it, the more opportunities you will see.

Why do you think serial entrepreneurs tend to get better and each go around? Because they learn each time from their mistakes and can recognize or create the chance of success because of their insight and experience.

If you look for the bright side of life, the silver lining, you will always find one.

Action item: look at your last big problem. Literally put it on the table, take it apart, and walk around looking at it from different perspectives. What other things do you see? Now try this approach with your problems of today.

Action item: look at your last big problem. Literally put it on the table, take it apart, and walk around looking at it from different perspectives. What other things do you see? Now try this approach with your problems of today.

02 FEBRUARY

"Opportunity is missed by most people because it is dressed in overalls and looks like work."

Thomas Edison

Do the work.

Grind it out.

Edison famously explained his 10,000 failures to create an electric light bulb as 10,000 ways to NOT make one. He kept doing the work, and that's why we don't use candles today.

The Master has failed more times than the novice has even tried.
Which blow of the axe fells the great oak? The 500th which ultimately fells the tree can not happen without the first 499.

Some work sucks, I freely admit it. Cleaning up chicken poop, puppy puke, changing diapers. Filling out mind numbing reports, talking to government employees that are just running out the clock until retirement in 2047, these are all on the list of not fun things. But you might have to do them.

Plow through it.

Cleaning up puppy puke and poop and training them leads to a dog that can be a great companion. Dealing with those sloths in the office downtown can let you build your dream. Are you going to give up on your dream just because there is a stack of paper taller than a beer to fill out?

Do the work.

There are millions of trade jobs available in the US that will create a good life for people. But you can't just enter them and be at the top, you have to go through being an Apprentice and learning, then Journeyman, and ultimately a Master. It takes years of work to realize the opportunities.

You shouldn't be handed a Black Belt. You should work for it, earn it with blood and sweat. In the old days the Black Belt was actually a white belt that had just gotten nasty over thousands of hours of effort and training. A true Master applies the discipline of what they have earned in other areas and masters their environment because they have done the work.

Action item: what is one area you could work a little harder in and see some results?

03 FEBRUARY
"Genius is talent set on fire by courage."

Henry VanDyke

We all have great ideas. Those who change the world dare to execute on them.

It doesn't matter if it is a self-driving car company, writing a poetry book for that special someone, or taking the risk at work. All advancement has come because someone dared.
When Picasso decided to change his style as a painter, he risked his reputation and livelihood. He took the risk and produced incredible works. He did so multiple times. The true embodiment of genius.

Jimi Hendrix had the courage to try something different with his flipped guitar and approach to playing. As did Tony Iommi after he had his fingertips cut off but refused to give up, creating the signature sound of Black Sabbath's guitars whilst in pain because it would have hurt him more to not play music. That was talent fired up.

The eccentric chess champion Bobby Fisher won his title by swimming and playing mind games instead of practicing like others, two things no one else had the courage to do because of the protocols and mores of the chess community. How many other chess players have movies about them?

If you don't have the courage to try something different, you'll end up middle of the pack. Average might be acceptable, but the talented and courageous can become exceptional.

Keats stated "I was never afraid of failure for I would sooner fail than not be among the greatest."

Take that risk. "You'll miss 100% of the shots you don't take" is an old hockey adage and if you are afraid to pull the trigger, to take the risk of failure you can never achieve the potential of your greatness in any way. Have the courage to risk, else you'll be one of those numberless high potential people that never translated their gifts into action and accomplishments. They are for the most part forgotten, while the bold are immortalized for what they dared to do.

Action item: what is that one risk you haven't taken that would change your life or the world? What is stopping you? Take a deep breath, be brave, and move forward!

04 FEBRUARY

"I have no special talents. I am only passionately curious."

Albert Einstein

Einstein contributed to areas of physics ranging from cosmology (the movements at the largest scales imaginable) to Brownian motion (molecular sized movements) down into the subatomic (photoelectric effect). And it was because he maintained the curiosity and wonder of a child throughout his entire life that his work is still garnering Nobel Prize attention a century later.

"Hmmm, I wonder what would happen if..." can lead to a Darwin Award if all safety procedures are ignored, but it also leads to innovations. Wondering, and then exploring those various rabbit holes of ideas and side paths, has created Post It notes, the internet, and bacon-wrapped everything. Or chocolate-dipped everything.

Zora Neale Hurston summed it up: Research is formalized curiosity. It is the child at play that records what they are doing for others to learn from. Many a PhD student in STEM has the email signature "It wouldn't be called research if I knew what I was doing." Looking right at you Dr. Karl Umstadter!

Many an educator has killed the future of a child by killing their curiosity, and luckily almost as many have encouraged that natural desire of children to understand the world around them and supported these kids in ways that have turned them into lifelong learners, regardless of their grades or natural aptitudes. The desire for knowledge, the need to learn and understand, is not limited by IQ or the walls of a university.

Curiosity literally knows no bounds.

A desire to understand the world around us created philosophy, science, and art, the backbones of civilization. The autodidacts (self-educated) range from the unknown person that rubbed sticks together to create fire, to the one that planted the first crop leading to agriculture, through Leonardo da Vinci to Eddie Van Halen and beyond. I'm one.

Curiosity is what continuously expands not just the borders of human knowledge and potential, but opportunities for individuals. Never let that quest to understand cease, and you'll continue to evolve as a person and remain mentally young until the end of your days.

Action item: what's something you've always been curious about? Go look it up on the internet and spend a half hour exploring!

05 FEBRUARY
"Be curious, not judgemental."

Walt Whitman

Ask questions. Play around. Try to understand. This is what children do all the time.

They also accept everyone, whether they are in a wheelchair or missing a limb or have different skin tone. Kids are kids, and will ask questions about why things are and then go "oh, ok" and move forward with no bias or baggage.

Kids also try to figure stuff out, and look at things based on their limited experience and fill in the gaps with some outlandish ideas. Like dwarves helping at your office or cookies taking four hours to cook. But sometimes this naïveté can be insightful, leading to new approaches to solving problems. The headline "Teenage Scientist Creates..." is fairly common because new eyes can lead to new ways of doing things. This is why Einstein and John Nash won Nobel prizes: they were curious like children. Be childish in this way.

And then like a child, don't judge. Judging is for people with expertise in specific areas, individuals that have experience and vast knowledge and can make well-grounded assessments of a situation. That is why the vast majority of us have no right to judge others the vast majority of the time, because we are only seeing small sample sizes over short durations with incomplete knowledge.

Yes, you can momentarily call someone a "crazy driver" for their swerving and weaving, but leave it at that instead of attributing it to their age or other factors. You don't know so don't presume to judge.

Unless you have a cool wig and a gavel and robes, let it be.

If you are the expert, lend your expertise to improve others so they can have better outcomes, not being a stern jerk and yelling "FAIL!" or hitting the gong. That doesn't help others get better and makes you look like an insensitive twit like the semi-reality talent show judges that build their persona off of being bad humans. You're better than that.

Just try to understand, maybe help a bit but don't impose your belief system or will on others. It will create friction and limit other people's growth and fun. It will also limit your ability to learn and grow.

Action item: today, you will be given the opportunity to experience something outside your normal zone. Enjoy it, ask questions about it, learn from it and appreciate it for what it is.

06 FEBRUARY

"Never judge anyone shortly because every saint has a past and every sinner has a future."

Oscar Wilde

"All the world's a stage, and all the men and women merely players" Shakespeare observed. Can we call someone a hero or a villain after the first or second act?

Today could be a bad day for someone. Their autistic kid could be having a meltdown while their aging parents aren't eating and their boss is screaming at them. That person might make a mistake because they are mentally overwhelmed, or are so tired that they miss something they normally don't. Does this make them a bad person, or a bad parent?

Evil people often hide behind magnanimity, giving sums to charity and basking in the do-gooder accolades while using the spotlight to hide what they are doing in the shadows. Does the temporary halo make them angels or merely hide their horns?

That badass covered in tattoos teaching Sunday school after three tours and a half dozen wounds? They probably have a lot of red in their ledger that they are working off, and the world will on balance be a lot better off for what they did and are choosing to do now. Who are you or I to judge that book by its funky cover?

In baseball the adage is that people will "play to the back of their baseball card". Anyone can get lucky or unlucky on a particular swing of the bat, or any given game. If someone is eight years into a career as a .275 hitter and gets off to a super start to the year hitting .500 over twelve games, you probably feel ok saying that they are going to cool off tremendously as the season progresses.

Same thing for a multiple time All-Star going through an 0 for 12 rough patch. Unless it is the postseason, the handful of games neither makes nor breaks their career nor reputation.

The truth will come out over time. Someone that is a thief will steal again given the opportunity, and will look for the opportunity unless they are fully reformed. Their pattern of fraud and misdeeds will appear as one looks over the tapestry of their story, as will the heroism of the continual quiet good deeds that are often missed in the flash and rush of life.

Cheaters hide in plain sight.

As Kahnemann reminds us in "Thinking, Fast and Slow", snap judgements are rarely accurate.

Action item: if you have a strong negative reaction to someone's actions today, pause and put yourself in their shoes for a moment and try to understand why they did what they did.

07 FEBRUARY
"Try to be better than yourself."

William Faulkner

"The time has come, to sink or swim. My only rival is within." Ruelle

Martial Artists for centuries have known that the battle is not against the physical opponent standing in front of them but against themselves: that mastering their fear and body and will, gives them what they need to be victorious even against great odds.

Simone Biles was the gold standard of excellence in gymnastics. She did not try to jump higher nor turn faster than the other competitors: she focused on herself and doing her best. That's why she IS the best. Same thing that Michael Phelps did in the pool en route to more gold than a pirate dreams of.

Kirk Hammett was a wickedly good guitarist with the band Exodus. Then he joined another band and decided good wasn't good enough, so he hired guitar god Joe Satriani to teach him to be even better. Kirk's understanding of music expanded, his ability to practice improved (yielding the obvious results), and that other band became the monster that is Metallica. What would the rock and roll world sound like if Kirk hadn't tried to be better than himself?

Actor Matthew McConaughey was asked who his hero was. His answer: me in ten years. And ten years later his hero was still the man he could be a decade from then. Keep benchmarking against what you could become and work towards it.

None of us are perfect. But we can all improve, whether as a parent or a friend or in our profession or avocation. We can do little things like visualizing not yelling at someone to increase our tolerance, or perform one skill slightly better by investing the time to think about it and improve. A little here, a little there, and over a few months we have noticeable improvement. Less stress, better health, the capability to do what we previously couldn't. These might not get us on the highlight reel or Youtube/Tik Tok fame, but they make us better and ultimately happier individuals.

Trying to be better than the you of yesterday is the ENTIRE premise of Every Day Excellence.

Action item: start challenging yourself to be better today than yesterday.

08 FEBRUARY

"Do what you have to do until you can do what you want to do."

Oprah Winfrey

Almost every musician has started with no skill but high desire, and perfectly emulated the sound of strangling a cat to begin with. Yet in their mind they were seeing when they would be good, whether playing piano in the high school auditorium or shredding their guitar in an arena filled with a hundred thousand screaming fans. You can't get there unless you start, and we all start with poorly developed skills and can barely make the instrument emit a decent note. But everyone has to start and suck to be great.

Want to build a multibillion dollar tech company? Well, you probably can't do so. But you can start building your website and product. It will probably suck as an MVP (Minimal Viable Product), and that's ok. Iterate and re-iterate and keep the cycle of improvement going and it could become a hugely successful company. Just be ok with it not being perfect or awesome to start.

Want to do a triathlon? Start by getting off the couch. That first step is the hardest. Start training each day, and add distance and intensity until you can do all three events in one day, even if it is only a 5km run instead of a full marathon. Keep the vision, keep working and stretching and eventually you can do a full triathlon. But do what you can, now.

Want to speak in front of crowds? Speak in front of a mirror, learn about speaking (maybe Toastmasters or other resources online), do more speaking, practice and put in the time and effort and then you're on stage like Joe Jordan or Walter Bond or Joel Osteen. But do what you can, today, with your current skills.

We learn to cook great meals by first learning to boil water. It takes time and energy to heat the water, and it takes more time and energy to become a gourmet chef. Start by boiling an egg, like so many have before. And you can't go instantly from room temperature to a roiling boil, you must go through each degree on the way up to being hot enough.

Repair that relationship? Start by talking to them. That is the first step back to love.

Where you want to be is not where you are now, but you have to get moving to get there. It might be slow, you will stumble, but you have to move forward to reach your destination. Start putting one foot in front of the other, even if it is slow and tentative to start. Move forward towards your goal and dream.

Action item: where do you want to be in three years? What can you do today so that you can do things then that you can't today? Take that first step.

09 FEBRUARY

"I may not be where I want to be, but thank God I am not where I used to be."

Joyce Meyer

We all started life as helpless, blind, probably screaming babies. Then we opened our eyes and started to see but were still helpless, completely dependent upon others to feed us, change us, protect us. Who was it that did that for you?

Probably your parents. Who had started off as helpless and blind as you, but grew and developed into functional human beings, hopefully loving and caring ones that raised you into a decent and productive member of society. You were able to grow because they had grown, and their fondest wish for you is that you could become more than what they had, to be better and live better. That is the American Dream.

When you were four you couldn't tie your shoes.

At ten you couldn't drive.

At 20 you weren't as emotionally developed as you are now.

Even a year ago you were less than you are today. What will you be a year from now, especially if you remember that having a growth mindset leads to increased happiness?

What could you become over the next five years, if you really wanted to improve your life?

Humans are special because we control our destiny, by our rational choices. We can look at where we are (physically, emotionally, etc) and where we are going and decide to alter course and end up at a different destination. It doesn't matter if you are born into poverty (Andrew Carnegie did and then gave away more money to charity than anyone to that point in history), lose your sight (Ray Charles), lose your business (yours truly and too many to mention): you aren't done until you stop so keep going, moving forward from something bad to something better. Until you give up you're not beaten.

Action item: where do you want to be in a year? What is the one step you can take today?

10 FEBRUARY

"Have faith in your own abilities, work hard, and there is nothing you cannot accomplish."

Brad Henry

The Horatio Alger-esque self-made success story is as old as the US, whether it is Ben Franklin or Andrew Carnegie (US Steel) or Donna Carpenter (co-founder of Burton snowboards). The ability to found a company, build it your way without having to pay bribes and relatively minimal government interference (for the most part) and reap the rewards for betting on yourself is as American as cowboys and Apple pie. In fact almost nine out of ten millionaires in the US are self-made, a statistic that inspires both here and abroad.

When you are self-employed, there are no paid days off. Days off mean that the money machine is turned off for the day, unless you have reached the point of having employees that can keep it going. Startups and small businesses are the engine of our economic growth and are responsible for most new non-governmental jobs in the country.

Startup means 9-5 is out the window. Half days though: any twelve hours will do. And that is typically six days a week, not five. The average Founder is working in the early days at least time and a half, and eighty-hour weeks are not unusual. With no guarantees of success.

As Peter Thiel (co-Founder of PayPal and Palantir) describes it: you are building an airplane while falling off a cliff. Time and speed are critical, as well as executing properly.

Albert Grey in the speech to The Million Dollar Round Table entitled "The Common Denominator of Success" points out that the secret of success is not a secret but that those who have achieved formed the habit of doing things that failures don't like to do. Like work very hard, put their money and reputation on the line, and give up a safety net for the chance to fly.

The story of the college kid building something in their dorm room (Gates, Cuban, Karthik Bala, Zuckerberg, etc) that eventually employs hundreds or even tens of thousands of people and makes them fabulously wealthy is almost trite because it's happened so often. Why can't you start something? Why aren't you?

The best investment is not going to be in some mega-corporation, but in yourself.

Action item: sit down and write an inventory of your skills. What do you do well? Looking at that list, where are your opportunities to turn your ability into additional cash flow?

11 FEBRUARY
"And now abide faith, hope, and love."

1 Corinthians, 13

These are the trinity of positivity. Always keep the faith, never give up hope, and do everything in love. If you hold to these three things, life will not be perfect but it will be better than the alternative.

If you saw *The Big Lebowski*, you know: The Dude Abides. You can wait, tolerate anything for a period if you are operating from a perspective of faith, hope, and love. Abide, the tide will turn in your favor eventually.

The National Institute of Health conducted research (plus a comprehensive review of publications) and found conclusively that faith, hope, and love in practice improve medical outcomes across the entire spectrum of illnesses and injuries.

On a biochemical level they help us heal, as well as on the mental and moral ones. They will not cure cancer or fix an injured back on their own, but as a supplement to medicine they will reduce stress and pain levels in addition to shortening recovery times.

Action item: sit in a fairly quiet, calm place with a piece of paper. Write on the paper "FAITH HOPE LOVE". What comes to mind for each of these? Write them down. Then try to model these better throughout your day.

12 FEBRUARY
"To live without Hope is to cease to live."

Fyodor Dostoevsky

Hope springs eternal: it is reflected in the young green shoots of spring and the laughter of children. It is what carries us through the dark of night, the depths of winter and doubt, and through the inevitable rough patches of relationships and any worthy endeavor.

Hope reinforces faith when we start to doubt because we are seeing no results from our efforts whether it is at work, dieting, or breaking bad habits. Hope gives us strength: it is the only thing stronger than fear. It allows us to hold the line for just a little bit longer.

Hope is what drags us out of bed on that rainy morning, and is reinforced when the rainbow appears after we slog through several wet, cold, nasty miles. It is that brief flash, the unexpected smile, that suddenly fills us with the energy needed to get through whatever hell we are experiencing.

Hope is not a plan, but a booster as we get bogged down executing the plan we have and start to think about giving up. It is hearing the cavalry is coming, so we can redouble our efforts and win the battle we are in, even if the cavalry doesn't arrive. It is tapping into the reserves we didn't know we had because we believe in something, and can draw it out of us in the worst of times.

Hope is innate, programmed into us from our earliest days as a people, and is culturally reinforced but as individually tailored as our thoughts and feelings. And when everything outside and around us collapses, we can tap into that inner spring to see us through the harshest of times.

Action item: think back, to the darkest night of your soul, when it seemed like nothing was right and you were ready to despair and give up. What kept you going? What gave you hope? Hold on to that. Embed it into your heart for when you need it again.

13 FEBRUARY
"Courage is like love: it must have hope for nourishment."

Napoleon Bonaparte

Hope not only enhances other positive attributes, it nurtures them and allows them to grow to their full potential. Courage and love are two of the highest ideals of humankind, and both achieve their full potential when fed a steady diet of hope, reinforcing what is already there until the full strength that was innate is revealed for all to see.

Like all great organic things, courage (or love) starts from small seeds that must be watered properly, encouraged with the right light and food, and then they can begin to sprout. Little acts of courage such as saying what you believe in low risk situations can either be squashed or supported, and if supported they are strengthened and reach higher. Courage in great things begins with courage in little things usually, and strength of character is developed not overnight but over years.

Many successful people achieved what they did because they had someone giving them the nourishment for their courage right along. It could be that grandmother that gave you tough love and challenged you to be better (maybe with the fear of a whoopin'), that coach that forced you to the edge of your comfort zone, or that teacher that declared "you can do better, I expect more from someone as talented as you." And you can now be the one that gives the encouraging word.

Giving someone else hope is a spectacular gift that costs you nothing out of pocket, just a little out of your heart.

As Aragorn proclaims in *The Return of the King*: "I give hope to Men." Give hope to someone else so that their courage can grow and they can do great things.

Action item: give hope and encouragement to someone else today. Reach out to that friend or coworker who just needs a couple of words of support, maybe a cup of tea or a pat on the back, instill hope in them for their coming battle.

14 FEBRUARY
"I didn't need discipline, I loved what I was doing."

Arnold Schwartzenegger

Do you love what you do? I mean really, truly love it?

Like can't sleep Sunday nights, not because you are worried but because you are excited to go into work the next day?

Most Americans dislike or actively hate their job. Instead of getting a new one (which makes sense if you can), why not find the aspects of what you do for a living and fully embrace them? By focusing on the positives, you can accept the inevitable negatives of every situation. You program your Reticular Activation System (RAS) to see the positives, and you will be happier because your mental filter allows in more of the good things and just ignores the blah or bad.

Attitude is not everything, but it certainly is a major proportion of not just our success but our happiness in work and life.

Find a few things in your work, and home, and other places you invest your time, to be truly excited and ecstatic about. As we only have so much emotional bandwidth, focusing on the positive must therefore squeeze down the negative. If the balance of the time is good, the overarching feeling will reflect this and you will approach the situation with more energy. You'll be more productive, and a good influence on those around you which can impact the culture at work and the vibe in your house.

Action Item: Make a list of five things you love about work and home. Read it several times today, and keep it somewhere you will see the list often.

15 FEBRUARY

"Gonna need a bigger boat."

Sherrif Brody, *Jaws*

How big is the fish you are going after?

Don't chase minnows all day. Choose a few hours every week to go after the Great White.
Take that moonshot.

"We chose to do these things, not because they ah easy, but because they ah hahd!" President JFK talking about putting a man on the moon by the end of the decade.

Google used to allow all employees to spend 20% of their time on pet projects that could be revolutionary. Gmail came out of it. As did AdSense and Google News.

3M endorsed 15% time and you might be using the output of this in some capacity today.

Go after that Great White (shark or whale: be Captain Ahab). Chase that dream client or huge idea or BHAG (Big Hairy Audacious Goal), that crazy career changing thing.

Put in small doses: it is easy to starve if you are elephant hunting all day, but if you do what you need to feed your family and run your business or please your boss, allocate some time around it for the Real Big Deal that could be the stuff of legend.

Action Item: What is your Great White? Allocate time in your calendar weekly to hunt it.

16 FEBRUARY
"Cast your net, you will catch many small fish where you least expect."

Ovid

Ok, so you are trying to catch your Great White, but what are you doing with the vast majority of your time? Are you catching enough small fish to feed you, or are you going to starve while hunting the monster?

The gestation period of an elephant is 22 months. Can you spend 22 months chasing and waiting and not have any success?

I have seen hundreds of young professionals with huge potential fail out of business because they exclusively focused on the "big deal" and ignored the little things that would cover their overhead. Not sexy cool cases or deals, but they would pay the bills and there are tons of them.

Also, doing the little deals builds your skill set. Get the little victories over and over and make your mistakes on the little things instead of the big things. Lots of little successes will build a good career, no matter what your career is. Focusing on getting that one huge victory is the surest way to fail overall.

Ichiro Suzuki and Ty Cobb are in the Hall of Fame not for heir power (even though they both showed they could hit homers if they wanted to do so), they are immortal for getting hit after hit after hit.

There is an old story of a father taking his son out to hunt for food for the tribe. A multi day affair, and on the first morning the father killed a small burrowing animal and gave it to his son, telling him to keep it so they could eat. The son threw it in the bush, disgusted. They caught no more game that day, and went hungry. They never returned to the tribe.

Catch and eat the little things to sustain you on the hunt for the big game.

Grab the low hanging fruit so you don't starve.

Take the easy things where they come, at work and home, so that you have the energy for the big things.

Action Item: what is one easy victory you can achieve today? Grab it!

17 FEBRUARY
"The secret of attraction is to love yourself."

Deepak Chopra

The greatest love is self-love. Not narcissism, but a well-grounded appreciation of who you are with all of your foibles, your strengths and weaknesses and weird little quirks.

Think of yourself as this: you are a precious, uncut stone. A diamond in the rough literally. Over time, the stone is shaped by a variety of events, both good and ill. It is rubbed (sometimes the wrong way!), and polished.

Are all diamonds perfect? Nope, their rarity makes them valuable.

Are all diamonds the old definition of clear and exceptional under that standard? Definitely not, and in recent years we have come to appreciate the diversity of colors in the gems.

Tiny diamonds can be as beautiful as giants.

And there are an uncountable number of ways that a stone can be cut, to remove flaws or accentuate strengths or bring out the inner brilliance.

There may be some "expert" and "accepted" standards of beauty but to the right people, and in the right light, all of these crystals have their own beauty, their own radiance to share with the world.

You are that diamond.

To the right person, you are the most beautiful thing in the world. And that person should be you. Create yourself, and show the appropriate facets to the appropriate people.

Love thyself.

Action Item: write 10 things about yourself that you love.

18 FEBRUARY
"True nobility is being superior to your former self."

Ernest Hemmingway

Ever watch a toddler learning to walk?

They fall, constantly. Bump: right on their butt. And they get up, again and again and again, wobbling and standing and pulling themselves along the couch then across open spaces and falling and rising, rarely ceasing their efforts to master the skill they see big people do all the time.

This is how we need to approach things.

Babies learn at an unprecedented rate, and have few fears. Act like a baby.

The Zen Buddhists have a concept of "shosin" or "beginner's mind", where we approach things with the eyes of a novice or child. Einstein was well known for his childlike joy and approach to the world, which led to some of the greatest insights into physics of the past two centuries.

When you were younger, you made great progress whether it was working your way through a video game or learning a language in school or an instrument. The martial arts have visual codification of advancement of skills with their belt colors. When you get advanced degrees and designations you put them on your LinkedIn profile and email signature. These are all easily trackable measures of improvement.

And note: they are not comparing you to others in a win/lose scenario, but against who you used to be.

Don't judge yourself against those who have been working in that space or on that skill for decades, judge yourself against yourself. Be better than what you were, and focus on what you could become.

Action item: find one thing that is core to your success. Grade your ability on it. Now what do you need to do consistently to improve your grade? That's your homework.

19 FEBRUARY
"Income seldom exceeds personal development."

Jim Rohn

It is said that you could take all the money in the world, redistribute it equally, and within a few decades we will be back to having 20% own and control 80% of the wealth, in line with the Pareto Principle. As Jordan Peterson has noted it is actually more extreme potentially, because in any group some work and some don't and the distribution of work ethic and talents is typically around the square root of the total number of people producing half the output for whatever reasons.

So if you aren't a member of the Lucky Birth Club and have great wealth bestowed upon you, what are you to do other than play MegaMillions and hope the balls take a lucky bounce? How do we remove as much chance from the equation?

Work. Work on yourself.

If you work 10% harder than others, and this compounds in output, at the end of a year you will be 10% ahead of average. At the end of three years it is roughly a third better than peer. A decade? 2.5x. 25 years and you would be over 10x more productive than those you started with.

Now what about working smarter and harder, improving your outlook and your skills and your vision and discipline and many factors of self-development, so you could outperform by 25% per year from your starting point. From an average start you would be 265 times the average person. Even if you were below average to begin with (such as the author you are reading!) the relentless work on YOURSELF will improve you and your economic outlook tremendously. That same personal development will make you happier, probably healthier, and live longer. All good things you would probably agree.

Action Item: Do that little extra at work and home. Just a little extra, it compounds.

20 FEBRUARY
"A wise person should have money in their head, not their heart."
Johnathon Swift

Money is not the root of all evil, the envy and idolatry of it is. And the lack of it can lead some to do illegal things to get it. But it is an inanimate, fungible thing that we should use but not be burdened by.

Money is a tool. It lets you get things like food and clothes and experiences.

More money lets you buy more or better, but are you going to eat 10 cheeseburgers instead of 2? Get a million-dollar car instead of a $50,000 one? Spend the rest of your life in Paris? Probably not. I can't even eat ten cheeseburgers a day, and I've tried.

Be aware of money and appreciate it. Think about it, and definitely understand it as you would any other tool you use in your work or leisure, but don't let it become like The One Ring where you obsess over it and are willing to kill for it.

And that includes killing yourself.

Don't sell your soul or your health for the thirty pieces of silver or the stock options. Work hard, but don't work yourself to death chasing a buck.

Like money, but don't fall in love with it.

Enjoy money, but don't become addicted to it or define your self worth by your net worth.

Master your tool instead of becoming its serf.

Action Item: if you are not money savvy, find a weekly blog or other service to teach you a little. If you are savvy, double check to make sure you aren't becoming obsessed.

21 FEBRUARY
"You were born with the greatest weapon in all of nature- the rational, conscious mind."
Robert Greene

Humans have the ability to manipulate their environment, be it making stone axes to understanding planting seeds to guarantee food in the future, or reading and writing. We can learn from over five thousand years of advancement, and access the most powerful computer created because it resides between your ears.

Use it.

We are not bound by the Crocodile Brain that separates the world into the Four F's (food, fight, flight, f... procreate), or our Monkey Brain that emotionally and intuitively separates others into Friend or Foe. These earlier brain evolutions allowed us to survive, but it is the complex, rational big front brain that has made us the dominant species on the planet.

As we have moved from an agrarian society to an industrialized one and now a knowledge and service-based economy, your ability to think is more critical than ever. Fear is neutralized by logic, anxiety by understanding and planning. Our ability to understand the potential outcomes of our actions separates an adult from a toddler or even a teenager.

Our ability to question instead of accept, to play "what if" so we can see potential consequences of actions and minimize poor choices, to synthesize new ideas from older ones is what separates us from the lower animals and will allow you to craft a better future by rationally thinking and executing instead of gut reacting and over reacting.

Action Item: what is one thing that scares you? Think about it, write down all the reasons why it shouldn't scare you, make a plan in case you encounter that thing or situation. Let your mind overpower your fear.

22 FEBRUARY
"There is more wisdom in your body than in your deepest philosophy."

Friedrich Nietzsche

When you are hungry, eat. When you are tired, sleep. A basic principle that we outgrow for some reason.

Sometimes, you'll be tired, mentally and physically. So rest and recharge.

Sometimes you have a ton of energy and can be super productive, in a state of Flow. Ride that wave baby until it's done. And if you tend to get that gift at a regular time of day (around dawn, early afternoon, whenever it typically hits you), arrange your day to take advantage of it.

Your body knows when it needs a cheeseburger to help rebuild muscle.

Those butterflies you get in your stomach looking at a particular person? Maybe you should embrace how important they are and go talk to them, or regret it forever.

Gut feeling? Learn the difference between subconscious biofeedback giving you a hint and indigestion from chili dogs.

The body is a giant sensory organ, interacting with the environment in ways we are starting to understand but martial artists have known for centuries. Let the body inform you what is going on, what you should be doing.

Action Item: stop. Breathe. Feel. What is your body saying right now?

23 FEBRUARY
"The only true wisdom is in knowing you know nothing."

Socrates

Shosen, the beginner's mind of Japanese Zen.

When most Black Belts are awarded their First Dan, they receive their black belt but also a white belt, to remind them of humility and their lack of knowledge.

The greatest scientists were ready to scrap everything that they knew to start all over again, as if there were no pre-established facts. This often led to revolutionary breakthroughs, from biology to physics to psychology.

Metacognition is the process of thinking about your thinking, and there are stacks of evidence, both anecdotal and scientifically verified, that shows that this capability of questioning and reviewing not just what you think you know but why and the processes that lead to it is one of the highest order mental skills, unlocking greater insight and productivity.

Children repeatedly show that coming into a situation with little or no presuppositions can lead to innovation and creation, new ideas and applications and explanations that those with a more fixed mindset are unable to perceive and achieve.

Many a dojo has a sign proclaiming "leave your shoes and your ego here" by the front door.
A bowl is most useful when it is empty.

Socrates is regarded as the Father of Western Philosophy, and was so humble in his assessment of himself that when strangers asked him to recommend a philosopher to teach them he directed them to other philosophers, never mentioning that he had had a thought or two in his life.

Put down the baggage of your ego so that you can pick up new ideas.

Action item: what area do you think you have mastered? Go learn one new thing about it, something that you didn't know that will make you re-examine your belief in your expertise.

24 FEBRUARY
"Education's purpose is to replace an empty mind with an open one."
Malcolm Forbes

Education is NOT indoctrination, or rather, it ought not to be. It should not be teaching you WHAT to think but rather HOW to think.

Education's most important purpose is to encourage learning and continual acquisition of knowledge that can be applied for self and societal betterment. This could be in a formalized, degree pursuing classroom environment, it could be in an at your own pace online program like through Coursera, or it could be a rigorous self-created program tapping into the library, discussions with experts (both live and recorded), and research/experimentation. The goal of real learning is breadth, depth, usefulness, and lack of bias or agenda.

Education is NOT about creating clones nor villainizing any particular individual or groups. It should be about understanding a situation from multiple perspectives and drawing lessons from even the worst examples of humanity for the improvement of the future, not cauterizing or covering unsightly parts of our past.

Education should lead to vigorous debate, especially over ideas that make you uncomfortable. As St. Thomas Aquinas said: "the unexamined life is not worth living." Even the Nazis should be understood, not out of sympathy for their beliefs but to understand how a minority group was able to take control of a country (divide and conquer, scapegoating, slippery slope actions, indoctrination, censorship, spying on their own people, stripping of rights, etc) and what we need to do to prevent such an atrocity from occurring again. To really understand, we need to look closely at something, no matter how ugly or evil. Avoiding leads to forgetting and parallel problems developing again.

Education should leave the learner wanting more, to be hungry for additional knowledge instead of checking a box so they can get a piece of paper and continue on as before. Like eating, learning should be a daily occurrence, a sustenance for the mind as food is fuel for the body. And unlike sweets or red meat, you can not over-indulge in study (unless it is never applied, and you develop a fat head for not using the information you have gained).

When you stop learning you stop growing as a human, and quickly start declining. To maximize yourself, maximize your knowledge.

Action item: learn one thing today. One new thing. Repeat daily. Alternatively, sign up for a class, so that you have a learning plan for the next few months.

25 FEBRUARY
"It is not the answer that enlightens, but the question."

Eugene Ionesco

We have all heard the old adage that there are no dumb questions. That might not be 100% accurate, but it is reflective of a curious and inquisitive mindset which is what leads to understanding.

"Take the attitude of the student, never be too big to ask questions, never know too much to learn something new." Og Mandino

The shortest sentences in the English language are usually questions: Why? What? Who? Where? How? They are the simplest expression of wonder and the most fundamental attempt to understand the world around us, and scale from the subatomic to the cosmic and cover the relationships between items, actions, and souls. The continuous search for meaning is inherent in the human psyche and will probably continue until the last person passes from the earth.

The ability to formulate a relevant and thoughtful question, tailored to the situation, is an indication of preliminary understanding, to start moving from "Unconscious Incompetence" to "Conscious Incompetence, knowing that you don't know and seeking to further your insights on a topic.

Knowledge is an expanding space, and understanding what your limits are and purposefully seeking to expand them is critical to preventing mental stagnation. Questions are casting light on an area to see it, and being able to not only know where to point the light but also how to create it based on previous knowledge (and questions) is the difference between a lucky discovery and true illumination.

Action Item: today, ask 10 questions that you normally wouldn't ask. Try for at least one of each of the 4 Ws and 1 H (Who? What? When? Where? How?)

26 FEBRUARY
"Your path is illuminated by the light, yet darkness lets the stars shine bright."

JLW Brooks

Only in the dark of the night can we see the stars and marvel at their beauty.

In the quiet of the night we can appreciate the wonders of nature around us, listen to the birds in the pre-dawn and not be overwhelmed by the hubbub of life.

In the calm of the night we are alone with ourselves, for good or ill. It is in this darkness that we can truly see our own light, unspoiled by the reflections or shadows of others.

It is the contrast against the blackness that allows the little pinpricks in the firmament to give us glimpses of heaven in the little actions and events, from the kindness of a stranger to the smile of a child to the remembrance of a love no longer here.

The contrast of the darkness allows the dimmer lights of the firmament to be seen and appreciated, instead of being overwhelmed by the sun.

Without the night, there is no sunrise, no chasing of the dark by the light. Continuous beauty and sun will blind us, numbing our senses and making us immune to the moments sprinkled around of goodness that we normally don't notice.

Action Item: Tonight, go outside and look at the stars. Feel the chill on your face, the wind against your cheek and the little wonders you would normally overlook.

27 FEBRUARY
"Everyone carries a Shadow."

Carl Jung

"What is Light, without Dark? What are you, without me? I am a part of you all." Tim Curry in *Legend*.

In Kenny Rogers' *Coward of the County*, the protagonist Tommy (known as Yellow for being a coward) refuses to fight because he promised his father that died in prison he would walk away whenever possible. Then his wife is gang raped by local outlaw brothers. He goes to the saloon and they make fun of him as he turns towards the door, until he locks it and mops the floor with them. "Because sometimes you've got to fight when you're a man."

A good man is one who has the capacity for violence and controls it, until it needs to be unleashed to defend those he cares about. Folklore of almost every country is riddled with the tale of the bad man turned good, embracing the light and becoming even more powerful for having right on their side but carrying the capacity for extreme violence, having embraced their Darkness and made it a source of strength to help defend the weak and innocent.

Those who have been broken and repaired themselves are stronger than those who were never weakened. They have faced the black voids of doubt and despair and no longer fear them. Those who have hidden in the shadows can see in them and see the other lurkers in the dark, to protect those that they would prey upon.

Frank Abernathy, antihero conman of *Catch Me If You Can* now helps the FBI because he can think like a bad guy, having been one. It takes a thief to catch one. White hats versus Black hats. Most intelligence operations rely upon people who have been on the line or over it.

Psychotherapist Jordan Peterson looked at the linguistic origins of the Bible's "the meek shall inherit the earth" and states: ...translations of the word "meek"... derived from the Greek...it meant something like those who have weapons and have the ability to use them, but determined to keep them sheathed...And that means people who are capable of force, but decide not to use it, are in the proper moral position." Bad men choosing to be good are the protectors of Society.

Embracing your inner demons and coming to terms with them, harnessing their power and being able to unleash Hell if need be to protect what you love. That is a powerful person.

Action Item: look into the darkest parts of yourself and ask what you are capable of to save those you love. Are you willing to go over the line? How far will you go for what you care about? Take your darkest needs and desires and use them as fuel and strength for good.

28 FEBRUARY

"I'm a bad man."

Muhammed Ali

Muhammed Ali was The Greatest. Before that he was Cassius Clay, and six-year-old Cassius Clay was champion of the world. At least in his mind. He set the standard for trash talk and backed it up, his lightning wit almost as fast as his hands. And he knew it.

Having an edge is a benefit if you are willing to go to the edge for your greatness. Ali trained harder and believed more than others, and fooled them into thinking he was a fool with his antics and poetry but the time he put in at the gym, on the roads before dawn, and in the ring made him not just a bad man but the undisputed Champion of the World, what he knew he was at six years old. Confidence was Ali's greatest attribute.

Confidence is not arrogance. Confidence is based on a rational understanding of our capabilities, based upon what you have done in preparation for what you are going to do.

A salesperson who has done $200k of production three years in a row, who knows her market inside and out and has the referrals to do the same production again is not being arrogant telling her sales manager that $200k is her base acceptable level for the next year.

Someone who has never done it before saying they will do it, or someone who did it once on luck instead of skill, planning, and grinding it out is arrogant. Recognize the difference whether it is in yourself or your team.

Confidence is knowing you can handle yourself in a situation. You don't seek out situations (like walking down the dark alley at night on purpose, or starting a fight in a bar, or poking the bear in any way) but if a situation arises you aren't scared because you have training and experience and can handle a fight (or a market meltdown, or the chaos of ten five year-olds, or meeting a quota, or passing that exam), because you have the skill set, will set, and experience to do what you have to do. Even if you haven't done it before, if you have done the requisite work believing you will achieve, it is confidence as opposed to arrogance.

Knowing your capabilities and being able to trust them is liberating and powerful. You don't have to declare it like Ali (part of his psychological games where he beat his opponents before stepping into the ring), but if you watch a former Special Operator or experienced martial artist you can quickly realize that they too are bad men even if they are not projecting it with their words.

And there probably won't be many bad situations around them (assuming a fairly normal environment), because others can pick up on their vibe of danger too and "don't start none, won't be none".

Having the capability to take care of yourself actually makes you less likely to be a victim. Bullies want easy targets, not ones that are a lot of trouble. A confident walk and awareness of your surroundings are two critical components of self-defense.

Action item: be more confident today. Before any situation (work relationship, etc) quickly review why you can succeed in it. Ten seconds of review, then picture yourself victorious, arms raised like Ali declaring "I AM the Greatest!"

29 FEBRUARY
"Confidence is the most important single factor in this game..."
Jack Niklaus

Golf is the most mental of the sports, with every single action completely under your control to begin (the swing) and then totally out of your control for the result (wind, bounces, other players, etc) until your next ball strike. You could have an ugly swing and get lucky bounces off the back of a turtle and have a great result, smash the ball perfectly and hit a bird (not the birdie you hoped for) and get a snowman (8) on a hole, or another player might have all the luck in the world that particular day and your great day is overshadowed by an epic one. As they say "that's golf."

But the most controllable thing on the course is not the six-inch putt on the green, but the six inches between the ears. That is the place golf tournaments are won or lost, and it is a perfect analogy for life.

Making that huge pitch at work? Did you prep properly, going over everything you can about the people that will be in the room, what they want and need and how they process information and what it will take to get a yes? If you haven't you are going out on the golf course blind, no caddy, and just hacking away hoping to not lose all your balls. If you did, you can have confidence as you swing away. There are things you can't control (the other people pitching, whether the decision maker is sick, etc), but the best golfers have confidence in their ability as you should in any situation you have done your prep for.

Golf is not a game of perfect. Neither is business. Nor relationships. Nor life. But if you have done your work, you can "grip it and rip it" and have faith that the outcome will be what you deserve and want.

Doubt is the enemy of excellence, whether it is on the fairway or in the rough of the golf course or the relationship with your significant other. But having that belief in the work you have done before, and being ready to take the risk of messing up your shot to get back to an easy stroke is the outcome of years of work and maybe having a good coach (and caddy to help with the lay of the land). Take a breath, clear the negative thoughts from your minds, play through the shot in your mind, then go for it.

Action Item: remember you don't need to be perfect until you are finishing the putt. Forgive yourself if you mess up on the way, but look at that one thing today that is giving you butterflies. Close your eyes, take a deep breath. Open them. Now go for it!

IF YOU DO YOUR BEST, DON'T MIND THE REST

Irish Proverb

01 MARCH

"As is our confidence, so is our capacity."

William Hazlitt

Sometimes we see the Cinderella Story in March Madness, where the unknown or little basketball school with no pedigree takes down a big-name traditional power and makes a deep run into the tournament. Often they are led by a good to great coach and a player who a few years later is an NBA All-Star. And it isn't necessarily their physical skills but their confidence, their belief in themselves and their team, that carries them several rounds into the Big Dance.

I know a martial artist, an incredibly talented one that I have trained with for decades. He is now higher rank than I am, but he can't beat me even though he is now better than I am. Because he believes he can't and so he won't. But the instant he believes he is as good as I know him to be, the moment he thinks he can beat me he is going to whoop my butt.

The Miracle on Ice, where a group of scrappy well coached college kids from across the US took down the mighty Soviet Team (that beat NHL teams and was the elite hockey machine) because they BELIEVED they could, even though the Soviets had absolutely shelled goalie Jim Craig previously. Do you believe in miracles?!

Want that promotion? Write down all the reasons you deserve it and then go ASK for it.

Your crush? Go and ask them out, showing what a quality person you are and that you deserve the chance to show them you'd be a good companion and more.

That potential big client? Rock out to your song and call them!

Action Item: Review your SWOT. Look at your Strengths. Add more things to that list, and focus on further improving them so that you can be awesome at some of them.

02 MARCH

"Leadership is unlocking people's potential to become better."

Bill Bradley

Some people are natural born leaders and are team captain and President of the Student Body and have God given abilities that the rest of us mere mortals can only dream about. These are unicorns, rare beyond belief.

Usually leaders are made, not born.

Most leaders have become what they are because another leader saw potential in them and mentored them, guided them and challenged them to become in reality what they had seen in potentiality.

Someone further up the ladder turned and reached down to help them climb higher.

The experienced salesperson who became excellent not just because of their work ethic but because someone a generation ahead of them sat them down early in their career and invested time, imparted wisdom and said "You can do this kid, I'll keep an eye on you." and that "kid" had a great career and now at the twilight of their career is sitting down with the rookies and trying to share what they've learned, to impart on the current generation the knowledge from all previous ones.

The senior engineer showing the recent hires how to trace a wiring diagram or the craftsmen showing a better way.

Mariano Rivera, the ONLY unanimous choice for the Baseball Hall of Fame, used to sit in the bullpen with young pitchers from other teams and teach them, imparting his experience and knowledge. This is what true leaders do.

It is not a title. It is not a special parking spot or salary, a leader is the one that makes others better because they see the hidden possibilities in another and help the other person realize and materialize them. Teachers, coaches, big brothers or sisters, all can be leaders and make others better than they think they can be by believing in them.

Action Item: who looks up to you, that says they want to be like you? Have a cup of coffee with them and show them how to be BETTER than you are.

03 MARCH
"Leadership is an action, not a position."

Cindy Pace

Too many people think that leadership is an elite skill that is as rare as movie star good looks. Not true, and leadership can be developed like any other skill, and comes in an entire spectrum across almost any group.

That nine-year old Cub Scout? Yeah, that Bear Scout is a leader and teaches the six-year-old that looks up to them as a model of what a Scout should be, on how to be clean and courteous and all the other components of being a good Scout.

The twenty-two-year-old volunteering to teach programming skills to teenage girls? She is what those younger women will remember as a "coder" when they head to college or the military, and subconsciously try to emulate her positive demeanor and good attitude towards tough problems.

That Sunday School teacher who teaches kids what it means to be a good person? Leader.

Your mentor at work who shows you a better way to move something, so you can work faster and make more money? Sounds like a leader.

Anyone that has any influence over another is a leader per John Maxwell. Even the newest recruit that exhibits an ability or attitude, that nudges their buddy and gives them emotional support, is a leader as much as the General or CEO that directs the grand actions. The green newbie won't receive the accolades of the grey-haired senior officer, but they are developing the skills that could lead to that corner office or stars upon thars someday. Even if their journey is along a different path, the leadership acumen they build will serve them and others along the way.

Every one of us is a node in the network of our lives. Every other person we touch (personally or professionally) is an opportunity to share insight and experience, to lead (and learn) so that the strength of the network is improved. It is not about being in the position at the top of the pyramid that once leadership was believed to be restricted to, because we are all the centers of our universe of connections. It is the actions we take, the influences we exert, throughout these links, that measures our strength as a leader.

Action item: look at how and where you spend your time, who you interact with. Choose one person and increase your attention toward them to help them become better.

04 MARCH

"Action expresses priorities."

Mohandas Gandhi

It is not our intentions that determine our future. It is not our pretty words that show what is important to us, nor even our thoughts. What we actually DO impacts the world. Actions are powerful.

What do you choose to do with your time? Do you invest in yourself by reading, or do you waste time watching The Bachelor? What you do determines your future and reflects your belief system. Do you not only tell someone you love them but show them, regularly, in actions large and small? Or do you only say you do but the malaise of effort reflects a lack of commitment and in reality they are tenth on the list of how you allocate your time and energy?

If you are tired but still drag yourself out of bed and to the gym, that action reflects your prioritization of long-range health over short term comfort. And it will be reflected in your body as well as other areas that depend upon your discipline to choose what you want most over what you want now.

Do you fill your cabinet with junk food so that it is easy to grab and constantly consume highly processed, calorie dense chemicals or do you purchase fruits and vegetables as snacks? Your action expresses your priorities, and will determine your outcomes.

Do you step up and take the hard project at work, or look for the shortcuts and take the easy way? Both are indicative of you as an employee and your bosses notice what your priorities are and whether they merit promotions or a pink slip.

If you cut corners and cheat, it shows that you don't value the integrity of the process or the commitment and prefer the quick shot of pleasure over the feeling of doing it right, even if it is more difficult and delayed in reward. It displays your heart, even if not for the entire world to see, because enough actions and it becomes obvious what your priorities are.

Do you show that you love someone by your actions, or just give lip service while not trying to make their life better (or actively harming them)?

Action Item: look at how you have spent your time so far this week. What do the activities you've spent time on say about what is important to you?

05 MARCH

"Your decisions reveal your priorities."

Jeff Van Gundy

Do you decide to be better or bitter when faced with adversity? Either path reflects back on your psyche and reveals who you are inside.

Do you decide to tell the person you really care for that you are sorry for hurting them, even if you didn't mean to and they bear some share of the blame for the pain and the miscommunication? Choosing to swallow some pride for the good of your relationship shows that you value the other person more than the ego boost of being right or stubborn.

Do you decide to go someplace you shouldn't, either physically or emotionally or on-line? It speaks volumes about you without ever saying a word.

Volunteer, and stay out of the camera's eye while doing so? Or look for the photo op? Almost as insightful as laying on a shrink's couch as to what goes on in your head and heart.

Do you choose to try something new, or stick with what you have always eaten? Says something about your openness to new ideas, and whether you'll adjust to changes at work easily.
Work out, or plop yourself down and relax?

Ellis' ABC model shows that every Activating Event will ultimately have a Consequence (often because of a Choice), and the intervening step is controlled by your Belief System. Which is a summation of your priorities, a codification of your philosophies and priorities. In the end, almost all of our actions are outcomes of our decision making based upon what is important to us, and is the reason why Facebook and other Big Tech gather so much data about our decision making to have insight into our psyches and belief systems so that they can exploit it for their financial gain. Maybe you should invest some time to understand why you make the selections you do, to understand what is really important to you and why.

Action item: look at your bank statement/credit card statement for the past month. What did you decide to spend money on? What does that say about your priorities?

06 MARCH

"Sometimes it's the smallest decisions that can change your life forever."

Keri Russell

"For the want of a nail the shoe was lost, for the loss of a shoe the horse was lost....and for the loss of the battle the kingdom was lost."

We have all heard of The Butterfly Effect, where the wings of a butterfly in Ontario create a typhoon in India. Where a tiny action creates a monstrously huge impact someplace else.

Did you smile at the person who gave you your coffee this morning, making their day a little brighter which was then passed onto a college kid later in the day? That kid that is going to invent a vaccine fifteen years from now and save your life?

Did you decide to spend an extra few minutes studying, thus passing the exam?

Decide to NOT drive after a few drinks, avoiding a DUI or killing someone?

Decide to check on your friend that you've been concerned about, and end up preventing them from making a huge mistake with drugs and saving their life?

Let that person know you like them?

Clean the plates off the table so your significant other doesn't have to, and improve your relationship because of the little sacrifices?

Start saving money right out of college, even a little bit, to start building a savings habit that eventually lets you retire in style because time was your ally?

Pick up that coffee cup and throw it out, and a little kid sees it and decides to pick up all the garbage around their block and the TV station sees it and does a feature and other kids start cleaning up trash and suddenly the city is a bit cleaner and nicer because you threw out one piece of garbage?

Admiral McKracken in his great commencement speech talks about making your bed as a way to start your day, so that the day finishes well and you sleep better to set up the next day for success. It is a little thing that instills a good habit and attitude.

Focus on the little things, because they can compound into big things that create great good.

Action Item: look around you. What is one tiny action you can take that will make the world better? Do it.

07 MARCH
"The secret of change is to focus all of your energy, not on fighting the old, but on building the new."

Socrates

How often have we seen the fireballer that threw almost 100 mph re-invent themselves into a pitcher as their velocity declines, going from the overly proud young stud to wily veteran that uses deception to make hitter look like fools, extend their career, and ultimately make the Hall of Fame because their second act was good for an additional decade?

How many companies realized that being only brick and mortar was inefficient and moved into cyberspace, even before the pandemic and were able to come through the worst economic upheaval in generations thriving? How many of their competitors fought the tide and drowned?

Time will march on, and we can't stop it. Nor should we try, because it is the decline of the old and rise of the new that leads to all things, including you sitting here right now reading this.

Do not fight the last war is a military adage that has existed since the days of Napoleon. He crushed the Prussians because they were fighting the last war still, and did not adapt. The French didn't learn that lesson in early WWII. The US forgot it in the War on Terror and Afghanistan became Vietnam 2.0 in many ways.

Twitter was a failed company that pivoted.

In business there is a concept of "blue ocean" markets, as contrasted to the "red ocean" that is filled with blood because everyone is fighting for market share in a limited space. Better to sail out and discover the new world and new opportunities where no one else is and build your empire there instead of having to claw and fight in a zero-sum game that is more Pyrrhic Victory than anything. Instead of fighting the old, risk and go find the new.

Adapt, and overcome.

Don't be the grumpy old guy on the front porch saying "back in my day..." and "get off my lawn!". The world evolves and those who don't change are called "dinosaurs" because they will go extinct.

Just like the dodo.

Action item: what is one new idea, technology, or technique that you are really resisting? Invest some time to understand it, and set aside your luddite tendencies to see if it might help you.

08 MARCH
"We build too many walls and not enough bridges."

Sir Isaac Newton

At the end of the Black Panther movie, T'Challa proclaims the same thing: "more connects us than separates us. But in times of crisis, the wise build bridges, while the foolish build barriers."

When was the last time you sat down with someone that you disagree with in many ways, to see where there are areas of agreement so that you can understand and create respect? Supreme Court Justices Ruth Bader Ginsburg and Antonin Scalia were known as "The Odd Couple" because even though they were on opposite ends of the political spectrum they had a deep respect and friendship that they built and maintained over decades that allowed them to examine their own beliefs and logic while remaining true to their ideals. While sitting on the most influential bench in the country. More people in the Capitol should follow their example.

Fight with your spouse or significant other? Instead of pointing fingers, why not ask "I hear you are upset about X, can you tell me why so I understand?" Won't resolve every argument, but it will reduce them in the future because understanding reduces conflict, in a family and among nations.

Talk to your boss or that coworker you have an issue with. "Hey, I noticed we are not progressing on Y, can you give me some insight as to this? I want to understand what we are doing and what you need from me so we can get the job done." A discussion like this over a cup of coffee (or adult beverage) will go a long way, not just on this particular project but also for your career.

That annoying neighbor (who probably calls you the same thing)? Sit down with them and break bread. Mending fences together instead of unilaterally erecting them is as old as our country and a way to improve relationships and neighborhoods.

Investing time in emotional infrastructure with those you interact with will allow you to have quicker movement of products, ideas, and emotions. Bridge the gap with others and you'll save a lot of time and heartache.

Action item: Who was the last person you disagreed with? Reach out to them and talk, to build a bridge over the chasms that separate you.

09 MARCH
"In every conceivable manner, the family is our link to our past, bridge to the future."
Alex Haley

Your family was there before you were born, and they will be here after you are gone. They are our foundation that we build up from, and the higher levels built on our own works.

Think about your own personality: you are an amalgam of your experiences and your earliest and strongest ones come from family: parents and siblings specifically. And your own children inherit bits and pieces of who they are from you, a transfer of attitudes and inclinations down through generations.

Your parents and lineal ancestors have passed you your eye color and shape, your base musculature tendencies, and (unfortunately) their proclivity towards (or away) from baldness. These genetic gifts actually account for about half of our manifested traits, be it how happy we tend to be or if we are born to be a sprinter. We can through our decisions (often modeled off of those closest to us) influence the ultimate outcomes (even skinny people can lift weights, and naturally morose individuals improve their outlook). Our genes deal us the cards, but we get to decide how to play the hand we are dealt.

If you have children (or grandchildren), you can act like a filter for them: you can stop some of the negative pieces of your family history from passing down. Just because your dad was an alcoholic doesn't mean that your kids are doomed to become one. By understanding the negative aspects of our family we can actively work against that predisposition with attention and awareness, with education and effort that can make sure the flaws in one generation aren't passed to future ones. Linking to the past does not mean being chained to it.

Your family tree has given you roots to draw nourishment from the past while you reach for the sky and branch out for the future. Deep roots will help you grow higher, but it is up to you as to what you draw from the ground laid for you to determine how sweet the fruit you ultimately bear is.

Action item: look at some old photos of your parents and grandparents today. What parts of yourself do you see in them? What are some of their better aspects that you wish you could emulate? What is preventing you from doing so, today?

10 MARCH
"Like a bridge over troubled water I will ease your mind."

Paul Simon

I don't think this comes as a surprise but life is not all rainbows and riding unicorns across meadows while fairies shower us with money.

Sometimes it's tough, and it seems like when things get tougher more problems decide "hey, now's a good time to pop up and pile on!". Maybe it's something at work, added to a relationship issue and economic concerns and then the car needs service, plus your kid gets in trouble in school and your seasonal depression is amping up....

Troubles seem to multiply like unmatched socks and move from mild annoyance to "I want to punch everyone in the face" level, and you start thinking about how much easier life in prison might actually be compared to what you are going through.

Stop for a moment.

Close your eyes.

Take a deep breath.

And another.

Picture the sound of a stream of running water. No, don't picture yourself holding someone under the water!

But picture the person who is with you, listening to that babbling brook.

Let them be your bridge over the troubled water.

Action Item: That person who you envisioned? Call them.

11 MARCH

"I am learning to trust the journey even when I do not understand it."

Mia Bron

Butterflies don't just appear magically in the spring.

They start as eggs, then pupae, then caterpillars. They then create a chrysalis around themselves and transform from an earthbound slow ugly thing to a fluttering bit of beauty that can move in three dimensions and literally fly away.

Joseph Campbell analyzes the journey of the hero, where our hero (or heroine) must undertake a perilous journey into darkness to grow as a person. Merida in *Brave*, Luke Skywalker, Samwise Gamgee, all must undertake the quest of discovery that is as old as human storytelling. Jordan Peterson breaks down the psychology underlying the Bible stories such as Jonah and the Whale (echoed in Pinocchio) that are reflected in essentially every other major religion, showing that the favored writer's analogy of "on the road..." is universal.

We are all on a journey and none of us know where the end destination is. And the GPS isn't functioning quite right, and there are construction detours everywhere. Plus the gas might be running low, and you need more coffee and a bathroom break.

Sometimes you might need to pull over and rest a little. Or take a break and stretch your legs and look at the butterflies in the meadow. That's ok. Heroes and heroines rest when they need to. Both Gilgamesh and Frodo slept.

As we struggle through our quest, we face trials and tribulations that give us skills and strengths for the rest of the journey. Like a video game there are side quests that sometimes distract us too much, but we have to get back to the main quest sooner rather than later.

Your path is not clear and straight and that's good, because that is where ambushes occur. The long and winding road, with bends that hide the surprises ultimately lead to better destinations.

Action Item: look back over the past five to ten years. What unexpected curves in your journey have led to spectacular sites or opportunities?

12 MARCH

"Faith sees the invisible, believes the incredible, and receives the impossible."

Corrie ten Boom

Faith is moving forward when you are surrounded by doubt. It is not always fiery, but the quiet voice in the back of your head that says "take the step. And again."

Faith sees the path in the dark, and gives the strength to walk it even in the shadows.

Faith is what allows startup company founders to work crazy hours and take risks while their friends and families say "you're crazy." Because these crazy founders can see a future that others can't, believe they can bring it into reality, and then receive the economic and social benefits of changing the world.

Faith is listening to the coach that knows how to bring out the best in you that you don't know is there, that knows how to win and has a vision of your team knocking off the powerhouse and becoming champions in the classic underdog story we have seen repeatedly.

Faith is sitting with your addicted friend in their worst moments, so they know you believe in them and their recovery and are willing to fight (even fight them) to help them help themselves and heal, to escape the hell they are in.

Faith moves mountains, both metaphysically and physically.

Faith lets you exhaust yourself today, then get up tomorrow to work on bringing the incredible into the everyday.

Faith is the difference between giving up and getting back up.

Have faith.

Action item: sit for a moment and reflect. When was the last time you believed and no one else did, where you did what you had to do even if no one else could conceive of what you were attempting? Capture that feeling, lock it into your heart to tap into later.

13 MARCH

"Vision is the art of seeing the invisible."

Jonathon Swift

Roy Disney flew over the orange groves of Florida and saw Cinderella's Castle rising above happy throngs of people.

Nikolai Tesla saw the electromagnetic waves transmitting information.

Ada Lovelace envisioned the computer.

Tori Amos and Billy Joel see music as color, and compose in pictures that they translate for the listeners.

Seeing that which others cannot yet comprehend is a gift which all children have but we forget as we grow up. Seeing what COULD be is as (or is even more) important than seeing what IS as an ability that creators tap into to improve our world in everything from art to technology to teaching. Seeing the potential in a block of marble (Michelangelo) or how a burger is made (Ray Kroc) or where the game will evolve to (Billy Beane) are all varieties of vision that have altered the way others see their world, and unlocked immense value.

Some people see the world through rose tinted glasses, others with X Ray specs. Some might have Rowdy Roddy Piper's glasses from Them, but seeing the same thing as others but in new ways is one way to understand the world and bring about changes by not accepting that which is currently seen is all that there is. It is the secret sauce of science and art, the impetus for advancement in all forms and the reason why we can do everything beyond subsistence. All human advancement has come from vision, from the earliest agriculture to people walking on Mars in the future.

See what could be, not what merely is.

Action item: what is your vision for your life? What do you see in your future that others cannot see yet? What do you need to do to manifest it, so that others can see your vision?

14 MARCH

"A question that sometimes drives me hazy: am I or are the others crazy?"

Albert Einstein

Those who see the world differently often are labeled as insane, or more politely called crazy. Whether it is groundbreaking work in science, pushing the boundaries in art, or trying to build a business from the kitchen table, anyone challenging the status quo needs to have a little bit of "not right in the head" in them to look at the mores and accepted standards and question them.

"Madness and genius are one step apart, I'm just not sure which foot to lead with." JRRT

Crazy like a fox.

"No great mind has existed without a touch of madness." Aristotle

The fact that Einstein was aware enough to question his own sanity while delving the most esoteric secrets of the universe is somewhat refreshing, as many other great minds have gone down rabbit holes and unfortunately not popped back up for decades (John Nash or Howard Hughes) or blew themselves up (Jack Parsons, Van Gogh, Kurt Cobain). Metacognitive awareness of whether our own thoughts are pushing us beyond the bounds of rationality is a key factor in creative longevity.

"Why is that so?" is a question that scientists, philosophers, and artists of all forms have asked since time immemorial. Having one eye on others and one on yourself is a difficult balancing act that requires energy and attention but preserves the dynamic tension required to expand the limits of our knowledge and expression.

"You want to do WHAT?" is a question that has halted great (if untraditional) ideas over and over, but is a sign that you might be onto something. Whether it is an app to let you get a ride with a stranger (Uber and Lyft), an unorthodox approach to a physical ailment (like the treatment for leukemia), or an attempt to finish a degree while working full-time and raising a family, having half the people (or more) tell you that you are crazy might mean that you are on the right track for something great.

Action item: what is something that you've thought of attempting that others said you were nuts to do? Dust it off and seriously take a look at it again and see if it really is that outlandish of an idea.

15 MARCH
"The people who are crazy enough to think they can change the world are the ones who do."
Steve Jobs

Think Different, the campaign Jobs launched soon after returning to Apple (the company he founded and was FIRED from, eventually returning after he matured and tempered his worst tendencies) starts with: Here's to the crazy ones, the misfits, the rebels, the troublemakers, the round pegs in the square holes...the ones who see things differently. All innovation comes from seeing the world differently, but then working to bring that vision to reality. And it is this translation where a lot of the real craziness dwells.

Hundreds of car companies were founded in the United States in a couple of decades. But it was Henry Ford that was crazy enough to go to backwoods upstate New York to learn about assembly line technology, institute a 40-hour work week, and pay well above scale to truly change the auto world and the entire face of manufacturing.

Althea Gibson: winner of ELEVEN Grand Slam tennis titles starting in the 1950's. A black woman whose talent and class rivalled the great Jackie Robinson and broke barriers, laying the ground for stars like Venus and Serena Williams and Naomi Osaka.

Jonas Salk foresaw a world without polio. The nameless man standing in front of the line of tanks in Tiananmen Square made the world see that a single person can stop an army.

Stan Lee and the Marvel Universe he helped create.

A big nosed author typing away like one of the infinite monkeys to produce this book, that hopefully changes at least your world. He is definitely crazy enough to believe he can make the world better. Alexander the Great slicing the Gordian Knot or any of thousands of inventors and company builders in garages or at kitchen tables with a head full of crazy notions that become everything from bomb sights to cancer treatments, novels to novel solutions to sticky problems. The ones who don't accept the status quo because it's just not good enough and we can do and be better dammit!

The crazy ones who have a dream and want to see the world improve so much that they bend reality to their will a la Jobs, that see "no" as not the obstacle but the way to "oh yeah!" They believe in the future more than the past and are ready to go against convention and tradition to bring about a brave new world.

Action Item: what do you rebel against? What area are you considered a "troublemaker" in because you don't accept "well, that's how we've always done it!" What can you do to change that little bit of the world? Go do it!

16 MARCH

"No matter what people tell you, words and ideas can change the world."

Robin Williams

Words have the power to harm or to heal, to light a fire that burns the world or to inspire and fire up others to do great things. Choose yours carefully, and guard your attention as to which ones you expose yourself to because of the power of words and ideas.

Ideas can spread like wildfire for good or ill, at a rate and reach inconceivable even a generation ago. An image or tweet can reach a million people in under a second, a billion in a few minutes. Revolutions are started by people but it is the ideas and the fiery rhetoric around them that touch off the powder kegs, for good or ill.

"I have a dream." "Tear down this wall." "Lock her up!" Each of these instantly evokes images and instills a visceral reaction, the words capturing the ideas and emotions of that particular moment that would influence history for years. The blazing passions can warm or burn, the classic dichotomy of powerful things.

We live in a time where words spoken a few years ago are dug up and used to cause harm, yet words that are used to heal or help are ignored. This focus on separation and division instead of unification and bonding, of alienating instead of allying for a greater good is dangerous and is purposefully utilized to acquire power via fear instead of creating hope for all. These are the most dangerous of words, and the First Amendment protects them, even the ones we disagree with.

Use your words for good. Choose to heal instead of harm. That is a radical idea in today's world and as such the world is ready for an old idea: that we can look out for ourselves and help our neighbor even if we don't agree with them. Seek to understand their ideas, their why behind the what. You might find their ideas are not so radical.

Action Item: listen to someone you normally disagree with. REALLY listen to them, to see if you can find common ground and build a better idea from your two parts.

17 MARCH
"Being Irish, I always had this love of words."

Kenneth Branagh

The Irish are known for their gift of the gab, and have contributed both "Blarney" and "shenanigans" to the lexicon. And as I have been reminded over and over by my relatives, to never ruin a good tale with facts!

Words allow us to weave thoughts into tapestries, to allow others insight into our inner world. Developing skill in working with them, in crafting phrases and concepts to communicate ideas and emotions is one of the critical skills for success. The capability to express ourselves and ultimately influence others has been valuable since the earliest societies. The ability to tell a story to teach a concept has been a staple of leaders religious and secular from the dawn of time, and will stay an integral part of being human for as long as we are human.

Words are the realm not just of poets and politicians but every person that wants to lead others in any capacity, from a couple of kids playing in the dust on a playground in kindergarten to the corner office. Language lets us shape our perspectives, literally the narrative of our reality and those we surround ourselves with.

Read.

Read more.

Read even more.

Anything from a comic book to a trashy novel to the encyclopedia or the complete works of Shakespeare. More words are like more Legos: you can build greater structures if you have more pieces to play with.

Action item: pick up and read something today you normally wouldn't read.

18 MARCH
"Poetry is language at its most distilled and most powerful."

Rita Dove

Listening to good poetry should make you drunk with feeling, unable to withstand the emotions that swell up inside you. Anger, fear, sadness, joy, love. All the emotions, unrestrained by the normal conscious restraints we have in everyday life.

"In wine there is truth" is an old Latin saying, and poetry is stronger wine than anything from a vine because it is made from the soul of the poet put on the page.

Shakespeare, Rumi, Jeanty all captured their supernatural inspirations of amorousness and shared them with us to partake of with those we adore. For as Robin Williams proclaimed: language was invented for one reason boys – to woo women. And poetry is the "liquor is quicker" of words.

I try to write poetry and fail miserably in distilling the message into the most powerful yet innocuous spirit. Too strong or too spicy, it burns the tongue instead of smoothly coating and warming. Yet it is the nature of the human heart and spirit to strive again and again until we have that fleeting taste of beauty…

Poetry Is

Poetry is the soul
put on the page
for others to see
and study, dissect
like you cut apart
my heart.

Feel the burn like a papercut to your soul, with the bitter juice poured into the wound.

Action item: read and write a poem today.

19 MARCH

"Calmness is the cradle of power."

Josiah Gilbert Holland

The person who can remain unperturbed as the storm rages without and within holds a tactical advantage in the chaos of life.

"Calmness is one of the beautiful jewels of wisdom." James Allen

What does it mean to be a samurai? To seek a stillness of your mind. Warriors know that being calm as the fog of war descends is the key to survival. It is this internal tranquility that prevents fear from paralyzing them, and gives clear vision and decisions in the pandemonium swirling around them.

Anger makes us stupid. It makes us react to external events and people, and give up our power to others.

"You have power over your mind not outside events, realize this and you will find strength." Seneca Think about the last time you were furious. How rational were you? How clear was your thinking, or your speech? Were you persuasive or just loud and belligerent? Would you have been more successful in that encounter if you had a slightly cooler head?

Think of James Bond. Is he ever angry, losing his cool? Or is he calm, controlled, polite, and deadly? Hot heads rarely get the license to kill, because they would wantonly use it.

When was the last time you were broken hearted, ready to cry? How well were you able to perform, whether at work or at home? Brett Favre's performance following his father's death is all the more epic for his poise on the field that night, a calmness he rarely possessed as a gunslinging daredevil.

Still waters hide the greatest treasures.

.

Action item: when emotional today, take three breaths, each deeper and slower than the last one.

20 MARCH
"Be like a duck. Calm on the surface, but always paddling like the dickens underneath."
Sir Michael Caine

They look placid, just cruising along on the surface, totally nonplussed. Balanced and demure, the epitome of cool and calm. And yet underneath they are struggling, fighting with all they have to move forward. Welcome to life. The most suave and seemingly perfect people are treading water and struggling under the makeup and illusion of a perfect life.

I once did a presentation with a young rookie in my office. It was a pretty big deal for him, his share being worth almost half his annual minimum quota in one shot. The client at the final decision point hemmed and hawed and talked himself out of it and into it and out and in. Three hours of vacillation and we walked out with the deal. The other guy looked at me afterwards and exclaimed: that was amazing! You were so cool. How many times have you done something like that? I looked at him and gave him my best Miyagi "Don't know. First time." He almost had a heart attack.

Just because internally my gears were going at redline level, doesn't mean I let anyone see it. That is one of the secrets of success: work like hell but make it look easy.

"One of the things about powerful people is they have the ability to make it look easy." Ice-T

"The definition of being good is being able to make it look easy." Hugh Jackman

I did a Tae Kwon Do demonstration at an activity fair on campus, when all the clubs got a chance to recruit and maybe show off a little. After I ran a mini class and some students do some forms and then fought, we brought out a couple of cinder blocks and put them near the front of the 30'x30' area. Then I laid a four-inch thick block of ice on top of the cinder blocks, like Stone Henge and stood facing it with my back to the large open area. Up went my foot, over my head, and down harder than a sledgehammer. WHAM!!! The block of ice exploded. Ice went flying, chunks bigger than your fist shooting ten feet into the air and ice cubes hitting the back wall. I bowed and we cleaned up as the crowd went wild.

Someone asked me how long I had trained for that break. "20 years and 20 seconds. The twenty seconds were deciding to do it and then doing it." The years of practice, the intense effort, was all hidden from those watching, while the students knew how hard I pushed them, not knowing I pushed myself five times harder when they weren't able to see it. Like the duck, I looked placid but only because of how often I ran my motor at red line. No matter your struggles, don't stop kicking.

Action item: don't let your boss see how hard you work, but work like hell today.

21 MARCH

"We forge the chains we wear in life."

Charles Dickens

We create our own boundaries and hell within our minds and hearts. We chose the path we are to follow with our decisions, and with our mindset.

Are you forging chains that hold you to a particular location, like the small town that you grew up in because your family is all there and no one ever really leaves?

Are you bound to a particular job because chains of fear keep you from spreading your wings and flying?

Are you staying in an abusive relationship (physically or mentally) because of your self-imposed limitations?

"Chains of habit are too light to be felt until they are too heavy to be broken." Warren Buffett

What habits are chaining you, whether to your cell phone or to a lifestyle that you don't truly desire? How do you break said chains before they are too strong and you are bound for eternity? We can use the chains we forge to hold us steady, like on the anchor of a ship in a harbor during a storm. These bonds of friendship and family can moor us to safety. Do not let the anchor stay down though when the time is right to sail out on the adventure, because you can always return to your home port with stories and treasures. Never leaving harbor is the opposite of what a ship is designed for, even if it is safe there at anchor.

We can use the chains to hold us together in the dark, keeping us from getting separated from those we need to survive. Climbing mountains requires holding fast to those that are there to support, guide, and help us even at risk to themselves.

Chains help us move through the winter storms, and can lock out the dangers in an uncertain world. But come summer the chains come off the tires and we can go further and faster. We can not open doors that are chained shut.

Know when to take the chains off.

Action Item: what are the chains holding you in place at work and home? Are they for your safety like the anchor, or restraining you like a dog that wants to run?

22 MARCH
"Innocence is like polished armor; it adorns and defends."

Robert South

The truth is simple to remember, and powerful even when others don't want to hear it. The simple truth will also protect you most of the time.

Yes, in business and divorce you need attorneys to protect you, mercenaries that are hired to defend you against the trickiness of their own ilk that look for chinks and weaknesses in your armor or to take advantage of the landscape. But most of the time innocence is the shield that unbreakably keeps you safe, deflecting all attacks.

Polished armor is beautiful, reflecting the rays of the sun and shining brightly. The light of the sun and truth is anathema to lies and evil in the great stories, and that is a reflection of reality: darkness covers many the misdeed and evil thought. Innocence is a protection in that the tendrils of evil can not penetrate and turn your heart nor mind to nefarious thoughts or deeds if your heart remains pure. The inability for malice to take root in you prevents the growing of bitter fruit.

Look at someone pure in heart, and see how they walk, often like an angel barely touching the earth. The armor of innocence is light (as opposed to the heavy heart of those with a guilty conscience). See how they almost dance in their movements. Innocence is light and bright raiment that is beautiful to gaze upon, mithril most fair and dear.

Over time, even the greatest of knights have their armor dented in battle. We have bruises from where our armor stopped the blow but we still felt the force of it, leaving us not as shiny even if we are still as protected as before. Battle after battle over time leaves us with knicks and scrapes and scars, but we are still ultimately safe if not as beautiful. Given time and peace we can polish our armor again, repair the little damages and be ready to fight again, but too many wars will eventually destroy even the innocent.

Keep your innocence wherever you may. Keep your words and deeds as pure as possible, to maintain the integrity of your person and the protection it provides.

Action item: today, tell the truth all the time. Remain silent if you must, but utter no falsehood today. Start recreating your innocence and the beautiful protection it provides.

23 MARCH
"Truth will always be truth, regardless of lack of understanding, disbelief or ignorance."
W. Clement Stone

Einstein did not believe in quantum physics until the very end of his life. Even if one of the preeminent minds of science did not believe the reality that quantum theory opened up, it did not change the facts that came to light over time.

It is a testament to Einstein that he could acknowledge that he had been mistaken for so long, and admitting we are wrong takes more strength than many of us are willing to admit we lack in the first place.

I screw up and am wrong all the time, I will always be paying the price for my ego and arrogance and ignorance, and I will unfortunately bear some of the losses from my stupidity and inability to accept the truth until the end of my days. That is my cross to bear.

"The truth is like a pancake. No matter how thin, there are still two sides" one of my close friends told me and I was too stupid (or arrogant) to try and flip it over and look at the other side. Having that understanding from the opposite perspective though has let me understand better. Too bad it took me so long to flip it over and look at the other side.

Just because we don't believe something doesn't make it false if it doesn't align with our world view. Cognitive dissonance is common, where our thoughts have major incongruity, a piece that is utterly out of place and we don't expend the effort to try and alter our current thinking to allow this new piece of information to fit well.

Instead we try to hammer it into place or just leave it sitting there precariously and unintegrated into the whole. We as humans are lazy and would generally rather just leave it then question our existing reference frames and change our beliefs to accommodate new information, especially that which contradicts long held beliefs.

We are for the most part the sum total of our experiences and exposures. If we have a significant amount of these that build one narrative of the world and later are made aware of new information that contradicts what we tell ourselves, we often don't believe the new information.

We may be in shock, we may reject it as fake or unvetted, we might just completely ignore it. And if the new information is small in amount, or relevance it just might not be enough for us to change and over time the lack of evolution leaves us significantly out of sync.

Or it could be so huge and frame breaking that we can not comprehend it and so narrow our focus to what we think we have and know because it is safer that way. Our belief system must grow over time with new knowledge, the same way the periodic table of elements has or the map of the explored world has been filled in over the years.

Our minds, our reference frames, our very ways of seeing the universe that surrounds us must expand in line with the increase in human knowledge.

Action Item: What is one thing you believed a decade ago that you now know to be untrue? Take a moment to think about your current thinking, and see if there is something that you have avoided integrating. Note it above.

24 MARCH
"Losing an illusion makes you wiser than finding a truth."

Ludwig Borne

Sometimes, we need to have the rose-colored glasses knocked off our face by reality. Sometimes we need to see the angel actually has horns and the rose has thorns.

The person we love when we first fall for them is an illusion, a combination of best behaviors (admit it, you were on your best behavior and covering your flaws too), and subtle mis-directions so as to cast themselves (and us) in the best possible light. But when the makeup comes off, when the stress of life causes the masks to slip, truth is revealed.

We live in a world that the Scottish psychologist Laird would love to analyze, a universal "False Self" of social media and SnapChat filters and internet envy that enables us to create whomever we wish and project it on the world. This is either a drastic overcompensation of our internal True Self or a repudiation thereof where the scrawny scientist becomes a powerful superhero, or the shy bookworm is the life of the party, where everything can be bigger (and better) than life. We can create an image that we wish we were, and move in and out of circles wearing costumes and swapping identities in ways that even a few decades ago would have been incomprehensible.

And then when you think you find The One (be it a person, or a place to live, or the company to work for; any person, place, or thing that can present itself in the most favorable way to woo you), emotionally you invest of yourself and become partially or wholly seduced. By an illusion, even if it is based on reality.

And then SMACK!

Truth hits and hurts. They aren't on a pedestal anymore. They aren't the most beautiful, or as caring as you thought. They aren't as wealthy, or as good. The apartment has bugs and is in the airport flight path. That manager is a slimeball and will steal your ideas and throw you under the bus.

Or even little things like she snores and leaves her hair in the drain, or he can only really cook three dishes and can't fold a sheet and really loves music you abhor.

Is there enough truth, enough substance to rebuild a realistically based relationship after the illusion is shattered? Or are the lies and flaws too deep to reconcile? You need to look at the situation and make a choice. But if you can move forward, it will be different and better.

Action item: this might hurt. What was the most important relationship that was not as true as it should have been? What did you do to contribute to the illusion? What can you learn for the next time around?

25 MARCH
"The more you lose, the more you want to win."

Brett Hull

Losing sucks.

Does it suck in a way that you will avoid losing by not playing the game?

Or does it suck enough for you to get up early and put in extra effort so you are better and lose less? Does a loss break you and make you avoid taking the risk of asking your crush out, or does it make you improve yourself so that you have more to offer and they become more likely to say yes over time?

Does not getting that sale make you give up that career, or do you sit down and figure out what you could do better, so that you have action items to practice and improve and next time your chances of getting the deal aren't 50/50 but closer to 100%?

Michael Jordan famously used getting cut from his high school basketball team as fuel to become one of the most spectacular players of all time.

Sugar Ray Leonard took his loss to Roberto Duran so badly he immediately started training for the rematch and came out so strong Duran famously quit, declaring "no mas!"

Do you put yourself in a position to lose more often so that you can win more? Is improvement from every day critical to your being so that you literally hate losing enough to make the sacrifices of time and money to hire people to make you better (coaches, courses, better nutrition and education and systems) so that you can win more and at a higher level?
Are you ok with losing, or allergic to it?

Action Item: Think about your last big loss. Dissect it, analyze it. What is one thing you can do better next time that would have changed the outcome? Do what it takes to make it happen.

26 MARCH

"Skate to where the puck is going to be, not where it has been."

Wayne Gretzky

Proactive planning, not reactive planning.

Teaching a 16 year-old to drive is a scary experience, partially because they think it's Mario Kart and partially because they are looking roughly a foot in front of the hood and by the time they realize it, they have hit the shopping cart. Teaching them to look out at a distance of five or six car lengths, and be aware of what is not just directly in front of them, is critical for them to succeed.

Great planners, be they financial advisors or business strategists or whatever, look to see what is going to likely happen five and fifteen and fifty years in the future and take that into account with what they design.

Good design allows for expansion and improvement over time, instead of having to rip out the old and replace it with new whatever in a costly and time-consuming manner every five to ten years instead of planning ahead. Designed in flexibility and the potential for growth is as important as protecting against downside risk.

Think like a chess player. They move here, then I move there, and then they do OH CRAP I don't want that!

Look ahead and if need be pause to think instead of reacting. Humans can project into the future and it gives us a tactical advantage over other animals. Plan ahead, don't just go after the shiny object right in front of you.

Action Item: play the "What if?" game. What if they do this, what will I do? What if they do X, what are my possible responses so I'm ready for the bounce of the puck?

27 MARCH
"A lion runs the fastest when he is hungry."

Salman Khan

A fed lion has no need to hunt down a meal. They get fat and lazy. Content.

The Challenger is always hungrier than the Champ.

Those fighting to climb the mountain strive harder than those in the corner office, especially after a few years when complacency sinks in.

Need creates speed.

What makes you hungry, makes your mouth water with desire and inspires you to kick in the extra gear?

What challenge are you going after, be it physical, mental, educational, or other?

Why are you jumping out of bed, ready to hit the ground running?

As Twisted Sister proclaimed in the 1980's: stay hungry!

Action Item: what gets your pulse pumping and ready to GO? Write it above, go get it!

28 MARCH

"Discipline is doing what you hate to do, but doing it like you love it."

Mike Tyson

Most people have no problem doing something that they enjoy, because the doing is a reward. This applies to kids playing, adults attending cocktail parties, religious people going to services. Doing what we like gives us a dopamine shot of pleasure.

Those things we hate? Most of us will do almost anything to avoid or outsource this if possible. It could be cleaning the toilets or running particular reports at work, or picking up the phone to schedule appointments (something that I hate and still will do anything to avoid even if I am arguably pretty damn good at it). Lifters usually hate cardio, and I don't think very many of us like to diet. But as fitness guru Jack LaLanne said, learn to love a sweet pepper as much as chocolate.

There are some people that look forward to doing what they hate because it makes them better at whatever is truly important to them. That young lady that is scared of public speaking so joins Toastmasters and practices speaking in front of the mirror that eventually does a TED Talk. That scrawny kid that can't press the bar that becomes a behemoth. The kid that hates the violin that makes it to Carnegie Hall. The stutterer who becomes President. These are all people doing what they hate to do until they love it.

You don't have to go to that extreme, but for a little bit each day can you do the important things you hate and do them with your whole heart? Can you pretend to love cooking or presenting in front of your boss? Dig down, give it your absolute best for a limited time each day so that you can get to do the things you love?

In *The Common Denominator of Success*, Gray states that successful people make a habit of what unsuccessful ones are unwilling to do. To put on a smile, suck it up, and go. Can you do this consistently to get what others won't?

I know someone who does Ragnars (200-mile team relay runs), marathons and even Ultramarathons. Because he hates running. OK, that someone is actually me. I hate running, I'm not built for it, I'm as fast as a 286 computer and sound like a sixty-year-old diesel engine and am an ungainly freak. And I do it with a goofy grin because I hate it until I stop. But I do it, because it makes me better at other things.

Can you fake it 'til you make it in aspects of your life that will help you grow? Or at least admit you hate them but do them with all your heart?

Action Item: choose the thing you hate at work the most, and do it like it is your favorite thing in the world for a week.

29 MARCH
"A champion is someone who gets up when he can't."

Jack Dempsey

When you get knocked down, it isn't your muscles that get you back up off the canvas. It's your guts. Your heart. Your spirit.

Babe Ruth said it's tough to beat a guy who doesn't give up.

Don't give up when life knocks you down.

Fight that cancer.

Fight for your kids.

Battle for that job or promotion.

As Rocky said "I didn't hear no bell." Come back out swinging.

Don't let yourself (or your corner) throw in the towel.

Find a reason to fight. James "Buster" Douglas took down the unbeaten and seemingly unbeatable Mike Tyson right after his mom died, because he promised her he would be World Champion and had something to fight for. He became a champion because he did what he couldn't.

Brett Favre went out and threw for well over 300 yards after his father died, because his dad would have wanted him on that field. Even though he couldn't even see because of tears in his eyes, he had one of the most dominant performances of his career because he had to go out and compete.

Steve Jobs built NEXT and PIXAR after being canned from Apple. He got back up, and eventually made Apple the first $1 Trillion company. Jobs got back up, as did the company that kicked him out. Beethoven went deaf and composed some of his greatest works.

You could stay there, laying on your back staring up as the ref counts.

Or you force yourself to stand. Stand and fight. And win.

Action Item: DON'T GIVE UP TODAY! ONE MORE ROUND!

29 MARCH

"Every champion was once a contender
who refused to give up."

Sly Stallone, in *Rocky*

If you are still standing at the end of the fight you are the winner, even if you are not handed the title. As Sinatra sang:

> *Not the words of one who kneels*
> *The record shows, I took the blows*
> *But I did it my way.*

If you can take all the abuse (physical, verbal, emotional, mental) and still be standing, you are a winner. A champion, and worthy of the title of "warrior".

Not every contest is in a nice squared circle, with cheering crowds and a multimillion dollar purse. The special needs parent that fights for their kid's IEP (Individual Education Plan) and has worrisome day after sleepless night because of their child's needs will never give up.

The single parent working multiple jobs to take care of their kids.

The broken-hearted fighting the darkness every day and refusing to give in.

The Vet battling his demons for just another day, or the abused woman that stands up and faces her fears to stop a walking evil.

These are the champions, the warriors around us. They refuse to give up.

"Never yield to force; never yield to the apparently overwhelming might of the enemy." Winston Churchill

"A Champion is defined not by their wins, but by how they recover when they fall." Serena Williams

My autistic son is my hero, because even when he is overwhelmed and starts to shut down from sensory or emotional overload, he fights it. He fights like a champion, and will be one someday in some way because he refuses to give up.

"True champions aren't always the ones that win, but those with the most guts." Mia Hamm

The kid fighting cancer.

The grandparent struggling with Alzheimer's.

The dyslexic trying to learn.

These are not truly physical battles, but the emotional reserves and courage of these people to not go quietly into the good night should inspire all of us as much as a boxer or a mixed martial artist. Less bragging than Connor McGregor, and many many more rounds because the fight does not end until the very end.

Refuse to lose.

The physically broken down former champ Rocky tells his now adult son that is complaining about being in his dad's shadow: "Let me tell you something you already know. The world ain't all sunshine and rainbows. It's a very mean and nasty place and I don't care how tough you are, it will beat you to your knees and keep you there permanently if you let it. You, me, or nobody is gonna hit as hard as life. But it ain't about how hard ya hit. It's about how hard you can get hit and keep moving forward. How much you can take and keep moving forward. That's how winning is done!"

From his time as a contender refusing to give up to his comebacks, Rocky was more heart and guts than technique but always embodied the warrior spirit of a champion.

Action item: refuse to give up. When life beats you down, keep moving forward!

31 MARCH

"Though the road's been rocky
it sure feels good to be me."

Bob Marley

Tired of hearing celebrities whine about how tough their life is while they have nannies and personal chefs and trainers? Bob Marley was shot twice, recovered, and then diagnosed with the cancer that ultimately claimed his life. And yet he maintained a positive attitude.

I know people that have broken their neck, were told they would never walk again, and even though they can barely dress themselves without help have run marathons. And they have gone on to be President of their trade association, sitting in front of Congress and answering questions about the very insurance policies that paid his bills while he healed.

The road has been rocky for my buddy John Nichols, but I know of few happier people. He feels good because he knows what it was like to not feel with a severed spine, and his good vibes rub off.

I have other friends that struggled for years, whether it was building a business or getting their degrees while raising a family. They finally succeeded after years of stress and late nights and wondering how they were going to pay the bills, and they are thankful for the opportunity to struggle.

People like this deserve extra praise because they could have given up and taken the easy road at any point but refused to do so.

Anyone that has chosen the difficult road is deserving of praise. And if they succeed, deserve all the rewards for the risks they took, the long nights and sleeping in the office then getting back at it, the day after day grind, the worry and ridicule and fear.

There is a reason why capitalism rewards those who take risks in aggregate, because each individual faces an incredibly difficult road to success.

Maybe your relationship has been rocky. Did you decide to get off and abandon it, or struggle on the journey together? You deserve praise.

"The bravest sight in the world is to see a great man struggling against adversity." Seneca

Come back from an injury? Kudos to you.

"The only disability in life is a bad attitude." Scott Hamilton

Supported someone as they break an addiction? This is incredibly difficult to watch a loved one struggle, and to not abandon them to their demons and their internal storm.

"If you want the rainbow, you gotta put up with the rain." Dolly Parton

The harder the path, the greater the feeling of victory. Think about when you worked all day in the hot sun, busting your butt. And then had a good meal and a nice adult beverage. Was there anything better than when it touched your lips after a hard day?

Earned rewards are the greatest.

Action item: today you will struggle at times, that is life. But as you do, stop for a moment and think how good you have it. Savor the struggle on the rocky road.

APRIL, DRESSED IN ALL ITS TRIM

HATH PUT A SPIRIT OF YOUTH IN EVERYTHING

William Shakespeare

01 APRIL
"The easiest person to fool is yourself."

Richard Feynman

April Fool's Day is a wonderful day in that people actually try to inject some humor into the world, to disrupt the monotony that seems to have spread. A day for newness and the unexpected with low risks and a chance to laugh at ourselves and those we spend time with. It is meant to be harmless and good-natured trickery, the most mild of Loki (or Puck, or any other infamous trickster) aspects to lighten the day.

But trickery and falsehood can be much darker. Loki brings about the end of days (Ragnarök) by tricking others, by using illusions and lies. And we all carry the trickster inside us, and the ones we fool most are ourselves.

"I'm just" is the start of the slippery slope. Anytime we tell ourselves or others "I'm just" it means that we are on the border of territory we probably shouldn't be in, and we are rationalizing our decisions to enter that unknown country. It could be just having that cookie to cheat on your diet, or just posting to a dating app to cheat on your spouse. "I'm just" is an ethical red flag.

"It's not what it looks like, I'm only" is another self seduction phrase for us to fool ourselves about what we are doing, to justify something that earlier we would never have even considered doing. We also believe our own rationale and abilities too much. "I'm ok to drive" after a few drinks, or "I don't need help" when we are struggling emotionally, or turning a blind eye to a friend or coworker's bad behavior and remaining willfully ignorant of misdeeds. These are negative examples of casting a spell on ourselves, of glamouring to lead astray.

Yet we can also fool ourselves into making better choices. Multiple Nobel Prizes in Economics have been awarded for behavioral psychology leading to better outcomes (Thaler, Kahneman, etc.) whether it is enrolling in our 401k or not buying those cookies. We can trick ourselves for our own good by convincing ourselves we just have to put on our running shoes and go out the door (turning into multiple miles), or instilling confidence by playing that pump up song and landing the deal, or even adding spices to a dish and reducing the salt and fat content and improving our health through little white lies of culinary chicanery.

In the end, the easiest person to fool will always be ourselves, because we have years of experience doing it.

Action item: stop and reflect for a moment. What lies are you telling yourself? Are they justification for bad choices, or are they making you better long range? Alter the story a little and use your illusion for your betterment.

02 APRIL
"Whatever you are not changing, you are choosing."

Laurie Buchanan

Sometimes, we accept things because it is easier to deal with the status quo than to poke the bear or actually fight against the flow of events. We might be tired of the fights, or just not care enough about the small issue we see that is seemingly unconnected with the greater problems of the world. In any case, what we accept is what we get, and if that includes heading down a path we might not like it is still because of our choice, or lack thereof. This could be staying in a toxic situation (at work, with a partner, a location, even a friendship) or poisoning ourselves with what we feed our mind or body. Apathy is dangerous because our tolerance for unfavorable stimuli will slowly grow until the negativity affects every fiber of our being, physical and emotional, unless we actively prevent it from happening.

Are you the boss? Do you allow people that work for you to cut corners or do you hold the line? If you tolerate shoddy work, guess what your people will produce? And remember: you are always the boss of you, and can set a higher standard instead of just tripping over the bar.

If you want to change your physical health, do you keep buying junk food? That's your choice, and if you make it easy to choose poorly you will (Thaler earned a Nobel Prize in Economics exploring this). Do you choose to sit on the couch and watch TikTok for an hour, or do you decide to watch it for a few minutes while walking around and getting your body moving and adding micro-activity that compounds into losing two pounds a month from doing the little things better? You decide.

Do you tolerate your five-year old being disrespectful, or do you take them aside and talk to them about choosing to be nicer to others and how to not be a little jerk? If you let them keep exhibiting the actions they are right now, they will grow up to be a big jerk because you didn't elect to help them alter their behaviors. You can change their behavior at five, by fifteen they are who they will be and it is too late to alter their attitudes without a radical external intervention (say like boot camp).

Do you wallow in negative thoughts, or do you feed your brain positive music and motivation? Yes, mental illness is real and medicine is needed in many situations, but re-programming the software in the brain by choosing to have a better environment and stimulus feed is real too and can positively interact with the drugs for superior effects. Buy a healthier snack, make the junk food more difficult to get to (like in a cabinet out of sight), play happier music in the background, or walk up that flight of stairs instead of taking the elevator. Little choices lead to big results.

Action Item: choose one tiny thing to change about your environment for a positive impact. One small change that you will stick with, and choose to be better.

03 APRIL

"Change before you have to."

Jack Welch

There is an old adage in business: the best time to borrow money is when you don't need it, because when you need it nobody will loan it to you,

The best time to polish your resume is when you love your current job and have no plans on leaving, just in case.

The greatest of pitchers start adding in off-speed pitches such as a curve before their blazing fastballs lose much velocity, so they can start mixing it up and still get hitters out even as their fireballs fade.

Be ahead of the curve.

Understand where your industry is going, and be prepared so that instead of being left behind, you can be one of the change leaders and become more valuable instead of unemployed. As Wayne Gretzky said: good players go to where the puck is, great players go to where the puck is going to be. There is a reason he's The Great One and some of his records will probably never be beaten.

If you have a kid who will be of the proper age to get their driver's permit in six months, NOW is the time to start getting your head around that fact and to begin teaching them the situational awareness needed to drive safely, to start discussing the theories and to model good driving behavior yourself. Before they start saying "but you....."

You probably baby proofed the house before the little one came. That was smart, but why did you stop planning ahead as your little angel grew into the terrible twos and beyond? Because you wanted to "enjoy every moment?" You can live in the moment and still plan for what is coming.

Keeping an eye on the future and planning for what is coming is not "dreaming", or being "unable to enjoy today". It is making sure you don't become a dinosaur.

Action item: take a minute and think about the last time you were embarrassed because you were not up to speed. How did it feel? Now what is something you see coming at work that you should prepare for?

04 APRIL

"You have to be odd to be number one."

Dr. Seuss

If you do what everybody else does, you will get the results everybody else does and be part of the pack. Now that's ok if your cohort that you are benchmarking against is your MBA class from a prestigious school, or your training class in ROTC, or any other group that is pre-screened to produce superior results. Just being an average professional athlete is not a bad deal. But what if you could be exceptional among them? Unless you are a genetic freak, you have to do things differently.

LeBron James spends a million a year on his body and does things that seem outlandish. And yet he is in discussion to be the GOAT (Greatest of All Time), and has a net worth of almost a billion dollars for putting a ball through a hoop and then playing even smarter off the court than on it. King James' approach to the game was unlike any before him, he has evolved along a unique arc, and his path post basketball is not what one would have expected. He is definitely odd.

Bruce Lee was one of the first martial artists to use electro-stim to force his muscles to work while he was doing other things, giving him the equivalent of hundreds of additional pushups a day. Odd, and a unique figure.

Mathematician John Nash and physicist Richard Feynman both built from fundamental principles to explore new territory, or old areas in a new light. Neither would be considered "normal". Both have Nobel Prizes. And the picture of Feynman playing bongos is as iconic as Einstein playing violin. Elon Musk was a weird kid. He became the richest person in the world. Other people who have been in that position include Jeff Bezos, Bill Gates, Cornelius Vanderbilt, J Paul Getty, Andrew Carnegie, and John J Rockefeller. All odd individuals.

The Beatles were the biggest band in the world and easily the number one act. Listen to Sgt. Pepper's Lonely Hearts Club Band or watch Yellow Submarine. Definitely odd.

To achieve different results, you need to look at the world differently. To process what you see in a way others aren't, and build a vision of the future based upon things others can't see yet. Unusual, or outlandish.

Not normal. Strange. Crazy. Weird. Odd, and in a good way.

Action item: what is unique or just very different about you? How can you leverage that?

05 APRIL

"Follow your own weird."

James Broughton

Not going to lie, my favorite Muppet is not Kermit the Frog or Animal: it is The Great Gonzo. Gonzo is a Weirdo with his own unique style and approach to everything, and a bizarre friendship with chickens. Read into that what you will.

That person that marches to the beat of their own drum? They are probably fairly happy dancing to their own tune, even if no one else can hear the circus music in their head. Maybe if you listened to the soundtrack in your head a little more and let your feet dance a bit more often, you'd be happier too. Just saying.

If you are a lover of Hello Kitty or weird socks, collect Pez dispensers or lacrosse trading cards, knit Cthulhu stuffies, or just want to be a pirate when you grow up (if ever), that is part of who you are. Don't hide your crazy, revel in your madness. As my running team says: do something crazy so you don't go insane.

So what if you love anime and insult your friends by calling them a potato? Attend Comic Con? Steampunk? Renn Faire? Go for it. If their weirdness overlaps with yours and no one gets hurt for it, enjoy the unusual because it will make you more confident and well rounded and stronger in other areas that directly impact your future.

We all need a friend that is weirder than us, and our real friends should be able to accept our foibles like a fascination with Thor (yes, yes, my office has multiple comic books and action figures) or those really bizarre people that put mayo on their fries. It is these little eccentricities that truly make us human and allow us to bond with other members of our "not all there" tribe while also giving us the opportunity to explore new things that our friends expose us to.

"Weird" comes from the names of one of the Fates, a spinner of destiny and the future. Something inescapable and intrinsically linked to an individual. It is who you are, and trying to avoid it is like Harry Potter dodging The Prophecy or Achilles' glory and demise. It is what it is, que sera sera, and so be it. Be weird, your own weird way.

Action item: What is your weird? Embrace it and let your freak flag fly!

06 APRIL
"Follow your dreams. They know the way."

Kobi Yamada

Psychologists say that dreams are flashes of insight as our subconscious processes information from a variety of sources. Some people think they are messages from greater powers, to inform us of destiny. Einstein likened it to the coming attractions of life, which is essentially a combination of the first two ideas.

Dreams show scenes of what could be. Sometimes the movie trailer has misleading scenes (Odin and Thor in an alley in New York is an example), but usually the trailer (or coming attractions) is snippets of what actually is in the movie to excite the audience. It is up to us to decide if we are going to attend that particular movie though. We might not be excited by the romcom or slapstick comedy or psychological thriller, and chose to avoid that show or path in our life.

We all have multiple dreams, ranging from that one where I turned into Godzilla and rampaged through Tokyo, to the one of my crush being a political operative and spy while wearing Pittsburgh Steelers gear, to the one where I built a successful writing career. I am not pursuing becoming Godzilla, no matter how cool that would be. But I am pursuing the writing one. We get to choose the dreams we pursue and make them reality.

As a kid, many of us dreamt of driving fast cars or riding horses or being astronauts. Maybe you didn't have the math skills or meet the physical requirements to become an astronaut, but to have a fast car or ride horses is not dependent upon genetics or training: it comes down to pursuing something you are good at that bears the economic fruits to have these things.

You can have a horse by working on a farm or being a rock star or an engineer, or even volunteering to muck the stalls and do the dirty work others won't. Remember: Hercules cleaned stables as part of his labors towards godhood. You don't need Olympian muscles but an Olympian heart to realize dreams.

Keeping the dream in front of you and working to achieve it is what is needed more than vast financial resources.

As we get older (notice I didn't say grow up, because we must keep that inner child around), some dreams pass into the mist (like my dream of competing in the Olympics did after various injuries and having kids) and new ones emerge (like running a Ragnar with my son or having 100 acres of woods to just disappear into).

Just because they are not the passionate world-changing epic dreams of our youth does not make them any less valid.

If your dream is a small house with a lawn, that should be as important to you as the idea of Olympic gold to an athlete, with similar focus and effort.

And no one else has the right to belittle your dreams and tell you they are stupid or small, just know that whether it is climbing all 46 High Peaks in New York or a single emotional hill in your life that to make dreams real requires you wake up and work for it.

Dreams become reality through action backing up the belief.

Action item: what was a dream from when you were a kid that you could still realize? What would it take to do so? Are you willing to do the work to see it happen?

07 APRIL

"If dreams die, life is a broken-winged bird that cannot fly."

Langston Hughes

Dreams are powerful. "I Have a Dream" instantly evokes an emotional response decades later because of the strength of the imagery in the speech, and the powerful vision it calls us towards. Imagine what it feels like to those who believe the American Dream has failed them, that are hopeless and despondent and broken like that bird?

Think of the high school athlete who gets up early every morning and trains, as she has for years and years. Who doesn't go out or party because she is focused on winning, and earning that scholarship so that she can attend college, maybe the first in her family and it is the only way to economic mobility. She dreams and works and sacrifices. And then in the big game she tears her knee up. She will never play again, nor be able to afford college. Can you just feel the deflation?

The couple that scraped and saved and worked, ultimately pulled together the money for their dream: a restaurant that they would run. They planned menus and décor, worked night and day to refurbish the space and create a place they and others would love. And then the Pandemic hit, and they lost everything. Everything gone. You can feel the heartbreak, the fear of bankruptcy. The sleepless nights. The soul crushing doubt and terror of watching it all go away.

The parent with the terminally ill child.

The parent with Alzheimer's, slowly fading away while still there.

The man in love with the addict that is spiraling down and down into the black depths, destroying themselves and those that adore them who are powerless to stop the deterioration and despair.

Some dreams we can not save.

The inevitable decline due to time can only be slowed, so that every precious moment left is treasured as an irreplaceable and priceless image and emotion. When my best friend Rich was dying from leukemia in our early forties, his wife Stacy (the strongest woman I met and one of my inspirations) took this approach and created memories my nephews and she will have for the rest of their lives. Even though my buddy is not here physically, parts of the dream are captured.

But if we can, we must fight for these dreams. In addition to cherishing every moment of that time with Rich, Stacy fought to save his life. In the end the disease came back and took a great man and better father and best friend, but they fought for that dream of another lifetime together and even on the bad days Stacy can be strong despite the breaks in her heart and wings because of Rich's fight for his family. She has to fly solo now, no longer having her wingman and dream companion.

Fight for those dreams.

Fight even those we love, to help them break their chains or break through their pain. Fight for them, when they can not fight for themselves and doubt is starting to dissipate their dream. Support them emotionally and motivationally so they can do the rehab (physical or otherwise) and get through the pain and back in the game, so they can face the chemo and side effects. Help them be strong and battle and live. Believe in their dream when their faith starts to waiver.

A dead dream kills the spirit. Resuscitate it, give it CPR and mouth to mouth if need be. Don't let the dream die, whether in you or in those you love.

Action item: what dream is someone close to you pursuing? What do they need to make sure their dream does not die? Help them.

08 APRIL

"Dream big. Dream without fear."

Randy Pausch

If you have never read or listened to *The Last Lecture* by Professor Randy Pausch and how he faced terminal pancreatic cancer, do so. His courage and poise are truly inspirational.

Tim McGraw had a song called *Live Like You Are Dying*, and some of the things the person does included: skydiving, Rocky Mountain climbing, bull riding, fishing, being a better spouse, and living like tomorrow was a gift. Have you ever lived like that?

If you couldn't fail, what would you do? Start that business, take that physical challenge, write that book? Ask your crush out? Seek forgiveness and to mend fences with family? Save your marriage? Fear is the thing that is holding you back, so listen to Professor Pausch.

Jim Collins in Good to Great talks about BHAGS: Big Hairy Audacious Goals. Every Day Excellence was a BHAG and is now in your hands because I dreamt big and then ground out the work. Putting a man on the moon. Becoming a tv star. Getting your college degree, or buying a house or building your career. Getting your kid through college, or pulling them from the depths of addiction. Losing that fifty pounds or walking the Appalachian Trail. Have the BHAG.

Every notable accomplishment of humankind was a big dream at one time. What if that person was afraid to tell others, to do what it took to bring their dream to the world? What would your life look like today without a smartphone, or electricity, or freedom or a home?

Dream big.

Action item: sit someplace where you can really think for a bit, maybe with an adult beverage or a tea/coffee. Take a piece of paper and start dreaming and writing, no restrictions, no constraints. Dream. Dream big. Dream without fear!

09 APRIL

"I am following my dreams to prove my nightmares wrong."

Synthia Beauvais

There is something called The Second Son Syndrome, where the younger brother has to prove that they are better because they start from a position of being smaller, less skilled, and do not have the same attention the First Son received early on. As such we work harder to try and win our parents' attention and adulation. Where we have to prove that we are as good as (and ultimately superior to) our big brother that picks on us when we are little and takes our toys and won't let us hang out with them and their cool friends when we are in preschool. So subconsciously we tell ourselves "well, I'll show him" and spend our first dozen or fifteen years trying to get out of their shadow, to prove to ourselves and everyone else that we are not just "J's baby brother".

Later on in life all of us (second son or not) get a job and we are like "oh crap, what the hell am I doing?! I'm not worthy of this." So we bust our humps, put in extra time after hours and in the early morning to make sure we don't screw it up. And maybe we keep at it for years, not only getting the hang of it but excelling and winning accolades. But we still keep working at it like we are brand new and the boss is looking over our shoulder, like we could screw up and get fired tomorrow even if we are one of the leading experts. That fear from the early days, that need to prove to ourselves and others that we deserve to be in that position, drives us as much in Decade 3 as on Day 2.

Tom Brady was still trying to prove he deserved the starting job when he won his 4th Superbowl. When he won his 7th he was trying to prove that it wasn't his coach (Belichick) that won those Lombardi Trophies. He was living the dream because the nightmare kept him motivated.

How many people in business have succeeded because they were so terrified of failing that they kept working like a startup even after they were a billionaire?

How many musicians were scared kids, afraid of performing so they practiced and practiced and faced their fears and practiced and played and now live the life of dreams because of facing those nightmares?

Something that terrifies you can empower you tremendously, make you work harder than anyone else and drive you to success, if you face the fear instead of flying from it. Instead of letting the nightmare frighten you into paralysis, harness it to your chariot and let it pull you to epic adventures.

Action item: what dream are you following as a response to an underlying fear? Look directly at that demon, that thing that scares you. Steal its power and use it to achieve your dreams.

10 APRIL
"History is a nightmare from which I am trying to awake."

Phillip Roth

Guess what? Humans are horrible to each other, and we have been since the dawn of civilization and will be until the last one dies. We lie, we cheat, we steal and we kill each other. This is what has always happened and unfortunately probably always will.

History? That is the story of humanity, written usually through the lens of the victor at the time with their perspective. Generally the winner won't give the story of the people that lost the battles and their land, the cultures destroyed and the innocents slaughtered. They prefer a sanitized version that discounts the lives and civilizations destroyed, whether it was in the Fertile Crescent 5,000 years ago, Ireland 500 years ago, or Africa a century ago. Even the textbooks we grew up with were one sided and fairly jingoistic. And that is not right.

We need to look at not just the Disney Fairy Tale version of what happened but the real stories, with all the ugliness on all sides. The hatred, fear, loathing, the abuses and horrors. It is the complete tale, the full R Rated story that will inform us and allow us to truly learn history's lessons better than "be pretty and powerful and live happily ever after." It is not a beautiful radiant dream but a complex epic with no true archetypes but complex and flawed characters everywhere.

Waking from the nightmare of history is being able to look at the past in the bright light of day and explore all sides of the situation, turning over facts and events in our hands and looking at them from multiple perspectives and angles, seeing the flaws and beauty both.

Waking from the childlike dream allows us to use a mature, rational eye to understand and discuss what occurred before, instead of drinking Kool-Aid and accepting all from the point of view of the Powers That Be, whether the ones that triumphed three thousand years ago or in the last election cycle. Understanding lets us learn from what came before and hopefully prevent the worst episodes from being repeated because those who are informed can help warn against the rise of the next Robespierre or McCarthy.

History echoes itself if we let it, meaning the lives destroyed in previous eras could be in vain. Opening our eyes and exploring the past in its complexity is the best way to understand our current world, and see without rose tinted glasses what is unfolding today and in the future.

Action item: google a historical event, and read about it. Now look for a different perspective on the situation, one not written by the victors. Expand your perspective by further opening your eyes. Now look at today with these new eyes.

11 APRIL

"History is a vast early warning system."

Norman Cousins

Modern Stoic and author Ryan Holliday has great insight into current events, hearing the signal in the noise because of his still mind but also because he has seen the patterns play out before. The Great Influenza of the early 20th century and the Antonine Plague that claimed Marcus Aurelius serve as lessons about how leaders should act and how people react during pandemics much better than the talking heads on TV trying to push their particular agenda or an internet filled with hate and fear. Deep dives into history prepares us for the future because human nature has not changed much in three thousand years even if technology has.

Income inequality, racial tensions, floods, recessions and depressions, legislature ineptitude, wars, famines. All have happened multiple times and will happen again. Do we react crazily or do we draw from the experience of those that lived through it before?

During the Bitcoin bubble one of my friends and I discussed how it was just like the real estate bubble of the 2000's or the dot com bubble or the land bubble or tulips or.... The madness of crowds is consistent across time even if the underlying assets change and we repeatedly hear "but this time it's different!" No, no it's not.

New technology is introduced. Many firms enter the field creating a highly fractured marketplace and significant innovation and adoption. Consolidation starts to occur, and the hundreds of firms in a handful of years become just a handful of major players dominating the space, and innovation slows. Internet Service Providers of the late 1990's? The Browser Wars? Automobiles in the early 20th century? TV manufacturers in the middle of the century? All of the above, and any new tech that comes along. History echoing itself, as it has done throughout human history.

Companies rise and fall. So too countries. Anyone that has studied the rise and fall of the Roman Empire and looks at the bread and circuses of modern America probably has some concerns about the choices of our past few and next few leaders.

What was old is new again. Fashion cycles back into vogue. The lessons of the past are forgotten after a few generations and the same cultural battles get fought again in new ways, and the wheel of time keeps rotating. Hard times produce strong people which produce easy times which produce soft people that create hard times that produce...

As John Le Carre said: if you spy long enough, the circus comes back around.

Action item: turn off the tv, and read about what came before and why. Now ask yourself what lessons should be remembered in the current environment.

12 APRIL
"To be ignorant of the past is to be forever a child."

Cicero

We all have that friend that is making the same mistakes in relationships today that they were making a decade ago. They have not learned from their past so are doomed to repeat it, until they learn the lessons, no matter how tough those lessons are.

If you haven't looked back at history (of the organization you work for, your country, or your own actions), don't be surprised when something happens and you smack yourself in the head for not seeing it coming. You made yourself willfully ignorant, and when you turn a blind eye to something you get blindsided. Do you have a family history of alcoholism or addiction? You should know this so you can try to take preventative measures and recognize the warning signs. Same thing with genetic predisposition towards diabetes or heart issues or arthritis. He who is forewarned...

If an athlete makes the same mistake over and over, they get burned by their competition and maybe even cut from the team. If you make the same mistake at work over and over you get fired. We are meant to learn and grow through our experiences; not doing so is willfully choosing to remain an emotional toddler or teenager for a lifetime. And while this might be a short term coping mechanism and amusing to others, it gets old real fast and leaves the immature person vulnerable to falling into a victimhood mentality because they lack the capacity to act upon their own behalf. The old tale Iron John illustrates the transformation from child to independent adult that a rational and evolved person must go through, including the separation from their parents and the facing of challenges and acquisition of knowledge in a foreign environment, including bleeding and getting scars, both physical and emotional. Those who don't undertake this sort of journey are stilted in their development and remain dependent emotionally (and maybe financially) until they are forced to undergo this growth on the road of life.

Being a child is cute at 5, as is playing like a child at 25. Still actually being an emotional child at 45 is lamentable. Individuals like this, sheltered from life in their towers, have not built the emotional framework to survive in the wild of the world and litter the gossip pages and trash tv shows because their inability to cope serves as a warning for those willing to see it as such. As a teenager your mom probably told you at some point "oh grow up!". Hopefully you have, because willfully remaining an ignorant teenager dooms people to a cycle of repeat failure until they learn their lessons and break that cycle.

Action item: today, take a page from the pros and essentially "watch game tape" after you have an interaction with your boss or a family member. What went well, where can you improve? Learn from this so the next time you are in a similar situation you have better outcomes.

13 APRIL
"History will be kind to me; for I intend to write it."

Sir Winston Churchill

History is written by the victors, or about the victors. It is also written about those who chose to thrust themselves into the middle of conflicts and other great events. Few people are remembered that were not involved in pivotal moments, and the way that individuals generally are positioned to be in a position of authority in those pivotal moments is by getting involved well before events are on a world stage.

We all have free will, to make decisions great and small. From when you get up to whether or not to study for that test to which job you accept, most of your life is determined by the decisions you make, even if some of the current choices are before you because of decisions you made decades ago. Churchill would not have been pivotal in WWII and the history of the world if he had chosen to stay in his study and just paint as he could have. He chose the life of politics as a young man, and as such got to help write the history of the world instead of just painting the past.

When you make the choice to be actively involved, whether it is in your child's school or local politics or your professional/trade association, you get to help craft the narrative instead of just sitting back and reading the story. There is much more work in being one of the characters than being a mindless twit sitting on the couch eating popcorn, watching passively as others go to work or battle, and a hell of a lot more risk, but those who are in the story are remembered well beyond their lifetime. Helping write history is one way to achieve immortality, even in a limited space like your local Scout group or ethnic club.

Even being a footnote is better than being forgotten.

Action item: as the Muppets sang "life is like a movie, write your own ending". Start writing your story today instead of reading someone else's.

14 APRIL

"Destiny is not a matter of chance.
It is a matter of choice."

William Jennings Bryan

Studies with identical twins have shown that about 50% of their ultimate happiness and health is based upon their genetics. About 10% is things beyond their control that happen to them (car accidents, winning the lottery, etc.). The rest? Determined by their decisions, their choices charting their journey in life. We determine our future as much as our past does.

I have seen individuals graced with God given talent I can barely comprehend, and they fail to have the success or impact that they could and should because they make suboptimal choices. The tragic story of Patriots' tight end Aaron Hernandez, who chose to be in bad situations with unsavory people that eventually lead to murder, prison, and his own death because of repeated poor choices is only one of the most dramatic examples of disastrous endings because of horrible decisions. We all have friends whose life can be summed up with the line from Indiana Jones and The Last Crusade: he chose poorly.

Contrast this with the child born in abject poverty, maybe with a fractured family and addiction rampant. Or in a war zone. Yet they create a positive outcome because of disciplined decisions with an eye on the long-term outcomes instead of opting for the short sighted immediate pleasure producing options. Jose Aldo and Kassim Ouma (fighters), Diego Maradona and Pele (soccer), Serge Ibaka (basketball) grew up in conditions and situations poorer and more desperate than you or I can comprehend yet have had success and for the most part make decent personal decisions. Their choices, while not perfect, lean towards the light instead of the dark, because they grew up in the dark and know what will happen if they decide to stay in that mindset.

One of the things that economist Dr. Thomas Sowell analyzed was genetic predeterminism versus individual free will and competitiveness. The numbers and history repeatedly show that although you as an individual (or a small collective group) may have a tendency towards an outcome, your ultimate outcome is determined not by religion or race but by individual choices and the mindset of rising above or falling to the expectations of those we surround ourselves with. If you chose to hang out with irresponsible lawbreaking disrespectful idiots you will adopt their behaviors and become one, just like if you decide to surround yourself with driven ambitious people they naturally wear off on you and raise your personal standards of performance, whether it is as a business owner, student, parent, or athlete.

Alan Page lost his mother at 13. She encouraged him to always focus on his education. He worked construction in high school in Canton OH, literally laying the groundwork for the Football Hall of Fame. His work ethic led him to Notre Dame on a football scholarship, where he won a National Title before becoming part of the Minnesota Vikings famed Purple People Eater defense of the 1970's. In the off season he attended law school. He became the first defensive player to win the MVP, and was eventually enshrined in the Hall of Fame he had helped build. He also built a name for himself as a judge until his age mandated retirement in 2015.

Alan Page lost his mother at 13. She encouraged him to always focus on his education. He worked construction in high school in Canton OH, literally laying the groundwork for the Football Hall of Fame. His work ethic led him to Notre Dame on a football scholarship, where he won a National Title before becoming part of the Minnesota Vikings famed Purple People Eater defense of the 1970's. In the off season he attended law school. He became the first defensive player to win the MVP, and was eventually enshrined in the Hall of Fame he had helped build. He also built a name for himself as a judge until his age mandated retirement in 2015.

Alan Page crafted his future through his choices to do the right thing and continuously push himself. He could have turned out like many other thirteen year olds that lose a parent and end up on the other side of the law, but Page wrote the story of his life instead of letting circumstance dictate it. Ever wonder why your sibling, who was raised in the same house as you, had the same parents as you, is so different today? Because you have each made choices that put you on different paths. You started very close to the same point, but your decisions created separate identities which then caused you to look at the world differently and select different options when presented with choices.

Biology and upbringing are the start of the life journey but you are the driver of the car in the end.

Action item: today, you will have choices. When presented with one, ask "what will give the best long-term outcome" and take that option, even if it is more difficult in the short run.

15 APRIL
"If you know and don't do, you don't know."

Dr. Mark Hillman

Knowledge is not power. *Applied* knowledge is.

Knowing that you shouldn't eat four donuts for breakfast and still doing it means you still ate four donuts.

Knowing what to do to improve your relationship and consciously choosing not to do so means that you really don't know what you really want and need to do because you are letting the short-term comfort or perceived risk overcome what you need to do, and that means you really don't know how bad it will be. You think you know, but you don't really know and allow fear to prevent you from action.

Knowing what the ethical move is and not doing it means you have surface knowledge of ethics, not a deeply held belief in and wisdom of right and wrong.

Knowing what you need to do to improve your business, be it firing that bad hire or investing in training or not entering into a partnership with an unsavory character but not taking the right action is being weak, being weak out of fear. Because you allow extraneous doubts to get in the way of the actions.

Know, then do.

Action item: Quick, what is the one thing you know you need to do to make your life better? Do it. Do it now.

16 APRIL

"Knowing others is intelligence,
Knowing yourself is true wisdom."

Lao Tzu

Meta-cognition is the ability to think about your thinking, and is one factor that separates greatness from the pretty good. The capacity to stop and reflect, to look at ourselves, our actions, and to literally separate from ourselves and look at why we are doing something as an independent, unbiased third person would but with our knowledge of our history is a skill that takes years to fully develop but opens untold potential for the future.

Almost all sports teams scout their opponents. The better ones scout themselves to see where their flaws are that their opponents could exploit, and look to apply strengths against weaknesses to gain advantage and victory. The best understand their own biases and can get in their opponents' heads as well as their own to truly see the playing field and potential.

Understanding that you are weak in an area allows you to compensate for it, whether by improving that area personally or outsourcing the work to another who is strong in that component. Great business teams do this by allocating tasks to those that are best suited (mentally, skill set, and temperamentally) to excel at them while filling out the gaps and making sure workflow and communication are operational.

You performed a SWOT analysis back in January to help you to understand yourself. Hopefully you have been playing to your strengths and taking advantage of your opportunities.

Action item: look at your SWOT, and choose one Weakness you can outsource.

17 APRIL
"Knowing yourself is the beginning of all wisdom."

Aristotle

"He who knows his enemy and himself will ever be victorious." Sun Tzu, *The Art of War*

Self knowledge is critical for a well reasoned assessment of your current situation, and to be able to create plans for a better future that can actually be executed upon. If you try to accomplish something great (such as running a marathon) but have not assessed yourself (health and fitness level, time constraints, financial commitments, etc.) you are doomed to failure because the most important component in your success is you. No one else is going to do the prep work and run the course and have to face and overcome the doubts that arise. Only you.

Maybe you don't have a photographic memory, like 99+% of us. Perhaps you have dyslexia and need to alter your studying (like attorney David Boies or financial wiz and NY Mets owner Steve Cohen), or have ADHD (yours truly). These aren't curses that will relegate you to a life of poor performance, they just mean you need to do things a little differently to succeed. People wonder why my days are structured and I rely on processes so heavily, it is because I know my limits and use the external reinforcements to keep me on track.

Bruce Lee was known for his wicked spin kicks in movies like *Fists of Fury*. Part of the reason was he had one leg slightly shorter than the other, something others might view as a disadvantage but Lee turned into a major strength. His self-knowledge let him maximize his potential.

Tony Iommi of Black Sabbath injured his fingers and learned his limitations, leading to that dark sound when he tuned down.

An athlete that knows they have a skill deficiency (such as a turnaround jumper) can then work on it and turn that flaw in their game into at least a neutral skill, maybe even a strength. Jordan, Kobe, and LeBron have all done so. It allowed them to evolve in their profession.

Knowing that you can be arrogant (yes, I am admitting it) means that shortfall can be worked on (and I am). Same too with a short temper, or patience with others, or empathy.

"Knowing is half the battle," as GI Joe reminded us in the 1980's. It's the easier half of the battle, but self awareness is the start of self improvement and the foundation of personal growth.

Action item: text someone that knows you very well that will be honest with you and ask them "what are some of my flaws?"

18 APRIL
"Humility is the beginning of true intelligence."

John Calvin

There is a concept known as "Circle of Knowledge", representing what we understand. If our knowledge is limited (say a unit of one from our center as a start), then the border of that circle where it meets the outside area of our lack of knowledge (or ignorance) is per basic geometry (circumference equals two pi r where are is the radius) roughly 6.28 units.

Now if we double our knowledge from one unit to two, our border of ignorance goes from about six and a quarter to over 12.5. Uh oh, more areas of uncertainty. More places for us to be proven wrong. The more we know, the more we realize we don't know.

The more we know about the Universe, the more we realize our knowledge is pitifully small by comparison and the more we look for knowledge.

When a student receives their Black Belt, they also receive a white belt to remind them that they are beginners on a new path, and that a lifetime is not enough to learn all that there is to learn and remind them to be humble. That is also why it was always my job as a senior student to sweep the dojang, to force humility. Even as an Instructor I would do so, because the lessons of humility are always helpful.

"The only thing that I know, is that I know nothing." Socrates

"The more we learn the more we realize how little we know." R. Buckminster Fuller

Maintain the beginner's mind, looking at things with fresh eyes and questioning what you know always. The arrogance of intelligence is dangerous and has led to mistakes that kill companies and destroy careers, leading to blunders that could be avoided by having the smartest and most experienced ask questions as if they were raw rookies.

Always assume that other people have more knowledge or skill than you do, and be ready and willing to learn from them. If you adopt this attitude, your circle of knowledge will continuously expand and you will still be comfortable not knowing an ever growing number of things.

Action item: make a short list of things that you don't know that you think might be important to start learning about.

19 APRIL

"Leisure is the mother of philosophy."

Thomas Hobbes

Maslow's Hierarchy of needs starts with Survival Needs (food, shelter, clean water, etc.) for a reason: if you physically starve to death or freeze to death it doesn't matter how warm and fuzzy you feel inside.

The greatest portion of human history has been struggling to meet these basic needs, and even today there is starvation and lack of clean water worldwide. We have worked very hard to help fill these needs and by the middle of the 21st Century the basic Utopian Dream could happen almost worldwide.

What does a human being do though if they don't have to spend their entire life scrabbling for calories and warmth and water? They can think.

Except for the past roughly two centuries, only the elite could read or had the time away from the battle for survival so had the time and mental freedom to actually think. So the leisure time created by agricultural and mechanical advancements of the past few hundred years (steam power, internal combustion engines, electrical power, etc.) has led to not only a population boom but an idea boom as even the average person in the US in 1950 had access to more knowledge than the emperors of Rome or the Founding Fathers of the US.

A ten year old today has more computing power than the entire US space program of the 1960's and more free time in a summer than most people in human history had in their entire life span. So even in the dog days of summer when it is brutally hot and they just want to swim, a kid has more time to actually think than did essentially every single one of their ancestors.

When every waking moment is not spent trying to survive, it is easy for the mind to start asking questions such as "what is the meaning of life?" because it is no longer "fight off that wolf". When a belly becomes filled, the mind can start becoming so too.

Too many people use all of their leisure time to fill their head with useless gossip or pursue distractions from video games to other banal amusements. And don't get me wrong: I love listening to a Yankees baseball game or watching Epic Rap Battles of History or running on a treadmill until I am ready to puke then having a beer and shooting the shit with my friends.

But I actively focus on learning and developing myself every day, listening to different ideas on a variety of topics and asking myself questions so that I can assemble an overarching philosophy that makes sense for me, instead of blindly following what I am told by some external expert talking head on TV.

Understanding that we can use Youtube to access hours of information with different perspectives about any subject from the engineering of a candy factory to Schopenhauer or interpretations of Shakespeare allows us to develop our minds and philosophies in ways that even a Pharaoh or Philosopher King like Marcus Aurelius would envy.

So why waste it on who is cheating on who in *90 Day Fiance* or *Real World* or whatever is the distraction de jour?

Action item: take five minutes at some point today, turn off all the distractions and just ask "why am I here?". It will move you along on your philosophical journey.

20 APRIL

"There is not enough time to do the nothing we want to do."

Bill Watterson

Calvin might be a six year old boy, but he embodies all of us and the lost innocence of childhood. His summer vacations of wandering around through the woods with Hobbes the Tiger, using his imagination and his environment, is a call back to the forgotten and simpler times many of us grew up in. And the wisdom of the kid resonates to this day.

Think back to those lazy hazy summer days from when you were growing up. The long days with no official bedtime and no alarm clock in the morning, just the light streaming in the window, eating corn on the cob and spitting watermelon seeds and not having to worry about what day of the week it was.

Hitting the local pool or watering hole, running through sprinklers and drinking from the garden hose before the sky is painted marmalade, the crickets and frogs start their evening songs, and the fireflies start blinking. Maybe a fire and making s'mores.

Picture it. Can you feel yourself relaxing into your childhood?

Every day was a lazy Saturday afternoon, an adventure if you felt like it or just chilling under a tree in the shade, maybe laying on your back in the grass and looking at cloud pictures.

And then POOF you're an adult. A grown up with a job and responsibilities and taxes to pay and road rage.

It sucks.

The saying that youth is wasted on the young is true in so many ways.

Go out and pretend to be six again. Wander in the woods, play Calvinball. Be a kid again.

Action item: be a bum for a while. Do some of the nothing you didn't get to do.

21 APRIL

"Rest is the sweet sauce of labour."

Plutarch

Nothing is as sweet as that shower beer after doing an entire day of hot, back breaking work outside and actually accomplishing something. That first taste of a cold lager, the moment the water hits your shoulders and the grime starts dripping off. This is the reward for what was done. You earned this.

That quick power nap after a long day, before hitting the next series of tasks after knocking off a huge to do list? Go for it, even Hercules rested part way through his 12 Labors.

Giving your all, whether on the home front or at work, is one of the keys to long range excellence and success. It is also exhausting, draining on the physical, emotional, and mental levels. Mind, body, and spirit all need to be recharged.

Even God rested on the seventh day, you are human and need to take a break at times too.

If you have or had multiple small children, you know the stress. Sometimes you need to just close the bathroom door and have five minutes of alone time to catch your breath and mentally reset.

Stressful work environments can be the same way, with each direct report or project basically being a toddler that is getting into everything and needs a constant eye on them while you are trying to do everything else that needs to be done. Sit on the couch at the end of the day and take a few deep breaths and let your mind rest from the stresses, especially if you now have to deal with your actual toddlers (or worse yet teenagers) that depend upon you.

Exhaustion makes cowards of us all, and mental exhaustion is just as bad as physical because then we get the dumbs. I can't tell you the number of conversations I shouldn't have had when I was emotionally and physically exhausted where I came across poorly because of not taking a few minutes to rest and reflect. And anyone reading this who knows me, yes I am apologizing to you.

Too many people don't truly expend themselves and so don't really appreciate rest. They haven't earned their Saturday nights, or are living on a semi-permanent vacation and have a malaise in their soul because they haven't traded enough sweat and effort to make the reward sweet and so subconsciously know that they don't deserve it. Earn it. Win the prize of a good night of sleep and a dessert by pouring out of yourself in all ways, then let Morpheus reward you for your efforts.

Action item: leave it all on the field today. Work your ass off until you have nothing left, empty the tank and then enjoy what comes after because you earned it.

22 APRIL

"Kindness is like sugar,
it makes life taste a little sweeter."

Carla Yerovi

A random compliment from a stranger can completely make your day, because the unsolicited, unbiased, and unreturnable show of appreciation and goodness from someone with absolutely nothing to gain from it immediately improves our outlook. From that moment forward things are a little brighter and better, because someone took a few seconds to give us an emotional uplift with no thought of anything in return. It is a sign of true agappe, love for all humanity.

We all try to have patience with our children. We have been taught to honor our father and mother. We are polite to coworkers out of unwritten mores of behavior in the office and to try and garner "points" for down the road. These are all conditional examples of affection. And they can be construed as kindness, especially when what we give is more than what we expect to receive from it. Therein lies the essence of the appreciation for true kindness.

Kindness is sweet to us because we as humans are social creatures and have a reciprocal nature in that we expect others to treat us in a similar manner to how we treat them, a tit-for-tat that maximizes economic benefit. It is when the returns are disproportionately low that our altruistic nature is kicking in, and because of how we are hardwired it actually makes us happier than quid pro quo actions. And kindness is doubly sweet because who benefits more from the unselfish action, the recipient or the giver? It is unclear, so one action creates two positive feelings that can then have a ripple effect for others around us.

My mother taught me that when I was in a bad mood or having a bad day, the best thing I could do was go help someone that could never help me. To go show some kindness to someone else who was having a bad day, and could never do anything for me. One of the single best lessons my mom ever taught me.

As I write this, I am having a really down day emotionally and physically so I am going to follow my own advice and do this action item.

Action item: go help someone's day be better. Randomly compliment someone or help someone that can do absolutely nothing for you.

23 APRIL

"Kind words can be short and easy to speak, but their echoes are truly endless."

Mother Teresa

Roses. Candy. Physical gifts that are gone in a week, take some planning to acquire and get to the person you care about, and carry an economic cost. Yes, they show how you feel about your sweetie and bring a smile to their face which is a good thing. But they are limited in effect and are too often an attempt to cover up other failures of appreciation and demonstration of affection.

When was the last time you texted someone important to you randomly and essentially said "I appreciate you."?

That person who inspires you with their strength of character and how they handle all the crap of life? A quick message of "hey, your example keeps me going when it's rough." They might be having a really rough day, and your acknowledgement, that kind couple of words might be the shot in the arm that they need but rarely get because everyone sees them as a paragon of strength.

Your best friend from high school? Send the random text saying "Thank you for putting up with me for decades." I did that this morning and made someone's day (maybe hers, maybe mine).

Your lover? A morning message reminding them that they brighten your day more than the sun rising over the horizon. A little thing that could brighten their day that much.

Sit on the stairs with a kid and encourage them, whether it is for them tying their shoes or picking up toys or trying really hard. Your positive words will help them grow for years.

The newest person in your office needs a pat on the back and to be told "keep it up, I know it can be tough or frustrating. I believe in you." That person will someday be a boss and your words today will echo across the decades.

That old man in the Veteran hat? Tell them "thank you for your service." You might not have supported the war they were in, but they probably are still fighting some of the battles from it and could use your moral support to quiet the echoes of the guns.

Actions are louder than words, but a quiet kind word is incredibly powerful and can make all the difference in the world to that person today.

Action item: a kind word is worth a thousand flowers. Text someone you care about and say something kind.

24 APRIL

"What you do speaks so loud that I cannot hear what you say."
Ralph Waldo Emerson

Actions are powerful, words weak.

Don't preach to me from the Gospel, show me how you love thy neighbor and do things for their benefit by giving of your time, talent, and treasure to make your community better. Get out from within the walls of your monastery and onto the street where the people are and do stuff, like they talked about in Sister Act or the Marines have repeatedly done on the streets in countries where they were fighting terrorists.

Win hearts to your cause through what you do as opposed to what you say.

The Marshall Plan that rebuilt Europe after WWII was more valuable than all the speeches of the politicians because it gave people hope. Not through words but through roads and electricity and infrastructure and jobs that gave people dignity and a path to independence and personal pride again. Contrast this with the burnt out areas with destroyed infrastructure and no economic prospects, whether in the Middle East or the Midwest. Giving someone an opportunity is worth more than a fly-in and pretty but empty words from a politician.

Show me you care, don't tell me.

Show me you care about the poor by doing something to relieve their suffering, be it helping to create jobs or donating to a food kitchen or choosing to serve in a charity that helps them. Just making statements is as useless as "thoughts and prayers" on Facebook, because poverty is overcome by effort.

Instead of complaining about your weight, stop buying junk food.

Instead of whining about having no money, improve your resume and Linkedin profile and sharpen your skills and apply for a better job. Even if you don't get one right away, you are taking actions to be able to improve your lot instead of moaning and creating a psychological sinkhole.

"If you are going through hell, keep on going."

Don't tell me you are going to change your life, show me you are with the little things that add up to big differences.

Action item: action. Show me and yourself you are serious by actually doing something that moves you in the direction of your goals instead of flapping your jaws.

25 APRIL
"Those who have ears to hear, will hear."

Dmitri Shostakovich

Beethoven was deaf yet could hear the music he composed.

Mozart heard the music of the angels and transcribed it.

Those who carry beauty in their heart can see it in the world around them, even when others cannot.

Entrepreneurs see potential and make it reality.

Writers see new worlds and write stories in their minds and put them on paper, while artists see similarly and put it on canvas.

What do you hear and see that others can not yet grasp?

Can you see the potential in someone else that they don't yet comprehend? How can you help them unlock this excellence?

Do you look at a yard and see the plants that could be there and the beauty they bring? Plant them and share them with the world.

Create. Make things out of nothing but your inner vision and spirit.

Action item: make something today.

26 APRIL
"Music can name the unnameable and communicate the unknowable."
Leonard Bernstein

Picture Darth Vader.

You probably heard The Imperial March, maybe even started to hum it and felt in your core the power of the Dark Side personified. You can feel it in your soul, even if you cannot verbalize it. This is the power of music.

Music can inspire. Think of The Rocky Theme, those horns blaring. Your heart is probably racing, your hands now over your head in the champion pose. You are ready to rumble.

The Hallelujah Chorus by Handel. Your soul soars on wings of eagles and angels as the voices unite in praise. The Wiggles, Barney, or Baby Shark elicit a visceral reaction. Could be the joy of childhood or the desire to poke your eyes out, maybe a combination of both.

You and your friends probably have "your song" that gets you amped up and ready to party. Anyone from The Castle (Pi Kappa Phi Alpha Tau) that is not yet retired that hears The Charlie Daniel's Band start in on Orange Blossom Special feels their heart race and is ready to put their arms around shoulders and rush in and celebrate Brotherhood and friendship in a way words don't describe.

Music is older than words, and carries primal power and ephemeral enlightenment.

If you are GenX, you made mix tapes. Older Millennials ripped CDs, younger ones put together Youtube playlists. All to say what we have trouble expressing, especially to that crush.

Wrestlers use entrance music, and anyone that was a teenager in the 1980's knows the Ultimate Warrior's frantic entrance while those a decade later know that breaking glass announces the arrival of Stone Cold Steve Austin. Music sets the stage emotionally, and can be used for intimidation: think Wagner's *Flight of the Valkyries* being blasted from choppers in Apocalypse Now or *Enter Sandman* from Metallica ringing through Yankee Stadium as Mariano Rivera runs out from the bullpen. Not what the opposition wants to hear.

Do you use music? I finish most races to Manowar's *Thor The Powerhead* and drop the hammer, and flip my mental switch for work with Queen's Theme to Highlander (*Princes of the Universe*.) Just the opening strain creates a psychosomatic alteration in my body and I am ready to go. Before I walk on stage (or turn on the Zoom presentation,) I NEED it to perform.

Action item: remember your theme song from back in January? Dust it off and start using it to flip your switch and unleash your primal power.

27 APRIL

"Music is a safe kind of high."

Jimi Hendrix

Ironic statement from yet another rock icon we lost way too early to overdose, yet the first album I ever owned was The Jimi Hendrix Experience *Are You Experienced?* Granted, I did steal it (as all good pirates and rockstar wannabes should), even if I ganked it from my mom.

I remember as a kid hearing Beethoven's *Ode to Joy* (technically the last movement of his 9th Symphony) and being mesmerized and carried away in a manner I never experienced before. That was the day my love of classical music was born (further reinforced by Bugs Bunny cartoons as has happened with so many other people born in the 20th century).

I wanted to make that kind of music that could carry people away. That same composition inspired Paul Robeson in the 1950's and was what Leonard Bernstein chose for the commemoration of the Reunification of Germany. The emotional high as the chorus ascends and celebrates still gives me chills a lifetime later. If you love music, you probably have that one piece, that one song that was your seminal love.

I have watched my friends that are real musicians on stage, playing and pouring their souls out. It doesn't matter if there are fifty people in the audience at a small club or thirty thousand at a rock festival, the passion they put into it is the same and transforms them from mere mortals into conduits of divine inspiration, tapping into infinite energies in ways that those of us in the audience marvel at. Music doesn't just tame the savage beast but unleashes the divine and gives us glances of all the heavens above and the alternate realities across the realms.

The Sorcerer's Apprentice was the pinnacle of Disney's Fantasia because music truly does alter reality.

Music helps create insight. Einstein and Feynman were famous for the instruments they played to relax and think, and Doctor Sir Bryan Maye of Queen or Dr. Dexter Holland of The Offspring are examples of scientists who leaned more into the art of music than their hardcore sciences and so guide with notes as opposed to numbers.

When I am struggling with a problem and can't go run five miles to let my subconscious play with it (typically while listening to Iron Maiden, and no apologies for it) the next best thing is to listen to Schubert (my preferred performer is mon amie Julie Sevilla Fraysse) or YoYo Ma performing the Bach Sonatas or Rostropovich and Dvorak's Cello Concerto and let my mind do what it does as it wanders. Generations of thinkers have used their own particular variation of this technique to solve problems, and I see no reason why you and I shouldn't learn from them and adopt their best practices.

Bad day? Play music.

Need an energy boost after five hours with toddlers? Play grown up music.

Need to set the mood with your sweetie? Play the right type of music. I will always be partial to Enya.

Music is mind altering in the best possible way, with no side effects or risk. Play it.

Action item: what is that one piece of music that transforms your spirit? Play it.

28 APRIL
"I think everybody wants to be a rock star."

Anna Camp

Nickelback sang it: we all just wanna be big rockstars and live in hilltop houses driving fifteen cars. It seems like rock stars have it all: fortune, fame, minions to take care of everything, groupies and whatever they want. "Money for nothing" as Dire Straits intoned back in the days when MTV played music.

I have some rockstar (or country star) buddies. Yes, they get to do glamorous things like date models or go off the grid for a month at a time. And the parties they can attend or throw are epic, just saying. But you know what? They have problems just like you and I.

My buddy Christian Lopez had his van broken into and his guitars stolen. That's just like a criminal stealing the tools from someone that works with their hands. Yes, they are replaceable but expensive and a pain in the tookus dealing with it.

Think about the last time your hard drive crashed and how much it disrupted your life. Now imagine it happening eight hours before a monster presentation you have to rebuild from scratch (been there, done that...). That is what Christian went through, and even though he is a star, looks like he belongs on the cover of a fashion magazine, and is engaged to a wonderful and gorgeous woman related to Hollywood elites, he still deals with the same crap as you and I. He just looks better doing it.

My other buddies have dealt with changing diapers and puking kids in the middle of the night, as opposed to puking band members as they did when they were younger stars. They struggle with meetings they don't want to sit through, have to file their taxes, and get jury duty summons just like you and I. Some days they don't want to deal with their crap, which although different than yours and mine is still a steaming pile of fecal material at times.

Also, do you realize how much time they have to spend dealing with lawyers? And not for bailing them out if they destroy a hotel room, but for contracts and more contracts. Tour logistics. Licensing. Contracts with band members and the label. Do you want to spend as much time dealing with lawyers as you do actually doing your job?! Even my friends that are attorneys get tired of dealing with lawyers.

And another thing most people don't realize: how these stars paid their dues and sacrificed along the way. Are you willing to dedicate thousands of hours to practice your craft, live near (or below) the poverty line for years, and have your economic future determined more by luck than anything else? That is what entertainers, athletes, and writers/artists do. Too many people see the tip of the iceberg of success and ignore the 99% that came before, with all of the rewards concentrated in a fleeting moment mainly beyond our control.

And then there is the press and social media. Are you still jealous of someone who as part of their reward also has to live in the fishbowl of attention and can barely go get a burger or take their kid out without getting accosted? Where if they put on a few pounds it is all over TMZ, and paparazzi harass them and their entire family. Would you intern for fifteen years to have a few years of public adoration that reaches the level of a gilded cage?

I personally don't want to be a rock star. Let my buddies have the gold records and mansions and throw the parties. I'd rather write the songs they sing and hang out in their kitchen the next day drinking a beer and not be under the bright lights, able to connect and guide and enjoy the quiet interludes. Because it is in those moments that rockstars are people and truly human.

Action item: instead of focusing on being on stage in front of 50,000 screaming fans, focus on your skills like a rock star focuses on their craft in the early stages. The hits will come when they come.

29 APRIL
"I won't be a rock star. I will be a legend."

Freddie Mercury

Have the BHAG (Big Hairy Audacious Goal per Jim Collins in *Good to Great*). Don't just try to make the team, practice and play to be an Allstar. Be the best you can be instead of just barely making the cut, whether it is in sports, the office, or your passion.

Be the best YOU you can possibly be, and others will see it. Live with passion. Work with passion, and play with passion like it is the closing seconds of Game 7 of the Stanley Cup and you have the puck.

"Begin with the end in mind" Stephen Covey admonishes us. Well, if you get to totally determine what that end is, and have the power to make it a reality, why not set your sights on something more than mediocrity? If you are going to have to sacrifice and struggle and believe in yourself, why not go all the way to 11 and be a legend?

What is the difference between adequate and excellent? On a daily basis it is a few minutes, just a bit more of your heart and soul put into your work. It could be asking that one extra question of the client to differentiate yourself, or picking up the phone two more times to try and book appointments. It could be five extra minutes of studying or preparation for that presentation, or doing the extra five push-ups each morning. Maybe invest a few minutes with your kid to help them with their homework or read to them before bed so they learn to love learning, or the moment to cut up veggies to snack on instead of grabbing a handful of chips as part of your diet.

The 1% difference, daily applied, creates tremendous results over months and years.

At six years old Cassius Clay announced he was going to be Champion of the World. He grew into The Greatest, Mohammad Ali.

Thirteen year old Bill Gates was writing computer code. Zuckerberg was 12. Mark Cuban was hustling as a kid.

Set your sights high and program your mind around being not successful but epically so. Then do the work to become a legend.

Action item: what do you need to do to become a Hall of Famer in your field? What little extra do you need to do daily to eventually become an immortal, remembered after your time? As Freddie sang: no time for losers, 'cuz we are the champions of the world!

30 APRIL
"If the legends fall silent, who will teach the children of our ways?"
Chief Dan George

There was a time when the Great Stories were told by the Elders, and children would harken to their lessons. The languages and cultures around these tales have evolved over the centuries, but the core issues remain fairly constant across time and distance.

Personal responsibility. Love of family. Defense of the weak. These are themes that appear over and over again in the myths and legends of most cultures, as explored by Joseph Campbell and JRR Tolkien. Repeatedly, the Hero must journey far, receive guidance from an elder, fight the dark spirit, and return to society a changed person for their sacrifice. From Gilgamesh to Luke Skywalker, Sigurd to Rama they fight against the darkness and inspire and inform the actions of those raised on their tales.

Our legends now include Washington ("I can not tell a lie") and Superman ("truth, justice, and the American Way.") They too embody protecting the innocent, sacrificing for the greater good of the community, and servant leadership even with tremendous power. Humility in victory and bravery even in defeat, lessons that were as appropriate three thousand years ago as three weeks ago. Students of history can read about Washington's foibles and debate the finer points, but the broad strokes of the myth used to be known by all Americans as part of our culture, the embodiment of what it meant to be a US Citizen and taught by the broad culture and adopted by people arriving on our shores for generations as part of the American Story.

Are our children today learning personal responsibility? Whose job is it to teach them? Not their schools. It is the obligation of parents and relatives, of coaches and cousins to model this behavior and unfortunately it is not being done, so the children are not learning this aspect of the ways that built the country. It takes a village to raise a child.

Defense of the weak was taught by the great religions and the folk tales of cultures for centuries. No more, and bullying is among the most dangerous threats in our schools because of the long-term psychological damage it does. Children used to learn that bullies were to be stopped through the stories they heard and the examples set by the grownups. Now they are learning that bullying is the way instead, and the online environment has unleashed trolls in the schools that all too often lead to violence or self harm. Who will show the kids the fair way again?

Action item: look in the mirror. Are you teaching the children the right ways? If not, what changes do you need to make to lead the next generation with a positive example?

AND ALL THE WORLD IS GLAD WITH MAY

John Burroughs

01 MAY

"Teaching is the greatest act of optimism."

Colleen Wilcox

Children are our future, and as the song goes "teach our children well". But learning is not restricted to just the little ones, and teaching is not restricted to those that are in our traditional educational facilities.

The wisest of the Greek kings Odysseus was nigh unto a god for his wisdom, and he learned much from a single person: his teacher Mentor. Through the Trojan War and his wanderings after, he survived not just because of his physical skills but because he had learned to think and adapt from his teacher. Hope burned in Odysseus because Mentor encouraged and fed the flames.

Seneca tutored Nero and remained in the Roman capital not because he wished for political power, but because he hoped to curb the Emperor's worst tendencies (he obviously did not succeed). Seneca hoped that Nero would become more like Marcus Aurelius and strengthen Rome while leading a better life, as multiple Stoic tutors had influenced Aurelius. Seneca maintained hope for his pupil right to the end.

Think of your best coach from when you were growing up, that former soccer player that encouraged you to channel your inner Mia Hamm or Briana Scurry and be a leader on and off the pitch, or the former minor leaguer that fixed your batting stance while teaching you about hard work. Or the teacher that saw through the ADHD or dyslexia and filled you with a passion for learning even in a non-traditional manner. Did your favorite aunt teach you to fish and open a lifetime of enjoyment to you, or your older cousin showed you how to cook and now you are teaching their grandkids what you learned decades ago and passing it down for generations?

Teaching is a path to immortality, to being remembered and improving the world long after we are gone. It is the ultimate affirmation of life and hope to give of ourselves to future generations.

Action item: who mentored you? If they are alive, reach out and thank them. Then find someone to pass this knowledge on to, so that your Mentor can continue to teach the future generations.

02 MAY

"Education is not the filling of a pail,
but the lighting of a fire."

William Butler Yeats

Your brain is never full, even if it might feel overloaded sitting through a Quantum Mechanics class. Your brain is not your iPhone whose memory is filled with 2047 pictures of your cat Tuna so you delete your banking app to still be functional.

We joked that my Fraternity Brother Harper was the first human being to fully utilize his brain, so to learn something new he had to forget something (like where he lived or social skills like showering or not randomly blurting out "I like ketchup!"). But that isn't how your brain works either, funny as Harper has always been. Oh, and he is now a Professor of Mathematics. Still forgets his way home sometimes.

Your brain is constantly rewiring itself in a phenomenon called "neuroplasticity", where we continuously create new neural connections and even as the brain ages it learns to become more efficient as an offset to cognitive decline, if stimulated. And that is the big "if".

A quarter of Americans read less than one book a year after completing their last year of formal education. This is not one educational book, this is ANY book above Dr. Seuss level. An additional quarter read one to five books a year (per Pew), so half of our citizens are barely reading or learning. That should scare you, but also give you hope that if you read only one book a month you can be above average and progress in life at an above average rate. I try to consume a book a week (reading or audio book while I drive or run to multitask). This puts me in the top 8% of Americans. Not bragging, but my parents instilled a love of learning that aligns well with my natural curiosity. And what it does is it keeps my brain young and revving almost all the time due to the continuous exposure to new information and ideas. That is the idea behind education.

Force your brain to accept new information and forge new neural pathways. Put yourself in situations that make your brain pause and have to work harder than normal, and just like your muscles it will become more powerful. This is what long form reading does.

Other ways to broaden your horizons and keep your mind limber include:

Listening to music. Especially music that you wouldn't normally groove to. I mix in such eclectic styles as Romanian manele, Mongolian throat singing, classic country, and sitar to supplement my heavy metal, classical, and Sinatra. Don't judge me.

Word of the day or fact of the day subscription services. Daily dose of micro-knowledge.

Learn a new language.

Learn to play an instrument.

Listen to podcasts, long form discussions between people with deep knowledge. Look for a variety of subjects that challenge you.

Museums. Virtual tours abound these days so you can tour the Louvre or the Guggenheim as easily as the one across town.

I have a buddy that is trying to qualify for JEOPARDY! (a LOT harder now than I was twenty-five years ago when another buddy won two nights in a row), and he says his focus is to learn a minimum of three new facts a day, every day. It is simple, but requires consistently exposing himself and learning new things. He might not be Ken Jennings, but he is certainly pursuing his dream with a good plan and keeping his brain active.

Learning is a lifestyle, not a goal. It's like eating healthy or exercising regularly, and just like consistent physical effort will keep you healthy and strong long past when your peers will be. Doing the same approach with your brain will keep it flexible and strong well past the point of grey hairs.

Action item: start reading a book today.

03 MAY
"Don't let schooling interfere with your education."

Mark Twain

One of my mom's favorite sayings. She was an educator and turned everything she could into a learning experience (even if it was painful). This is the woman who taught us about cooking and chemistry, farming and biology, and applied philosophy. She bought us bug jugs and magnifying glasses (which of course I misapplied), and taught me to read a book with an index card and pen so I could take notes and look up any word I didn't know.

If I didn't know how to spell a word, she'd say "There's the dictionary, figure it out yourself." And if I replied "If I knew how to spell it, I'd look it up!" I'd get smacked in the back of the head a la Gibbs in NCIS (which explains the flat spot on the back of my head). As I've said, sometimes knowledge is painfully gained but remembered forever.

Today, I tell my kids (or people I work with) that ask the same thing to "GTS". As in "Google That Stuff", the equivalent of my mom telling me to look it up or figure it out myself. The information becomes much stickier in the brain if worked for, and sometimes leads to side quests with additional knowledge as the reward.

Grades were important to me but not to my mom because she knew that an A didn't mean that there was understanding, nor that the concepts could be applied when needed. With my own kids (who are wicked smart), I repeatedly tell them I care about two things with their education: effort and attitude. If they have a good attitude and give their best efforts they will succeed and I will be proud of them, regardless of their grades. But when they don't give good effort they know I know and I am disappointed, because they are lacking in professional pride and discipline in their studies and there is a carry over effect into other areas of their life.

Do you learn for learning's sake, is it for progress with work, or is it to check a stupid box someplace? I have taken more than enough absolutely mind-numbing and useless Continuing Education (CE) classes for work in my life. Probably anyone that has ever taken a CE class can say the same thing, and so when I teach these I make sure that they are the finest in edutainment (a term stolen from Patrick Bet David, meaning learning and laughing or at least enjoying wrapped in one package) and applicable. Hopefully so far in this book it's met that criteria of being mirthful, memorable, and instructive.

Action item: picking up a book might be a boring way to learn something. So go learn something you didn't know via a more entertaining method.

MAY THE 4ᵀᴴ
"Much to learn, you still have."

Master Yoda

"The only true wisdom is knowing that you know nothing." Socrates.

"You can not learn that which you think you already know." Epictetus.

In the Japanese martial arts traditions there is an ideal of "beginner mind" (Shoshin), where things must be approached with openness and the wonder of a child experiencing it for the first time. Sometimes we get this feeling of awe with a sunset or standing over the Grand Canyon, but a true beginner's mind looks at even the morning coffee with appreciation (and not just because of the caffeine). The way the steam curls up, the vortexes as it is stirred, the smell. All things are new, as if experienced for the first time.

What if today you looked at your partner like you had never seen them? What little beautiful things would you notice, from the little mark on her cheek to the way his eyes dance when he smiles? What would you ask them if you weren't burdened by your experiences together?

At work, would you do things the same way you have been for years or would you approach the tasks differently, both from a process point of view and an enthusiasm perspective? Can you remember the excitement you had on the first day, and recapture some of that wide eyed spirit?

Five years ago you were working to get where you are today. Yet because of hedonic adaptation you still want more and maybe don't appreciate what you have as much as you thought you would. Mentally go back to the beginning, to the crappy apartment you lived in with smelly furniture and barely enough to eat. Then look around your current surroundings and realize not just how good you have it but how good you could make it if you were to work and think and act like when you were hungry.

Believing we have learned all we can, that we have capped out or are too old (or tired, or stressed, or...) to keep learning is one of the quickest ways to go from green and growing to ripe and then dying. Our brains can continuously adapt through neuroplasticity, where we are building new neural connections and flexibility that staves off aging. There is a reason why Lao Tze was known as "The Old Boy" and Yoda and Einstein acted like children in many ways: they kept Shoshin.

Action item: learn something completely random today, and try to fit it into your worldview or work. Repeat daily to stay mentally young and flexible.

05 MAY

"Who's more foolish: the fool, or the fool that follows him?"

Obi-Wan Kenobi

We all have that ringleader friend that for some reason can talk us into anything, good or bad. Maybe you are that person, just saying. How do you use your powers of influence?

Do you lead the gang out to the bar for drinks, and keep people out until late o'clock and disrupt their schedules to the point it messes with their studies or work? Or are you getting them out for a hike, checking out a new art exhibit or restaurant, and getting them to expand their horizons?

Do you lead to greatness or lateness?

Leadership is a special privilege and should not be abused, because those that chose to follow you trust you. Maybe they trust you to lead them into interesting experiences that lead to great stories, but if too often they deteriorate into a drunken bacchanal festival that ends with regurgitation and multiple visits from the police, people will opt out of your negative pied piper routine for the good of their livers and careers. I have a close buddy that this seemed to be a regular occurrence with and so the amount of time I spent with him seriously dropped, not because I was a stick in the mud by any means but sometimes it is better to avoid constant foolishness that reaches an epic level. Discretion can be the better part of valor, especially when the pattern of going to extremes is more regular than politicians lying to the public.

Sometimes, cutting loose is good, it builds bonds and reduces tension. Especially if you have kids, sometimes you need "grown up fun". But when fun is interfering with the important things like work or relationships, it needs to be reeled back in a little and if the ringleader consistently pulls you into that danger zone, it might be time to reduce exposure to that person.

If you are the ringleader, lead for a reason, guide those around you for growth and personal development. And if your ringleader is leading you astray, maybe it's time to find a new circus.

Action item: look at the people you spend time with. Are any trying to lead you on the wrong path? Maybe it is time for addition by subtraction.

06 MAY

"I find your lack of faith disturbing."

Darth Vader

Faith is a uniquely human characteristic, because it entails having forethought and at the same moment having belief. Being rational and simultaneously suspending rationality, in that grey area lives the most powerful of human creations: faith. Why does an expectant mother go through the bodily changes and suffering of childbirth? Biologically based belief in what lies ahead. That is faith.

Why do teachers invest years in getting the education that they need, the licensing, and then work with children to learn everything from their alphabet to calculus and nutrition and philosophy? Because they have faith in the future. Before you started your job, someone had the faith to hire you.

Even if the person that you love is off on a wrong path right now, you still love them and believe that they will do what they must and that they will come back, even if they are wandering lost for a while. That is faith.

Every new business owner has faith in their ability, and their plan. Every coach should believe in their players, knowing that they have done all they can do to help them grow and develop and that they should execute as trained. That is faith. Every person entering a hospital has faith in the medical science and doctors, even if they don't know what is wrong yet. Every time I see one of my Cub Scouts do a good deed to help someone else just because they know it is the right thing to do, I have my faith renewed.

Many people use religious faith to strengthen themselves and guide them, especially through dangerous times and rough patches in their lives. Faith supports us and strengthens us in times of trouble. Faith is why we get up and push ourselves every day, because we believe we can be better. That is faith applied, and rewarded when you look back at how far you've come.

Faith is hope with a plan. It is not as dependent on the whims of the universe but on executing what you have carefully thought about. It is hope that is internally driven or dependent upon non-supernatural support.

Faith, true faith, gives quiet strength instead of screaming from on top of a soapbox or mountaintop. It quietly whispers "trust and do".

Action item: take a moment and think about who and what you have faith in.

07 MAY

"No man is disturbed by things, but by his opinion about things."

Epictetus

The sun rises. This is a fact. Is it good, or bad? That depends on your point of view. If you are a farmer, or planning on going to the beach it is probably a good thing. If you are a vampire it is not. You don't get that bank loan. Are you devastated and just give in, forfeiting your dream or do you take a deep breath, grab a coffee and sit down and brainstorm ways to still do what you are planning but without the external financing?

The person you love (maybe you yourself) makes a self-destructive choice. Do you freak out? Abandon them? Attack them? Or do you continue to love them, and do whatever you can to help them through the consequences of their action? Do you fly away, or rush to their side in the time of need and work on strengthening the bonds and being there for them, even if their choice shatters your soul into a million shards? Is your opinion of that person strong enough to overcome the hurt? Do you love yourself enough to evaluate what you've done and try and fix things, or do you abandon hope and just keep on the path of doom?

Your favorite restaurant on your birthday is out of your favorite dish. Do you let it ruin your evening, or do you see it as an opportunity to try something new?

One thing the Stoics teach us is that it is ok to not even have an opinion. I don't care what is happening on reality tv (unless by reality tv you mean the Yankees game). So I have no opinion. Same with almost anything outside of my control. What is happening in countries like Afghanistan and Palestine and Iraq. I can't do anything other than vote and give money to charities to assist, and so that is what I do and don't get too worked up over things beyond my control.

I can't control the weather so unless the Yankees game is rained out, I can easily switch gears to something else and have little emotionally invested so don't get upset and can use that mental energy elsewhere on things more important to me.

Same with if someone tries to engage me in a debate about The Electoral College or if a candidate for governor in another state is good or bad. Notice how much of politics revolves around opinion and emotion, designed to stir us up and separate us as opposed to uniting us to work for the good of our communities. George Washington warned about this in his Farewell address.

Care less and you will have less stress in your life. You'll also be able to care more about the bigger things. Author Mark Manson (The Subtle Art of Not Giving a F*ck) talks about going on an information diet (as does Tim Ferriss): consume a lot less empty mind calories by cutting down your consumption. Just look at the headlines, or the front page of a few news sites for under ten minutes. You have basically all you need to know about "the news".

Not having an opinion is a result of being disciplined in your awareness and where you spend your mental units. Saving them for something more valuable than what some celebrity said or did that will be replaced by the next scandal within two days as the news cycles through its endless dirty laundry is worth it.

Napoleon used to wait weeks to read the mail, knowing that the surface opinion driven chatter of the day would have been replaced by the new distraction, and so was able to keep his cool more and dedicate mental bandwidth to military issues by knowing to ignore the equivalent of today's social media.

Action item: opinions are like buttholes (everybody has one). Stop checking out and engaging with other people's rear ends today. You are a human, not a dog.

08 MAY
"You can have your own opinion, but not your own facts."

Talib Kweli

"Alternative facts" is an oxymoron and a dangerous idea. As Indiana Jones said, there can be many truths interpolated but facts are indisputable and immutable. Rarely are wars fought over facts, but constantly over "truth".

A diamond is made of carbon is a fact, which facet you look at presents your interpretation of the truth and how beautiful or not what you see is. Changing your position will change your perspective and your truth, but the chemical composition of the diamond is unaltered. Fact does not change based on how you look at it, only with additional information that has been vetted.

It is the job of science and logic to sift through feelings and opinions and data to come up with facts. It is the responsibility of those that present facts to present facts, not interpretation thereof or their opinion of it. This is one thing that has caused issues for our media over the past two plus decades: spin obscures clarity. And it happens on both sides of the aisle.

Look at the source data and who is presenting it to you. Ask what their bias could be and why. Who paid for the research? Who could benefit from the information presented, and are they presenting all of the information or cherry-picking points? Does it stand up against scientific scrutiny, and is it repeatedly demonstrated? Does the information have integrity or has it been manipulated?

Think like a scientist, and question your own biases.

Action item: look at your news sources. Add in at least one that has the opposite bias so that you can see if something is a fact, or merely someone's interpretation of truth.

09 MAY

"Science is simply common sense at its best."

Thomas Huxley

Science is the universal language, because biology applies equally on every continent and physics on every planet. And from the moment we open our eyes, we start experiencing the world around us, collecting data and synthesizing an understanding of it. Enough observation allows us to start to develop ideas about our surroundings, and that is the basis of understanding and common sense. A child quickly learns that unsupported things fall. They don't need the mathematical rigor of calculus from Newton to understand gravity, they just "get it". The mathematical modeling merely captures what is seen, and then lets us extend what we see to what could be possible, like sending a man to the moon through higher level thinking based upon what the average five-year old knows.

For thousands of years science was advanced not by PhD's and multibillion dollar research budgets but by tinkerers, by people with a vested interest in making a water wheel grind better or a crop more productive. Observation and contemplation were the key components of technology creations, an extension of the human capacity to understand. As we advanced from the most primitive creations of bows and arrows and flint through bronze and iron to information, we refined the process and thoughts and built upon existing levels of information and thought to create the codified science and near wizardry we now have. Yet its core is still common sense, looking at the world around us and asking "why" and "how" and "what if". It is questions that lead to answers and more questions, and have created the world we enjoy today.

"Any sufficiently advanced technology is essentially indistinguishable from magic" as Arthur C Clarke said, and the danger is that the average user no longer understands the basics from which it is built up from. Fifty years ago a car manual came with instructions on how to change the oil and spark plugs, now it comes with warnings to not drink the fluids. This is definitely a lack of common sense and the dangers of disconnecting people from experiencing their environment (both good and bad) that Carl Sagan warned about is becoming evident.

Action item: put down the electronic device and go experience something like taking apart an old motor, reading an instruction manual, or jumping in a puddle and observing how the ripples work. Play with string and rubber bands to get a feel for how the world functions, then sit down with a piece of paper and explore the cause and effects of an action. DO science instead of watching it.

10 MAY

"Common sense is not so common."

Voltaire

In fact common sense is so rare these days it should be classified as a superpower. "I'm Basic Thinking Dude! I basically stop and think for five seconds before taking action, based upon my previous experiences and common sense." Save us, Basic Thinking Dude, you're our only hope!

Let's actually reflect on this for a moment. Common sense says that "from my experience, if x then y" and is dependent upon continuously learning from experiences so this very short decision loop is improved. When you were a kid, you learned early not to touch a hot stove because of the quick feedback loop. The more varied your experiences (like walking down the street alone, or trying to cook eggs at five, or reading history, or playing with your parents' tools), the broader and deeper your background knowledge and your ability to start connecting the dots between different actions and outcomes.

Not only is the range of your exposure greater, but the recognition cycle time can decrease to the point of being intuitive, like tying your shoes or a hedge fund whiz able to calculate a yield curve nearly instantaneously. Now calculating a yield curve is pretty esoteric (but common in their world), but understanding that water under pressure shoots out should be fairly everyday knowledge, but how many plumbing disasters occur daily because people "didn't realize it would happen". That's because they didn't have enough exposure to have that feedback loop of common sense working properly.

I blame the parents.

Seriously, I do. When we were kids in the 1970's (when everyone wore polyester bell bottoms and dinosaurs roamed the earth according to my kids), we always had a relative or neighbor that was working on their car and would show us what they were doing. Parents cooked, and we learned by watching and helping. We knew that tie dyed and whites don't go together either because we were shown and told, or we did it once at six and never did it again because we had to wear pink underwear as a result. Too many people in their 20's don't know how to do laundry or cook a basic meal, let alone change a tire, not mix bathroom chemicals, or how to read an instruction manual.

And it shows.

Common sense is a building power, in that the knowledge acquired in one area (say how to take care of your bike), flows into other areas (car maintenance, understanding traffic patterns, looking at the sky and weather to make sure not caught in a storm, time management) and becomes more of a habit as you acquire more knowledge on a variety of subjects and learn to make better, quicker decisions.

Common sense is more mental muscle than model because the more you use it, the stronger it becomes.

We see the effect of this decline: the run on the stores for toilet paper or other items, dead people getting elected, car accidents and financial frauds. As people become afraid to make mistakes when they are young, they don't get the lessons and wisdom from these errors and are set up for greater failures in the future.

Scars are permanent reminders of lessons learned. That cut on your finger from trying to slice an apple but cutting towards yourself instead of away, the little burn mark on your thumb from touching hot metal in the shop, the nick on your leg from the barbed wire as a kid (I have this one). The small psychic scars from losing your parents on the playground or failing a test because you played video games. These little scars prevented us from having terrible injuries later because we developed common sense from the experience.

Bubble wrapping your kids (or self) actually sets them up for more harm and failure, and is the reason why the deferred pain of stupidity due to lack of common sense is so great and widespread.

Action item: what was one lesson you learned early on that would be important to share with those around you, so that they don't need to get any fresh scars?

11 MAY
"Common sense is the enemy of romance."

Eric Jerome Dickey

If it's logical and rational, it's probably not love and romance. Romance is often about casting a spell, suspending the normal rules of our drab and hectic world and bringing the magic into the everyday, whether it is through poetry or flowers or music or changing the scenery (candles, a trip,...).

Common sense is meant to be rooted in everyday experiences, learning from the mundane and having routine. Romance is the breaking of this, creating excitement and newness. It is the splurged dessert when on a boring diet. The rush of sensory feedback, the sugar and alcohol in the blood, the slight naughtiness even. It is submitting to momentary pleasure, regardless of the future and consequences.

It feels good to be bad, even if it is not wrong. Maybe more so if it is.

Create (or re-create) the magic. Strike a spark, to keep the flames going amid the soul dampening drudgery of our everyday lives.

Careers and kids suck away our spirit, extinguish the flames, drain our energy and make us forget our passion that once burnt hot. Rekindle it. Somehow.

Even if it seems impossible. That is your logical mind operating, the common sense you've developed over time. Shut your neocortex down and let your spirit flow to unlock the love.

Forget the odds, even if they are million to one. If they are worth it, they are a Pascal's Wager and worth any risk.

Hopeless romantics know in their heart, believe to the depth of their soul that there is a way to overcome all the odds and weave magic. Romance is that magic. From Sapho to de Bergerac to Rumi they tap into powers beyond our normal ken for the greater purpose of love. Learn from them.

Action item: suspend all belief and dream. Channel de Bergerac and weave a spell, suspend common sense and the grey every day and show them your heart.

11 MAY

"Common sense is the enemy of romance."

Eric Jerome Dickey

If it's logical and rational, it's probably not love and romance. Romance is often about casting a spell, suspending the normal rules of our drab and hectic world and bringing the magic into the everyday, whether it is through poetry or flowers or music or changing the scenery (candles, a trip,...).

Common sense is meant to be rooted in everyday experiences, learning from the mundane and having routine. Romance is the breaking of this, creating excitement and newness. It is the splurged dessert when on a boring diet. The rush of sensory feedback, the sugar and alcohol in the blood, the slight naughtiness even. It is submitting to momentary pleasure, regardless of the future and consequences.

It feels good to be bad, even if it is not wrong. Maybe more so if it is.

Create (or re-create) the magic. Strike a spark, to keep the flames going amid the soul dampening drudgery of our everyday lives.

Careers and kids suck away our spirit, extinguish the flames, drain our energy and make us forget our passion that once burnt hot. Rekindle it. Somehow.

Even if it seems impossible. That is your logical mind operating, the common sense you've developed over time. Shut your neocortex down and let your spirit flow to unlock the love.

Forget the odds, even if they are million to one. If they are worth it, they are a Pascal's Wager and worth any risk.

Hopeless romantics know in their heart, believe to the depth of their soul that there is a way to overcome all the odds and weave magic. Romance is that magic. From Sapho to De Bergerac to Rumi they tap into powers beyond our normal ken for the greater purpose of love. Learn from them.

Action item: suspend all belief and dream. Channel De Bergerac and weave a spell, suspend common sense and the grey every day and show them your heart.

12 MAY

"Speak low, if you speak love."

William Shakespeare

Love can be the grand gesture that has others talking, whether the special cupcakes shaped like roses to show your love in a tasty way, or writing a song for your crush and having musicians record and perform it for them. These are wonderful and very public generally, but they are not the sort of thing that can be repeated continuously.

Doing the dishes so they don't have to look at them is repeatable.

Bringing her a cup of coffee every morning so that as she awakens it is to the wonderful Joe, and shows you want her to start her day in a good way because you care.

Always telling them "goodnight, I love you, sweetest dreams" so that they greet Morpheus with a smile because you showed that little bit of consistent caring.

Making eggs the way they like instead of your preferred way. Agreeing to New England clam chowdah instead of Manhattan (this is a big deal!) A random text of a picture of plumeria or a daisy or whatever their favorite flower is. "Saw this, thought of you." Maybe a meme, something about their favorite sport team or athlete, a piece of art, or something completely random that makes you think of them.

Send them a Youtube link to your song, with a note "thinking of you and smiling." A hug on a bad day, no words, just holding them. A note on their pillow or in their lunch "I Love You" that they will see hours later when you aren't physically present.

Taking their hand and looking into their eyes and smiling, for no other reason than they bring you joy and you want to reflect it back to them.

As 1 Corinthians reminds us:
>*Love is patient;*
>*Love is kind;*
>*Love is not envious or boastful*

A picture of a rainbow after a storm or a gorgeous sunset, no words, just God's canvas with something that makes your soul sing as much as your love does. These are how to speak softly of and to your love.

Action item: quietly show them today. Make it a daily habit.

13 MAY

"You, as much as anyone in the universe, deserve your love and respect."

Buddha

It wasn't all your fault. Even if the breakup was horrible, the divorce nasty, or the leaving the company an epic disaster, that is no reason to think you are worthless. Stuff happens. Maybe your business partner had the work ethic of a sponge. Once you discover this, if you did everything reasonable (or even more than reasonable) to help get them up to speed and encourage their production and they could not evolve into a productive team member, that is not your problem. Learn from it and get a better winger next time. But don't destroy yourself.

Your ex is battling you in court and it never seems to end and you are like "who is this person?!" Don't let it crush your soul, and if they are lying about you don't start to believe the horrible things they say. They loved you once, and you should still love yourself even though the relationship ended.

You are still a human being, and deserve the dignity of one even if things are rough in your world. All people deserve love, even if they have made mistakes. "Let he who is without sin cast the first stone", and we have all screwed up at least once today alone. Don't flagellate yourself. If you mess up at work didn't lead to people dying, it is recoverable. "If it's not fatal, it's fixable" applies. When PIXAR was in its first handful of movies, someone accidentally deleted a chunk of the code, thousands of hours of work vaporized with the stroke of a few keys. They weren't fired. That is probably worse than anything you could do.

Mistakes are teaching moments, and one of the most important lessons a good leader should be focused on is that to err is human. Mistakes are part of the growth process, and give an opportunity to rethink a situation and solve problems that sometimes lead to even better outcomes. It is not an excuse to abuse someone, nor should the punishment be disproportionate to the damage. Tough love is still love, and is done with respect for who the person is now and has the capacity to become. The destroyer USS Decatur ran aground in 1908 while under the command of a young ensign. He was court martialed, admitted fault, and was reprimanded. He received some lousy assignments, but his love of the Navy and his belief he could be of service kept him in. You might know his name: Chester Nimitz, later Fleet Admiral and the single most important officer in the history of the US submarine fleet as well as Commander in Chief of the US Pacific Fleet in WWII. Even though Ensign Nimitz messed up, he deserved love.

Jack Welch blew up his lab at GE Pittsfield. He later became one of the most famous and powerful CEOs in US business history. Jack loved himself (maybe too much, but still deserved love.)

Action item: you deserve love. Write yourself a love letter, telling yourself why you like you.

14 MAY
"Self-respect is the cornerstone of all virtue."

John Herschel

Low value people repeatedly self sabotage because they do not believe they are worthy of love, respect, or success. Their lack of belief in themselves (which they often cover by going to the other extreme of narcissism or outrageous but faked apparent self-love as a coping mechanism) leads them to have flash in the pan wins at work and short-term relationships that repeatedly fail because of their issues that make them screw it up. And they are often repeatedly taken advantage of by predators that see this and use the person lacking in self-respect for financial, sexual, power, or other reasons.

Self-respect is so critical to being a properly functioning and independent member of society that it is Jordan Peterson's first rule in his 12 Rules For Life, and the neurochemical basis of it traces back hundreds of millions of years, well before we stood upright or Tiktokked. As a clinical psychiatrist he has seen thousands of patients with low self esteem leading to addictions ranging from needles to the phone to neophilia that ultimately weaken or destroy the psyche and have poor overall outcomes. A cursory glance at the literature shows a distinct relationship between low self esteem and criminal records, low educational outcomes, affairs, divorce, and addictions. Self-respect based on fact (not fluff) is one of the key components of sustainable success.

Developing decent self-respect early is one of the most important reasons behind many early childhood and pre-kindergarten programs, and the statistics bear out the positive effect of these programs (with the caveat that the rest of the child's environment can't be utterly destructive). Teaching kids that they are capable of tying their shoes, then learning the alphabet and reading, then showing them that they can figure out and solve problems of increasing complexity lays the foundation for their emotional and intellectual growth. Maslow's Hierarchy of Needs moves from safety needs (food, water, shelter) into emotional ones because all higher levels of self awareness and empowerment depend upon having self-esteem and respect.

We have all heard tales of a coach that takes high risk kids and gets them to focus on a sport, teaching them about the relationship between hard work and success, who has high standards and believes in them more than anyone else. The coach teaches them to have faith in the process and models self confidence and teaches them to respect the game and themselves. Often these kids catch up to their peers that they were trailing, and take the lessons from their sport into other areas of their life and many of them break the bad cycle they could have been caught in because they replaced low self-esteem with valid self-respect.

If you don't respect yourself, you will have trouble respecting others. This is why martial arts and pledging programs and Scouts and the military teach all sorts of basic skills and challenge people over and over to develop self-respect that is earned. People who have gone through these programs for years tend to outperform their peers, because of the fundamentals that are instilled. If you respect yourself you will make better choices, because you have more internal strength to not choose what makes you feel good in the instant but sacrifices the long term.

Self-respect allows someone to believe in themselves enough to invest in deferred gratification (dieting, investing, studying, training, working on their relationships instead of just flying away) because they understand in their core that even if it isn't easy right now it is the better choice overall, and a little temporary uncomfortableness will yield much greater positive feelings and results later. The low self esteem person needs the fix now (a like on social media, a hit of narcissistic supply, a drink, etc), and the focus on the easy quick blast of positive neurochemicals leads to a path of bad choices and ultimately self-destruction.

Action item: what is one thing you have done that has helped build your self-esteem? Why? Did it work so well you stopped doing it? Should you do more of it?

15 MAY

"Virtue is to herself the best reward."

Henry More

We have all heard "no good deed goes unpunished." So be it.

Virtue can be its own reward.

Doing the right thing because it is right, not because of a pat on the back or because it will impress someone else, is the right thing. Even if it hurts you financially or otherwise in the short term. I've gone through it numerous times.

I am not going to lie or try and sugar coat it and make it less of a bitter pill to swallow: sometimes doing the right thing, being virtuous for the greater good, will cost you. Friends. Potentially your job, or even a relationship with someone you hold dear. Maybe a ton of money. But integrity is priceless, even if it really sucks in the short-term doing the proper thing. You will second doubt yourself and hear it from friends and associates and family that you should have done something less honorable, maybe more Machiavellian and beneficial to yourself. Ignore them,

"To thine own self be true." Shakespeare

"When truth looks in the mirror, virtue looks out." Matshona Dhliwayo

Just because you can do something doesn't mean you should. Choosing to not indulge (in alcohol, or those forbidden fruits, or those luxuries that you know will fade in feeling immediately) is more than just satisfying. Avoiding or resisting temptation makes us stronger and better able to continue to do so, even when it would feel oh so good to give in to that pleasure that we think no one will know about....

You will know. And eventually so will others.

In the end, we all have to live with ourselves. Some people look into their accountability mirror and their own souls daily. Some never do. Avoidance behavior compounds the issues, so those small sins grow and cascade and can bury our internal light beneath tons of debris that was brought down on our heads by our own actions, because we started the avalanche. Little choices have great outcomes, so the continued discipline of staying the course and walking the line, even when it would feel so good just to cross that one line once, is the secret to avoiding being buried by guilt and letting shame crush us.

Action item: there are lines you know you should not cross. Are you close to any of them? Step back and look at the situation and back away from the temptation.

16 MAY

"When was public virtue to be found when private was not?"

William Cowper

We see the story repeatedly on shows like American Greed: the public figure that does so much good for the community through their charity and public service that secretly was living a double life, lining their pockets and doing horrible things. From Boss Tweed to Bernie Madoff, the publicly perfect individual that is corrupt to the core that eventually is revealed like the Portrait of Dorian Grey is a lesson and warning for us all.

A building with a cracked foundation cannot stand for very long, it will eventually collapse. So too with an individual that papers over their faults in public and lives two faced, because eventually someone will discover their other side and reveal the unpleasant truth, with the natural consequences.

Those who cheat will cheat, and will eventually be discovered. The repeated scandals of New York governors (Cuomo, Patterson, Spitzer) may be an indictment of our political system (especially here in NY), but also forces us to ask about the people we give power to in general. Every level of politics is seemingly rocked to its core annually with a scandal, only to have another one pop up soon thereafter, then another, then another. Maybe we should look more at the private virtues before endorsing or promoting people, because the private sector has the same issues without nearly the press coverage.

Power does not necessarily corrupt, but rather attracts the corrupt and easily corruptible. More attention to the personal standards and backgrounds of those moving into positions of influence might be a solution, as is accountability and openness as people move up the chain of command. More light on a situation generally keeps the cockroaches away and keeps the mold from growing as strong.

"It is a well known fact that those people who most want to rule people are, ipso facto, the least suited to do it... anyone that is capable of getting themselves made President should on no account be allowed to do the job." Douglas Adams in The Hitchhiker's Guide to the Galaxy.

Servant leadership was how this country was built, people being willing to step forward to serve and sacrifice. Of the 56 signatories of The Declaration of Independence:

Five were tortured and killed.

Nine fought and died of wounds or hardships.

Eleven lost everything financially.

At least six lost a son, spouse, or other close family member due to battle.

They signed their death sentences when they signed their name and agreed to "mutually pledge to each other, our lives, our fortunes, and our sacred honor." If you are in a position of trust in the community (political, religious, volunteer), keep your honor. It is the American Way.

Action item: do you live up to the ideals of your organization? Start being better.

17 MAY

"Having these colossal accolades and titles, they get in the way."

Bob Dylan

It's safe to say Bob Dylan was not burdened with a golden voice. That lack of greatness allowed him to explore his talents as a songwriter and focus on what he was good at, ultimately winning the Nobel Prize in Literature.

Ego is The Enemy contains multiple tales of glorious rise and fantastic fall, more dramatic than that of Icarus, told by Ryan Holiday with discussion about how to keep the ego in check. Success is a danger he warns, because we can end up believing our own press clippings. We destroy ourselves by believing in our abilities too much.

Accolades and titles are external trappings that can trap us, bind us into believing our own greatness. This is a tremendous danger, as all too often in the Greek myths pride leads to the wrath of the gods and tragic downfall.

Tom Brady and Michael Jordan are in the discussion for GOAT (Greatest of All Time) in their sports, and almost immediately after winning a championship they would start prepping to win another. They collected immense personal accolades (11 Superbowl/Finals MVPs alone besides a litany of regular season awards and astounding net worths), but only one thing mattered to them: winning. Not ego. Not personal paychecks. Not individual stats. Rings, and doing what it was needed to be in a position to get another.

We have all seen the person with some early big wins in their career who starts to think they are entitled to success, that it will be easy and then WHAM! Life hits them. And their past successes, instead of reminding them that they can get up and get at it and do it again, make them bitter and they are just a flash in the pan and a warning for others, a warning however unheeded as the cycle repeats.

Work like a novice.

Work like you're trying to earn the job.

Listen to your significant other like it is your first date.

Pretend it is the first time, every time.

Action item: set aside the successes of the past and ask "If I were to start today, what should I do to be the best?"

18 MAY

"Leadership is an action, not a position."

Donald McGannon

There can be only one #1 in any organization. But all highly functioning organizations have multiple leaders, and the best exhibit leadership among all of their members. From the young woman on the phone interacting with irate customers to the corner office, the best performing groups ingrain leadership into their people so that they can all through their individual actions and examples move the collective towards its goals. This is what leadership is in essence.

Leadership is that kid helping carry groceries for their neighbor.

Leadership is not a bunch of people in suits and pantsuits in a conference room talking, taking some notes and patting each other on the back and then releasing a statement. That is empty and self-serving. Yes, I am calling out all the politicians and their photo ops.

Leadership is the cop playing with the kids on their beat and making sure they understand right from wrong not because of what they are told but by what they observe in the way the men and women in blue listen and respect and perform.

Leadership is the little old lady volunteering to help at the Seniors' Center or being a surrogate grandma for high-risk kids.

Leadership is telling your friend to knock it off, to stop messing around and screwing up their life even if they get pissed at you.

Leadership is not telling your team you need them to pull extra time for a week to hit the goals. It is saying that, bringing them pizza and doing whatever you can to assist them in getting the job done and managing their stress. Being empathic and empowering and knowing when to say "go home, your dog needs you more than the project right now." And making coffee for everyone.

Dictionary.com says it is "a person who guides a group". It doesn't talk about title, or experience, or innate ability. The definition is based upon the action of an individual influencing others. Not someone with a gold star on their chest or a crown upon their head or the special parking spot.

Leading is like living. It is what everybody does to some extent. The more fully you lead, the more fully you can live.

Action item: look for a chance to step up today. Make it easier for someone else to do their job. Help someone out. Lead by example.

19 MAY
"A boss has a title, a leader has the people."

Simon Sinek

Have you ever heard a kid yell "you're not the boss of me!"? Typically it involves stomping, maybe some screaming and very little actually getting stuff done. Maybe after kicking and pouting, they can be dragged at extreme effort and embarrassment to wherever you need them to be. Not the best way to get what you want out of them.

Then what does the same kid do the next day? Probably plays "Follow The Leader" and will traipse all over the place, over and under obstacles and exhaust themselves cheerfully.

A boss has leverage because they can fire you. A leader has power because they can fire you up. Boss implies a superior position, looking down and ordering. Leader implies being on the same level, and leading the charge after rallying the troops. Which one creates heroes out of ordinary people, and which just creates animosity? Bosses crack the whip. Leaders get cracking with their team.

Both lead to throwing. Bosses throw temper tantrums and insults, leaders throw themselves into the fray with their people. A boss will throw people under the bus, a leader will throw their people's name in for rewards and positive spotlights and accolades.

This is not to say there is no hierarchy or command structure. But a boss depends primarily on the hierarchy to get those below them to achieve, while a leader might employ the chain of command but is trying to bring those they lead to their level, at least in thought and vision and opportunity for impact.

Defense Secretary James Mattis didn't like the nickname "Mad Dog", but was widely known among Marines (and other military men and women) as "Chaos" for " Colonel has another outstanding suggestion", a call sign given to him by a man that would become a 3-Star General in his own right. Even as a 4-Star General and then the man right below the Commander in Chief, Mattis was idolized for how he led from the middle of the pack to earn the position to be in charge. Even as THE military leader he rarely had to boss people around.

Leaders lift others up or pull them up to a higher level. Bosses sit on high and expect to be raised up higher by those below them. Bosses seek the credit, leaders give it to others. Boss Bad. Leader Loved.

Action item: look at how you interact with those that you have power over, be it at home, work, or elsewhere. How can you get them to do something without resorting to "because I say so!"?

20 MAY

"The sign of a beautiful person is that they always see the beauty in others."

Omar Suleiman

You might have heard the quip that "beauty is skin deep, but ugly goes straight to the bone." Probably true, but the beauty in many people is not apparent at first glance and takes seeing with more than eyes to experience.

We tend to project ourselves upon others. So if we have been hurt in love we project that and the doubt it creates onto our partners in new relationships. If we can't be trusted we won't trust others, even if they are eminently trustworthy and always honest to us because liars believe everyone else is as false as they are.

That honest person probably also can't comprehend (or purposely overlooks) the lies in the other, because they are projecting their positive interpretation outward from their soul. This bifurcation and radicalizing based on our own mindset applies everywhere.

There is a lot of psychology behind the halo/demon effect, but we tend to see the world not as IT is, but as WE are. We resonate with things in others that are internal to ourselves, so if we have a negative feeling about say manele music or politicians we will subconsciously push this belief on others such that if they are neutral or negative towards this they will align with the dislike at some level and we glom onto this.

Basically we send out a signal and if it is returned we hear our own projection amplified and reinforced so we perceive the other as sending it. Same with a positive emotion around bunnies or butterflies: we see and feel what we are predisposed towards and recognize it in others.

So we see ugly or beauty in others based upon how we see ourselves and the world, based upon our mental filters. This is part of the reason why narcissists and empaths are attracted to each other, or conmen (women) and too honest marks because the good side cannot even comprehend the bad exists, so when the darker oriented individual finds this naivete they can exploit it, often until the other side is jaded and disillusioned.

The defense is to still keep the positive outlook without being Pollyanna, to understand that there are bad people (or just negative and untrustworthy ones). To keep your positive outlook but not go 100% until others have proven that they deserve it.

Seeing beauty may take work if you are in a negative headspace or emotionally hurt. But it is a skill that can be developed, like being able to assemble a jigsaw puzzle: see the patterns based on having the vision, and slowly assemble the pieces. It takes effort, it takes time, but in the end you have something more beautiful than the pieces that made it up.

Project your beauty onto the world, even if the world is ugly at times or others don't see it at the moment. Some people will connect with that vibe, and like the nodes in a communication system the more people participating in the appreciation and sharing of beauty, the more powerful the signal.

Action item: today see the beauty in someone else. Try to focus on someone that is in emotional pain (especially if they strive to hide it).

21 MAY

"Beauty is a light in the heart."

Kahlil Gibran

Beauty is in the eye of the beholder, but when it is in the heart of another its light can be seen by all, even the blind.

Beautiful hearts brighten the world around them. They lighten your life, and warm your spirit.

Surface beauty grabs attention, but deeper soul beauty inspires adoration.

Are you beautiful on the inside, or are you like The Portrait of Dorian Grey and perfect on the outside but rotten in your soul? This will be seen eventually, as the dark heart slowly poisons the mind and body. Just like the pure, the bright and just one shines through the eyes and makes others see Heaven when they look upon this person.

Radiance comes not from the perfect pearly smile, but from the spirit inside.

Action item: spend time today around a beautiful person. Not physically but emotionally and spiritually, and reflect their light into the world.

22 MAY

"If light is in your heart, you will find your way home."

Rumi

We all look for the external lighthouse to guide us through the storm and avoid crashing on the rocks. And external beacons can definitely reinforce what we are carrying inside us, maybe even re-ignite something that has started to fade. But outside motivation or guidance is not sustainable and will lose power over days and weeks, this is why people go back to religious services even though it is the same messages repeated. It is why physical trainers or coaches repeat the same phrases and practices, to remind and reinforce until the outside influence has sunk into the inside.

Our hearts can get us in trouble as they can be fickle or fooled. Our intentions might not be as pure as we think or wish that they were. We all struggle with our version of the heart of darkness, but we also know that we carry at least a sliver of light in us no matter how black things seem. And it is this bit of light that is our internal beacon. It will help us find our way.

Focus on feeding the flame in your heart that produces the light. The old story of the two wolves (the dark one and the light one) that live in us has been repeated enough that we don't have to go in depth on it, but try to feed the light one because it will guide you to where you should be, where your heart dwells.

Having a light heart will lift you up instead of dragging you down, but it will also buoy others that might be experiencing the rough seas of life and need a beacon. Even if they look fine, say they are happy, appear to have it all; others around us are struggling mightily and doing what we need to do to feed our light (often through little acts of service or kindness or gratitude) have the ancillary effect of lightening others hearts too. Making our world a little better place, a bit of heaven and home for all.

Action item: what makes your heart light? A picture of a sunset? A particular flower? Someone's voice, or a song? Helping someone else? Choose one thing and experience it, and if possible share it to spread the light.

23 MAY

"Home is the nicest word there is."

Laura Ingalls Wilder

It rolls off the tongue and just feels right, a warmth in the soul and the smell of mom's kitchen. It feels like your favorite aunt and your birthday rolled into one emotional embrace.

Home.

Home is different for all of us but universal in that it is safe, where we could hide from the world, and is tinged with love.

"Home is where the heart is." Pliny the Elder

You know the place, where even as you approach you feel your soul soar. Where your body starts to relax before you arrive, a Pavlovian response a lifetime in the making. When you hear the word "home" the image instantly leaps into your mind from your heart, and the weight of the world seems to decrease as the feelings well up, supporting your psyche and buoying your mood.

Home.

It might be the house you grew up in, or your family cabin. It might be a relative's place, or the house that you have purchased and made your own with your choices and love. Where little trinkets key off waves of remembrances, like that kid in the bathtub with their pet frog plaque or that glass you got at McDonalds that is still in the cabinet.

The little things that you discovered over time, like the squeaky floorboard you had to be careful of so you didn't wake up mom or the hidden compartment in the closet where you hid things. The tree you carved your first love's name into. That scribble on the wall from the toddler getting ahold of the Sharpie marker. The priceless memories that only those who were there share.

Home.

More than a house. "I like how it feels here at home, Dai (Dad). It feels like love." As spoken by my then six year old. I can think of no better way to describe it.

Action item: go home today, at least in your mind if not body.

24 MAY
"Leaving home in a sense involves a kind of second birth, in which we give birth to ourselves."
Robert Neelly Bellah

There is an old European tale about the leaving from home and becoming an adult known as "Iron John," that like many tales is entertaining but carries tremendous psychological weight in that the leaving of the protection of the parents on a journey to adulthood is a universal human story. From the Spartan krypteia to US military boot camp or simply going off to college and having both physical separation from the parents and a cutting of the figurative umbilical cord, the right of passage to adulthood and the rebirth or recreation of an unique adult identity independent from the parents is universal and timeless.

The transition to adulthood is a time for exploration. As a freshman in college there is a banquet of new experiences beyond anything a high schooler could dream about. Want to learn to juggle (more than just your schedule), or learn to code, or try a martial art? What about taking a course in world philosophies and trying 1,000 different types of tacos? If you never leave the farm (or stay home and have mom continue to do your laundry) and don't start accepting the individual personal responsibility of adulthood (with all the tiny scars and bruises that come with it as reflected in the tales by pinching a thumb or ritualistic scars/tattoos in various cultures), you will remain a teenager even if you are in your 40's if not forced to metamorphosize.

Here's something really cool though: even if you are more than a few years past your high school days, you can still "leave home" and rebirth yourself. Take on additional responsibilities at work that force you to grow. Step up as a volunteer and go outside your old comfort zone to develop new skills and mindsets. Enroll for a degree or certificate program to expand your mind and vision. Sign up for that Spartan race nine months from now and change your identity from couch potato to runner and badass. Leave the comfort zone you've been in for a while and force yourself on a new journey of discovery, which like Deadpool in the med facility will force your adaptation to survive (albeit not in the way of Dr. Killbrew or the Spartan youth fighting wolves).

You can always choose to face adversity and remake yourself in the image that you want, but it becomes more and more difficult over time because the walls of our castle (external societally driven expectations and inner walls we build ourselves to keep new/foreign ideas out). Force yourself to travel mentally at least a little, and you can go further afield as you start evolving into a new you.

Action item: how can you mentally remove yourself from your current situation and expose yourself to something new, to force you to grow?

25 MAY

"All we are given are possibilities - to make ourselves one thing or another."

Jose Ortega y Gasset

What did you want to be when you grew up? A doctor? An astronaut? President? Firefighter? The probability is you are not what or who you wanted to be at 6 or 16. Maybe not even at 26. According to the Federal Reserve, about three out of four people end up working in something not closely related to their college major, something they usually spent four years and a bunch of money on only to earn their living elsewhere. Why is that?

Many use the skill sets learned to enter new areas, like physicists going into computers or finance, or the psych major ending up in sales. Many start businesses that follow their passions or gravitate towards them within an established company. Too many just take what they can find and regret over time not using their skills and abilities because they became pigeonholed. But it doesn't have to remain that way. We can make ourselves into something else, something better.

There are tons of stories about the person working their regular job and building a company from their kitchen table (or in the proverbial garage), then going fulltime with it and never looking back. Amazon, Microsoft, Boston Beer Company (Sam Adams beers), Khan Academy, Spanx. Every one of these founders worked nights and weekends on their passion, then made the leap from employee to boss and have reaped the rewards. What is preventing you from sitting at your table and starting to explore something that lights your fire? These founders worked 60+ hour weeks at their regular job and cared enough about their ideas to sacrifice a little sleep. Brew some coffee and get to work!

Arthur Conan Doyle (Sherlock Holmes creator) and Robert Frost (poet) held day jobs (doctor and teacher respectively). Sir Brian Maye of Queen has a PhD in Astrophysics. Before he became Han Solo, Harrison Ford was a carpenter. Arnold Schwartzenegger worked construction all day, lifted, then took acting classes. So if you just want to stay in bed do as Ahnold says: sleep fastah!

The entire world is available to you on the internet. You can learn anything on YouTube, you can access via your library online essentially any book. You can learn skills, find experts, play with concepts and explore ideas easily. Why don't you? Why are you sitting on the couch eating Cheetos and numbing your brain with reality TV all the time instead of doing SOMETHING to create a better future for yourself?

If your life is perfect as it is and you are ecstatic with it and your future, keep at it but the probability of that is negligible so don't fool yourself.

Action item: what is one thing you enjoyed earlier in life that you don't do anymore that is fun and could help you be more passionate or successful? Pick it up again!

26 MAY

"We either make ourselves miserable, or we make ourselves happy. The amount of work is the same."

Carlos Castaneda

Abraham Lincoln is often misquoted as saying "folks are usually about as happy as they make up their mind to be." Honest Abe didn't say it, but that doesn't make the saying false. Truth can come from unexpected places.

"Happiness is a choice that requires effort at times." Aeschylus

Some days ARE rainbows and extra sprinkles and finding a surprise $20 bill in your jacket pocket. Some days are blown out tires and broken heels while it rains. Let's remove these extremes though and look at the middle three-quarters or so of the time, when a day is a mixture of the coffee pot overflowing and stepping on cat puke in bare feet (squish!) but also getting a great parking spot after catching all the lights just right and getting a free donut.

Did you let the coffee pot destroy your entire day, so you bitched that the donut had sprinkles? Or did you shrug off the mess, say "oh well" and move forwards and be pleasantly surprised at catching the lights and realize a free donut is a FREE DONUT and be happy? Same day, which set of filters (positive or negative) did you decide to adopt?

Rose tinted shades, or grey glasses?

It can take mental and emotional energy to bust out of a funk. About the same amount as it takes to get into one, but generally the downside is a slow and constant decline that we don't notice happening as our energy is leached away by all the little things that add up and can just be summarized as "life". It is rarely the great big obstacle like losing a job or the car engine blowing up, and those large events are somewhat forgivable for their short-term negative impact. The step on the cat puke and then the internet going out for five minutes and the neutral (instead of loving) text from your significant other and all of the sudden you want to punch everyone in the face and your energy is sucked away and you're miserable. OR you invest the energy yourself to laugh at the cat puke pedi and use the internet outage to stand up and stretch and take a couple of deep breaths, then look at your lovey's text and pause and try to ask why it isn't all lovey dovey, and work on empathy for a moment.

Same amount of mental effort ultimately, but which leaves you happier? And which is better for the other people around you?

Action item: the instant your day starts to go sideways today, (and it WILL,) stop! Pause. Take a deep breath, and look for something to laugh or smile about. Do so. Repeat throughout the day.

27 MAY
"Work on yourself more than you do your job."

Jim Rohn

The job market changes constantly, companies rise and fall. But skills will stay with you, and habits of excellence carry forward into new situations, allowing you to adapt and overcome as the world changes around you.

"Give a man a fish and he eats for a day. Teach a man to fish and he will never go hungry."

I knew a salesman that was dependent upon his manager to give him the leads from the company website every day so that he could talk to them and hit his weekly quota. But while he was actually selling these clients he was developing his sales skills and looked for similarities among the ones that bought, and started to develop some language to ask for introductions to other potential buyers. Then the sales manager went on vacation for a few weeks, so she couldn't give the salesman any leads. But he had developed his skills and took a deep breath and applied them, then had his best two-week period even without a lead from the boss. He had worked on his skill set and will set and out-grew the crutch he had been using, and he and the company were better for it.

How much have you worked on improving your communication skills, so that you can clearly and concisely convey ideas to those several layers above you in the hierarchy? This gets noticed even more than the work output.

How much time have you spent pushing yourself to the edge of your comfort zone (maybe through physical exercise, or having the difficult conversations that yield better results, or studying new skills) and as such expanded your capabilities? Those that just skate by at work are those first on the chopping block, those that exhibit a commitment to improvement get promoted.

Make yourself so talented and valuable that you become irreplaceable. Then you have the power, because even if the Powers That Be at work decide that they are going to reduce headcount, you are now so much more talented that leaving that company would be a good thing for you, and you might have a little trepidation but no fear because of well-grounded confidence earned through enhancing yourself and your capabilities over time.

When you then go out into the market again, you will be leagues ahead of your competition that sat on their duff and didn't develop themselves.

Action item: look at what you do for work. Is there one area that you can improve yourself, to become the best in your company? If it is a skill that is sought beyond the walls of just your current employer, start improving it.

28 MAY

"The last thing you want is to look back and wish you had worked or played harder."

Derek Jeter

Rookie of the Year, 3,465 career regular season hits (5th all time), five World Series Championships, elected to the Hall of Fame with 99.75% of the vote (who DIDN'T vote for him?!) and one of the few regrets of his career? Joe Torre didn't come to him earlier with ideas to improve his defense (even though he won five Gold Gloves as shortstop) that could have maybe helped the Yankees win another championship. Professional all the way through.

We have all heard that youth is wasted on the young. That you don't know what you have until it's gone. It's true, and the pain of regret for not taking a risk or doing something is almost always greater than the regret of having messed something up when you actually tried.

Errors of omission versus errors of commission are more painful, the "what if" that gnaws at the soul for the rest of your life. "What if I had applied for that job?" "What if I had asked my crush out?" "What if I had worked a little harder in my 20's instead of partying?". Eliminate the what ifs to live your life to the fullest and get the most out of your career.

When you are working, be fully present. Don't be mentally on the beach someplace and only half working. It's not fair to your employer, your co-workers, or your future self. If you are on the clock, focus on the task at hand as Marcus Aurelius would say, and give it your all. When you clock out and are with your family, BE with them with your heart and mind. Don't be physically with them but mentally in the office, because your kids deserve all of you when you are with them, even if those stacks of paperwork are calling you. Play with them hard, the work can wait until they are asleep.

We are not built for laziness. The human body was designed to move, not lay on a couch eating bon bons and watching the tube. We are meant to push our limits, both physically and mentally. "Taking it easy" is a break from the action, a respite and relaxation not the normal function and attitude. Recharging is ok, but only when you've exhausted yourself.

Look at little kids. They go full out and then crash, sleep, and repeat. They learn and grow and play and live at a rate we should be envious of and emulate, because life is not a video game that you can just reset and give it another go. You get one go around, and might as well make the best of it!

Action item: just today, push a little harder. Work a little bit more to get better, and play a little harder when you take a break. Be a little more extreme, because it will give you results and memories that last the rest of your life.

29 MAY
"Baseball is 90% mental. The other half is physical."

Yogi Berra

Professional athletes are great physical specimens, with hand eye coordination that is amazing. Putting a round bat, a tube about 2.5 inches wide, on a ball less than three inches wide moving at 90+ miles an hour is impressive. Returning a 100mph serve in tennis or stopping a piece of hard rubber traveling at a similar speed while standing on knives on ice are "normal plays" for athletes, not even worthy of mentioning. So is sinking a ten-foot putt for a golfer.

Now imagine thousands of people watching you do it.

And knowing that millions more are watching/listening at home.

And if you make it, you get $1,000,000.

But if you miss you get nothing.

Welcome to the mental game of being an athlete.

You probably felt your heart start racing just reading about the pressure, empathetically experiencing what pros have to manage regularly. All the physical skills in the world don't matter if they can't be executed under pressure.

Welcome to the world of the soldier, the first responder, the surgeon and the saleswoman. Perform, or there are negative consequences.

The mental game is what separates the amateur from the professional from the greats. The stronger the mental game, the more successful even if the physical skills are not the absolute best. The mental conditioning is the differentiating factor.

How do you prepare for your mental game? Do you preplay in your mind (visualization), and play what if (alternative scenario planning to avoid surprises)? Force yourself into stressful situations so as to raise your level of comfort with discomfort (almost all practice and training)? How do you make your mind sweat and condition it like your body? This is where the champions are made.

The game is won or lost between your ears, not between the lines.

Action item: find one way to challenge yourself today by making yourself uncomfortable and stressed, then calm your mind and focus so you can execute.

30 MAY

"Physical fitness is the first requisite of happiness."

Joseph Pilates

When was the last time you were really sick? Like wickedly tossing your cookies and chills with nasty fever and pain everywhere all the way through and wishing you could sleep or be shot and just put out of your misery? That was probably the opposite of your idea of happiness.

But what about at a lower level of discomfort? When was the last time you were out of breath after playing with a kid or puppy for just a few minutes? Doesn't that inability to keep playing lessen your joy, negatively impacting your happiness?

When were you probably happiest? As a kid, playing? Running around with your friends, doing stuff, being active? Physical activity is integrally connected with the experiences and the fun.

When we work out, we raise the heart rate, strengthening the cardiovascular system for the future. We reduce cortisol (stress hormone), relaxing the body and reducing inflammation. You also produce dopamine, the happiness hormone. You don't have to spend hours in the gym every day nor run a 10k then do yoga every morning before eating chia seeds and kale washed down with wheatgrass, but some activity every day to raise your heart rate, metabolism, and mood is a key factor in not just longevity but improved life appreciation.

Sir Richard Branson has long believed that exercise increases productivity and happiness, and encourages all members of the Virgin Empire to spend time on fitness because of how it impacts the bottom line.

Bobby Fischer swam every day to improve his cardiovascular health and mental endurance as part of his preparation for winning the world chess title.

I run, and then the words flow. Whenever I am struggling with a problem I go workout. Afterwards my mind is sharper, my thoughts clearer, and I can find solutions. These make me happy.

The ability to work long and hard at a high level professionally is partially based on your physical stamina. It is intuitively obvious that being successful work-wise can improve happiness (albeit not as much as most people think, as shown in the Yale Science of Happiness course), and physical activity allows the mind to reset and recover after stress, so working out actually allows you to work harder and enjoy life more.

Action item: get up and move around. Every hour get off your butt and walk around for a few minutes as a start, and find some physical activity you enjoy and start doing it regularly.

31 MAY
"The reason I exercise is for the quality of life I enjoy."

Kenneth H. Cooper

Dick Van Dyke once said about exercise: In my seventies, I exercised to stay ambulatory. In my eighties, I exercised to avoid assisted living. There is an anecdote that he later said "And in my nineties I do it out of spite." None of us hung out with Mary Poppins, but we can emulate what has kept Van Dyke spry and mentally on point.

Exercise makes you happy on a neurochemical level. Even if you hate exercise, getting your body moving regularly for at least thirty minutes will stimulate telemeric health (keeping you fit at the subcellular level) and keep your metabolism going, counter the natural muscle and bone density loss that occurs over time, and potentially expose you to other people in a socially helpful way that further staves off the aging process.

Look, we all know the reasons why we should exercise regularly. They are all over the popular press, the news, the internet. So instead of giving you the science-based rationale, here are some emotionally driven reasons to get more exercise regularly that might be more meaningful.

You want to be able to play on the floor with your grandkids. You want to walk up stairs without getting out of breath and red faced. You want your ex to think they made a mistake. You want to beat your boss in the company events. Your teenager called you "old man" or "old lady" and you need to show them what for. Your high school reunion is coming up. So you can earn a donut.

Sex! It's better and more likely if you're in shape. Because your high school wardrobe is coming back into fashion. If you don't, you won't be alive for your kid's wedding. The Covid 19. It's more than the Freshman 15. So you can buy new clothes. To woo your crush better. Because diabetes sucks. If you run, you can eat more. New swimsuit. Just no banana hammocks!
So you can hike up that mountain and get a spectacular view.

This is by no means an exhaustive list, but hopefully there's something on there that gets you motivated to motivate.

Action item: get 30 minutes of exercise today, of whatever form you want.

JUNE IS THE GATEWAY TO SUMMER

Jean Hersey

01 JUNE
"Quality means doing it right when no one is looking."

Henry Ford

If you put your name on it, it better be the best you can do.

We have all heard the story of the carpenter that was ready to retire and was asked by his boss to do one last job that his heart wasn't in. He cut corners, did sloppy work, basically dreaming of retirement while working. When the house was finished, the boss presented him with the key proclaiming "this is now yours." Would you want to live in that poorly built home?

If you are doing a job for someone, that means someone else isn't. That client will trust that you did the job right, fully conscientious and up to code or standards. If you didn't, someone could pay the price. Someone could get hurt, or sick, or not be taken care of properly.

Do the job. Do it right.

Show professional pride, even in the little things that no one else will see.

Attention to detail carries into other areas.

Excellence is contagious.

My kids used to make fun of me for cleaning the bathroom and scrubbing everything down until it sparkled. And it wasn't because that's what I had to do or my mom would smack me in the back of the head (that was for a hundred other reasons), but because it was just the right thing to do. It felt good to do it right, even if it was going to get messed up again. Just because. Hopefully they adopt this attitude, because quality effort will always show to others and yields better results in the end. The Scout Oath (for Cub Scouts and Boy Scouts) states: I will do my best. If a six-year-old can learn that (and even hang up their uniform) can't you as a grown up strive to do so too?

Action item: the next task you undertake, focus on doing the best you can, even if it is something as menial as cleaning your bathroom.

02 JUNE
"Art resides in the quality of doing, process is not magic."

Charles Eames

Picasso spent a lifetime becoming Picasso. Da Vinci noodled and scribbled and started (and stopped, and restarted) on hundreds of pieces of art. Writers have waste baskets overflowing with crumpled pages as they struggle to write that masterpiece.

Martial artists all start as a white belt with no knowledge and build their skills over hour after grueling hour of practice covering decades. The excellence is not because of drinking a magic potion but from the blood and sweat they have poured out of themselves.

Mozart was preternaturally gifted, but still practiced from the time he was a small child and even he improved over time into the musical master he would become.

The great cellist Pablo Casals was asked in his 90's why he kept practicing and he stated "I think I am getting better."

All art is created, not through the waving of a magic wand (even a paint brush), but by effort expended over periods of time to hone skills that are then captured for an instant on a page or other medium. The finished product is what we see, but it is the heart of the artist in creating the work that we should celebrate.

As Nike says "just do it." Draw a line, or write one. The beginning is the hardest step. The second hardest is to keep going. So keep going.

Writers write, and most write every single day. Painters paint. Do it. Do it regularly.

There is joy in the work of creation.

Create.

Action item: what art do you love (drawing, writing, music, etc.)? Do it, even if you don't think it is beautiful today.

03 JUNE

"Art is a sense of magic."

Stan Brakhage

Have you ever watched someone take a piece of flattened wood pulp and a bunch of semi-sticky carbon, and out of only their mind create a beautiful image, a drawing that makes you say "wow!"? How about someone sitting at a piano and summoning music from the air?

Wonder about a writer pounding a keyboard like one of the infinite monkeys to produce a poem that captures their soul, to share with the one they adore and achieve immortality for their heart on a page? Neither muse nor maker will last a century, but the work could live on forever.

Someone opens their mouth and out comes the sounds of angels?

Art is the highest form of communication known to humankind, and the most difficult in that it takes decades of honing natural skills that few have to then attempt and fail and attempt and fail over and over in the hopes of a moment of excellence that can be captured and shared.

The true magic of "The Sorcerer's Apprentice" is not the wonders that Mickey dreams of, but the vision on the screen for us all to wonder at; not the water washing over him but the music washing over the audience. Think about what it took to bring this to life like that broom, and how this magic flows down generations.

Art can inspire the soul, awaken desire, impart sadness and wisdom. Different forms are called "mediums" because they bridge the gap from the immaterial to our world, the divine to the mundane. Those that channel this power deserve appreciation, even if we disagree with their creations. The output, the art, is an embodiment of things beyond mere mortals.

Action item: go online, and find something created by someone. A symphony, or a drawing. Maybe a sculpture or a poem. Find some art that you would not normally seek out, and expose yourself to it so that your soul can wonder at the magic of others.

04 JUNE

"Magic touches people in the way great art does. It lets them see the world with new eyes."

Drummond Money-Coutts

Fantasy is alluring and seductive. Being unbound by normal rules of physics or society changes a person's perceptions in such a way that even when they return to the "normal world", they are enhanced in unquantifiable ways.

Ask any astronaut after they have returned to earth why they are different and they will talk about seeing our planet and people in new ways.

Art is the earthly gateway to such new visions.

Look at a Dali painting such as "The Persistence of Memory" (the melting clocks) or Bosch and the suspension of rules to paint a new vision of reality is apparent. So too with playing peekaboo with a baby or Harry Houdini defying death or early quantum physics. All make us look at the world a bit differently.

Technology is magic incarnate, as our quantum physics driven electronics show scientific wizardry that even fifty years ago would have been considered science fiction and a few hundred years ago would have been called magic. Do you look at your new phone in wonder? Do you marvel at the power in your hand and the new worlds it can take you to?

What about books? Dragons in the skies, wizards bending reality and fantastic powers. This is the gateway to infinite new worlds, the escapism of children of all ages and the inspiration. Reading opens the doors of perception and is an equalizer across all economic and social classes and across the globe.

Fantasy can change your reality.

Magic is literally all around us, if we can open our eyes and senses to experience it and let it change us for the better.

Action item: close your eyes. Take a deep breath. Another. Think about a magical place for you. Feel the air. Listen to the sounds. Put yourself there. Experience it. Now open your eyes and bring some of that world into this one.

05 JUNE
"Meditation is the soul's perspective glass."

Owen Feltham

The first looking glass was a calm mirrored pool of water, still and silent. This was where people could first see their reflection, and the stillness of water to truly see yourself is an analogy used by meditators around the world.

Our world is hectic to say the least. Always on and on the go, rarely pausing to breathe let alone truly relax without the distractions of work and kids and advertising and spam calls about your car's warranty. Think about it: when was the last time you had ten uninterrupted minutes alone with yourself, no phone or partner or fur baby or anything to encroach upon your thoughts? This time alone with the most important person in your world (you) is critical for the development of metacognitive (and meta-emotional) understanding and development. Shutting it all out for a few moments will allow you to reset your emotions and recharge your mental battery, because life is draining and most of what is outside of ourselves can force us to be out of control.

Meditation can be either passive (sitting like the Buddha and contemplating the cosmos or your navel while breathing slowly and letting the mind and body relax) or active (like martial artists doing patterns or dancers engaged in their dance or runners experiencing the runner's high and laboring hard but not even noticing the effort.) Both are good in their own way, and have their place in your life. It might be slightly easier to close your eyes (and door if possible) at work and count from 12 to 1 than to go run around the block usually, so keep that in mind.

As you meditate, your mind will probably wonder. That's normal. Bringing it back to center and on what you are contemplating (the flame of a candle in the dark is a good tool for focus, but might not be copacetic at work) is something you will become better at over time. Give it time.

Some people meditate by trying to empty their thoughts and become one with their breathing or the world around them. Others instead intensely focus on one thing, be it a koan (Zen riddle), a math problem, their love of someone, or actual prayer. Both empty and full intent are good exercises, and just like you don't work the same muscle group constantly by just doing the same physical exercise, same with your mental exercises of meditation: mix it up for max results. Varying how you approach this will improve your techniques and bring you more stillness and tranquility within your inner pool and allow you to see yourself better.

Action item: put your feet flat on the floor. Take a deep breath. Now another. Close your eyes, and take ten slow deep breaths. Repeat three times a day.

06 JUNE

"Sleep is the best meditation."

HH the Dalai Lama

Sleep is nature's greatest remedy. It allows your body and mind to heal.

When you sleep, your body encodes memories, sorts through the events of the day, cleanses the soul, and allows the wall between the subconscious and conscious to come down so you can dream and understand what you do not understand when you are awake, be it losing that person you don't acknowledge is important to you yet or working out that weird work problem. In sleep we find peace and clarity in the blessings of Morpheus as the cerebrospinal fluid circulates and washes away the cares of the day on a biochemical level.

"A good laugh and a long sleep are the best cures in the doctor's book." Irish proverb.

How often have you heard someone say "let me sleep on it"? What they are really saying is "This is a lot of information that I need to sort through, and I need to see what not just my mind but my gut say is the right thing to do." This is not the person deflecting, but making sure that they are bringing their full faculties to bear on the problem.

August Kekule couldn't solve the problem of the shape of the benzene molecule until he fell asleep in his chair and dreamt of the molecule dancing, then becoming a snake and grabbing its own tail. Voila! The benzene ring.

Srinivasa Ramaujan, the most brilliant mathematician of the 20th century had no formal training but said the goddess Namagiri would come to him in dreams and he would write what she taught him: almost 4,000 advanced mathematical proofs that still stretch the mind a century after his death.

Dmitri Mendeleev's Periodic Table of the Elements.
Samuel Taylor Coleridge's *Kublai Khan* (also called "A Vision in a Dream").
The Rolling Stones' *I Can't Get No Satisfaction*, Jimi Hendrix's *Purple Haze*, The Police's *Every Breath You Take*, Berlioz's *Symphonie Fantastique*.

All came from sleep, allowing their minds to noodle and play while the body rested.

Once the mind is filled with facts and figures, it needs sleep to separate the signal from the noise and sort through for the true insights.

Action item: if you are struggling with a problem, set a timer and take a 20 minute power nap.

07 JUNE

"Writing is a very focused form of meditation. Just as good as sitting in a lotus position."

Alan Moore

To write clearly, one must think clearly. Thinking clearly is one of the goals of meditation, so it makes sense that the intense effort to write powerfully and succinctly is a parallel path to traditional meditational methodologies with many of the same benefits.

Various forms of meditation use different tools to assist in the effort. A candle, the sound of windchimes or a gong. Water over rocks, or even electronica/house music to alter the mind and state of the participant.

Some writers fuel up on coffee and cigarettes (Voltaire or Wilde), others smoke weed (Stephen King), do coke (Robert Louis Stevenson and Hunter K Thompson), or drink (Tennessee Williams and Ernest Hemingway) to achieve their altered state. Some just throw on some heavy metal music and pound away, others prefer the dawn light and birds warbling in the trees for a more natural backdrop. I personally run then write. Just like meditation or the writing itself, the facilitating methodologies to get in the flow is as personalized as the writer themselves.

Psychologist Jordan Peterson has repeatedly discussed the importance of writing for self-clarity whether it is goal setting for the future or journaling as a reflective exercise. Marcus Aurelius is better known to us today because of his "Meditations" (his personal journal) than for his tenure as Emperor of Rome.

Writing makes a person think, and there is not enough of that today.

Writing becomes stronger and more effective with practice, much like meditation. And like the Zen monks that would have sudden insight (satori), over time as a writer you can get flashes of insight; lines of poetry popping into your head fully composed, concepts and insights appearing out of nowhere based on your previous efforts. These flashes of understanding, of preternatural intuition and comprehension, are fleeting and wonderful and intensely beautiful all at once.

Take the time to develop the mental strength to clarify and convey your thoughts as it is a skill applicable daily in the real world.

Action item: carry some paper or index cards with you. Stop and jot something down, a thought or observation. Repeat. Repeat. Repeat.

08 JUNE

"There is nothing to writing.
All you do is sit down at a typewriter and bleed."
Ernest Hemingway

The best writing is the soul on the page for others to read and experience.

"Good poetry lets the reader feel the poem, great poetry lets the reader feel themselves." JRRT

Writing is one of the most exposing activities a person can undertake, for authors bare not their physical form but their psyche to the world. Every fear, every flaw, every shattered dream and fantasy is revealed to complete strangers in a way few other creators do, letting others see into your core and judge. Rarely do other artists become this vulnerable.

Yet writing gives strength. It takes courage to not only use the painful experiences to power yourself, but to also document and interpret them for others. To inspire and share that strength with others that may be struggling through their own journeys and wrongfully believing they are alone in their heartbreak or wars within is one of the greatest gifts you can give to someone you may never meet.

The heart of the author on the page is a horcrux, a piece of their soul that is split off and captured. It is there to influence others beyond the mortal span of the writer, but also to be studied and dissected and debated, an immortality of exposure that can influence others but will never let the darker aspects of the wordsmith be buried nor forgotten.

So dear reader, the mere thought of writing may fill you with butterflies and excitement and fear all at once, like any great new experience. Like the early stages of love, with all of the joy and heartache it can bring. In love and writing you can only influence others, but have control over what you reveal to the outside world. The greatest loves are fiery and passionate and open and true, echoing what the most powerful writing is. Are you ready to bleed for your beliefs, to put your heart on a page that will be rejected by some and adored by others?

Action item: sit at your computer, open a document and complete this sentence "Even though it hurts me, I am glad I..."

09 JUNE

"I see dance being used as communication between body and soul, to express what is too deep to find for words."
Ruth St. Denis

The instant most people hear rhythm we begin to dance and sway, a primal connection between the music and ourselves. It is not rational or logical but older and deeper, reaching into the depths of time and our souls. From the newest baby responding to their mother's heartbeat to the most senior citizen, we move and dance unknowingly and unconsciously when we can.

It doesn't matter the music, it doesn't matter the physical capabilities of the individual, music draws our soul into our muscles and we reflexively shimmy and shake and shiver, moving to the music in ways that make sense to the dancer. Sometimes others can feel what the dancer is trying to communicate. Other times we (meaning I) look like a freak. Doesn't matter, the dance moves the dancer and the feelings and emotions are more powerful than our social mores.

Maybe you grew up in the 80's and watched the break dancers on MTV (back when it had music). Maybe you are older and remember Soul Patrol or American Bandstand. Or maybe you groove to Dancing With The Stars. Across generations and genres, dance is a unifying power be it tap or Irish Step dancing or a haka. Movement is universal and regional and personal, and it is all good.

One of the greatest stories about dancing comes from my friend Chuck, a 6'4" redheaded goofball Irishman. The oldest son in a family of eight kids, Chuck was totally uncoordinated if he didn't have a basketball in his hands and was definitely rough around the edges. Yet for several months before his sister's wedding he secretly took dance lessons, and then asked his mother to dance at the wedding and waltzed with her. Four decades later his family still talks about the beaming smile on his mother's face. He wasn't Fred Astaire, but the pride of that one dance and the joy it brought to Mrs. Ranney cannot be expressed by words.

Action item: put on some music that makes you happy, and dance like no one is watching.

10 JUNE
"Work like you don't need the money. Love like you've never been hurt. Dance like nobody's watching."
Satchel Paige

Whatever you do, do it for the love of it not for external reasons. Not money, not revenge, not accolades from others. Be self actualized and do it because it makes you happy and harms no one else.

Professional athletes often say they'd play for free, because they love what they do. And after a few years many actually don't really need the money, and if they can maintain the wide-eyed wonder of the rookie freshly called up they are a joy to watch because they have joy playing their game. This is how to live life.

Being unable to sleep on Sunday night, not out of anxiety but because you are as excited as a six-year-old the night before her birthday. That is the essence of Satchel's quote.

Giving unquestionably of yourself and your capabilities, letting it pour out of you in whatever manner you express yourself (art, poetry, dance, cooking, etc.) and then being ready to do it all again with your entire being because it is who you are. That is arete, the Greek concept of excellence in life. The Japanese call it ikigai, the happiness of doing what you do for the good of the world and yourself. The joy of a child engaged in something meaningful and wonderful, where time has no meaning. "Flow" as defined by Csikszentmihalyi in *Flow: The Psychology of Optimal Experience*.

You know it when you feel it, when you do it, when you simply are it. When the dancer becomes the dance, and the words write themselves, when you are totally in the moment of doing and nothing else matters: not the past or future, just the Zen-like now that is wonderful. Achieving this even for a fleeting moment is a touch of Heaven, and consciously choosing to have the attitude of taking actions towards this is a path to greater happiness in all endeavors.

Action item: no one can see you right now. Get up and dance, let your body move in joy of life. Smile! Now carry that feeling into whatever you do next.

11 JUNE

"Failure is a part of success."

Hank Aaron

Hammerin' Hank (the REAL Home Run King and a classy human being) never struck out like Reggie Jackson did, or any of today's sluggers do. It was a different era, one filled with much more difficulty and less safety nets. And as a man that became famous because he literally swung for the fences (and achieved it 755 times) and is to this day the all-time leader in total bases and RBI, in an era still filled with racism and a childhood of hardship, Hank Aaron embodied the American Dream because he believed in himself and was willing to take the risks to become great.

Bob Dylan was a commercial failure as an artist for years. Part of his charm, part of his story and ultimately part of his success.

Twitter was a failed project.

Space X's first several rockets exploded. Or rather experienced a "Rapid Unscheduled Disassembly" per CEO Elon Musk.

Becoming comfortable with failure as an outcome of attempting to become great is a mindset that is not common, and because of that the positive outcome (great success in whichever endeavor) is rare and celebrated because too many people avoid trying so that they are guaranteed to not fail. From the ancient Stoics to Mohammad Ali to the kid playing guitar in their room working towards becoming the next Eddie Van Halen, falling in love with the process of becoming great with all of the stumbles and mistakes is one of the surest ways to guarantee success by embracing repeated failure.

I knew an insurance agent who was among the leaders in history of his company, Gay Davis. Even thirty years into his career, his goal was to lead his office in the number of times he was told "No" each month. Because he knew that if he was told no forty times a month, he would have enough people saying "Yes" to be successful. Inverting the mindset allows every failure to be celebrated instead of being perceived as an obstacle to success.

"Fail early, fail often, fail forward."

Action item: what are you avoiding out of fear of failure? What if you failed at it ten times, but succeeded on the 11th? Would it be fatal in failing? Would you be able to recover financially? If it is a risk that you can accept, try it! And again, and again!

12 JUNE

"Above anything else, I hate to lose."

Jackie Robinson

Hating to lose makes you willing to do the hard prep work beforehand to win. It makes you run one more wind sprint, shoot five extra free throws, do that little bit extra on that project because somewhere the competition is working just as hard. Hating to lose makes you play every moment like it's the Championship Game, like it is the biggest presentation of your life, like it's the tryout for Julliard. Hating to lose changes your attitude and removes the complacency that often creeps in with success.

I HATE to lose. So much so that I put forth the effort to improve so I can consistently win, especially on the little things that others probably overlook. Winning feels better than sleep, because it recharges you more than an extra hour of rest. "I'm tired, but it's a good sort of tired" is something only those who give everything and exhaust themselves over and over to become exceptional and win can feel and appreciate.

Hating to lose forces you to have deeper internal reserves than the person you are going up against, whether it is in the interview for the job promotion or playing minigolf with your kids. Bringing your A game all the time, giving your absolute best, becomes a lifestyle and mindset that seeps into everything you do, an attitude of excellence that impacts all aspects of your career, relationships, and life.

Hating to lose is NOT cheating, but respecting the integrity of the game and using all legal and ethical means not to cut the other guy down but to maximize yourself. It is the sacrifice of things that don't contribute to your winning long range, whether it is the negative friends that can lead you into trouble (you lose every day you're in jail) or that relationship that sucks your soul out, or the yummy tasting but incredibly bad for you foods that are your vice. Hating to lose means sacrificing the Good for the Great, embracing delayed gratification, and falling in love with the process of improvement so that when the test comes, you can confidently execute on your training.

Hating to lose is altering your perceptions and establishing an environment that supports your success, like not having potato chips in the house so you can lose weight or avoiding the smoking area if you are quitting. It is removing those apps off your phone that lead you to waste time or lead you astray with temptation. It is looking yourself in the mirror and acknowledging your lack of perfection, so that you can then face your shortcomings and work on overcoming them.

Action item: what is the most important game you are playing? What are one thing you need to eliminate/reduce and one thing you need more of to consistently win this game (work, relationship, school, etc.)? Do it.

13 JUNE
"Losing feels worse than winning feels good."

Vin Scully

Psychology tells us that we need five to seven positive thoughts to offset every negative one to maintain a neutral mental position. Because losing hurts. Badly.

That is why so many people are afraid to take risks: it hurts to fail and it hurts worse when others talk about it and compound the pain. So too many people avoid it altogether.

However you can harness that feeling to get better. Michael Jordan famously got cut from his high school team and he carried that pain inside to fire his drive, to become one of the greatest basketball players ever.

The Polish psychologist Dumbrowski studied people that had trauma, and found that for many of them it was a seminal event that forced their improvement and made them good or even exceptional. When was the last time you failed? Did it make you bitter or better? Victim, or force your evolution to victor?

Tom Brady has won seven Lombardi Trophies as Super Bowl Champion, but it is the three losses that stick in his craw and pushed him to improve and modify his training and game to win again. Losing the biggest game of the year is a pain that not many of us know, but to those that have felt this loss it is often what pushes them to the next level of performance because they never want to feel that again (sorry Buffalo Bills of the early 1990's).

Losing sucks. And the greater the stakes of the game, the more the pain of loss. But the ability to put yourself into position to experience that feeling, and if need be to harness it for personal growth, is what separates those on the couch from those in the game. The willingness to take the risk of tremendous loss is part of the deal to feel the ultimate joy of winning. It is how you recover from the great losses that determines your ultimate legacy.

Action item: when was the last time you lost? How did you feel, in your gut? If it made you sick, what did you learn from it to improve your game that you should remember today?

14 JUNE
"I don't mind getting beaten, but I hate to lose."

Reggie Jackson

If you did all of your preparation, and showed up ready to give your best efforts and then did so, do not be upset if a better person or team beats you. If however you were not beaten by a better performance but lost because you did not bring your best to the table, that is on you and you should be upset.

Losing is part of life, and an intimate part of winning. It is the greatest teacher in that it reveals flaws that winning covers over, and shows the character of the individual that suffers the loss. Did you go down meekly, or did you fight to the end? Did you give away points through mental mistakes? Did you miss things because of lack of attention to detail? Was your entire team fully committed, or was there dead weight (or worse, counter-productive people sabotaging your chances)?

Losing is necessary to the process of winning. It is a painful part, but it is the catalyst for continued growth and eventually excellence. Anyone that has never experienced losing has never tried to achieve anything significant.

"Winning cannot become your habit unless defeats have torn you apart..." Chetan Kumbhar.

"Champions realize that defeat, and learning from it even more than from winning, is part of the path to mastery." Rasheed Ogunlaru.

Learn to hate losing so much that you do the hard work outside the game to win, be it sharpening your speaking skills or the extra reps in the gym. Hitting the books increases the breadth and depth of your knowledge, and pushes your comfort limit to be better and deserve to win in the future.

Action item: when was the last time you lost? Feel the pain, the emotion. Wallow in it; open that wound! Experience it all over again, the punch in the gut and desire to throw up. Don't run from it, embrace it. Hate it all over again. Now get to work so you don't feel it again.

15 JUNE

"To give anything less than your best, is to sacrifice the gift."

Steve Prefontaine

One of the greatest and definitely the most flamboyant competitors in American distance running history, "Pre" ran and lived fast and gave everything he had from the moment the gun went off, be it in a race or life itself. "High speed, low drag" was an understatement of his attitude, and his willingness to push himself to the point of puking is legend and inspiration.

"Not to use your talent is a sin" I was told early on and so follow Prefontaine's lead in other arenas. Usually ones where I'm not dry heaving at the end, but definitely the mental equivalent.

We have all seen athletes with God given talent who never truly succeed because they don't give their best consistently, on the field and in their preparation. These "I coulda been a contender", the ones that we look at after their career and say "If only they had..." are the most disappointing of all because they never translated their potential into success. Not because of injuries (highly unfortunate in any case), but because of lack of effort or attitude. "He chose poorly" is one of the worst possible indictments of a person's career, in sports or other professions.

What does giving it your all mean? Going flat out, red-lining and pushing beyond your limit and pegging it there for as long as you can over and over again? Collapsing after because you have nothing left in your tank physically or mentally?

Win or lose, maximum effort!

My mother (the former nun) told me early on that not giving my best was a sin. I don't care how successful I have been, I still give my best and use my talents wherever I can to assist others because I know I'll have to answer to her if I slack off. Anything less than my best is not good enough even if I succeed, and if I give it my all and don't succeed it was a worthy effort and all that can be asked of me in that situation.

Professional pride in all you do, from running reports to preparing your space to that sales pitch. Flat out, hair on fire, everything you got and then the extra gear you didn't realize was within you. That is how to not sacrifice your particular gift.

Action item: what is your next task? Do it with all your heart and soul, as if your entire career will be judged on that one thing.

16 JUNE

"To give the best of the day to your work is most important."

John le Carre

I get up at early o'clock, something I have done since I was a little kid. Typically with the birds before dawn, and from then until around lunchtime I am at my most powerful: most creative, sharpest mentally, and highest energy. In fact I had to tone it down for my 7:00 am meetings for decades because I'd overwhelm people not used to my energy and enthusiasm that early. Now I learn and workout and write before most people are stirring because that is when I am at my best, so I try to capture that energy.

My brother on the other hand is a night owl: he would roll out of bed at the crack of noon and we would often pass each other as I'd get up with the sun and he was going to bed. Different strokes for different folks, even with the same environment.

There is a lot to be said for getting up early. Marcus Aurelius, The Rock, Apple CEOs Tim Cook and Steve Jobs are examples. Trevor Noah of The Daily Show gets up at 6:00. That's pm. Painter Jackson Pollock was a comparatively early riser at one in the afternoon.

Da Vinci slept in 20-minute increments and averaged about two hours of sleep a day. This polyphasic sleep cycle is rare but new moms and Ragnarians get it, as do RPI and MIT alums.

Winston Churchill knew the value of taking a nap in the afternoon to recharge and then get back to work until late.

It is not my place to tell you when to go to bed (unless you're my kid), but figure out what pattern works well for you and stick to it. And when you are awake and in your "power stroke", at you best, take advantage of it. Could be eight am or three pm (or even am) whatever works for you, do it, as long as it fits with your expected work schedule. If your most productive time and workplace requirements don't align, look at changing jobs because it will be better for you and you'll ultimately be more productive and successful working on the time scales that are coordinated with your rhythms.

Action item: what two-hour time period are you most awake and productive? What are the most critical things to your long-range success and happiness can you do then?

17 JUNE

"Win the morning, win the day."

JRRT

Do you have to drag your butt out of bed after fighting the clutches of the covers, hiding from the dawn? Or do you roll out of bed and into action, taking advantage of the silence and stillness to get to work on yourself and your dreams?

Most people are at the height of their mental and creative powers a few hours after waking. If you get up at early o'clock, you can get in a workout while the birds are still singing and then be productive while most people are still in bed. Which means you can pound through a huge chunk of work before they start messing up your day, because if you think about it most of our distractions or problems come from other people asking things of us. If you can accomplish most of your important work before anyone else has a chance to interfere with your vibe and flow, you'll be well ahead of the game early and so have built in time for their disruptions.

Dwayne Johnson is famous for being a physical freak and his work ethic that chiseled him into The Rock. He is up and lifting at 4:15, even when a hurricane is blowing through Florida where he lives. He does his second workout (cardio) while most people are hitting the snooze alarm. That's why he was the "Most Electrifying Man in Sports Entertainment" and a two-decade box office superstar. Can you smell what the Rock is cooking? Only if you're out of bed!

Many business successes swear by starting work before 7:00. 9-5 is for those that want to be average: those that want to be great and focus on hitting their base threshold of activity/production before most people stroll into the office. This lets them have time on their side to win the day in case something doesn't go right early, and if things go according to plan they can be in the "bonus round" (exceeding daily expectation) by noon so are in a state of relaxed (and hence superior) performance for half the day, just by shifting their schedule earlier.

That half hour before the kids wake up? That is probably your best time period all day. Do you waste it, or squeeze what you can out of it so that you are ahead of the curve?

Action item: set your alarm for tomorrow for a half hour earlier, and don't hit the snooze button. Get up and start going!

18 JUNE
"An early morning walk is a blessing for the whole day."

Henry David Thoreau

To properly interpret and express this, I took a walk this morning in the chill of the late Spring, as the sun was turning the sky gold and the birds chattered and chittered back and forth. Before the world was truly awake. Nature still in control and human problems but vaguely remembered dreams, I strode along the gravel path bathed in speckled shadow and communed with the world around me, peaceful in my soul for a moment.

Doesn't that sound better than a blaring alarm and chaos?

Morning, before the cacophony of humanity ramps up, is an unappreciated gift that is there to be opened daily, a juxtaposition to Pandora's Box in that all the beauty and serenity and wonderful things come out first. Open it and let the ephemeral benefits surround you and cleanse you before the stench and stain and strain of society and work can corrupt your good mood.

"The Golden Hour", that time from before the sun is visible over the horizon until a bit after, when the light is dispersed and the navy blue of night changes to the periwinkle of morning through a constant slow shifting of colors, is the most precious time of the day. Do you take the time to appreciate it?

Even in the nasty winters of Upstate New York, with the biting winds and snow and cold that can leach into your bones, I try to get out early if even for a few minutes. The cold wakes you up ("bracing" as my stiff upper lipped friends would declare), and the movement gets your blood circulating and the shock awakens the brain. In the summer it is not yet blistering, the birds are warbling and chattering, and as your legs move you can enter into a Zen-like state of active meditation as the brain slowly moves from dream to waking for the day. Every morning is a good day for a walk, even if it is miserable because the finishing makes you appreciate a warm dry house. All mornings reveal blessings if your mind is open and receptive to them.

Action item: set your alarm so that tomorrow you can enjoy The Golden Hour.

19 JUNE

"If you're changing the world, you're working on important things. You're excited to get up in the morning."
Larry Page

Do you ever have trouble sleeping on Sunday night, not because of anxiety but you are as excited for the next day as a kid before Christmas? That the chance to do something great lays in each day, and so you are charged up all the time?

Do you find yourself getting up before your alarm clock and saying "well, I'm up so let's get cracking, I got important stuff to accomplish"?

Wake up at early o'clock and say something like "woohoo! I love what I do!"?

Something like three quarters of Americans don't love what they do for a living. That's over 180 MILLION people rarely get up and look forward to doing what they do. In the land of opportunity, that is a travesty.

Google began as Page and Brin's Doctoral Thesis. I guarantee they didn't like a chunk of their required grad classes, but where they had a choice they decided to work on something interesting and build something that changed the world. Why aren't you choosing in your free time to work on something interesting around your boring job? It probably won't be as big as Google, but it could light your fire and be a passion project that makes you happier in other areas of your life and puts the spring back in your step.

Start that online store.

Start writing that book.

Record that demo.

Start that side gig.

The act of creation will awaken things in you that have slumbered, and will wake you up daily with a mission that is more powerful than the allure of the covers and snooze button. As the saying goes: why not change the world?

Action item: what is one thing that really excites you that you could work on regularly and build something significant? What is stopping you from taking the first small steps?

20 JUNE

"A man with money is no match against a man on a mission."

Doyle Brunson

The rags to riches story of the kid growing up with nothing and becoming incredibly successful is American folklore and as common as burgers at a cookout. Grit, determination, hard work, hustle: call it what you want but the man or woman that is working for something bigger than themselves, who is willing to do the little things over and over, that is going to keep going past the point of exhaustion and hope again and again, is probably going to make it in this world.

James "Buster" Douglas took down the undefeated Mike Tyson, because he was on a mission having promised his mother on her deathbed mere weeks before that he would. The now rich and distracted Tyson stood no chance against the man on the mission.

The wolf climbing the mountain is hungrier than the one on top.

If someone kidnapped your child and told you you had 30 days to come up with $100,000 cash, you would find a way to make it happen. Little would stand in the way of you getting your little one back. Yet if given a year but no pressure, no massive reason to work and risk, you wouldn't scratch together the same hundred k. The mission makes the man make the money.

We've all seen the young salesperson who needs to hit their quota or be canned, and all of a sudden they are constantly on the go and have the resolve of a missionary and miraculously squeak over the threshold, doing four months of production in a week. And then they relapse, because they are no longer on that mission.

You don't have to be one of the Blues Brothers and be "on a mission from God." But you do need to truly believe in who and what you are working for, and be willing to take risks because the pain of failure is greater than the pain needed to achieve. You need to have faith in the outcome and be willing to go to the legal and physical limit, expand your envelope of comfort and capability, and have the zeal of a preacher (quietly or overtly) to not waiver, because the mission is more important than your temporary comfort or pride.

You need to believe, break your internal barriers, and then bust your butt. Then you too can be Buster.

Action item: what is your mission? What is that BHAG (Big, Hairy, Audacious Goal) that fires you up and makes you steel your nerve and move forward because it is so important?

20 JUNE

"Without gambling, I would not exist."

Hunter S. Thompson

The chances against you existing are roughly 400 Trillion to one. You have already won, just by existing.

You were born in an era and a location that gives you distinct advantages over almost everyone that was born outside of the 20th or 21st centuries in the First World. You are the 1% right out of the gate.

You have won the game already, before you even get to start playing. Now the question is, what are you going to do with the house's money since you are already ahead? Are you going to sit over on the side and wait for a waitress to bring you free drinks, or are you going back to the tables to have some fun and maybe win big?

Even if you lose it all on an unlucky roll of the dice, you are still better off than 99+% of the people ever to walk the earth, or walking the earth right now. So what else are you going to do to try and walk out of the casino at least entertained, maybe a winner, potentially even a legend?

Every one that attempts something great is taking a risk, gambling with their money, their time, their reputation. Garth Brook released an album under the name "Chris Gaines" because he didn't want to risk his reputation as a country superstar while trying out a different genre. Michael Jordan walked away from being a three-time world champion in basketball to try baseball.

These gambles didn't payoff in the traditional sense, but both of them have experiences they would never trade and Jordan's fire for basketball was relit and led to a second threepeat and one of the greatest teams of all time. Both Gaines/Brooks and Jordan were willing to take a risk, instead of the millions that are unwilling to put themselves out there and potentially fail.

No risk, no reward.

Many best-selling books were rejected a dozen times, even two dozen times. That is the risk of an author: put your soul on the page, expose yourself and be rejected over and over and over. Happened to JK Rowling. Then she made over a billion dollars with Harry Potter and has given away hundreds of millions of dollars. I think her gamble paid off. Maybe mine will.

Anyone that pushes the boundaries of their field is gambling. It doesn't matter if it is a radical concept in science (too many Nobel prizes to list), creating a video game company like my friends Guha and Karthik Bala did with Vicarious Vision (acquired by Activision), or Bob Fosbury flopping over the high jump bar (the now eponymous Fosbury Flop).

Anyone that pushes the boundaries of their field is gambling. It doesn't matter if it is a radical concept in science (too many Nobel prizes to list), creating a video game company like my friends Guha and Karthik Bala did with Vicarious Vision (acquired by Activision), or Bob Fosbury flopping over the high jump bar (the now eponymous Fosbury Flop).

Taking a risk is one way to earn immortality (or notoriety) because no one remembers the names of the sheep that finish in the middle of the pack and end up like everyone else because they did what everyone else did, even if a little better. A horrible failure (if not fatal) is still remembered whether as a tragicomedy or a case study.

Risk takers are not with the cold timid souls but earn a place in Valhalla, Hall of Heroes for those that attempt great deeds. Dare to do something awesome (or stupid as Weird Al Yankovich would challenge), just be willing to take the risk of greatness.

Action item: what is a non-fatal risk you could take on a personal basis? Do it.

22 JUNE

"The only risk is not taking the risk.
You've got to take that step."

Jaycie Phelps

Life is fatal. You are going to die. Or as the Stoics say "memento mori". Now that we have that happy fact established, it is not a question of "if" but "when", and so the real question is how are you going to live so as to get the most out of the indeterminate amount of time that you have? As Sebastian says in The Little Mermaid: kiss the girl! You never know if she is your Twin Flame true love unless you give it a shot. Better to find out she doesn't like you now than to waste years wondering.

Want that promotion? Review why you should get it and go after it young lady, you aren't going to get it by sitting and waiting for it to be handed to you on a platter. Worst thing is they fire you, and if you really are good enough to take the risk of asking and being turned down, you're good enough to leave the company and upgrade your position so it really isn't a risk except to your ego to be told "no". Call that potential huge client. Worst thing is they say no, and you'll have overcome some fear and be better for the next big call. And if they say yes....

Life is a risky game, and since you were born you are playing it. Hedge your bets where appropriate (like buying insurances, getting legal documents in place, not eating from a street vendor in a third world country that is serving something you can't recognize, etc.), but remember: if it isn't fatal it's not final. If you can recover, the short-term discomfort you might experience is the tradeoff for the potential of something much better than the current situation. Don't gamble the mortgage money, but eating Ramen for a few days for a chance at filet mignon for a month is a good gamble.

Some of us seem to avoid risk at all costs, willing to give up all upside potential to avoid any losses. Unfortunately, these people are usually forgotten by history as they rarely do anything of significance and generally don't have a great life by taking the safe paths.

As Theodore Roosevelt proclaimed in the "Man in the Arena" speech at the Sorbonne:...if he fails, at least fails while daring greatly, so that his place shall never be with those cold and timid souls who neither know victory nor defeat.

Don't be a timid soul, boldly go forth and battle for what you want. Empires are not inherited but built, and cowards rarely have songs sung about them.

Action item: what is one low risk gamble you could take that has a disproportionate return (Pascal's Wager)? If the loss is tolerable (albeit a little uncomfortable) but the reward is worth it, why are you waiting? Ladies and gentlemen, place your bets!

23 JUNE

"Only the really young are fearless, have the optimism, the romanticism to take unimaginable risks."

Olivia Wilde

They say that the only thing that babies are innately afraid of are loud noises and falling, and I have seen many ones that due to exposure to these stimuli overcome all fears early on and are truly courageous. It is a beautiful thing to watch because these kids believe they are invulnerable and have no limits, and as such are able to achieve things that the rest of us look at, tilt our head and say "how the hell did they do that?!"

Back when I was a kid, all the boys wanted to be Evil Knievel the fearless daredevil (except me, I wanted to be Albert Einstein): gutsy, pushing themselves, and doing the impossible to the celebratory roar of the crowd. The ones who crashed and burned (typically with some great stories and scars) but got back on the bike (literally and figuratively) are the guys that have gone on to accomplish things; the ones that gave into the fear and didn't re-engage are more "normal" in their expectations and experiences because they no longer have the belief in themselves that they had when they were mini-Supermen.

When you were a little kid you probably kissed the cute boy or pretty girl right on the cheek and maybe blushed but that was the extent of the embarrassment. At five years old I called Becca Fisher's house at 7:00 am on a Saturday to talk to her (the scandal!) and saw no issue with it. I still have no issue calling her or any other pretty girl, or that potential huge client, because the worst thing that can happen is they say "no". The enthusiasm and optimism I had at five remains, and is probably the reason I can sit here writing this book with the romantic belief that millions of people will read it. If they don't, oh well (insert shrug here).

"If you knew you couldn't fail, what would you attempt?" is a question we've probably all heard and maybe even asked ourselves. Removal of fear instills confidence, and dreamers tend to be in that camp. Whether it is the garage band dreaming of arena glory and cheers of the masses (like Evil Knievel but less scars but more tattoos), the woman turning her passion for cookies into a business (Kathleen King's first endeavor went bankrupt, then she built Mrs. Tate's Bake Shop Cookies and sold it for half a billion bucks), the teenager striving to be the first in their family to go to college; all must remove fear and be young in their heart and attitude to succeed in something great. If they could overcome obstacles as they have, what is stopping you? A little fear?

Action item: what is the one thing you want to do but are afraid to do? Write out all the negatives, the worst-case scenarios, everything that frightens you about it. Now rank them, scariest to least. How do you overcome these fears and take action?

24 JUNE
"The only thing we have to fear, is fear itself."

Franklin Delano Roosevelt

Fear is more contagious than any virus, and can cause more damage than anything else because we create more demons in our minds than exist in all the circles of Hell combined. Humans are an anxious species, and this was good when we had to worry about saber tooth tigers in the woods or Viking raiding parties but those constant threats are nonexistent. We are living in the safest time in human history, no matter what the media screams in an attempt for attention and advertising dollars. Hearing a noise in the night? It's not a burglar or the monster under the bed: it is a mouse, the wind, or your teenager (which actually is a reason to worry, just saying).

Shark Week is fun to watch because they are the apex predators of the ocean and absolutely gorgeous, fearsome killing machines, but they aren't going to kill you. You are more likely to die from a vending machine falling on you. Are you afraid of vending machines? Why not? Because there was never a movie designed to instill fear with an awesome tuba theme where the vending machine is unseen until after it takes out a dozen people in the office?

Fear is good in small doses because it prevents us from doing stupid things and can keep us safe. But when it starts to spiral out of control and move from rational and reasonable (a wildfire in the next county means pack up and leave, a wildfire a thousand miles away should not freak you out), that is when it becomes not a self-preservation mechanism but a hindrance and harmful.

Y2K was going to be the end of the world. People were prepping for the collapse of society, stocking bunkers with canned goods and shotguns. And nothing happened. In the early part of the Coronavirus Pandemic there was a run on toilet paper because people thought that the world was going to end or something. If the world was going to end, the shotguns and canned goods probably would have been more helpful, just saying. Every election cycle is stoked by fear of what "they" are going to do as each side points across the aisle and riles up people with fear. You too probably wish for some civility and quiet, fact-based discussion and analysis instead of screaming and demonization across the board.

The impact of fear is scarier than what people are afraid of. The biochemical impact can linger for days or even decades, putting stress on the body that causes ongoing harm. But instead of worrying about this too, know that intellectual action will neutralize fear, as the brain really can only think or fear (not both) at any time. So rationally thinking about fear will make it dissipate like mist in the sun of morning.

Action item: what are you afraid of? Write it down. Now start writing all the reasons why you shouldn't be afraid of it. Actively break down your fears into their smallest parts, and you will see how small they really are.

25 JUNE

"Fear ain't nothing but a thought."

Master Daniel G. Grant

Fear for the most part is not an instant and automatic response to the fearsome dog growling, nor the adrenaline rush of the near miss car accident. Even though your heart is racing and you are in fight or flight mode, that is a preparatory physiological position and it will quickly fade, and can be utilized for positive outcomes. Fear is a hindrance, an anchor emotionally weighing us down and slowing us down, tethering us into a limited space of capability like that growling dog chained to its house.

Fear is for the most part self-generated, and is created because of the unknown beyond our experiences and control. We fear terrorists, soulless politicians taking things from us, murder hornets and alien invasions. These are things beyond our control and/or so unlikely in terms of happening that we are wasting precious energy and time on something that Zen Buddhists, Stoics, the faithful of the major religions, and most scientists would laugh at.

We create most of the demons in the world in our minds, and let them grow monstrous by feeding them our fears.

We fear spiders because of how they look, even though they are our allies in that they eat hundreds of times their weight in bugs over their lives. And unless you mess with the spiders they will leave you alone, so why fear them?

We are afraid to speak in front of crowds, until we practice our speech and get up and face that fear a dozen or more times, then we look forward to it with excitement.

We are afraid of rejection, or loneliness so we never really let people in beyond just the surface so we don't become vulnerable and potentially get hurt. We avoid the loss by never truly bonding with others, so rejection will not hurt any more than pulling a bandaid off, as opposed to risking being cut through the soul.

We are afraid of our own greatness, what we must sacrifice to achieve it and the inevitable failures along the way, so we talk ourselves out of attempting significant things.

Yes, getting punched in the face in the ring hurts, and getting punched in the gut via rejection hurts more. But it toughens the body and spirit and eventually you don't fear the hits. Exposure to your fears, repeatedly choosing the small bruises in preparation instead of the monster blow that inevitably comes from avoidance. Face the demons when they are tiny and confront them before they grow in the shadows and tower over you. Little acts of courage, be it facing the spider or making that first little attempt at human connection with the person that leaves you tongue tied, is how to squash fears before they paralyze you.

This is not an easy thing, but rarely are things of significance easily achieved. And it might not be visible, no accolades like the big trophy for defeating the visible opponents in front of the cheering crowd. Overcoming fear is the small, often unseen decisions and actions where usually it is only you and that shadow. Casting light into the creepy cobwebby corners of our mind and past reveal that there is nothing there but our own thoughts turned dark and negative, figments of our imagination, and we must continuously sweep the mind of these with exposure to sun and focused attention. We created these shadows, and it is up to us to remove them.

Action item: grab a piece of paper. Write down your biggest fear. Look at it, let the words start to make you uneasy. Now circle them. Now put a slash through them, indicating they are banned. Write three to five little steps you can start taking to eliminate this fear. Choose the easiest and implement it.

26 JUNE
"Change your thoughts and you change your world."

Norman Vincent Peale

If you listen to any Tony Robbins for more than fifteen minutes, you will probably hear him mention the RAS (Reticular Activation System), our filter that determines how we interpret the stimuli for the world. The RAS like most brain systems is semi-preset at birth but almost half of its ultimate orientation is programmable over your lifetime by what you CHOSE to expose yourself to, what you design your mind to be biased towards through exposure and repetition. Jim Rohm, Norman Vincent Peale, Napoleon Hill all echoed the wisdom that has been discussed in culture after culture over millennia and around the earth: as a man thinketh, so he becomes. And applies equally to women too. Your future is partially a toss of the dice of fate but as much your choices to the rolls. "No fate but what we make."

So what do you want your thoughts to be? Happier? Look for things to savor throughout the day, share small acts of kindness with others, exercise daily, and when you catch negative thoughts starting forcibly stop and ask yourself "Why am I thinking this negative thing?" and explore it for a moment. You will trend toward happier thoughts over the weeks and in a year be unrecognizable due to the smile on your face. Want to be less prone to anger? Look for what triggers your anger and pre-play these scenarios. Close your eyes and take a deep breath. Avoid the worst incidents if possible, or learn to recite the alphabet before taking action. A pause lets anger subside, and practice will make it happen faster and dampen the strength of the negative emotion. Want more patience? Similar to anger in many ways. Also focus on speaking slowly and lowly instead of shouting because it will prevent escalation of the situation, especially if a tired toddler is involved. Be a better leader? Study leadership, listen to Youtube videos of leaders and actively look for leadership opportunities. Ask yourself "What Would (insert leader's name) Do?" Practice being a better leader and you will become one.

Your brain is not just a lump of electrical connections in your skull, unalterable and destined for whatever the factory settings predetermine. It is under your control the same way your waistline is, reflective of your daily choices. If you choose to fill your house with ice cream and chips you will probably have poor physical health. If you feed your brain with crappy romance novels and trash tv and negativity your outlook on life will be clouded by the poor decisions that are clogging it up with bad stuff, worse than the arteries of the ice cream fiend. Your body, your mind, your choices.

Action item: search Youtube for clips about whatever characteristic (patience, bravery, stronger relationships, whatever) you want to exhibit more of. Listen to at least five minutes of this a few times a day, and start actively examining your thoughts and see how you can improve them towards what you want to be.

27 JUNE
"You must be the change you wish to see in the world."

Mahatma Gandhi

A lawyer who gave up that profession to become a leader and eventually an icon. That is an example of modeling what you want the world to become.

Lord Baden Powell wanted to give young men a chance to develop themselves better. So he founded Boy Scouts and led them for essentially the rest of his life, tweaking and improving so that kids world-wide could have a proven path to becoming independent leaders. That is the change.

Want your spouse and kids to be healthier? Remove the junk food from the house, start exercising more and making better choices and ask them to join you. By starting on the path to health and inviting them on the journey with you, you are becoming the change you want to see in that small part of the earth that is your world.

Want to protect the environment? What are you doing? The politicians that scream about climate change yet ride around on private jets (as opposed to flying commercial or bringing more people on their planes, both of which reduce the impact per person per mile) are not really modelling the change they want. The person that makes little choices around reducing, reusing, and recycling and uses a bike instead of a vehicle for short trips, who bunches their errands to reduce the number of trips, and uses a push mower instead of a gas one is actually a much better model.

World need more love and kindness? Start being kinder, showing more love and tolerance to everyone from your kids to co-workers to the annoying Karen in the store. Might be really difficult as she screams for the manager, but change is not easy.

Some people can create companies to leverage resources for change, whether it is a technological innovation that means less processing (and less waste), or reduces energy consumption, or saves people time. Other people volunteer their time and talent to assist others, be it reducing gang violence or helping Vets cope with what they've experienced.

Use your abilities to create change for the good of others in the world instead of just improving the little slice of our planet that directly impacts your life.

Action item: what is one thing you'd love to change in the world? What is the smallest action you can take to start making that change? Go take that action.

28 JUNE
"The world is my country, all mankind are my brethren, and to do good is my religion."
Thomas Paine

The wings of a butterfly create hurricanes a world away. What we do here, now, impacts people for generations and across the globe. Our actions (or lack thereof) send ripples and waves everywhere, and everyone influences us to a lesser or greater extent no matter where they are.

The American Revolution, one of the most important events in human history, can not be described completely as "uniquely American" because John Locke and the Iroquois Nation influenced Jefferson and the other Founding Fathers. Locke and the Founders were influenced by ancient Greeks and Romans and the Magna Carta and the Dutch. The Founding Fathers have influenced people around the world and for two and a half centuries. "All Men are created equal", if not explicitly stated, is an underlying theme in governments and organizations of impact everywhere.

If we are all equally human, endowed with the same inalienable rights, that makes someone on a different continent as much of my family as my cousin in the next state. That makes people across the country and those across a geopolitical imaginary line still part of the interconnected web of humanity that depends upon each other in countless ways. We are our brother's keeper and have a responsibility to not needlessly harm our extended family when it can be avoided, and to lend a helping hand where we can.

This is the "do good" part of the quote. Not "be good" and sit in our compound and read our particular Holy Book, but "do" good, as in get out from behind the walls and take actions to improve the lot of others, whether it is donating blood, working in a soup kitchen, volunteering professional services, or choosing to not support a company that you don't believe in their decisions (plus letting them know your choice and why so they get the message).

In the New Testament Jesus says that the 10 Commandments boil down to two principles, one of which is "Love thy neighbor as thyself". Doesn't matter what Holy Book you ascribe to, that precept applies equally to all major religions and love (per Mr. Rogers et al) is an action verb. Showing love for thy neighbor, be they across the street or across seven time zones, is what Paine (and most great leaders, secular or religious) called for.

Action item: go online and find 2 ways to do good today. One should be local, one outside your country. Big or small, do something for your brethren.

29 JUNE
"Every country has the government it deserves."

Joseph de Maistre

Oh, you hate the person sitting in the White House? But did you vote? If not, you deserve them. You did vote, but your candidate didn't get elected? Did you do anything to support them like talking to undecided voters and trying to sway them? Good! Were they the best candidate from your Party? Oh, they weren't? Did you vote in your Primary? Did you do anything to support the candidate you thought best in the early stages?

Are you involved on the State level, to help get the candidates you believe in to the big stage and a chance to influence the Nation, whether in Congress or the Executive Branch? No? You deserve the choices you were forced to pick from, because you didn't help create a better list of candidates. Do you know your State and local representation? Do they know you? Why not?

Do you attend local meetings of planning boards or other organizations that are the grassroots of politics on all levels, and get involved in the campaigns in whatever appropriate capacity on the smallest possible level because you know the person and believe they are in it for the right reasons and can do the job properly for the good of We The People?

Then you get what you get and you don't get upset as every kindergartener learns.

I'm not saying you become a political junkie or a cog in a huge election machine. I am saying that you need to invest some time as it makes sense to have input more than showing up once a year and pulling a lever or filling in some bubbles. Active involvement in the political system keeps it accountable to the people it is meant to serve.

I hate politicians as much or more than the next person. But I also go and get involved, know the issues that are relevant, and invest time to go and meet with the elected officials that serve us, even if I have to keep a hand on my wallet and take a very long shower afterwards. I make the sacrifice so that even on a micro level I can improve the outcomes overall. It's not perfect, but it is better than bitching and moaning and not doing anything about it.

Action item: what is the next political race in your area, be it dog catcher or Governor? Invest some time to understand the issues, and then donate a few minutes of your time to assist the person you think is best for the position.

30 JUNE

"Canada is a good country to be from. It has a gentler, slower pace - it lends perspective."

Paul Anka

"The True North, strong and free" as their anthem declares. A place famous for saying "sorry", even when they are not at fault, the total opposite of the typical New Yorker. And as the antithesis to NYC, Canadians do take things a little slower and are more appreciative, not just of the world around them but the people around them.

There are times when the high-speed attitude of the Big Apple is appropriate and even needed. But if your engine revs in the red constantly you will have a breakdown, be it mental or physical. Taking your foot off the gas once in a while, slowing down to enjoy the world around you and experiencing the view is the best restorative for your body and spirit. Even if you only switch from miles per hour to kilometers per hour (roughly 62% of your 'normal" hectic pace) for an hour or two once in a while, it will prevent you from overheating and being on the roadside broken down on your highway to success, and you won't appreciate the landscape or bother to smell the roses. Sometimes you can get there faster by going slower.

Just as importantly as the ability to slow down and smell the poutine is the capacity to appreciate it, and the person that made it or brought it to you. Not only pausing and acknowledging the crunch and golden color of the fries (savoring is a critical component of happiness per numerous studies), but showing gratitude to another increases overall joy both short term and longer range, something people in the US should adopt from our northern cousins. A heartfelt "thank you" to an overworked and stressed server can improve their day; a "good morning" to someone on the street who is in a foul mood or holding the door for someone and pausing long enough for a smile is not going to cause you to miss your train or lose a multi-million dollar deal but will make someone else feel better (if not like a million bucks, maybe just a little more human and that is priceless).

Unless you are Wayne Gretzky, everyone in Canada is just another person, whether you are a politician in Ottawa or run the fly-fishing shop in Kootenay or drive the Zamboni in Moose Jaw. People are people, we all have to deal with the weather and put on our shoes (or skates) one at a time. Even if you are running at Manhattan velocity with the hustle and bustle of Wall Street in a trading frenzy, you can stop and take a breath and give another person a few seconds of attention so they know that they matter. You don't have to hold them 'til the morning comes, but almost anytime is a good time to shift your perspective and appreciate others a bit more, eh?

Action item: tell five people "thank you" or some other small show of respect today.

JULY IS A BLIND DATE WITH SUMMER

Hal Borland

01 JULY

"Canada is a balloon puncturing country. You are not really allowed to be an icon unless you also make an idiot of yourself." Margaret Atwood

Canada has produced some spectacular comedians, a disproportionate number for a country with the population of New York State. Rick Moranis, John Candy, Phil Hartman, and an All Star cast of Saturday Night Live. Plus William Shatner.

The ability to laugh at yourself is critical. Whenever someone's ego gets too big, the Universe inevitably says "hold on there kiddo" and smack! right in the back of the head. So being able to handle the world (and ourselves especially) with humor (humour for Canadians) is one of those skills that are ancient and relevant. As Seneca pointed out: all things are cause for either laughter or weeping. Mel Brooks put it as "humor is just another defense against the universe."

Many civilians will look at the dark humor of Veterans as borderline rude and darker than last night's boiled down coffee (which they will gladly drink btw), but it is a coping mechanism that allows them to assimilate the horrors of war without sacrificing their humanity. How many people bought cases of Corona during the Pandemic to essentially flip the bird at the fear that was creeping in? To use laughter as a shield against the darkness, as Shakespeare repeatedly did in his plays?

Laugh at the darkness or cry until dawn.

Maintaining humility, understanding that even if you have great influence or power or wealth that eventually we will all be like Yorick allows us to appreciate what we have and others, to laugh like a child and find joy even in uncertainty. Warren Buffet still eats a McDonald's Egg McMuffin and small coffee as he drives to the office from the home he purchased many decades ago even though he is rich enough to buy all of McDonald's and Nebraska. Plus he certainly knows how to laugh at himself; his self-deprecating humor is legendary.

Elon Musk can be a jerk, can build trillion-dollar companies, and still is a quirky eccentric genius that isn't afraid to make a fool of himself. The ability to laugh at yourself is priceless. Shaquille O'Neal and Peyton Manning were champions, among the best ever to play their relevant games, and outside the lines of their respective field/court total goofballs that have no problem getting a laugh at their own expense. And they are still relevant well after their playing careers for that reason.

Even...Bill Shatner...can make fun OF...himself. If Captain James T Kirk (and Spock) can laugh at themselves, why can't you?

Action item: do something stupid today. Laugh at yourself for being human.

02 JULY

"I am not an Athenian or a Greek, but a citizen of the world."

Socrates

As the communication revolution swept the world it became smaller and smaller.

200 years ago you probably wouldn't have gone more than a score of miles from your birthplace.

100 years ago you probably didn't leave your time zone, and maybe read a newspaper.

50 years ago with TV people could see what was happening a world away.

Today you can interact with a friend halfway around the globe in real time.

In the book ZConomy, Villa and Dorsey point out that a teenager in the US has more in common with one in Europe and one in Japan than they do with their 50-year-old next door neighbor.

Fashion and food are, if not homogenized, at least exported so that anyone anywhere in the First World can get essentially the same thing as their peers, be it McDonald's or jeans or that cool new app. Interactive online games let a crew assemble for a battle from four continents speaking six languages easier than getting into the DMV. Social media allows a teen in Topeka and one in Taiwan to see the same dance or trick played on a GenXer. There truly is more binding Millennials across the globe together than separating them at this point.

When Socrates declared himself a citizen of the world, his world was what he could see and touch and feel, what he could read, and tales he heard from travelers that might have gone a few hundred miles. Today we can speak with people from Romania to the Republics of Korea and Congo simultaneously, taste their food, hear their music, and ask their thoughts about everything from world events to their favorite memes. We can email anyone and visit any museum via live stream. We have an obligation to be citizens of the world, to measure our impact not just in our neighborhood but in Newfoundland and New Guinea.

We are all human, and we are indeed our brothers' (and sisters') keepers.

Action item: reach out to someone with a different background as you and ask them what they think about some things. You'll be amazed at how similar we are.

03 JULY
"The earth is but one country and Mankind its citizens."

Baha'u'llah

In the movie Independence Day, aliens come down and try to destroy everything and the last remnants of mankind band together in a desperate last attempt to stave off annihilation. President Whitmore declares: "Mankind. That word should have new meaning for all of us today. We can't be consumed by our petty differences anymore."

The Covid Pandemic swept over borders and crossed all human made barriers, be they political or religious. The world economy suffered a ten trillion-dollar multi-year hit, over three times the annual US federal budget. That nasty little virus destroyed small businesses and large, closed religious institutions of all forms, and cancelled sporting events everywhere. For the first time ever, every single human being had to cope with the same exogenous event simultaneously. For once, all of us experienced something from the First World to Third World and across all economic and demographic slices around the globe. Think about that.

How did you emerge from this trial? Did you put up additional walls in your mind and heart, cutting off other people and focusing on yourself and your narrow sliver of humanity, or did your heart and spirit and thinking expand to encompass others you hadn't considered before? Over 40 million US citizens lost their jobs and close to half of us saw a drop in income (plus all the parents turned teachers struggling with kids at home), so you know many many people that were severely negatively impacted while everyone made sacrifices during this. From this are you now in an untrusting, bunker mentality, eyeing others suspiciously, or are you embodying what de Tocqueville wrote about American expansive charity and connection over a hundred years ago?

Are you bitter or better?

"The universal brotherhood of man is our most precious possession." Mark Twain

"The world is now too small for anything but brotherhood." A Powell Davies

"The most important thing in the world is family and love." Coach John Wooden

Action item: reach beyond your normal walls. Find someone different from you (age, race, religion, whatever) and talk with them, try to understand this member of your extended human family.

04 JULY

"Independence is happiness."

Susan B. Anthony

There were two birds. One sat in the gilded cage, singing sad songs of longing from her safety as she looked out the window. She might as well have not had wings, because she could not fly and lamented her gilded cage. The other sat on a branch outside in the winter, cold but able to soar and touch the sky, search for food and feel the wind. The second had to contend with the elements and risks and probably has a shorter overall life but actually lived, and experienced true happiness. Which bird are you?

"Those who sacrifice liberty for security deserve neither." Ben Franklin We all make choices, many of which give up some personal freedoms (such as wearing a safety belt or deciding to post to Facebook and letting them scrape your data) if we perceive that what we receive in return (not being thrown through a window, or being able to see alien cat memes) is of sufficient value we will make the tradeoff. The concern is when we trade too much of our freedom for the illusion of security and reach the point of being unable to reverse course if need be, where we are no longer free to make choices and mistakes.

Free will is the ultimate human freedom. The ability to choose and face the consequences (good and bad) of them is what being an adult is about, as opposed to being a child with the limitations of curfew and not leaving the yard or being able to watch what you want. Those freedoms come at a price (financial, time, etc.) and are often non-returnable, and the law of unintended consequences is almost as strong as gravity or Murphy's Law.

Remember in *Toy Story 2* how Woody had the opportunity to go and be nice and safe in a collection, never to have his arm torn off again or scuffed but also never to be played with again? And he chose to feel alive instead of hiding behind glass, protected but unloved. Maybe it's the Cowboy Way, but choosing independence as the way to happiness is pretty American, from our founding roots to today.

This is why there are so many entrepreneurs in our country, why second chances are part of our cultural fabric. The chance to try and fail, to take that shot and experience risk to be alive and potentially achieve something is as American as apple pie. With independence comes responsibility, comes the potential to be harmed, but it also brings the potential for the pursuit of happiness. Total protection from risk removes the freedom of choice and consequences, and is called "prison". The bird's gilded cage from above.

Action item: what is something that you can choose to do today that makes you happy? If the consequences thereof don't outweigh the joy, go do it.

05 JULY
"It is difficult to free fools from the chains they revere."

Voltaire

We create the strongest bonds that bind us, be they of the heart or mind. Our belief systems can give us power and freedom, but they can also limit our perception and vision and chain us like an anchor holding a ship in place, preventing it from sailing over the horizon to new adventures.

We all have our chains. Some of us are too bound by traditions, by doing things "the old way". Even these old ways were new at one point though, the most conservative of beliefs being radical when first introduced. Just because something is traditional is no reason to get rid of it, but it is also not a sufficient reason to keep doing something unproductive, self-destructive, or hateful.

Some of us embrace change so much that we don't look at the good aspects of what came before and see how to make them the core of something new, an iteration instead of a whole scale replacement. Eliminating the past means we can't learn from it.

Some people stay in abusive situations because they are scared of being alone, or losing the financial benefits even though they are being emotionally or physically hurt. Others are unwilling to open up their hearts again because they are chained shut because of what happened last time.

Too many are bound to political parties or ideologies, unquestionably following the chain without pausing to think or evaluate the individual candidate. George Washington warned against this.

Sometimes we are psychologically tied down to a particular place where we grew up or went to school. There is no invisible electric fence keeping us in place, only the shock of actually leaving.

We forge our own chains with our own choices. We can break them with our choices too, but all too often we blindly accept the chains that are placed upon us. And once we are used to the lack of freedom, of the weight and restrictions of the bonds, we cannot break them.

A baby elephant is chained into place with a stake driven into the ground. As the elephant grows and develops strength, eventually reaching maturity, it is easily powerful enough to rip the stake out of the ground but does not because the mental chain is too powerful to break. Is this you?

Action item: what is holding you back? What chain binds you and prevents you from reaching that goal? Look at your chains, and see where the weak link is so you can snap it and break free of your fetters.

06 JULY

"When we lose the right to be different, we lose the privilege to be free."

Charles Evans Hughes

Mel Brooks was a comedic genius and equally hit everybody: Jews (both his parents were Jewish immigrants), Catholics ("but no Irish!"), racists (almost everyone in the town in Blazing Saddles), politicians, homosexuals and homophobes, and even Darth Vader and Hitler (decades before Epic Lloyd and Nice Peter launched Epic Rap Battles of History). No subject was taboo but could be skewered because as they say in Romania: the truth is told through jokes. Part of accepting people's differences is to be able to satirize them, and George Orwell restates this as "if you want to know who rules over you, look at who you are not allowed to criticize." Comedy has always been the wittiest way of criticism, and has long been the preferred methodology of questioning social mores.

When everyone looks and acts the same, groupthink comes into play, innovation decays, and iconoclasm becomes the norm. Think of the most tightly knit social groups, be it a cult or an upper crust island (or building, or firm) or ethnic enclave. If everyone looks the same or thinks the same, if everyone has the same background or the same focus with no tolerance/expectation of individualism within the group, suboptimal results are guaranteed because progress comes not from identical efforts and outcomes but from continuous micro-experiments and different ideas interacting.

Differences create the spice and flavor in a dish, and variety (even within the constraints of a severe diet) is required to avoid utter violations and breakdown of all discipline due to pent up hunger and frustration and temptation. So in dieting, so in societies.

As I was reminded early in my tenure teaching martial arts: I'm not Bill Durkhee (6'3" and a cold hard military machine) or Danny Grant (5'5" and built like a fireplug and harder than stone). I'm me, a thin intellectual goofball. I think differently, so I fight and teach differently.

Learn your own way, win your own way. "To thine own self be true" as Shakespeare admonished.

Cookie cutter clones are the worst thing for an organization. It leads to short term performance but a lack of adaptability, and halts evolution which leads to organizational decay and death. Freedom to be different leads to acceptance of "radical" ideas, the key to adaptation and survival. It may take one generation or four, but stifling differences will strangle the organization (or country) eventually.

Action item: look at your work. What is one place where you feel you could express yourself and your personality more, to enrich the organization while being YOU?

07 JULY

"A hero is someone who understands the responsibility that comes with his freedom."

Nobel Laureate (Literature) Bob Dylan

Freedom isn't free. It comes at a cost. That cost is different for every generation and each individual, but ultimately we must all pay something for anything as precious as freedom.

For some, it is time to study and earn their degree after they put the kids to bed and have worked a full grueling day. For others it is joining the military and making the ultimate sacrifice to protect our way of life. Each is a hero in their own way.

Freedom is one of the greatest opportunities presented to us. When you have a free day, what do you choose to do with it? Do you sleep in late, watch Tik Tok all morning and then play video games all afternoon while eating Cheetos? If you do that once a year it probably isn't that bad, but if that is your normal Saturday I don't think you'll fit in your spandex supersuit very long.

Just because you can do something doesn't mean you should. You can eat a dozen Boston Crème donuts in a day or drink three forties of bad beer or smoke an entire carton of cigarettes today. Once you get a driver's license you can play real life Mario Kart. None of these are a good idea because they are poor choices that endanger people. The donuts won't harm others like the driving straight out of a video game does, but you in thirty years with a heart issue and arteries filled with cheese might have something to say to you today about it. About more responsible choices.

Freedom of choice does not absolve you of the effects from your choices. Your actions have impacts on you and others, and there are no rights without the corresponding responsibilities. Heroes understand that their rights don't extend to the point that they interfere or supersede another's rights, and consciously choose to restrain themselves and their actions. Else they would cross the line from hero to villain, using their power and the freedom it gives them to do bad things.

Action item: where is one area where the responsibility you assume is not on the level of the freedom you are enjoying? Click up your discipline, your restraint and self-control here a notch so as to move closer to hero status.

08 JULY

"Accept the terrible responsibility of life with eyes wide open."

Jordan Peterson

Playing ostrich by sticking your head in the sand to avoid seeing the harsh realities of life or scary situations does not work well for extended periods of time, because out of sight might mean out of mind but it does not mean the problem is out of your life. You have to look right at it and figure out how to solve the problems before they grow to the point that they cannot be solved.

Keeping your eyes open means paying attention to things, and not just those things directly in front of us as we focus on the road we have laid out for ourselves. Anyone that lives in a semi-rural area knows to keep an eye out for deer jumping across the highway because even though they are not the cars ahead of us that are our primary concern, a deer can destroy your vehicle in an instant. Or even worse: driving through a neighborhood and a kid chases a ball out into the road and…

Better to have your eyes wide open beforehand than have to squeeze them shut and still have a terrible vision there in your mind's eye.

Life is a journey and it is fraught with dangers. Only in fairy tales does the Princess live in the tower, get rescued by her Prince, and live happily ever after with no worries. Closing your eyes to reality is dangerous, and will only shock you more when they are forced open and things have gotten worse for the avoidance or lies we tell ourselves that have spun out of control. You have to face it like a grown up, even if it is horrible.

"Accept the bitter truth, but never give up hope" is the essence of the Stockdale Paradox and the way to face the terrible responsibilities you will encounter on the way, Because life is going to suck at times: we will all get sick, we will watch loved ones die, We will have economic strife and personal tragedies, We will get divorced, or at least see one of our close friends/family members go through it. We will experience addiction and self-destruction within our inner circle of people we care deeply about. It is inevitable.

Looking away from these things will lead to denial, lying to ourselves and others and escapism, be it in a bottle or the arms of a stranger or something even worse. Unflinchingly looking into the void, be it in someone we care about, ourselves, or the emptiness where someone once was in our life is the only way to confront this darkness and dispel it before it overcomes your soul and life, leaving only doubt and despair. Look into it before it grows into something monstrous and ravenous that devours you from within. Face it, unblinkingly.

Action item: what is the one thing you don't want to address, that monster that has grown that you refuse to stare in the face? Look at it. Look at it! Now face it and deal with it.

09 JULY

"No rights without responsibilities."

Paul Havemann

As we teach teenagers, having the right to drive a vehicle is a big step towards freedom and adulthood, but it comes with corresponding responsibilities such as taking care of the car, paying for gas, and removing distractions while driving so that they minimize the danger to others, plus helping get the younger kids to their various events or picking up milk to make it easier on the parents. If they are not willing to accept the responsibilities, they are unable to have the rights.

The Constitution guarantees the right to free speech. The responsibility is to not abuse it by spreading lies, or hurting other people with it. In a world of Twitter and SEO'd websites, one can easily reach the equivalent of the US population at the turn of the 20th Century in minutes, and this awesome power and right must be personally restrained by responsibility.

The right to vote should be celebrated but also informed, so as to not just click a box without thought. As a voter you bear the responsibility to invest some time to see which candidates align best with your beliefs, regardless of political party.

I have the right to eat a half dozen Boston Crème donuts (and I do on my monthly cheat day, it's epic!), but I have the responsibility to not do so all the time because of the consequences. As Wilfred Brimley said: die a bee tus! Or as my Tae Kwon Do Master taught us: you dig your grave with your teeth. The right to eat whatever you want comes with the responsibility of maintaining control, or if you are going to be out of control (say on your 21st birthday or bachelor party), there is someone else there to ensure that the lines to danger are not crossed when you can't be responsible within your rights.

I have the right to own a gun under the 2nd Amendment. As a responsible firearms Instructor, I am beyond anally retentive about my responsibilities for safety around these powerful items.

The great rights we enjoy bear an equally awesome responsibility, whether it is having kids or voting or The Bill of Rights. Expecting rights without the responsibilities is the illusion of a spoiled teenager and will lead to being grounded and loss of those privileges, maybe even irrevocably.

Action item: freedom isn't free, and choices have consequences. Before you say "I have the right to", ask yourself "what is my responsibility?"

10 JULY

"Service to others is the rent you pay for your room here on earth."

Muhammad Ali

"Each of you should use whatever gift you have received to serve others" Peter 4:10

"Trees refuse no one their shade, even the woodcutter." Hindu saying.

"Help one another" Quran 5:2

Every major religion echoes this: you were put on this earth for a reason. Multiple reasons probably, and one of them is to try and make the world a better place for others in some way. "From each according to their gifts", to others according to their needs.

Can you serve your local school by reading to kids, or supporting the building of a playground?

Can you serve your community by helping that old man clear the snow, or the senior center by helping to deliver meals?

I had an eight-year old Cub Scout tell me he wanted to help others and asked if we could do a small food drive. I put him (with the assistance of his parents) in charge and the boys collected eight bags of non-perishables from people, and got the local convenience store (thank you Stewart's Shops!) to donate a couple of crates of razors, toothbrushes, et al to help members of our community. Elliot (the Scout) is paying his rent by helping others.

Maybe you can volunteer for an open source project using your programming skills.

Or the local veteran's home could use someone to play games with the former servicemen and women, to help them re-acclimate.

Carry your neighbor's groceries. Help run the local sports group's concession stand. Knit hats or blankets for newborn babies.

As my favorite Fraternity song says: two hours of pushing broom, lets an 8 by 12, four bit room. You can pay your rent for your room here on earth with so much more than money, and doing so makes everyone better.

Action item: google "service opportunities near me". Find something that appeals to you and use what you have been given to help others in some way today.

11 JULY

"There is no higher religion than human service. To work for the common good is the greatest creed."

Woodrow Wilson

"Ask not what your country can do for you, but what you can do for your country." President John F Kennedy summarized what service over self meant.

Peace Corps, military service, volunteering as a coach or teacher. Scouts (Boys or Girls), poll sitter for local elections, helping at the food bank. Donating blood, or shoveling out the little old lady up the street. These are all service to other humans, and make the world a better place and serve as examples for others to model after, especially the youth in our communities. Love thy neighbor as thyself...

Alexis de Toqueville of France observed: I have seen Americans making great and sincere sacrifices for the key common good.

From the earliest days of the Colonies through today, the most American of attitudes is to help your neighbor when they need it. And it might be part of our culture because it was part of the magnetism that has drawn to our shores those that not only want to build a better life for themselves and families, but for their community.

John Roebling drove himself to the point of destroying his health to get the Brooklyn Bridge built. Nikolai Tesla sought to make power free, for the good of humanity, dying broke but of service to others.

Joseph Salk gave up his rights to the polio vaccine to get it produced widely and protect others.

Pat Tillman gave up his NFL career to serve his country after 9/11, paying the ultimate price.

Service can be the grand gesture with painful sacrifice, or it can be the consistent little things to improve your neighborhood. All service to others accumulates on the cosmic balance sheet.

Action item: as we teach the Cub Scouts: do a good turn daily. Help someone, in some way, today.

12 JULY

"The most effective way to preach the gospel is through example. If we live according to our beliefs, people will notice." Dieter F. Uchtdorf

We have all seen the individual that wraps themselves in faith and flag to cover the fact that they are a horrible human being. They preach and talk about what they do for their church, and how they are a patriot, and at the same time are enriching themselves through lies and thievery and violating multiple Commandments and laws. They look down their nose at others that don't give the proper image of following whatever mores and standards, while behind the scenes violate all principles that they espouse and are the greatest form of hypocrites. I stupidly entered into a business deal with a convicted felon who had changed his name but was still up to his fraudulent ways, using his (limited) service to the USMC and his involvement in his church as camouflage for his evil ways. I was duped, but it was my fault for falling for his illusion and theatrics.

Contrast this with someone you know, They rarely speak about their religious convictions, yet they volunteer countless hours in service of others. They aren't a screaming eagle of patriotism, but they do the little things like vote, support the volunteer fire station, help with the schools, and maybe even served the country, in uniform or out. They are the ones that you just say "they are a good man/woman" and they go about doing what they do to improve the world without a lot of fanfare. They don't like the spotlight even though they are the type of person that should be put on a pedestal as an example for others. If the spotlight does rest on them, they will deflect with something like "aw shucks" and point out other people that they think are more deserving of adulation. They'll say they had good parents and are "just doing my part." They are the unsung heroes and quiet leaders and the people we should teach our kids to look up to.

The coach who teaches kids the proper way to play the game, and be good sportsmen. The lady at church who knits hats for preemie babies at the local hospital. The Marine working behind the scenes at the Toys for Tots warehouse because they grew up poor and believe in duty and are honor bound to help the next generation, but not talk about it because it is simply "what we do." The volunteer tutor, helping prep people for the Citizenship Exam or teaching English to immigrants so that they are ready to contribute to the fabric of the country.

The doers, not the talkers.

Those who quietly model what it means to be a responsible citizen or person of faith, without ever having to raise their voice or their profile while making the world a better place every day.

These are the people who preach, without ever saying a word. And their message is powerful.

Action item: who is that quiet example of service to something bigger than themselves? What is one way that you can emulate them today to improve your world?

13 JULY

"Example is leadership."

Albert Schweitzer

One of the great leadership labs is a Boy Scout Troop, where 15 year old boys are running meetings, planning camping trips, and modeling leadership to younger kids, showing them what it means to grow into a self-reliant and dependable individual and member of a group. For the most part the adults are in the background, guiding and watching, because teenagers are teenagers.

Fraternities and Sororities used to operate in very much the same way. The seniors and juniors would run the House, everything from collecting rent and fees (often a hundred thousand dollars a year), plan events, coordinate schedules and herd the cats while simultaneously going to school and having other extracurricular activities. The job of a pledge was to learn how to do what needed to be done to run the organization, and develop into a leader for those coming up behind them. I have met senior military leaders, Fortune 500 CEOs, and startup founders that cut their leadership teeth when they put on a pledge pin and then learned how to coordinate cooking for 50 people as a 19 year old while still finishing their thermodynamics homework.

For over a decade I would show up early to my Tae Kwon Do class, and as senior student and assistant Instructor I swept out the dojang. It was my responsibility because I had seen the ones who came before me do it, and so it became my responsibility and a teaching tool. Over a dozen former students have told me over the years that they remember repeatedly seeing me do this, and that it taught them a lesson in quiet leadership that they could model.

As a parent, older sibling, or cousin or aunt (or funcle), little eyes are watching you to see what they should do. Always remember that.

There is a reason why over and over again the team captain in high school or college sports is not the best player, but the one that does all the little things right and embodies the proper attitude and will work to the maximum of their limited ability. If you have watched the movie Rudy, you can picture what I'm talking about. And yes, having met him, he is that small and his motor doesn't stop. Lead by example, even if five foot nothing.

Lead is an action word, not a passive verb.

Lead others by doing what you know to be right.

Action item: what is one way you can set a better example for someone coming up in your footsteps?

14 JULY
"I don't know any other way to lead but by example."

Don Shula

Coach Shula is still memorable for the only undefeated Super Bowl season in NFL history. His teams were tough (not Ditka tough, but blue collar and fundamentally sound) and consistent and hardworking, like their coach. He came from a huge working-class family and had to grind it out to succeed on the field, and beyond the lines he embodied the hard scrabble attitude with a constant desire to learn and improve. Making six Super Bowls as a coach was the outcome of doing the little things right consistently.

We all have that one person in our life who taught us many lessons, without saying a word. That Veteran who gets out of their wheelchair to say The Pledge of Allegiance. The lunch lady who models respect to all of the students. The rabbi or other religious leader who quietly serves their community (and not just their flock). The principal who greets all the students with a good morning by name. They lead by example.

The black belt who cleans the training facility.

The coach who stays in shape by running laps with the players.

The CEO who is polite and enthusiastic to everyone in the organization.

The Senior Partner who shows up early and makes the coffee before anyone else is there.

I was taking a Southwest flight back from Washington DC, and waiting patiently in line was Congressional Representative Chris Gibson. A retired Army Colonel with multiple combat tours (and a PhD too, he is now President of a small college). Gibson stood in line like everyone else, didn't want any special treatment (even when offered), and embodied the quiet, polite leader. By his example. I mentioned it to him a few years later at a talk he did, and The Colonel didn't remember the incident, because doing what you are supposed to do was a habit as opposed to a special occurrence. Too bad this isn't the norm among our elected leaders.

Do what you are supposed to do. Actions speak louder than words, and being a model for others through the little choices and activities will speak louder than an article in the paper or an appearance on tv.

Action item: what are the little things you can do that will model leadership, that without saying a word will send a message to others?

15 JULY

"A coach is someone who can give correction without causing resentment."

John Wooden

The Wizard of Westwood was able to take some of the biggest personalities (and men) in the game such as Bill Walton and Lou Alcindor and get them to buy into a system that produced an unprecedented run of greatness. Decades later Bill Belichick did the same with the New England Patriots, on the heels of Joe Torre's Yankees dynasty. There were amazing egos on those teams and they weren't always hoisting the trophy at the end of the year, but they were consistently great and attracted good players that wanted to play for them because they would improve under the coach's tutelage and have a shot to win the big one.

One way these legendary coaches succeeded was by getting the players to buy into their tough love, that anything the coach said or did was for the betterment of the team and the individual. They had enough wins and experience to have the gravitas (remember, Torre won an MVP and a batting title as a player) to have the authority to give suggestions for improvement, and as they achieved success they refined their system and insight as to how to improve, attracting great assistants that could further enhance the coaching and thus improvements of their people. There is a reason why Belichick's best coordinators returned to work with him again and again.

A good coach will believe in their players. A great coach will get players to believe in themselves, and the process to maximize themselves and their teams. A great coach will instill in their people a desire to have the negatives pointed out so that they can be improved upon, because as Herm Edwards famously ranted: you play the game to WIN! The greatest coaches have their players desire to win more than they want comfort, or accolades, or their own egos.

Champions want to be coached, and coaches need people that want to be champions more than they want to be coddled. The ability to look someone (player, partner, child) in the eye and say "I love you, but to be better…" and have the other person thank you for it is a rare skill that should be honed and carefully applied to build champion teams in your life.

Action item: who are you in a coaching relationship with, either as the coach or the one being guided? How can you make this partnership better, to focus on improved outcomes with less emotional tension?

16 JULY

"Dogs have boundless enthusiasm but no sense of shame. I should have a dog as a life coach."

Moby

Dogs are always happy to see you if they know you. Unless they have been conditioned otherwise, they are friendly and love to be on the go, experiencing new things and running around with little care in the world. They will bark at and chase squirrels, never catch them, and still do it again a few hours later.

A dog that wants off a leash will find a way to escape. And if it is loved, it will always find its way home.

A dog will fiercely protect "their kid" from any threat. They will also let that kid pull their ears, eat their food, and cuddle up with them. Think about that as a model of unconditional love.

A dog if shown love and early discipline will be well trained, and be able to take care of themselves even without you watching them 24/7. And when you return from work, they will be waiting eagerly at the door, missing you more than is reasonable and yet it is the most natural thing in the world.

A dog will play with you until they are exhausted, chasing whatever you throw and bringing it back. Even if they miss the tennis ball and skid out of control as if they were on ice, they are still going to get that ball and bring it back. Or that stick. Or sometimes a different stick, but that's cool because they want to share that one with you because they found it interesting. If someone brings you something cool to show you, appreciate it even if it wasn't what you had intended.

A dog will meet others, trying to run up and say "hi". They are social creatures like we humans, and they gain joy and energy from interactions the same way we do. Just don't go sniffing strangers' butts because that's ok for dogs but weird for people.

When tired a dog sleeps. When thirsty they drink. Dogs were Zen before Zen was cool.

Action item: today, act like a dog. Be enthusiastic and forgiving and curious.

17 JULY
"Money can buy you a fine dog, but only love can make him wag his tail."

Kinky Friedman

Love can't be bought, only freely given. Dogs and children know this, but unfortunately we forget it as we become adults.

Dogs will play with a stick or sleep on the ground. They don't need $50 chew toys or $300 beds, they'd rather curl up on your lap. They want the attention, the time, the things that money can't buy that shows that you really care. Same with kids: making a tank out of an old box and playing with them for an hour one evening is worth more than a several hundred dollar toy to most eight year olds. And deep down, it's the same with most people. Giving your spouse a BMW will get them excited for a bit, but giving them your time (especially if you are busy) and a single rose is more meaningful. The best things in life don't have price tags but rather represent a little bit of your soul.

One thing about dogs and kids is that they understand consistency, even though they can not verbalize it. They get the fact that if someone picks them up every day, that if someone takes them for walks and/or tucks them into bed every night, then the person who does it cares. That having breakfast regularly together and giving that little one (puppy or person) full attention on a schedule is recognized, much more than sporadic attention. An apple a day keeps the doctor away, and a dose of love daily is worth more than once a month over the top display that fades over the days and weeks.

Show that you love them in the little things: petting the dog, rubbing your kid's head and smiling at them, bringing your love their morning coffee and leaving it on the nightstand to slowly awaken them. Take a few moments out of your day to message the one you adore a picture of their favorite flower, or a meme that they would like. Talk to your kid about dinosaurs or ponies or whatever they are fascinated about. Get down on the floor and drive the cars or play with the Legos for two minutes when you get home, it will be the highlight of their day and something they will talk about when they come back from college fifteen years later.

The little things are the big things when magnified by the emotional lens.

We effuse praise on our pets (Who's a good boy?! You're a good boy! Yes you are!) and play with them. When was the last time you did the equivalent to your team at work, or your kids? Just as your cat will purr if you give her attention, or your dog wag their tail wildly, so too will the people in your life if shown genuine affection and attention.

Action item: what is one little and free thing you can do for the people closest to you to show them you love them? Do it.

18 JULY

"It's not the size of the dog in the fight, it's the size of the fight in the dog."

Mark Twain

My son Liam (curly red hair, big blue eyes, total heartbreaker) was by far the smallest kid in his day care classes. Every six months when he was moved into the next older class he would walk in, look around, and go knock over the biggest kid in the room. Three times in a row, each time with me getting a call from the Director of the center.

"Don't you know what he's doing?" I finally asked her.

"What?"

"Like the new prisoner, the fresh fish in the jail. The littlest kid is showing everyone he's the toughest and not to be messed with. He's asserting that he might be small but he's not to be messed with." She didn't realize that my mini-me was asserting his authority and sending a message to any would-be bullies: I might be tiny but my spirit is bigger than you can ever beat.

The story of the underdog outperforming and winning because of heart and guts is ancient. David versus Goliath. The Spartans at Thermopylae. The Colonies versus The British Empire. The Miracle on Ice. Buster Douglas taking down Mike Tyson. Erin Brockovich.

Right makes might, not the other way around.

The little guy who believes in their heart and soul has an advantage over the big guy that is used to winning, because the little guy will tap into everything they have, and because they have been disadvantaged, has more inside to draw out and use. The poor scrappy kid will become the best salesman or fighter because they HAVE TO. Chris Gardner's life is the script for the movie "The Pursuit of Happiness", and he succeeded against the longest of odds because he had to for his son. I dare you to watch that movie and not root for him.

The scrappy start up taking on the entrenched giant conglomerate? The nerd with the huge heart winning the love of the beauty queen? The poor teenage genius enters the science fair with her idea that leads to a new cure and the scholarship, allowing her to be the first in her family to attend college.

We want the underdog to win, because we see ourselves in them and wish we had the resolve to take on and beat the giants. It makes us alive, and instills hope. We vicariously live their victories.

Action item: find an underdog movie and watch it.

"I always want fighting spirit first."

Claudio Raineri

The Boston Red Sox team that broke The Curse of the Bambino was a bunch of Idiots. They were a scrappy bunch, who came back from three games down against the New York Yankees, the first team in baseball history to claw back from a 3-0 deficit. Even now it hurts to write about it. But they did it, fighting back from down 4-3 in the sixth inning of Game 4 to avoid the sweep and win four games in a row, then went on to win their first World Series in 86 years. Fighting spirit exemplified. Never admit you are licked.

"Do not go gentle into that good night" as Dylan Thomas raged. "A true champion will fight through anything." Floyd Mayweather Jr.

Guts and grit will carry someone further than lazy natural talent. The little kid on the playground with something to fight for will stop the biggest bully, because they have fighting spirit that they unleash against the larger opponent that is dominating others out of a position of internal weakness instead of strength.

"Never give up. Never surrender!" Commander Taggert. "Never, never, never give up." Sir Winston Churchill. "Can't stop me!" David Goggins

The fighting spirit is what allowed 300 to stand against the might of Persia. It led a scrappy bunch of poorly trained and equipped farmers to hold off the British. It is the Veteran fighting their PTSD. You are not alone, do not give in!

The fighting spirit has helped countless single mothers and fathers study into the wee hours of the night to get a degree after busting their butt all day, to give their family a better life. It has kept that kid with cancer fighting, even when their own body has turned against them. It is what keeps the parent of the special needs child going day after day and year after year, fighting an unbeatable foe but refusing to give in because it would mean their child loses. It is the lover of the addict that will fight that demon with them minute by minute, knowing that it can come back at any time but refusing to let the person they love succumb to the darkness.

Fight. Do not go gentle into the good night.

Action item: we all have a demon we battle, an enemy that could overwhelm us at any point. What are you fighting? How, or from who, can you draw strength and increase your fighting spirit so that you can look at that darkness and say "not today"?

20 JULY

"It is good to be competitive and have a fighting spirit, but one should not go to extremes."

Karishma Tanna

As Kenny Rogers sang: you gotta know when to hold 'em, know when to fold 'em.

The hardest thing is to surrender, to let go of something or someone. To let a dream dissipate, because it either no longer suits you or because you realize that it is unattainable. This is a situation every athlete faces at some point, the realization they are not good enough to compete at the next level (college, pros, Olympics, etc) or that they no longer have the physical skills and desire to do what it takes and retirement beckons. And it is even more difficult with a relationship.

Knowing when not to fight is as important as knowing when to fight. When the person you love is all twisted up and just wants an excuse to explode, it might not be the best time to point out a flaw or make a comment. It might be better to just back away slowly and give them space.

Hunters and snipers learn when to not take the shot.

It is at times more difficult to not get into the verbal engagement, because even though emotionally we want to fight we know intellectually that no good can come from it and it is better to say nothing and let the emotions dissipate. This applies in the office and the home. And especially on social media.

If you have been competitive your entire life, learning to take it easy because of a back injury or after a surgery is maddening. Tapering before a marathon when you've been pushing hard for months takes more effort than lacing up your shoes and doing a 10km, but is better for you at that point. Rest is as important as training, and the elite athletes know this.

Learning to say "yes dear" and take one for the team (even if you are right) will avoid a Pyrrhic Victory that will land you on the couch or in the doghouse. Winning by losing is an ancient tactic in war and love. Avoiding a trap or battle is a smart maneuver. Not fighting means you can't lose.

As Bruce Lee demonstrated in Enter the Dragon, The Art of Fighting Without Fighting is sometimes the best way to win. Avoiding the dangerous situation is the best way to not get hurt.

Action item: what are you fighting for with all of your might, that you need to let just happen?

21 July

""Every day is a major balancing act that I have to figure out and coordinate."

Jocko Willink

People look at high performers and assume that they are machines, that every day is regimented and perfect. This is hilarious to those of us that know that every day we are juggling flaming chainsaws while jumping on a pogo stick through a field of gopher holes that randomly shoot lava or slime into the air.

Successful people are not masters of everything in our world, much to our chagrin. We are like everyone else, doing the best that we can. Maybe we just have figured out how to screw up less often. Maybe we have used habit stacking (per James Clear's Atomic Habits) to at least have some predictably decent outcomes every day (workout, read a little, eat a decent breakfast) before the chaos spins things out of control as all too often happens. Maybe we are just good at not letting any one thing get too far out of control, and being able to shift gears and give the extra attention when needed so that on average we end up producing decently overall. Maybe we just win really big in one arena and it allows us to paper over or compensate for the other shortfalls. Every successful individual has their own story of their success.

Every morning after my initial routine (that gives me at least a baseline of physical and mental activity), I write down the most important things I have to achieve that day and the few things that I'd like to get done. Typically these include something physical (beyond my fifteen to thirty minute baseline), writing, a few key work tasks and one or two personal items. Then I try to get all the critical and most of the "nice to do's" done. Does it happen every day? Nope. But does it happen often enough for me to make consistent progress overall? Yep.

Some days I'm in full-on work mode and mentally dead after a fifteen-hour day. Some days I get to run ten miles. Other days I'm Dad of the Year for what I do with the hooligans. Am I ever all three in a single day? Yeah, right. And monkeys might fly out of my butt (Wayne's World! Wayne's World! Ruhr rur rur ruh ruhhhh!).

Someone told me once that we are all juggling balls of health, family, finance, relationships, etc. Some of these balls are glass, and must be kept in the air or else they will shatter. Some are rubber and can be dropped and either bounce or be picked back up when appropriate. Or someone can grab the ball from us and hold it for us until we are ready for it. Whatever makes sense in your situation. That is the secret to balance, and it takes time and mistakes to figure it out.

Action item: what balls are you juggling that are glass, and which are rubber?

22 JULY
"Focus on being balanced-success is balance."

Laila Ali

Being single minded and relentlessly myopically focused is what it takes to become a champion in any particular field, but being the absolute best in one field but a dumpster fire in everything else and a horrible human being is still a tragic failure. Having other outlets, other passions creates a more rounded human being, and a sphere is perfectly round and balanced.

Massachusetts Institute of Technology (MIT)'s motto is mens et manus: mind and hand. Balance of mental and physical.

The college athlete who focuses just on athletics and not the education (often at a very well known educational institution) is out of balance, and even if they make twenty-five million dollars but don't learn and complete their degree is unbalanced. So too with my brethren nerds that spend fifteen hours a day with their nose in a book (or computer screen) but can't partake in the joy of physical play and develop their body enough to support that incredible cerebral cortex they have. You might be on your way to being a super success in your profession, but do you have meaningful friendships that keep you grounded and your ego in check? Do you have that friend that is almost the opposite of you in many ways, but balances you out and makes you better?

Balance, Daniel-san. Must have balance!

I admit: I am uber-driven, overly competitive and don't relax well. I am probably borderline psychotic in my demands of myself, and expect others to raise their game to achieve their potential. I am in many ways "too much". So I work on developing balance: enjoying sunrises and sunsets, savoring the time to cook a healthy meal, doing non-competitive things for the joy of doing them. It takes a lot of effort for me to stop trying to win at everything. And I suck at it, I admit. So I spend time with some people that make me slow down and enjoy the moments.

The human body exists in a state of homeostasis, a dynamic and ever changing balance with our environment. We adjust somewhat to heat and cold, darkness and light. We thrive in a variety of places and manners, unlike most other animals. We adapt easily, and this resilience is because we do not exclusively evolve for a limited niche, be it in the world or workplace or our society. We do not exclusively have one function in the universe, nor in our relationships with others. We are meant to have and be a variety of things at different levels, and broadening those horizons in a balanced manner creates a better human being.

Action item: grab a piece of paper. What are your most extreme traits, that those closest to you would tell you (good or not so much)? How can you smooth those out a little, to become more balanced as a human being?

23 JULY

"The delicate balance of mentoring someone is not creating them in your own image, but giving them the opportunity to create themselves."
Stephen Spielberg

My mother cursed me. She wished upon me a child just like I was. And as she said, I got three of them. Heaven help me. Before my mom died I apologized to her profusely.

Creating clones is not what we want, either with our kids or the people we mentor. Even a near perfect replica of ourselves is not what the world needs, because everything grows and changes and evolves or it is left behind and becomes less competitive and eventually antiquated. My mini-me is somewhat different than I am because the world he is growing up in is not the one that I did, and what my kids need to grow into independent and productive young men is different than what it was like during the 1970's when we rode in the back of pickup trucks and were able to go in the General Store and pick up cigarettes for Mom on our own.

Better to be a perfect, optimized version of yourself than 90% of someone else. Yes, adopt good qualities and ideas from others but personalize them to yourself and make them your own. Adopt and adapt instead of cut and paste copying because the latter loses some power and won't exactly fit the situations, whereas maximizing yourself (influenced and informed by others that have succeeded) is a more sustainable and flexible approach. I want my mentees to have some of my aspects and language and insight, but to be themselves at full power.

One of the most important things we can do for those that come after us is to make sure they understand we are not perfect, to not build a cult of personality around us but to understand the why behind the what that we do. Why I am obsessive about tracking my numbers (work or workout) to hit minimal thresholds and what it means to me, so that they can discover their own numbers and build their own consistency. Why I say "I love you" probably too often, or won't drink ice water. Understanding these things lets those I am developing to see the rationale (or totally irrational reasoning) behind my choices so they can see why or why not these make sense to how I operate, and how they will choose to work going forward.

"Do not seek to follow in the footsteps of the wise. Seek what they sought." Basho.

Our mission for our children (biological, adopted, or influenced) is not to make them perfect for the life we lead, but better prepared for the lives they will lead in the future.

Action item: what is one aspect of your personality, or foible in your actions, that you took from your parents? What about your mentor? Now look at your children (or younger people in your life): what from you are they adopting, and why?

24 JULY

"A mentor enables a person to achieve. A hero shows what achievement looks like."

John C. Mather

A mentor helps you to develop a vision, and trains you in the skills needed to achieve said vision. But the actual achievement thereof? That's all on you. No one else can be the hero for you. That's your job, to slay your individual dragon and fight your nemesis. Because that is what heroes do.

Traditionally the mentor is an old man, typically one who has been there, done that, and made some mistakes that we later discover as they move the plot along. Think Obi Wan Kenobi helping Young Skywalker, partially to make up for his failures to Old Skywalker. Or Dumbledore and Harry Potter. Sirs Freddie Laker and Richard Branson. Jobs and Zuckerberg. The younger one learns from the battles of the older one (sometimes even against the same opponent like Voldemort or hubris) and goes beyond the achievements of their wizened advisor. The tale is ancient yet relevant to every new generation, as those of us who were the young Chosen Ones slowly become the silver haired mentors and teach the next generation of heroes and heroines.

The mentor trains the hero, pushing them beyond their limited beliefs. Obi Wan putting the helmet on Luke and then telling him to "trust his feelings". Sir Freddie teaching young Richard the Lionhearted about the ins and outs of the British airline industry. The transfer of skills and lessons down from one generation to the next, which personalizes and enhances them based upon their individual strengths and experiences, is a core tenet of the hero myth across populations and eras. The hero then fights, facing potentially insurmountable odds like both Vader and the Emperor, or a world unready for social media (and no monetization plan). Often the hero fights a more powerful version of the foe that humbled the mentor, so needs their talent and belief combined with the wisdom of those that came before to achieve victory. The hero must travel (a classic theme in the great stories), leaving all they know (including family) to grow into what they must be to turn the tide against darkness, be it an embodiment of evil (like Voldemort) or conquer numerous opponents to carve out an empire (inefficiency, byzantine regulations, nature, apathy, etc.). Rarely is the hero left unscarred or unchanged from their battles, because great victories are never without risk or sacrifice. The hero always pays a price.

When the student is ready the master appears. The master then steps aside and lets the student fight their battle. This is the way it has been, and will be.

Action item: who is your mentor, and how have they prepared you for your battles? Who are you mentoring, so that they can go and fight their own battles?

25 JULY
"A hero is someone who has given his or her life to something bigger than oneself."

Joseph Campbell

A hero is an idea made flesh, that will sacrifice that body for the idea.

Scrawny Steve Rogers became the embodiment of the American Fighting Man because the Super Soldier Serum enhanced his body, but he was already dedicated to those ideals, trying over and over and over again to enlist and serve because he didn't like bullies and believed in the ideal of freedom. Take away the uniform and shield, and he is still Captain America.

Beowulf was the embodiment of the ideals of strength and courage for his era, the pinnacle of manhood. He died as an old king, protecting his kin and kingdom in a heroic battle. The cycle from young warrior facing down monsters to old leader dying with sword and shield in hand to protect his people. A thousand years later he is still sung about and serves as an archetype.

Hawk and Dove, representing the balance between peace and aggression. Cloak and Dagger for the dark and light. Both partnerships represent contrasting but necessary approaches that when combined defeat enemies as varied as the imaginations of the authors.

Mahatma Gandhi. Jackie Robinson. Nelson Mandela.

Some heroes are created as the embodiment of the beliefs and myths of the people. Some are people that step up and do heroic things and risk themselves because of an idea worth fighting and even dying for.

There are millions of relatively unknown or unsung heroes. The football coach that shielded kids (Aaron Feis) with his own body. Vacationers Alek Skarlatos, Spencer Stone, and Anthony Sadler stopping a massacre on a train in Paris. The man in the picture in front of the tanks at Tiananmen Square. The officer that gets the kids out of a dangerous family situation, and the foster parent that takes them in. Not all heroes wear capes, nor appear on the news.

The little boy facing down the dog to protect his kid sister, or the older sister sacrificing in a variety of ways to take care of their little brother. Stories that happen across the country daily that will never be heard over the noise of politics and other negative fear mongering "news". These heroes do not get held up publicly as they should, to serve as a beacon for other regular people that step up in dangerous circumstances to save others.

Action item: who are your heroes? Why? What positive attributes do they embody?

"You are only as good as your team."

Dominique Wilkins

Dan Marino never won a Superbowl. Ted Williams and Barry Bonds never won the World Series. Charles Barkley never won the title either. They may be Hall of Famers, even MVPs. But none of them can be called "Champion".

Darren Fenster won a World Series with the Angels. Bobby Bouchey (not the Waterboy) won a Stanley Cup with the Canadians. Who?

Who are they?

Champions. Because TEAMS win championships, not individuals.

My kids are reminded that they play for Team Templin, and we win or lose together. If one doesn't do their chores, no one gets to go to the amusement park. I drove into the gates of The Great Escape and turned around in the parking lot (on my birthday!) because one of them wouldn't behave. We all lost together that day.

SEAL teams all win (everyone comes home safe) or all lose together, and winning is dependent upon each member doing their job.

Fraternities and Sororities know that if one of their members does not live up to the academic or moral/legal standards of the group (and those set by the Dean of Students), they will all lose because that Chapter will be shut down. So yes, you become your Brother (or Sister)'s keeper. Because the team wins or loses together.

The best small offices or business teams I have seen have a shared bonus pool. If the team wins, everyone gets part of the rewards, the spoils of victory. This is the way pirate ships operate and the profit incentive is powerful (as is the survival one of startup companies) to get everyone going above and beyond to win as a group.

There is an old African proverb: if you want to go fast, go alone. If you want to go far, go in a team. Teams can do things individuals can't, and in the end winning as a group is more fun than winning on your own.

Action item: is your team (work or family) committed to winning together? How can you be better prepared as a group to win your particular championship?

"Bad attitudes will ruin your team."

Terry Bradshaw

It was once said that Terry Bradshaw couldn't spell "CAT" if you gave him the C and the A. But he could win Superbowls, and his Steelers teams of the 1970's loved playing with him for his attitude, even if they had some of the baddest men in the league (Mean Joe Greene, LC Greenwood, Jack Lambert). Attitude will destroy a winning team or allow a mediocre one to triumph.

Attitude is not everything, but it is the differentiator. It is the margin of victory or defeat.

Cancer will spread and destroy your body, even if you look healthy from the outside. A bad attitude will destroy a company, even if the stock price is high. It will rip apart a family, even if their holiday card shows smiling faces and the letter that comes with it is all glowing and chipper. The bad attitude will rot all of them from the inside until the disease finally shows to the world, and then it is too late to correct.

Dave Mustaine was a great guitarist. But he was kicked out of Metallica because he was too out of control even for a band nicknamed "Alcohollica" for their drunkenness and antics. His attitude was so bad, it overwhelmed his talent and the band had addition by subtraction when they removed him.

Hell Week is designed not just to push someone to their limit, break them down and rebuild better but to also weed out those with bad attitudes.

Walt Bettinger, the CEO of Charles Schwabb, takes candidates out to breakfast and ensures that the staff mess up the order, to see how the candidate reacts. He purposely applies pressure as an attitude check before hiring someone, to prevent a bad hire due to a bad attitude.

Herb Kelleher's joking attitude about himself but super serious approach to his job (and commitment to customer happiness and retention) is baked into the very essence of Southwest Airlines, two decades after he stopped leading the organization he helped found.

Attitude determines altitude.

Great attitudes produce great results.

Action item: check your attitude. Is it positive, negative, or neutral? What would it do for your team if you had a slightly better attitude for a little bit?

28 JULY
"People may hear your words, but they feel your attitude."

John C. Maxwell

Roughly 7% of verbal communication is the words that are used. Over 90% is tone, body language, cadence, and the other unspoken but apparent messages. Just like a dog can feel your fear, another person can feel your attitude even if you don't roll your eyes.

Intent comes through. If your arms are crossed in front of you (closing you off) you send a message of unwillingness to listen or learn. If you are open standing, you convey a willingness that can change the dynamic and discussion.

I know a woman that is an engineer, and comes across as angry in everything that she does. Her negative attitude is in her tone and volume, her body language screams that she is ready for confrontation, and she wonders why she is not considered management material. Or is divorced.

One of the things I remember from my initial sales training was that we should smile before we started, and take a moment to look in a mirror and smile multiple times throughout the day. The smile is heard over the phone (pre-Zoom world), and alters the conversation if the other person can hear your positive attitude through the line.

Salespeople are also taught to have confidence, to assume a Superman or Wonder Woman pose for a few seconds before going into a meeting. This decreases cortisol in their system, thus making them more relaxed and increases the probability of success measurably. The attitude influences the outcome.

Attitude literally is everything in communication, which is the backbone of interactions, persuasion, and sales. Learning to communicate better will yield superior results across multiple dimensions, and it is all rooted in the attitude.

One way to have a better attitude is to be grateful. The fact that you can get out of bed. The fact that both your eyes work. The fact that you have clean water. These are all things to pause and be grateful for.

Or show some kindness to another. Text that friend that is having difficulty. Send a meme to your siblings. Hold a door for someone, or compliment a total stranger. One moment to brighten someone else's day will instantly improve your attitude, thus making your day better and more productive by whatever measurement you chose to use.

Action item: do five things today to either appreciate what you have, or help someone else out. It will improve your attitude and your effectiveness.

29 JULY

"No matter how busy you are, you must take time to make the other person feel important."

Mary Kay Ash

The golden rule says do unto others as you would have them do unto you. The platinum rule says do unto others as they would wish was done to them.

The most beautiful sound to someone is their own name. Use it, even if it is the waiter or the Uber driver. Make them feel important (because they are), and they will have a better day. So will you.

I met the CEO of one of America's Most Admired Corporations a few decades back. He wanted to meet all of the interns, to shake their hands and make them feel welcome to the company. Those interns became among the most productive members of the company over the next two decades. Maybe it's anecdotal, but that company was chosen as a Top 10 Internship program from that point to the end of the CEO's tenure and beyond, partially for making these rawest recruits feel like they were important.

When someone new wanted to join our Cub Scout Pack, I remember the old Packmaster getting down on one knee and talking to the boy eye to eye, making him feel like he was special (because he was). Even decades later his former Scouts remember him fondly for how he treated them from before they signed up to the day they finished.

The handyman in our office always gets a hello, and if possible a few minutes of time not because I want to make sure my roof doesn't leak but because he is a human being, and the moments I spend with him improve his day and can ripple out to help others. Butterfly effect in a positive manner, because we can do little things to brighten the world in ways we can't measure easily but can execute easily.

Imagine if your young children felt important and empowered by having a couple of chores that were "their job", and they knew how critical it was for the family that they fulfil these duties. They would start developing professional pride early, they would want additional responsibilities, and they can relieve the overall burden sooner than otherwise would happen. Make them feel important, and they become important. They contribute.

Action item: today, use people's first names if they are helping you in any way, and tell them "thank you" and "good job."

30 JULY

"The most important thing is to try and inspire people so that they can be great in whatever they want to do."

Kobe Bryant

How many players in the NBA today say that Kobe was their favorite and their inspiration? Just like Kobe said Jordan was his.

How many Major Leaguers wear #2 because of Derek Jeter?

How many young women went into law because of Ruth Bader Guinsburg?

Eddie Van Halen inspired thousands of guitarists, some professional and others who just play for fun.

Teachers can inspire kids every day, by encouraging them and helping them read and exciting their imagination and making them want to learn.

At work, are you an inspiration to the newer people there? Or are you a jerk, a curmudgeon, and a selfish individual who serves as a warning or worse?

Even a little kid can inspire others. The kid that rakes the leaves of his elderly neighbor and others see it (even grownups) and go and do a good deed for another. The kid courageously battling a disease that makes people appreciate their kids a bit more, and spend some extra time with them. How many people have entered the military because of a book they read, or because of the example of someone in their community?

Bill Nye the Science Guy has helped tens of thousands of kids want to be engineers and scientists. Even a geek in a lab can inspire that one kid that goes on to change the world with an invention or innovation, because they saw someone doing research and said "that's so cool!" and started studying for a reason.

Be excellent and inspire the next generation, whether it is your kids seeing you always be polite to people or taking the new intern at work under your wing. Eventually you will be the wind beneath their wings and they could fly higher than you ever could.

Action item: choose one person in your circle of influence that you can help become better than they thought they could be. Invest a little time and see what grows.

31 JULY
"A good teacher can inspire hope, ignite the imagination and instill a love of learning."
Brad Henry

We all know that teacher that is the dream killer, that tells kids (or told them like my 5th grade teacher told me) that "you can't". Be the polar opposite of that person.

Make someone see the world with rose colored glasses full of potential.

Make the kids dream bigger, that they could go to space or build a company or be a great leader, if they are willing to learn how and do the hard work.

Make them confident, so they can stand up in front of a group and convey their ideas. Maybe they will be a business founder, maybe they will be a performer. Maybe, just maybe they will be a teacher because of you.

Let them chase tigers in red weather and imagine dragons, sail on pirate ships of the mind and ride Einstein's light beam. Make the Magic School bus be a vehicle to explore their world and things beyond their current limits. All art, all technology was once just a dream so let them dream big to build a bigger future.

Encourage your kids to read, to draw, to think. To explore. To capture lightning bugs and turn over rocks and listen to birds and other creatures, because inspiration comes from all over.

Instill in them a desire to learn that has nothing to do with school and everything to do with understanding and growing. Plant the seeds and water them so that their curiosity is never sated, so that questions lead to more questions and more. Put them on the path of never-ending learning, of exploring new areas just because they seem interesting. Even if the knowledge does not check a box for a curriculum or a degree, it could be as useful as Steve Jobs taking a calligraphy class in college that led to the extensive fonts available today. Who knows where their educational explorations could take them?

Spark their fire, so they can light the world with their burning desire to learn.

Action item: do something today to teach someone, and inspire them to go beyond and learn more.

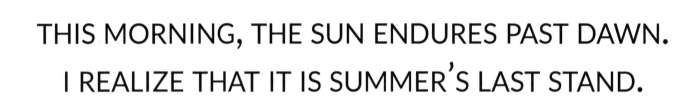

THIS MORNING, THE SUN ENDURES PAST DAWN.
I REALIZE THAT IT IS SUMMER'S LAST STAND.

Sarah Baume

01 AUGUST

"You are only given a little spark of madness. You mustn't lose it."

Robin Williams

One of the premier comedic minds of the past fifty years, Robin Williams made the world laugh but hid a dark secret of pain and self-hatred that ultimately claimed his life and light, and the world is much darker for it.

That spark of madness can light a lamp of hope in yourself and others. It can ignite a passion that will influence others and bring aid or joy for generations. A single candle can light a thousand others and brighten the night. How many charities exist because of a small spark?

That spark is all that it takes to make an engine turn over, rev, and take you places. You might not be a Formula 1 Race Car, but a 1972 pickup truck with a good spark can still be functional and do some solid work. Even an eighty-year old with spark can get up and go.

That spark of madness can be the gleam in your eye that leads to a joke that gets someone to smile and changes their day. Share that spark, because at some point you will need to have it shared with you.

Be an imp. Play the trickster, to keep that little spark going and spread it. There are times when disrupting the status quo and routine at work is what is necessary for an organization to advance. Keep that secret flame burning, that little weird passion that others try to blow out. It could be what lights your fire and leads to your next career when the nameless faceless corporate suits decide to "strategically reduce headcount" i.e. layoff a bunch of people to save money and protect the stock price.

That little bit of madness could inspire you to write a book: The Lord of The Rings universe began with a line on the back of a paper "In a hole in the ground there lived a hobbit." That line was the spark that Tolkien turned into a flame that has reached music (Led Zeppelin), movies, and dreamers the world over. Is it madness to brighten the world with your light? Tesla had a spark of madness and you have lights because of it, even more so than Edison.

Everyone of us has that little bit in us that is off, a slight syncopation of jazz in our classically trained thoughts and expectations. It is that discordant bit that drove Frank Zappa to create his off kilter and brilliant music. It can make your world sweeter and more interesting too, and be the inspiration for others. Keep your madness and share it.

Action item: what is that one really weird thing you hide? Why hide your light under a basket, when you could brighten someone else's life with your spark of madness?

02 AUGUST
"I may be crazy, but it keeps me from going insane."

Road Hazards (my running team)

We all suffered during the Covid Pandemic. Kids missed a year of school, almost half the restaurants closed permanently, and mental health concerns will be carried for decades as the entire world was upended. Yet we survived.

Cookie baking Fridays at lunch? Yep. Extra chocolate chips. Blanket forts? Of course. Even if you didn't have kids. Remember the fascination with Tiger King? Yeah, Carole Baskin probably did it. And everyone watched. It was crazy but kept us from going totally off the deep end. For the most part.

In the kingdom of the mad, the half crazy can be queen. Or king. Or as I prefer to be called "Lord High Imperator of All Existence, Known and Unknown." You can choose your own title in your little patch of madness, to keep from going totally crazy. Many started drinking too much, divorce rates went through the roof. Domestic abuse cases will be uncovered for decades. These are the bad examples. Insane more than crazy.

Having "Dress Up Day" at your work video conference? Harmless and fun. Nice tutu and Darth Vader mask. Glad you wore a matching tie. Playing "Elf on the Shelf" through the summer? Weird but ok. Playing Calvinball with your kids while wearing viking helmets? Been there. Yesterday.

Photoshopping yourself into National Geographic pictures and writing stories about your adventure with your crush in Tahiti so you don't go Jimmy Buffett and shoot the refrigerator? Beats the alternative to cabin fever, which people in the Northern latitudes certainly understand from experience. Add the sunlamp, Haiwaiian shirt and some sand under your toes. Run a backyard marathon (even if it is only 26.2 times around the postage stamp backyard), with local kids giving you lemonade every couple of laps and a cheering section? That's next Saturday. Have to make a medal the size of a garbage can lid because as the only participant, I win!

Countless people have survived worse than what we are dealing with by taking mental refuge in offbeat things. Political prisoners, Holocaust survivors, and Prisoners of War have all used this technique. We can get through whatever rough patch with a little bit of craziness.

And you can apply these ideas in the middle of winter, or school break when you have had it up to HERE with the kids, or on a rainy day, or just because the office needs a jolt. Crazy is not to be contained.

Action item: make a weird hat or outfit. Wear it. Laugh at yourself.

03 AUGUST
"It doesn't hurt to feel sad from time to time."

Willie Nelson

Know what you call someone who is ALWAYS happy? Detached from reality. Even Mr. Rogers was sad sometimes, it is a normal part of the human condition. Not feeling sadness at times is actually a sign of something not being right upstairs, because the world is filled with bad things and bad breaks, and not acknowledging this and dealing with it is avoidance behavior at the highest level and unhealthy. When reality crashes into them, it will be bad. Very bad.

Everyone has negative things in their life: it is not all cute puppy dogs wrestling or butterflies fluttering around while a Disney Princess sings. We all have some forms of trauma, whether it was losing a parent early or poverty in childhood or injury/disease or something random ruining a dream. And if you haven't had someone rip out your heart, you've probably lived bubble-wrapped in an ivory tower or never tried to actually share deep relationships with another person. These things happen, it's called "life", and it sucks at times. But as my dad says about old age: it beats the alternative. Dealing with negative emotions is like having shadows that contrast against the light. It is like having winter so that you can appreciate the summer more. The contrast is what makes the good times so wonderful.

We have all struggled with darkness at some point. The blues that we can't shake for days or longer, when getting out of bed is between difficult and impossible. When the clouds gather in your head and everything presses down, and your brain is fuzzy with negative thoughts. As Mark Manson says: assumed inability to solve our problems causes us to feel miserable and helpless. But the flip side of this is true too: when we feel bad and are having a horrible, terrible, no good very bad day and can find a way to work through it, to suck it up and go through the rough patch, we build the capability to handle future difficulties. We build our resilience for the inevitable bad days and events that will occur.

Our society has become much like Brave New World, where everyone is on Soma (whether in a pill or on their phone or other source) to evade negative emotions. Instead of avoidance behavior though, we need to embrace the dips of emotion, the down times that build our resolve and prepare us for the future. To look at the darkness and not flinch, knowing we can handle this, and whatever else will come instead of hiding from our demons and the environment in a self deluding haze. It's ok to be angry or sad at times, just like it is going to rain so we can have flowers.

Action items: what was the last thing that made you truly sad, to the point of crying? Think about it, embrace that emotion and all the memories around it, because there are probably some positives around it that you have forgotten in burying the negative.

04 AUGUST
"Johnny Cash has always been larger than life."

Kris Kristofferson

The Man in Black was not just a star, or even a superstar. Cash was and remains an icon. Even among The Highwaymen (Kristofferson, Waylon Jennings, and Willie Nelson with Cash), Johnny was the powerhouse of the supergroup with the recognizable gravel in his voice.

The man lived a hard life: cotton picking and a flood and losing his brother to a sawmill accident as a child, the failed marriage and drug abuse and numerous incidents with the law before struggling and earning redemption. These shaped his world view (and that gruff baritone) and led to hits like Folsom Prison Blues and a life of activism for the poor and downtrodden. Many of the issues throughout his life were of his own creation through his decisions, but Johnny Cash's successes (musically and personally) were his own too and serve as a template for other troubled geniuses struggling with early life trauma and the succubi of success.

Johnny's last series of Albums were called *The American I-VI*, and his comeback story is as American as they come. There is something uniquely American about the poor country boy coming from nothing and becoming somebody, or messing up their life through poor choices and straightening themselves out to achieve peace of mind and return to the top but as a more humble and better version of themselves. The arc of Cash's story, the rise from abject poverty to the heights of fame, the decline through his falling to temptation and then facing his demons to rise again is almost out of folklore, and serves as both warning and example for hungry and talented young performers.

Cash represents a forgotten, hardscrabble era of our history where family was the center of life and society, where even a radio was a luxury and hard work combined with self entertainment was the rule instead of the exception. Where people would do whatever it took to survive in a dangerous environment, and the grit in his voice reflected the grit in his soul that gave Cash the emotional strength to serve his country, overcome his issues, and use his fame to help the less powerful. His life was an epic adventure and morality tale, and just one of a multitude of complex individuals from this timeframe in our history that are fading in the distance like the cowboy into the sunset. Before the Man in Black fades into the night, check out his music and legacy and see what resonates in you like the strings of his Tennessee flat top box.

Action item: use whatever music app you prefer and listen to Johnny Cash. Feel his voice and the emotions, listen to the stories he poured his heart into. Having more Cash is always good.

05 AUGUST

"I was a bigger-than-life persona before I was anyone in my own mind."

Raquel Welch

Six year old Cassius Clay was the champion of the world in his mind. When he knocked out Sonny Liston the world realized what young Mohammad Ali had already known and spent his life to become.

A scrawny ten year old in Kalamazoo Michigan was already wearing pinstripes in his heart. He later won five World Series titles with those New York Yankees and became The Captain: Derek Jeter.

Steve Harvey believed in comedy so much he quit his job, ended up living in his car for three years, and ultimately became one of the most recognizable comics on the planet. Similar to Steve Martin two generations previously. Before the world knew who they were, in their minds they were on center stage.

Shania Twain started singing in bars at eight years old but saw herself on stage too.

Belief in yourself without work is just dreaming, but seeing yourself as you could be early and slaving away for years and decades to achieve your vision is the most common path to success known. It doesn't matter if that vision is the attorney studying for the bar picturing themselves as a partner in that big firm downtown, or the little girl collecting bugs and dreaming of being a biologist. Having a clear picture of who you can become and then daily working to become that image in reality is inspiring, both to the individual and people around them.

Think about your friends that have achieved their childhood dreams. How motivating are they, and how proud are you for them? Try to capture part of that and apply it to yourself. Just because you aren't five years old anymore doesn't mean you shouldn't have a vision for yourself and your future that you work towards becoming.

Action item: who do you want to be when you grow up? Start thinking like the YOU of five years from now, acting like that person. Be that person, until others see you as you see yourself.

06 AUGUST

"When something is important enough, you do it even if the odds are not in your favor."

Elon Musk

As Han Solo said: don't tell me the odds. If something is important enough, it doesn't matter how long of a longshot it is. You will take the risk and make the sacrifices to try and make it come true, whether it is building a business, getting into that college, or making that long distance relationship work. Because the payoff, the prize is worth the risk and the pain along the way.

Remember that the odds of something happening is based upon randomness in the universe. But not everything is independent: one choice leads to others, cutting off branches of potential outcomes and narrowing the list of results. Making good early choices influences the future steps and can reduce the odds and lead to more favorable outcomes.

Example: you want to build a business. Instead of just getting the licenses and permits, renting space, buying inventory and equipment and hoping to not be in the 90%+ that fail, maybe go about it a little smarter to bend the odds in your favor. Invest two hours on the internet in market research as to the profitability and pitfalls of the type of business you want to build. Search for competitors. Put together a list of needed assets and also assess your skills and shortfalls. Then look at how you could dip your toe into this venture in a low risk manner so instead of blowing your life savings you only risk a couple of weekends of work and a little bit of cash. Then when something goes not to plan (as ALWAYS happens) you can quickly learn and adjust and improve, and in the next mini-cycle be better, and then better, then better...

Break the HUGE thing into tiny pieces that you can control better, and your odds alter dramatically. There will always be risk in anything worthwhile. You take a risk walking out of the bedroom in the morning, you take a risk going to work or school, you take a risk every time you get behind the wheel or take public transportation. But you accept those risks with no question, and for relatively low payoff. Would you take a bigger risk to build a great company, or have an amazing experience, or for that person that you care deeply for? If the reward is worth it, any risk is acceptable.

The mathematician Blaise Pascal had a famous wager: would you bet a little bit of time for a potentially infinite payoff? The logical answer is yes. Now, would you bet an hour a day of your time for an incredible life, a top 5% of the population type of life? You are asked to make that sort of wager every day, with how you allocate your time through your daily choices. Even though only one out of twenty can be top 5% by definition, you can increase your odds by making better little decisions each day, and if that goal is worth it the sacrifices and little risks are all worth it.

Action item: what are you willing to take tremendous risk for? What is worth the pains and sacrifice to achieve, no matter how long the odds?

07 AUGUST
"A new idea must not be judged by its immediate results."

Nikola Tesla

1901: "Man will not fly for 50 years." Wilbur Wright. Guess Wright was wrong. 1926: TV will never be worth the investment. 1977: "There is no reason anyone would want a computer in their home." Ken Olson, Founder of Digital Equipment Corp. Early 2000's: Online shopping will never be significant.

Cars, cell phones, and even light bulbs were all ridiculed as wastes of time and money by the establishment. The "experts" that are entrenched are almost always wrong. Women voting. Equal rights for all Americans. Support for neurodiverse individuals in the marketplace. All of these were not considered rational and reasonable at the outset.

Some of Tesla's ideas were not able to be implemented for over fifty years. Some of Einstein's predictions were not seen for a century after he proposed them. They were both still right. You probably have an idea that can make your workplace better. Guess what? It will be ridiculed and rejected. People will be scared of it, maybe even saying you're being lazy or that you are corrupting the youth. Your boss won't force you to drink poison a la Socrates, but it is definitely not going to be a picnic. Hell, they might not even implement the brilliant idea that radically improves the company until after you leave (nooo, that never happened with me. Nope, never.). Still take the risk and bring the idea forward, because it will make things better and if it is implemented while you are there you get to reap the benefits. It might take years to overcome the office inertia, but when it does happen you'll rightly pat yourself on the back for your contribution.

When you start a workout program, within a few days you are probably sore, tired, and always hungry. Should you abandon the plan to improve your health just because the scale doesn't reflect the effort for weeks? Is the negative of muscle discomfort or hunger pangs for a little bit worth not fitting into that outfit, or eventually having a heart attack? The toughest part is a little bit after you start anything worthwhile, when you are expending energy and effort and literally have nothing to show for it (or even have moved backwards a little).

Don't give up, you are on the right path. Whether you are quitting smoking, building a company, or trying to improve the dynamic with the love of your life, you will have to fight the tendency of people to NOT change even if it is critical for success. Have faith, time is your ally.

Action item: what is a relatively new idea that you have dismissed as preposterous? Take a few minutes and explore it again to see if its time has come.

08 AUGUST

"The future isn't just a place you'll go. It's a place you will invent."

Nancy Duarte

There is a really bad Jean Claude van Damme movie from 1993 called *Time Cop,* in which the lead bad guy travels back in time and tells his younger self to take a particular unethical action which enriches the future one tremendously. The elder version also tells the younger one "and knock off the candy bars", petting his own ample midsection. Imagine if future you could come back and give current you instructions, not like Bill and Ted in their Excellent Adventure but real guidance so that you can have a much brighter future.

It can happen. You can project yourself forward ten or fifteen years into the future that you want to see. Feel it, experience the life you want. What sort of house, where in the world? What does your career look like? What are you doing when not working, and who with? Soak up every detail of that future. Commit to memory the neighborhood. Hear the sounds and bask in the emotions. Now come back to the present.

What would the older you in that nice house tell the you from today? What warnings do they have (candy bars or otherwise), and what are the actions that you need to take to build that house in the future you have seen?

Einstein said that imagination is like the previews of the future, the coming attractions in the movie of your life. Now that you have seen it, you need to get to work to bring it to fruition.

And knock off the candy bars.

Action item: take a piece of paper. Write on the top the date a decade in the future. Describe your house. Write about your family at that point. Tell yourself about what you are doing for work. Be explicit about your future life. Now how do you get from here to there?

09 AUGUST
"For every moment, the future is becoming the past."

Thor Heyerdahl

Of the four dimensions we live in as humans, Time is the only one that moves in a single direction. From past to future it inevitably flows onward, and nothing we can do can halt the stream.

Those of us who are parents wish we could just capture those moments of joy with our kids, whether it is their first steps or carrying them asleep from the car, their arms around our neck as they snuggle into us and sigh. But we can't and those beautiful babies become obnoxious teenagers (probably just like we were) and eventually rational grown ups that we are proud of and who acknowledge we were right (if we are lucky).

That date we look forward to that eventually we look back on. Maybe tell our kids about how I met your mother, or wistfully because she got away, or the comedy of errors that happens so often. Under all scenarios it becomes a memory.

Stop.

Take a moment to appreciate that sunset and reflect on the day, both good and bad. Review and learn so the next day can be better on average than the previous ones, but savor the highpoints.

That sunrise. The little kid on the bike with their huge smile. The great piece of corn on the cob. That message from a friend you haven't talked to in too long. All the great little bits that are sprinkled throughout the day like gems sprinkled in a mine, flashing and beautiful sparkles.

Now what were your moments of weakness, where your temper got the best of you when someone wasn't doing their job right or that idiot driver? When could you have shown more patience to your kid, or empathy for that co-worker? Where in your day could you have been a better human or professional, and how do you modify yourself and your environment to make the next few days have less dips than today did?

The river of time is flowing. Instead of just floating along where the current takes you, take control of what you can in the stream of time and be captain of your ship.

Action item: What was one thing you can learn from yesterday so today is better?

10 AUGUST

"We must learn from the past, but we cannot dwell in the past."

Gina Haspel

If you don't learn from the past you might as well be a goldfish, floating around in your bowl and excited every time someone drops crumbs of food to you with no plan for the future until they find you belly up and flush you down the toilet.

If you are trapped in the past you are just as hopeless as a hamster, a furry little thing running on the wheel endlessly and not progressing until your heart gives out and they put you in a shoebox in the ground.

We are generally much more like the mice from Who Moved My Cheese by Spencer Johnson. Some people sit down and mope like Hem, or adapt like Haw when forced to do so. Both have learned from the past and refuse to let it go or only do so slowly. Even better you can be proactive: if you are reading this you are probably more like Scurry (the quick adopter) or even Sniff in that you are a change leader for yourself and your organization (work /family). The first two learn from the past but try to dwell there, the latter two learn from the past to craft the future.

The Japanese Kaizen idea of short cycle learning and adapting is easily repurposed to everyday life, whether in the office or your home. Learn from what you do and do it differently if need be. And don't be afraid to experiment a little to see if the process can be incrementally improved, such as cutting onions with a fan blowing the vapor away so you don't cry, or leaving a cup of coffee in a mug in the fridge (with the pot prepped and ready to go as you microwave your mug for that first jolt of Joe), or recording your sales activity so that you can deep dive into the numbers and improve your performance month over month.

Balance is the key, being informed by what has passed but not bound to it. Your genetics influence your future health, but do not automatically determine it. Through your choices (based on understanding and learning from others and your own experiences) you can exercise and diet appropriately to reduce the chances of obesity or heart disease, stave off the worst effects of Alzheimer's, and even extend both quality and quantity of life. But only be using that past as guidance for the present and future but in an adaptable manner.

Action item: what is something that happened last week or month that is still gnawing at you? Roll it over in your mind, study it. Learn from it, but then let it go.

11 AUGUST
"I live in the moment. I can turn the page and move on."

Nadia Comaneçi

One thing about great athletes is that they rarely dwell upon losses but rather learn from and improve because of them. From this Nadia was the first to be PERFECT, with her 10.0 at the Montreal Olympics in 1976. How many times did she fall getting to that point? She turned the page over and over to become perfect.

Michael Jordan famously can tell you he missed over 9,000 shots in his career, including 26 game winners. And he'd take the game winning shot the next night if need be. Abraham Lincoln failed over and over before being elected President and saving the Union. Elvis Presley failed his music classes and was told early in his singing career to go back to driving a truck. He couldn't even make it as a member of a quartet. He became The King because he kept moving. Fred Astaire? Was assessed as "Can't sing. Can't act. Balding. Can dance a little." He certainly moved on.

Turn the page. Move on.

The Master has failed more times than the novice has even tried.

I have failed more times than I can count. And hopefully I can fail again today, and tomorrow, and the next day.

Even more important than being able to move on after you fail is to turn the page and move on after you win. How many people have you seen get lucky and then sit back and relax until they go "OH !#$%!"? And it's too late, they have lost whatever momentum they had or overspent and are behind the eight ball and unable to catch up, because they were looking in the rearview mirror. How often have we seen someone knock off the Champ, and then lose their very next fight? Or someone has a monster game and then disappears again? Learning to savor the victory but to get back to work the very next day is the key to building sustained excellence, whether it is in business or sports. Even relationships. What would your spouse say if you proclaimed "Well, I changed the baby. They're good for another three thousand miles!"

Winning is temporary. Losing is temporary. Every day is a new page on the calendar, a blank page to write your story. Write the best tale you can today, regardless of how good or bad the previous page was. That is the key to becoming a Champion in Life.

Action item: erase your mental and emotional hard drive. Today is a new day, and a new opportunity. Close your eyes, and picture a calendar with yesterday's date (August 10). Rip the page off in your mind. Crumple it up. Throw it out. Oh look! A new, blank day!

12 AUGUST
"You only live once, but if you do it right, once is enough."

Mae West

The biggest secret of life? None of us are getting out of here alive.   All people die, will you REALLY live?   "How long are you going to wait before you demand the best for yourself?" Epictetus

Watch a kid or a puppy. They have two speeds: full tilt and sleep. These are the two most joyful groups on the planet. What is preventing you from doing whatever you are doing (work, play, relationships) with your whole heart and then crashing at the end of the day, exhausted but happy like a kindergartener?

As Hunter S Thompson says the goal of life is not to go gently into the good night or leave a pretty and perfect corpse, "but rather to skid in broadside in a cloud of smoke, thoroughly used up, totally worn out, and loudly proclaiming "Wow! What a ride!""

It is to crack the bones and suck the marrow out as they mention in Dead Poets Society. It is to leave it all on the field, day after day, so that as the last sands drop there are no regrets.

Have that ice cream.   Ask the person out.   Take that risk at work. Neal Young: it's better to burn out than to fade away.

When was the last time you saw a beautiful sunrise or sunset, paused at its beauty and said "wow"? Why so long? When was the last time your heart was pounding with excitement? Why not today? When was the last time you talked to that friend that you had all those crazy late night adventures with? Call them and relive some of the memories, or better yet create some new ones!

"I'm going on an adventure!" screams Bilbo Baggins in The Hobbit. What was your last adventure? We were not meant to sit on the couch and watch other people have adventures while we snack on hyper-processed fake foods and empty calories in a climate controlled environment. We were born to take risks, get scars, break our hearts and skin our knees as we experience life.

To LIVE.

Action item: do one thing today to get your heart racing with excitement.

12 AUGUST
"You only live once, but if you do it right, once is enough."

Mae West

The biggest secret of life? None of us are getting out of here alive.   All people die, will you REALLY live?   "How long are you going to wait before you demand the best for yourself?" Epictetus

Watch a kid or a puppy. They have two speeds: full tilt and sleep. These are the two most joyful groups on the planet. What is preventing you from doing whatever you are doing (work, play, relationships) with your whole heart and then crashing at the end of the day, exhausted but happy like a kindergartener?

As Hunter S Thompson says the goal of life is not to go gently into the good night or leave a pretty and perfect corpse, "but rather to skid in broadside in a cloud of smoke, thoroughly used up, totally worn out, and loudly proclaiming "Wow! What a ride!""

It is to crack the bones and suck the marrow out as they mention in Dead Poets Society. It is to leave it all on the field, day after day, so that as the last sands drop there are no regrets.

Have that ice cream.   Ask the person out.   Take that risk at work. Neal Young: it's better to burn out than to fade away.

When was the last time you saw a beautiful sunrise or sunset, paused at its beauty and said "wow"? Why so long? When was the last time your heart was pounding with excitement? Why not today? When was the last time you talked to that friend that you had all those crazy late night adventures with? Call them and relive some of the memories, or better yet create some new ones!

"I'm going on an adventure!" screams Bilbo Baggins in The Hobbit. What was your last adventure? We were not meant to sit on the couch and watch other people have adventures while we snack on hyper-processed fake foods and empty calories in a climate controlled environment. We were born to take risks, get scars, break our hearts and skin our knees as we experience life.

To LIVE.

Action item: do one thing today to get your heart racing with excitement.

13 AUGUST
"He who has a why to live can bear almost any how."

Friedrich Nietzsche

Simon Sinek has one of the most popular TED Talks of all time exploring the WHY and how it made some of the most impactful leaders powerful and effective.

"Find your WHY and you'll find your WAY." John C Maxwell.

"When you know your why, you can endure any how." Viktor Frankl.

Most of us have had a relative that was told that if they didn't stop smoking, they would die and not see their grandchild born or their daughter walk down the aisle. Those are really big "whys" to change behavior and they did stop smoking and live to see what they desired. Didn't matter how intense the nicotine craving or the social cues to grab a cancer stick, they stopped because the "why" was so powerful and strengthening.

People run marathons for Leukemia & Lymphoma Society, raising money for research and going the 26.2 miles because of the "why." They trained me for my first marathon when my then-wife's grandfather was battling the disease. If he could take chemo, I could take the miles to raise money to battle the disease that would later claim my best friend Rich. To this day I run long distances in the purple of L&LS and think about both of them, keeping my why so I can get through the how on the long, long road.

Our men and women in uniform do superhuman things because of their "why," their belief in our country and their duty to it and the members of their unit.

The firefighters on 9/11 who ran up when others ran down. Father Mychal Judge will always be remembered because of this.

The parent working three jobs to support their family knows their "why" and it strengthens them every day, giving them the strength to do what they need to do.

The student studying day and night to rock their exams so that they can earn a scholarship, be the first one of their family to go to college, and help their younger brothers and sisters? The "why" is strong with this one.

The startup crew hammering away day after day to bring a vision to fruition and change the world.

The teenager training before dawn because of the burning need to be an Olympian.

The ten year old with the paper route so they can buy their own bike.

"Why" makes us immune to the pains and fears along the way, whether it is picking up the phone 100 times or knocking on 50 doors in a day, or the potential ridicule from cleaning toilets or getting on a treadmill while 100 pounds overweight.

"Why" creates Will.

"Why" makes us superhuman in bursts or over the long haul and the daily grind that would break other people down that have a less robust belief system.

"Why" is the only reason I can type day after day after day to put this book in your hands, knowing that I was put on this earth to improve the world and this work is one way to positively impact people.

"Why" is the most powerful of the five W's, and will create the H for you. You just need to have that

"Why" as part of your raison d'etre, an integral part of your being and soul.

Action item: what is your WHY? Get a piece of paper and watch Simon Sinek's TED Talk, and take notes about it. Then write down your WHY, because it will make you powerful.

14 AUGUST

"I am not afraid of a storm
for I am learning how to sail my ship."

Louisa May Alcott

Ships in harbor are safe. But they are meant to sail the seas, looking for adventure.

Hiding in your house is safe. However life is not meant to be lived bubble wrapped, but rather to experience the wonder, the excitement and awe and love. To get hurt, garner scars, and see sunsets. To taste that unusual dish or drink that bizarre liquor while meeting strangers and opening your mind and heart.

Live. You're going to screw it up no matter what.

If it's not fatal it's fixable, and the lessons learned will be more powerful than a diagram in a textbook. Mistakes are how children learn early, but as soon as they head to school they learn that mistakes are bad and to be avoided. It crushes out their willingness to take risks and produces cookie cutter clones. Better to try and build a fort and fail and hit your thumb with a hammer and learn the principles of engineering that will stick with them from hands-on experience than wait until high school, take a CAD class and have a theoretical understanding of how stuff works.
Being comfortable with failing is the best way to ensure success.

Once you learn from making mistakes, from sailing your ship and surviving storms, the easy seas are that much more pleasant and the storms are no longer terrifying but exhilarating. The challenges that you have come through already position you better for the hurricanes of the future.

This is why my mom took me out to do donuts and drive on icy parking lots after storms, so that I could learn to handle the car slightly out of control and recover, to understand the warning signs and be able to adjust before crashing.

This is why we have our kids do things right at the edge of their capability, so that they build confidence and expand their abilities and can learn to believe in themselves and build resolve and initiative.

This is why we take the risk at work or asking the pretty girl (or cute boy) out. It could fail and often does, but the ability to sail through the corporate chaos and relationship tsunamis allows us to reach the sandy beaches and enjoy the sunset instead of sitting on the cold rocky shore wondering and dreaming.

Action item: what is one storm you can sail INTO today that won't sink your ship?

15 AUGUST

"A ship in the harbor is safe, but that is not what ships are built for."

John A. Shedd

Sit on the beach and look at the horizon, or sail over it into adventure? Sure, you might go beyond the edge of the map and encounter monsters, but think about the stories you will have and the person you can become overcoming the adversities? Think of the capabilities you will develop for the future, and the treasures you can collect. Toes in the sand with a drink in your hand is a nice break from the rough seas, but we were built for challenge not leisure.

Safety is not a natural condition of enduring stability, but rather a temporary reprieve from the struggles of humanity. Thinking that it can be the norm as opposed to the exception is foolish and will lead to devastation, both physically and emotionally. Better to be a warrior in a garden than a gardener and slave as the old saying goes. Prepare yourself for the battles and rough seas so that when there is calm you can be relaxed.

We are built to learn and live. Look at a child and see how they absorb the world around them, exploring with their senses and bodies and trying to experience everything they can. Even when they fall down they usually bounce right back up and keep at it, especially if they are focused on achieving something (like the cookie jar). Little kids are constantly learning and growing physically and mentally, and the scars on their knees are visible signs of boo-boos that made them cry for a second until they were distracted by the next shiny object or moving animal that grabbed their attention and took them on their next quest. Why do we outgrow this mentality?

Early in The Hobbit, Bilbo Baggins turns his back on tradition and home and the warm hearth and heads out on the road crying "I'm going on an adventure!" He faces trolls, goblins, giant spiders, and dragons. He meets elves and parties with dwarves, befriends a wizard and risks everything including his soul. Hobbits are more built for leisure and rest than humans are. Why should one of these little people have the stimulation and excitement that we big people are afraid of for some reason?

Do not recklessly rush off to climb Mount Kilimanjaro or run with the bulls in Pamplona, but at least get out of your home and comfort zone and feel the rush of excitement from new experiences and locations, expose yourself to new ideas and foods and music and concepts. Because sitting there at anchor in the gentle sway of the harbor is nice after the adventure, but should be a gentle homecoming after going away on the journey.

Action item: what can you do today that is a little adventurous without being dangerous?

16 AUGUST

"Now and then we had the hope that if we lived and were good, God would permit us to be pirates."

Mark Twain

Confession time. I've always wanted to be a pirate. I STILL want to be a pirate when I grow up (even though my theme song should now be Jimmy Buffet's "A Pirate Looks at 50").

Pirates live by a loose code unlike polite society, but much more meritoriously based, where a man (or a woman) could become a Captain through their own success and everyone shares the spoils from capturing booty. A true meritocracy living under a skull flag and a code of honor among thieves but without the work for work's sake ideal of the British Navy, where as long as everything was in fighting shape then for the most part all was good and fair.

Pirates appeal to the sense of adventure most kids crave, of loose order and excitement and treasure. Of few rules, and not having to have too much manners. They are honest thieves. Or as Gilbert and Sullivan wrote:

Many a king on a first class throne
If he wants to call his crown his own
Must manage somehow to get through
More dirty work than I ever do.

There is more honor on a pirate ship than in most offices, and a hell of a lot less politics and more rum. Sounds like a better career to many of us.

Those of us who have to wear a tie or uniform for a living crave the individuality, the lack of regimentation and standardization (or forms filled out in triplicate that even the lawyers can't comprehend), desire the freedom of the open sea and the salt air as opposed to the hum of a copy machine while yelled at by a boss with suspenders and coffee mug micromanaging us. Oh, to be an HONEST scallywag! To be the most fair corsair, cutlass in hand and lass on me mind as the ship rolls beneath me boots and the wind whips the sails, no deadlines in sight!

A Pirate's life for me!

Action item: today at work, abide by the code. Mutiny if need be, and take what ye can, give nothing back!

17 AUGUST
"The Code is more what you'd call "guidelines" than actual rules."
Captain Hector Barbosa

There is no written Pirate Code like there is the Uniform Code of Military Justice. There is much more situational ethics involved, where one of the most important things is self-preservation. Just like the stewardess will instruct you to place the mask over your own mouth before assisting others, because those who cannot help themselves are unable to truly come to the aid of others. Good advice, as any mental health professional will agree.

Other guidelines that pirates followed include leaving a comrade who fell behind to their own devices, because it is better to lose one man than the entire crew. Maybe Mr. Spock was influenced by pirates when he told Kirk "the needs of the many outweigh the needs of the few, or the one."

But when it comes to rewarding the crew after capturing a prize at sea, The Code was eminently fair in that each member of the crew received equal shares of the spoils, as divided up by the Quartermaster that was essentially the Chief Operating Officer (COO) of the ship. Men (and women who became pirates) would be promoted internally due to death as next person up, or through their merits in certain areas of expertise. A successful pirate could eventually become Quartermaster or Captain completely independent of their birth rank or nationality or religion. Not a bad career path, other than getting shot at and the potential to be hung.

Yes, they were often scoundrels and knaves with poor hygiene. They killed as their profession, but so did many others of their era. It was a violent time, and piracy often provided the best means of survival and chance to build wealth without the advantages of noble birth.

Life would be short and intense for Pirates, and we can learn from their example of seizing the opportunities presented and taking risks where appropriate and avoiding the fight when the odds are not in your favor. Sailing fast, having your shipmates' backs in battle, keeping your powder dry and keeping a weather eye on the horizon while avoiding the shoals is a pretty good set of guidance for success in twenty-first century corporate America.

Action item: as The Code requires, look lively and do your duty so the ship can sail and capture the prize. How can you be the best crew member you can be today?

18 AUGUST
"If you know the Way broadly, you will see it in everything."

Miyamoto Musashi

From one thing you can know many things.

The universe is patterns that we interpret, whether it is the cycles of history or the Fibonacci Sequence in the nautilus shell. It is the Golden Ratio appearing over and over again in seemingly disparate pieces of the grand puzzle we are part of.

Maybe it is our Reticular Activation System at work where our internal filter causes our attention to catch on what we look for, be it opportunities or somebody trying to do us wrong at work.

Maybe it is a methodology of thinking, heuristics that allow our brains to be in energy saver mode so we default to seeing kindness if we are kind or solving everything like an engineering problem (for my friends from Rensselaer Polytechnic Institute). A Special Forces Operator will remain on high observance even years removed from deployment because the habits that were critical to survival are so deeply ingrained that they are not forgotten when their uniform is off.

If you are filled with love, you will see it in the world around you. Unfortunately so too with hatred. But which of those two opposing emotions you embrace will be resonant in the world around you, so you choose how the world is. What do you wish to see in others?

What do you know that colors the way you see the world? Do you see the chance to help others and do good, or are you projecting your own fears and attitudes and seeing everyone as a liar because that is what you do yourself? Are you looking for patterns that lead to inevitable success, or are you doomed in your own mind and see dark clouds everywhere?

Your attitude will influence how you see the world, will make your glasses rose tinted or dark and shaded.

If you know The Way, your decisions are easy because you are in harmony and balance, internally and externally. If you don't know your Way, you will continuously struggle because you have not figured yourself out and so will be out of control in the world. If you have a grasp of the great in the universe around you, the little choices and actions are naturally aligned as opposed to contravening your long range goals and intentions. Lacking this you will experience stress in your life.

Action item: are you in balance between the great and small things in your life? Do you spend your time on things that are in harmony with your Way? Get in, or out of the Way.

19 AUGUST
"There is no way to happiness - happiness is the way."

Thich Nhat Hanh

"The Way that can be seen is not the True Way." Tao te Ching. Happiness is like a butterfly: if you pursue it, it will always flutter off out of reach. Stop chasing it and it will alight on you and bring joy. Too many people look outside themselves for happiness, whether it is external validation from the BMW and nice house to plastic surgery or retail therapy. Sometimes people peg it to external events like your favorite tennis player winning or getting a promotion or how many likes an Instagram pic gets. These are all shallow and fleeting at best, dependent upon the whims and actions of others and ephemeral.

Those who can be happy with little can be happy with little, while for those whom nothing is enough then nothing will be enough. Happiness is a choice (assuming no biochemical imbalance and even then your choices can still mitigate a portion of the effects), and as (wrongly) attributed to Abe Lincoln most folks are as happy as they make up their mind to be.

You can find happiness in the little things. A beautiful sunrise, or the sound of the rain in the morning. You can choose to miss it, or be negative about it or you can look on the bright side of life (as Monty Python sang while being put to death). Take joy in movement, in getting out of bed and being able to walk down the hallway. If you've ever had a knee or back injury, you no longer take this simple thing for granted as others might.

Instead of saying you'll be happy when you get promoted or win X, fall in love with the process of preparing yourself to get promoted or becoming a champion. As a martial artist it is always nice to win; yet it is not about another piece of hardware that collects dust but the daily training and effort, the attempt to improve and for a second touch perfection, to make myself better than I was.

The process of improvement towards something (promotion, title, whatever) that is where the happiness lies, of pushing yourself and then sitting back after the huge effort and basking in the exhaustion of a good job done, over and over. Here lies happiness, whether it is in the office or the weight room or studying or on the couch after an exhausting but good day with the kids. This internally focused excellence is repeatable, expands our confidence and our vision, and is earned rewards. The race shirt from a marathon is worth more than the newest piece of high fashion because it was bought with sacrifice and effort instead of AmEx.

Happiness is not a target to be fired at but the process of practicing to hit any target. It is the actions, not the outcomes. Joy is in the effort, not the effect at the end. The journey instead of the destination.

Action item: don't chase the butterfly. Today, focus on "doing" and enjoying the process towards something, and on that path you will find unexpected happiness.

20 AUGUST
"The journey matters as much as the goal."

Kalpana Chawla

Arnold Schwartzenegger loved training, loved lifting weights and pushing himself. Yes, he had dreamt of being Mr. Olympia since a teenager in Austria, but he ended up loving the process of lifting to the point that he hid weights in the tank while in the Army so he could sneak in workouts. That kid that loves reading so much you have to take the flashlight away because they are reading under the covers? They love reading and learning for its own sake, and this desire should be encouraged instead of squashed.

The family road trip of days done by (maybe in the Family Truckster with wood panels as we had) is as much about the time on the road together, teasing your kid sister and getting truckers to blow their horn and the random experiences as it is getting to the place you were going.

The process of researching and writing the Masters or PhD thesis is more important than the document or defense, even if those endpoints are required to complete the journey.

Love the process.

The metamorphosis of becoming a champion remains with you after you have won and lost the title. The skills needed to improve your skills, the meta-cognitive tools, the work habits and mindset needed to win are valuable assets that can be repurposed after the path they were developed on has ended.

The transformation that we undergo on the road is the reward itself.

Once the dragon is defeated, the hero gains the treasure but the real wealth is what it took to face and overcome the dragon, not the shiny things in the hoard.

Falling in love is a greater adventure than being in love, and so continuously re-falling for each other, discovering new fascinating things about your partner, is the key to keeping the relationship green and flowering.

Action item: Instead of focusing on the goal you have been shooting for, focus on the process today. Look at the journey, and enjoy the steps along the way towards the destination.

21 AUGUST
"Like a band of gypsies we go down the highway"

Willie Nelson

Sometimes you only need 12% of a plan to be successful, especially when you know where you are to begin and where you want to end up and are determined to enjoy the journey. Where the moments on the road are more important than reaching a specific place at a specific time for a specific reason, so taking side quests and going down the road less traveled is not counterproductive but really the entire point of the odyssey.

Oh look, the World's Biggest Ball of String or Dinoland or something else that looks cool. Go check it out. Who knows what you'll find?!

Hey, a cool winery or brewery only ten miles out of our way? Sounds good to me, maybe we'll discover a new favorite.

Oh, you're from Romania? Let's sit down and tell me about what it's like, because meeting friends that you didn't know were friends yet on the road of life is an unexpected joy.

Ask someone what book they are currently reading instead of "what's new?" because you'll get a more interesting response that could help you on your journey more than hearing "nothing much, how about you?!" Better to go deep and be real and uncover a buried treasure than to have yet another meaningless surface discussion that adds no value to anyone involved.

Eclectic musical styles and friends open our minds to new concepts, and allow ideas to cross pollinate in ways we can never predetermine. Exposure to new concepts and being able to go with the flow between Point A and Point B is the most organic growth style available, an approach that led Steve Jobs to study calligraphy in college and led to fonts and design ideas Apple still uses to this day.

As Bilbo Baggins declared "I'm going on an adventure!" And as he later told his nephew: It's dangerous business, Frodo, going out your door. You step onto the road, and if you don't keep your feet, there's no knowing where you might be swept off to. Bilbo was half warning and half cajoling Frodo to follow in his footsteps, because shouldn't life be an adventure that we later regale the younger ones with tales of?!

Action item: plan an unplanned detour. Drive a different way to work or go exploring today, just to see what is out there. You never know who you might meet.

22 AUGUST

"A companion loves some agreeable qualities which a man may possess, but a friend loves the man himself."

James Boswell

Or as Robin Williams said: a friend is someone that will listen to your BS, tell you that it is BS, and then listen some more. Because that is what friends do. We all have that friend that we absolutely adore, in spite of a couple of really bad flaws (and worse than liking IPAs instead of real beers that don't taste like a cat peed on a Christmas tree). Whether it is their arrogance (yes, that friend is me and I'm still working on it), the repeated poor relationship decisions they make, or their mental laziness that makes them always try to take the easy route; if they are a real friend you will love them just the same. In spite of their flaws.

We all have dear friends of every political affiliation, and across multiple economic strata. Hell, some of my best friends are part of the Red Sox Nation, and as a Minnesota Vikings fan I even tolerate my Cheesehead friends from Wisconsin don't cha know? We'll have a brat and some suds and agree to not talk about Brett Favre. Good fences make good neighbors Frost said, and agreeing to disagree on certain topics is part of being an emotionally mature adult.

A friend has a relationship that goes much deeper than the surface trappings. It requires time and exposure to see how they act in different situations from the waiter messing up their order to how they perform when sick to how they treat their significant other. There is trust, and respect, and a willingness to work through temporary or non-earth shattering differences because the relationship is more important than short-term illusion of comfort. Real friendship survives and adapts.

Sometimes, the flaws in a friend are so deep that it cracks the foundation your friendship is built off of. Lies and deceit will do this, or repeated actions that endanger another, or violating closely held moral principles that are a bright line of our core being could all force the dissolution of a friendship, but anything short of these truly irreparable differences we accept and even joke about as weird foibles and "Just Frank being Frank". We all have that one friend…

Think of that handful of people that you really can call "friend", that you can call up and they would drop everything to help you whether it is listening to you vent about your partner or help you move that ugly couch for the fifth time. I guarantee that they are not perfect. But they are there when you need them and you probably will choose time with them over almost any other activity. That is real friendship, not the 752 Facebook "friends" who you rarely interact with and might not recognize in the grocery store. They are like a piece of cheap sugary candy that might give you a momentary rush but a friend will continue to feed your soul over and over.

Action item: who are that handful of true friends? Why? Reach out to them today.

23 AUGUST
"You've never had a friend like me."

The Genie (Robin Williams in Disney's *Aladdin*)

You probably don't have a friend that lives in a bottle and has cosmic powers. Hopefully though you have one that knows you well enough to conjure up a smile or magically know the right thing to say when you are down. Having a friend that knows you better than you know yourself is a blessing. Curse too because they can see when you are going to horribly screw something up in a relationship or at work because they know you so well. But they probably can also bring out your better nature, inspire you to do things you normally wouldn't that are at the edge of your capabilities and force you to become an even better version of you.

A friend is different from an acquaintance. An acquaintance will stop you on the street and talk for a few minutes about the kids or work or what have you, asking "how have you been?" but not ready to go in depth on it. A friend will ask the same thing and really want to know, will push off whatever they were going to do (or if they can't push it off they will call you within a day) to get you to open up so they can truly be there for you. The acquaintance will maybe check on you in a few days, a real friend will reach out via text and FB Messenger and another platform at two am and send memes and gifs and BE there for you, even if across a border.

We all have that couple dozen friends within the circle of acquaintances that are progressively closer to us and more intimate, like the rings of a bullseye. Those that get Christmas cards are a larger number than those that come over and have drinks, and the closest are those handful of people that will do anything for you because the friendship is at such a level that they are family if not blood.

An acquaintance knows some about you. A really close friend knows way too much and doesn't care because they really do care about you, no matter what. They might have even crossed over from just friends to being someone you love. They will tell you when you are screwing up and be there to help you, whether before the explosion or afterwards to help pickup the pieces. Maybe make some snide comments, but they will BE there with and for you. They will also be your biggest cheerleader when things go right for you and celebrate your successes even more than their own.

A true friend will fight for you, and even fight you if need be. They will hold up the mirror to let you see the truth, and the mask when you need an illusion. They will pump you up or calm you down, and even if you disappoint them they will believe in you, probably even more than you believe in yourself. And that is truly magical.

Action item: who are the friends that you didn't call yesterday, that were on the border of you reaching out to? Reach out to those ones today.

24 AUGUST

"A friend is one who knows you and loves you just the same."

Elbert Hubbard

We all have secrets. We all have done things we are glad our grandmother never knew about, and things we'd never want to explain to our parents. Maybe you hurt someone, or killed people in the line of duty, or were sexually assaulted, or had an affair. You can tell a true friend these deep dark secrets because they honestly care about you and will keep their mouths shut, will listen and advise and if they judge will do so with compassion and empathy for you instead of harshness and cruelty like the rest of the world. They will care about the damage to your psyche and help you heal more than anything else.

A friend will see you at your sobbing worst, tears streaming down your face and snot dripping out of your nose as you break down crying. They will hug you and not care about what you get on their shirt as they hold you and cry with you.

A friend will take your call at late o'clock and listen to your drunk complaints about your ex or your current flame, as well as the early morning random pics of you having too much fun. Both extremes come with the territory.

As Marilyn Monroe said "If you can't handle me at my worst, you don't deserve me at my best." And your real friends will be there for the worst, just like you should be for them because of the reciprocal nature of friendship.

Those real friends will sit there when you are sick, be it mentally or physically. And the worse the sickness the more important these friends are, to lend you a helping hand and their mental and emotional strength. We will be there for depression and addiction, for breakups and breakdowns and breakthroughs. We might even be there when you die, because even though it shatters our heart we need to be there and treasure every last moment, and we will carry you in our hearts for the entire rest of our lives, never stop missing you, and visit you in our dreams because we miss you that much.

A friend will look straight into the black parts of your soul and maybe flinch but keep staring into it because they believe in your light, and will pour theirs into you even to the last bit of themselves because you are that important to them. They will keep seeing you with more than eyes, but with the heart that you have filled over time and will always be a part of, no matter the distance or barriers or BS.

Action item: what should you do to be a better friend? Do it.

25 AUGUST
"Know thyself? If I knew myself I would run away!"

Johann Wolfgang von Goethe

As Carl Jung says, we all have a Shadow within us that polite Society would not smile upon. But polite Society was built by violence, by war, and by those willing to break the rules to create something better.

The Shadow is the true power behind the throne, the steel under the velvet that is rarely recognized because nice people don't talk about their dark desires that give strength and when integrated with the lighter aspects of our psyche produce a balanced, adaptable, and powerful person.

Most people don't want to look in the mirror because they have not faced their Shadow, instead burying it and ignoring it so that it grows and is uncontrolled, lurking beneath the surface of smiles and fashion.

Being unembraced and untamed, it looks to break out a la Mr. Hyde and when it does so it can be uglier than any monster we can comprehend because we recognize that this monster lurks inside of us too. That scares most people, and so they run away instead of standing and facing their fears and passions and desires, their negative aspects and blacknesses in all of our souls.

Col. Jessup (Jack Nicholson) in A Few Good Men rages: "and my existence, while grotesque and incomprehensible to you, saves lives. You don't want the truth because deep down in the places you don't talk about at parties, you want me". A truer self declaration of The Shadow in us has rarely been expressed: we fear the power and potential within.

If we never face this darkness though we are vulnerable. We all have the capacity to do horrible things, it is just that strong individuals have faced this and know they are capable of intense violence and even evil, and understanding it are able to keep the Shadow controlled and in check. Those who have never wrestled with this demon do not know its strength and how it could be made manifest by external events.

Almost every genocide of the twentieth century was perpetuated by average people whose darkness was brought out by evil leaders that normalized bad behavior and dehumanized others, and one reason was because of populace that were not integrated in their souls with both the light and the dark. Face and fight your demons to become powerful, and resist the temptations when the mores around you shift.

There is a saying: to stop a bad guy with a gun, you need a good guy with a gun. To stop evil, you need someone with the potential to do wrong that then has the capacity to recognize the evil, confront it, and stop it. Thoughts and prayers on Facebook won't do it, begging for mercy on your knees won't either.

Only by standing against evil, by being ready to harm and hurt will we protect the innocents. And most of us don't want to face that fact. But those who accept their Shadow, who fight it and keep it in check, are those that will protect polite Society when the order breaks down, when a bad person pops up in a church or shopping mall, that will face their own fear and fight for others or themselves even if it is frowned upon.

Action item: look in the mirror. Look into your own soul, remember all the horrible things you have done and thought of. Look right into your own heart of darkness and embrace your Shadow. Now master it.

26 AUGUST
"One of the perks of being a psychologist is access to tools that allow you to carry out the injunction to know thyself."
Steven Pinker

The internet can be a dangerous thing for people with anxiety, because they can go to webMD and all of the sudden they've got bubonic plague and an allergy that only three other people on Earth have. For people with curiosity and a healthy dose of self awareness though, it can open doors of growth that were undreamt of a generation ago.

There is so much psych, self-help, and guidance out there that it's sort of amazing that you are reading this book. Maybe it is because of my sense of humor or the action-oriented filter I passed tens of thousands of hours of learning through. Or maybe you were just looking for a different tool to help you understand yourself better, a new mirror that brings out different aspects of yourself that you were looking for. No matter what, I'm glad I can help you in some small way.

Poetry and prophecy are open to interpretation from the person that hears them, much the way psychology and self help are. We project pieces of ourselves into the words, and interpret them based upon our frame of reality.

Two friends or identical twins will read the exact same page and derive radically differing interpretations from the words. And this is good, because the actions that we need to take to improve our outlooks and outcomes are as varied as humanity itself, so you will be able to take what you need now and maybe if you reread these words a year from today or five, you will have different insights because at that point you will be a different you.

Probably your very core will not change significantly, as our general attitudes and beliefs are typically internally solidified before we are legally allowed to drink. Some things might change like if you go from addiction to sobriety (or the other way), experience tremendously traumatic losses (illness or injury, death of a close friend or family member, divorce, etc.) or a great positive experience (good marriage, birth of a child, significant investment in self-development). Maybe you went to war, or found religion, or went through significant counseling to heal something from your past. No matter what, you should evolve as a human being and hopefully continuously improve on a going forward basis.

This book is a decent tool, but there are so many others out there. Go take a personality assessment online to give you feedback. Do something physically challenging, whether martial arts or marathon (two of my favorite growth vehicles) or learning to dance or fence or swim. Take an art class. Read a lot, and even better discuss the books with friends or colleagues to swap insights and challenge your assumptions. Talk to people radically different than you, especially those much more advanced in years. All of these experiences will help us turn inward and question ourselves, which is a good thing.

Most of all, ask people that you trust to give you feedback, to tell you what they like or not, where you are making good decisions and ones that are not great. Be ready to "open the kimono" as Steve Jobs said and reveal more of yourself for a deeper discussion.

Not because exposing yourself is fun, but making yourself vulnerable to others' sight and feedback will help you see yourself as others do (not perfect, not disgustingly horrid, probably imperfectly perfect but improvable) and you then have a better, more realistic and grounded picture of yourself to work on improving.

Action item: look in the mirror. Look into your own soul, remember all the horrible things you have done and thought of. Look right into your own heart of darkness and embrace your Shadow. Now master it.

27 AUGUST
"Become aware of your own insufficiency."

Jordan Peterson

Socrates said "the only thing I know is that I know nothing."   One of the most insightful minds of history acknowledging his shortcomings. If more of us did this, we would all be better off.

In whatever field you excel at you pass through four stages:

Unconscious Incompetence: Not knowing what you don't know.
Conscious Incompetence: Knowing what you don't know.
Conscious Competence: Knowing what you know.
Unconscious Competence: Not knowing what you know.

As an example, when I was a mid-range Black Belt I was fighting a brown belt in front of a class of beginning and intermediate level students, and I whipped out a technique they had never seen me use before (a spinning ax kick. It was cool and just brushed their nose) and afterwards they were like "What was that?!" as they had never seen it let alone experienced it.

They went in that instant from Unconscious Incompetence to Conscious Incompetence, and once I spent fifteen minutes teaching the brown belt after class they moved into Conscious Competence and that kick later became part of their arsenal. I hadn't even thought of throwing that kick, I just DID it. I was Unconsciously Competent, as all high performing professionals become in their area of expertise.

How often do you force yourself to explore the border of your knowledge and look outward from what you know well into the uncertain areas beyond? This is where scientists regularly dwell, pushing the boundaries of their understanding in the quest for knowledge. And the greatest scientist realizes that we have barely scratched the surface and the Universe has an untold number of secrets for us to discover.

Writers get this. We spend our entire lives improving our craft, to try and convey the non conveyable emotions and thoughts to others, often getting pissed at how pale our words are compared to our subjects.

Knowing you suck is the first step to improvement.

Dave Grohl (Foo Fighters and Nirvana) has a lesson for young musicians: just start. You'll suck. Practice and have fun with your buddies. Know you suck but keep at it and suck less. Keep at it and play some crappy gigs. Understand you still sorta suck, keep practicing and get better and play better gigs. Repeat the cycle and you eventually won't suck, and maybe even end up in Nirvana.

I admit: I suck at relationships. I am supposedly some guru, but I'm not on point all the time. I get tired and frustrated and say things I shouldn't. I expect too much from myself and others. I fail to do the little things at times and miss the big signs, even when they are flashing red DANGER.

And because I know I suck I try even harder, to be a better listener and more empathetic and less of a hard ass. I still try to fix my friends, even though I am flawed. It's in my nature, especially since I went to a technical school where everything is a problem looking for optimal solutions. And so I have to fight that tendency, and I too often lose that fight.

I'm not perfect, but I try.

And that really is the point. We are all human, and admitting that and being ready to work to become a better one is the idea. Acknowledging when you are on the border between Conscious Incompetence and Competence, and being ready to do the work to make the transition, is where the struggle and rewards are for all of us.

Action item: what is one area that you are Consciously Incompetent in that with some work you could get some good results?

28 AUGUST

"The greatest of faults, I should say, is to be conscious of none."

Thomas Carlyle

I am arrogant.

I am somewhat conceited.

I live in a fantasy world where I am a great writer and will someday have an immense impact on the world and be able to hang out on a beach in Tahiti a few weeks a year. I am too focused on the future way too often, and I put achievement of goals and benchmarks of creation ahead of enjoying, of stopping and smelling the roses and appreciating the people that are important to me. And I'm scared I will never live up to my potential, as too many of us that were identified as "gifted" when children struggle with in adulthood.

I like cheeseburgers, donuts, and beer. And Oreos. ALL of the Oreos!

I try to save the world and as those close to me remind me: I don't have to love only the broken ones.

I am easily distracted and it takes a ton of effort for me to focus and finish, unless I hyperfocus and then will work to the point I forget to eat. Then I get hangry and really snippy.

We all have our faults. Being able to identify them is a critical first step.

Action item: What are some of your faults?
Some of my faults are:

29 AUGUST

"Self-awareness is not self-centeredness, and spirituality is not narcissism."

Marianne Williamson

Knowing that you need rest is not selfish, because if you get burnt out you are no use to anybody. One of my close friends told me this (pretty blatantly) today because I am emotionally, physically, and mentally drained. I'm not as funny, my productivity is lower, and my temper is much shorter. Taking a little "me time" is not being self-centered, it is an investment of time for mental maintenance on the machine to make sure it doesn't break down.

When you ride on an airplane, the flight staff gives the safety briefing and demonstrates putting on the oxygen mask with a declaration of "if you are traveling with children, please put your mask on before assisting others", because if you can't breathe you can't really help others. This goes for many areas in life.

Get your $h!T together, then you can help others get theirs together.

Catching your breath is not stopping, nor is it being lazy. Knowing you are running low on energy, or patience, is not being self serving. It is knowing you are reaching the point of the check engine light coming on for your body and mind, and scheduling an appointment to get yourself serviced and tuned up is important so you aren't broken down on the side of the road, steam pouring out, useless to everyone.

Action item: go take some "you" time.

30 AUGUST
"If we do not lay out ourselves in the service of mankind whom should we serve?"

Abigail Adams

The woman who laid the groundwork for the active partner model of First Lady, Abigail Adams was no moral or professional slouch and was guided by principles as strong as any of the Founding Fathers. In addition to what her husband did for this nation, look at her son John Quincy Adams: even though he was not a great President by most standards he was a servant leader unparalleled in US history.

After his term as POTUS, he spent 40 years in the House of Representatives. He had served previously in the Senate and as an Ambassador to several countries. John Quincy literally died on the floor of the Congress, having a stroke while fighting against slavery after six decades of public service to the young country. We all have the bedrock of our beliefs laid by our parents, would yours look at what you do for others and be proud of their child?

What master do you serve? Are you constantly chasing The Almighty Dollar, or do you allocate a portion of your time for community service and helping others? Even the most die hard of capitalists knew that doing things for the public good would be good for their bottom line, that doing things for others was a good way to help themselves.

Benjamin Franklin helped form one of the first fire brigades and libraries in the Colonies, and spent his life in service to the American People. He also accumulated immense wealth, so much so that by his early 40's he was dedicating the vast majority of his time to service, and his charitable trusts he established two centuries ago are still educating kids. How many of today's entrepreneurs are ready to dedicate a significant portion of their lives to others once they have their billions? When do we stop serving Mammon and start serving our brothers and sisters?

You don't have to sell all of your worldly possessions and form a commune to take in wayward youth. You don't have to abandon your corporate job and work in a soup kitchen or become a teacher for high-risk kids. These would be unreasonable expectations. You do have to do something for others because as Mohammad Ali said: service to others is the rent you pay for your room here on earth. Charities and community service groups across the country and the world need help. They need your help.

As we talk about in the volunteer world, everyone has at least one of the Three T's: Time, Talent, Treasure. If you can't write a big check, can you use your unique skills to assist a group that helps others by programing a website or volunteering as Treasurer or using your other talents to assist them in their mission of serving others? Can you volunteer to coach, or work the concession stand? Bag toys for Toys For Tots, or cleanup a neighborhood park? Read to people in a nursing home, or volunteer at a museum?

There is always a need in our communities for volunteers. The United States has had a tradition of personal choice to serve in some capacity to improve our localities since the earliest days, and is something that other countries have always looked upon in awe. It is more American than apple pie or baseball, because it is ingrained in our culture and codes. It is also from a purely psychological (or religious) point of view an excellent investment in your own future.

Service is the way to leadership.

Giving is the way to ultimately get.

Aid others, and you will have it when fortune turns and you need assistance in some capacity. Bank some good karma. Serve others.

Action item: find one way to serve others today. No matter how big or small, give of yourself to help another that needs it.

31 AUGUST

"Always render more and better service than is expected of you, no matter what your task may be."

Og Mandino

"It's never crowded along the extra mile." Wayne Dyer

Professional pride has almost been forgotten in our mass produced, disposable world. The pouring of one's soul into their work like the craftsmen of old, whether someone was a carpenter or an attorney, of giving your best because your name was on the work, has faded in the era of hyperspecialization and automation. And yet the principle that was ingrained in many of us through sports or Scouts or other manners is timeless: always do your best.

"One of the most important principles of success is developing the habit of going the extra mile." Napoleon Hill

Yes, "good enough" is often good enough, especially in a fast moving environment like a start-up tech company or a high volume restaurant. But if something is not intended to be replaced almost immediately (upgrading and improving the computer code, my cheeseburger that will be in my belly in four minutes, the rebound relationship, etc.) then there should be more attention to detail, more effort to create something that will last as long as needed instead of shoddy cheap plastic crap that falls apart in under a year.

All word processing programs have spell check. Use it. And the grammar check too. Plus there are numerous apps to help improve writing clarity without you having to grab a copy of Strunk and White's "The Elements of Style".

For the person that has your heart, going overboard is never enough. Give more than you will ever hope to get back, and if both sides do so you will have something beautiful and sustainable, an epic friendship and relationship that poets will extoll.

Whenever I invoice a client for consulting work, there is unbilled time included because I always do more than I am paid for. It costs me a little in the short term economically, but I get repeat business and create advocates for my work out in the marketplace. They are part of my marketing effort because they talk about what an awesome job I did and the more than fair cost. Word of mouth is by far the best advertising, and the only way to really earn it is to do as you say and more so that the client not just feels but knows that they got tremendous value.

"There is no advertisement as powerful as a positive reputation traveling fast." Brian Koslow

One of my mentors when I first entered the business world told me that the secret to success was to "under-promise and over deliver". To make sure that whatever the expectation of the client was, it needed to be met and exceeded so that not only would they be blown away, but so that I had the internal standard of excellence in everything I did associated with my business.

This was in alignment with what I have been taught for decades as a martial artist: the tiniest details matter, and there is always room to improve on the quest for perfection. Having the kaizen mindset (continuous improvement), applied to work carries over into other areas of your life because discipline and attention to detail to create excellence (arete as the Greeks called it) is an exportable skill that improves all areas of our lives if you let it.

Ask yourself this question: yesterday, did I do everything in my power to do the best possible job? Was I conscientious? Did I pause and plan for a moment to make sure I wasn't just rushing headlong into it, so that I didn't miss a little critical detail? Would my father be proud of how I performed, or would they be disappointed with my effort and attitude? Did I do my best given the constraints of the situation?

Action item: before any task today, pause and take a deep breath. Ask yourself "how can I do my best possible job on this?" Then do it.

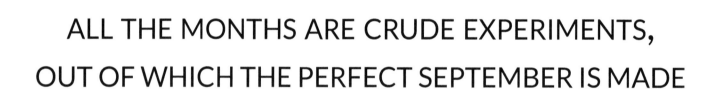

ALL THE MONTHS ARE CRUDE EXPERIMENTS,
OUT OF WHICH THE PERFECT SEPTEMBER IS MADE

Virginia Woolfe

01 SEPTEMBER

"Do the best you can in every task, no matter how unimportant it may seem at the time."

Justice Sandra Day O'Connor

There were two bricklayers working side by side. A woman walked up to them and asked what they were building. The first bricklayer snorted "Just a stupid wall."

The second one looked up from his task and fixed a gaze filled with passion on the woman. "Ma'am, we are laying the ground level of a glorious cathedral. Our bricks will support the walls holding the beautiful stained-glass windows in twenty years."

"But you won't ever see it!" she replied.

"No ma'am, I see that beautiful building every day, in every brick I lay!"

Who will be better in their craft? Who will enjoy their work better? Which one will be a better contributor, and probably a better all-around person? Those low level bricks are critical to build the towers reaching to the sky.

"Do it, and do it right." My mom (all too often when I wasn't giving my best efforts).

Admiral McRaven in his commencement speech for The University of Texas at Austin reminisced about SEAL training and the lesson of making the bed perfectly every morning. Not because the bed itself was important, but because it instilled a habit of focusing on the details and making sure that even the smallest of tasks were completed and completed well, an attitude that in the military can save lives and in business or at home save your butt.

Professional pride is one of the differentiating factors between good and great. It is the baseball player legging out every ground ball, because you play the game hard all the time and they might get lucky and turn an out into a base hit.

And because there are kids in the stands at their first ball game, and they will remember that particular play and give their all, all the time because of that one innocuous plate appearance that a decade later the kid talks about when they are a rookie.

Zen and Stoicism and Taoism are all similar in that they talk about doing tasks with your entire Being, of becoming one with your work. As you become a better person (or more connected with the world), your work improves as a reflection thereof.

There is no careless, poor workmanship because you are not a careless person.

"The devil is in the details" may be true when lawyers get involved, but the details are also where the angels and opportunities lay. Steve Jobs' father was a carpenter, and would still use high quality wood for the back of drawers that no one would ever see. Because he refused to cut corners, and that is the standard Steve brought to Apple.

The little details and jobs are critical for the overall aesthetic and success.

Action item: what is that one task that you dread? Put your heart into it, give it your absolute best for today.

02 SEPTEMBER

"Never help a child with a task at which he feels he can succeed."

Maria Montessori

There is a saying in the rehabilitation community: never do something for a patient that they can do for themselves. It's because this creates a limiting mentality for them, a dependency attitude that ultimately weakens their resolve and strength.

Let the kid struggle. When they solve the problem (mathematical or physical), they will have the pride of accomplishment and strengthen their "can do" belief system. Or you can make it easy for them and they will grow up weak and needing help forever instead of figuring out their problems on their own. This is what the "Snowplow Parents" have done for a decade and it shows.

Do you want your kid still living at home and dependent on you at 45?!

The job of a coach or teacher is to expand the abilities of the kid, and get them to believe it. To improve them and push them without breaking them by going too far. To take them to the edge of their capabilities, over and over so that their envelope increases. Muscles grow from being stressed, not from relaxing on the couch eating Cheetos brought by the butler Jeeves. All aspects of human development are from challenges, not ease.

Challenge the child, you'll be amazed at what they can accomplish and the adult they will become. Positive self-worth is not from being awarded participation trophies, but from overcoming obstacles and earning success instead of having it handed to you. Learning to fail is a good skill because it builds resilience, the potential to rebound from setbacks and to keep trying until they succeed. It is one of the most underrated skills in business and life.

Action item: next time you see someone struggling and want to help, sit on your hands. Let them struggle as long as they aren't in danger. Let them figure it out themselves.

03 SEPTEMBER
"Yesterday I dared to struggle. Today I dare to win."

Bernadette Devlin

The efforts of today bear fruit in the future.

The sweat of the morning earns you your dinner that night.

We all improve at things if we stick with them, whether it is the toddler learning to walk, the five-year old learning to ride a bike, or the teenager trying to master geometry and drive a car. Even someone in their forties can become more empathetic and a better partner and friend, with work. We all start as pitiful in any endeavor, and if we stick with it we can become decent or even great.

All martial arts Masters started as novices. Almost every performer started in their living room entertaining family, long before they thought of the big stage and sold out arenas. Struggling is a natural part of growth in any field. Failure is the best preparation for success.

Few people have truly achieved greatness on natural talent and a clear path. The road to success is filled with rough patches and obstacles. Overcoming these develops character and resilience needed to have the ultimate success.

You might not be ready to win yet. You might need to get right to the edge and fail. Maybe fail again, so that you become more hungry then change your habits and your mindset. To get over the hump and finally breakthrough to victory. "Lefty" Phil Mickelson finished second in multiple Majors in golf (six times at the US Open alone) before finally breaking through after he changed his diet and training. In 2012 he was inducted into the World Golf Hall of Fame and in 2021 became the oldest winner of The PGA Championship at almost 51 years old.

Simona Halep reached three WTA majors finals and lost them all, before breaking through at the 2018 French Open and then taking Wimbledon a year later. Her struggles forced her to master her fiery Romanian temper and eventually be #1 in the world.

Two thousand years ago Seneca observed: the bravest sight in the world is to see a great man struggling against adversity. Struggle comes first, victory follows. Victory without struggle is hollow and not nearly as sweet.

Dare to struggle, because those that do earn the accolades of winning.

Action item: what is so important to you that you are willing to struggle with it, to wrestle it for weeks or months to be victorious? What can you do today to tip the balance in the battle towards you and your victory?

04 SEPTEMBER

"Only those who dare to fail greatly can ever achieve greatly."

Robert F. Kennedy

Or to quote his brother Jack from his speech announcing we were going to the moon: we choose to do these things not because they ah easy, but because they ah hahd!

Elon Musk took his entire fortune from the sale of PayPal and dumped it into two longshot companies: Tesla and SpaceX. He was literally sleeping on friends' couches and in the office because he risked everything he had on his dreams. Again, after building PayPal. These bets paid off for him and his investors.

Call your crush.

Pick up the phone and call that potential huge client that scares you.

Enroll in that class. You can find the time to get the work done, once you get over the fear of commitment.

Ben Franklin left Boston area with almost nothing for Philadelphia.

Jackson Pollock tried something different with his painting. If he hadn't dared to be different, he'd be forgotten.

The first apes that came down from the trees dared greatly. Aren't you glad they did that?

You don't have to take your life savings and pour it into a business idea. But if you want to build something great you have to start and take a risk, even if that risk is just taking some time to flesh out your idea and do some market research. A few hours of time to potentially create something really cool is worth it, wouldn't you say?

Dare to look stupid by taking that dance class so you can impress your mom or sweetie.

Dare to present your boss that bold idea that could make the company a lot of money, or make your job a lot easier. If you don't dare to speak up, you definitely will miss out.

Daring is courage on exhibit. It is what earns people a place in history, and creates the stories your friends will talk about for decades when they say "hey, remember when you dared to...."

Action item: what is one small thing that you are afraid to do that could have great positive results? Do it.

05 SEPTEMBER

"To achieve great things, two things are needed; a plan, and not quite enough time."

Leonard Bernstein

Parkinson's Law states that a task will always expand to the amount of time assigned to it, generally with no improvement over a certain threshold time frame. Everyone has seen term papers done the night before, or a work project finished at the 11th hour over and over again. Deadlines create pressure and incentive to finish.

Just enough pressure is one of the keys to achieving Flow, the state of Zen like performance and creation when we are operating just at the edge of our capacity for something we desire in a space we are experts in. Like Bernstein getting an orchestra ready for a performance, or a writer working under a deadline on their book you are now reading. A deadline just shy of what would be considered reasonable is perfect to excite and stimulate the creative faculties to the point of optimum output.

But it can't be all willy nilly. You have to know what you are doing, be it an outline or a clear goal that you fill in the steps towards. Even 12% of a plan with a clear objective is enough guidance if the deadline is important enough to you. A more complete outline is better, but never should it be a perfect plan because that requires too much time planning and not enough time doing, and the plan will go off the rails inevitably because that is the way of the world. A rough guide with important checkpoints and a clear objective is superior in most situations.

Black Sabbath recorded their namesake debut album in a single day. Still one of the greatest of all time.

A Christmas Carol by Charles Dickens was written in six weeks.

On The Road by Jack Kerouac and *A Clockwork Orange* by Anthony Burgess were written in three weeks.

Startup Weekends abound, taking ideas to basic companies in a three-day period.

A great idea, a decent plan, and a closing window of opportunity to get the adrenaline flowing and you have the recipe for success.

Action item: What is something you want to accomplish that really motivates you? Write out a plan for it, then shorten the timeline by 10% or more. Go get it!

06 SEPTEMBER

"We cannot waste time. We can only waste ourselves."

George Matthew Adams

86,400. That is the number of seconds in our day, whether you are President of the United States or assistant coffee fetcher of the mail room. We al have the exact same allocation each day, and once that day is done we have either made something of those seconds or not. Those seconds are our lives, so either you created something with yourself, or you wasted the gift of life.

One of the worst wastes is to not learn our lessons. And I admit this is an issue for me as an overly stubborn thick headed Irishman who has trained in fields where persistence pays off. But sometimes I don't learn and instead of making the same mistake twice I make it over and over and over again.

Better to let someone else make the mistake first and learn from them (for example reading histories and case studies), or make them when the stakes are low (role play sales situations and presentations, scrimmages in sports, playing the "what if" game for difficult conversations with people close to you or decisions with work) so that the downside risks are reduced and you don't waste days or months of your precious life correcting mistakes or chasing something (or someone) that can't be caught.

I also need to avoid the sunken cost fallacy, where I throw time at things well after the point where I should, believing that "just a bit more" will save the situation or finally get the results I seek because we are close to a tipping point. Have a friend that will smack you out of this to save you a ton of energy and heartache, and you will learn your lessons much quicker and save yourself.

Robert Greene (author of *The 48 Laws of Power* and other great books you should invest time in reading) splits the world into two phases: dead time and alive time. Alive time is when we are doing, growing, utilizing the diminishing asset in a positive way. Dead time is when we are wasting ourselves and not using our sands of time for good purpose.

Catching your breath on the couch for a few minutes after a long day of work or tough workout or to text someone close to your heart is still alive time, sitting there for an hour and at the end saying "where the hell did that hour go, what did I do?!" is probably dead time. The more of your day you can spend in alive time, the more truly you live and more alive you feel, and even the downtime is not truly deadtime if you don't waste yourself in it.

There are many productivity "hacks" I use like listening to educational clips while driving or lifting or prepping food, so that I can get extra use out of those precious seconds. I also often ask myself "does this need to be done, and if so should I be doing it?" Little things like this make me not only more efficient but more effective, because I am investing more of my time on things that can bear fruit instead of barren, dead time.

Tim Ferriss introduced the concept of DEAL in his book *The 4 Hour Work Week*: Delegate, Eliminate, Automate, and Location. There is work that doesn't need to be done (eliminate it), can be programmatically repeated by computer programs (automate), or done by someone else at a much lower hourly rate (delegate). Embracing this concept will remove busy but not truly effective tasks from you, thus giving you more time (and mental energy) to focus on the important things in work, your family, and life in general.

Action item: how can you eliminate 10 minutes of dead time today, to not waste yourself but rather grow?

07 SEPTEMBER

"Decide who you are and what your goals entail – then go for the roses. Life has little regard for those who waste time." Jon Huntsman, Sr.

If you are going to fail, fail at something worthwhile instead of a tiny, meaningless goal. Better to swing for the fence than to keep the bat on your shoulder the entire time, walking back to the dugout after wondering what happened to the boos of the crowd.

When you work, work your butt off. Don't mess around, don't be disorganized (and hence inefficient and less productive than you should be), don't waste time gossiping or misusing your time. Work, and work hard. THEN go play, and don't let the two cross where inappropriate so that you can get the maximum effect and enjoyment out of each.

Figuring out what you want to achieve is the first step in this. Is it to lead your office in sales? Increase your production by 25% this year? Run a 10k in under an hour? Be able to buy that house, or pay for your kid's college? Whatever the goal is, first be VERY clear on it. Crystal clear. Like "I am going to be able to pay for Danielle's four years at RPI starting in three years at the current cost of $XXk per year, from savings and cashflow without impacting my lifestyle."

As clear as a newly cleaned fish tank.

Then go for it.

Do the things, both huge and miniscule, that directly contribute to achieving that goal. Get the resources lined up (new running shoes, buying books on a subject, hiring a coach, investing in technology, whatever it takes) and start working towards the goal while measuring your progress as appropriate (save $Y by end of the year, get Z number of leads, run Q miles three times a week). And be able to say NO to the things that distract from that goal. Going out until late o'clock means you can't get up early to study for the exam or do your miles. A shopping spree reduces the money you have to allocate towards that Big Thing (trip to Paris or tuition payment). Eliminating the waste (time, or money) is critical to achieving that goal and going for the roses of the victor.

The most successful in any field of endeavor eliminate that which does not help them win their particular races, because it does not bring them joy to not win in the end.

Action item: what is that goal? Put it on a sticky note, and put it on the fridge, and by the TV, and on your computer and steering wheel to remind you of what is worth winning. Make it the lock screen on your phone so you see it hundreds of times a day.

08 SEPTEMBER
"The sharp thorn often produces delicate roses."

Ovid

Little good comes without risk, without pain. Champions are remembered, not the people in the stands. And champions sweat, and bleed, and struggle before attaining victory. The cheers of the crowd come after the grunts of exertion and the pain of practice. That moment of adulation come from sacrifices and pains no one will know of, but that feeling is worth all the hours and years leading up to it.

Love is not easy if it is to be lasting. It takes work to get through sickness and health, richer and poorer. Few things that are worth it are easy. The toughest guy might have the biggest heart and cry over lost puppies, and will kick your ass if you tell anyone. Because the external walls are strong to protect the highly vulnerable interior of deep feelings.

The most difficult to acquire client can be the best one because they will be loyal because no one else can get through the labyrinth and earn their trust. That cold hearted woman with RBF could be the friendliest person you'll ever meet but is forced to keep her guard up because of abuse in her past that she won't talk about until she vets you and determines it is safe to start letting you inside the defenses she has erected to protect herself. That punk kid who writes poetry for his mom, who is fighting cancer. The songwriter who distills the pain of their breakup into a song that haunts and speaks to your soul with its beauty.

Dabrowski researched how trauma can create strength, that those who go through the worst can become the best. Stress creating growth. Pain producing power. Adversity developing excellence. Michael Jordan getting cut from his high school team laying the groundwork for one of the greatest competitors of the 20th Century.

The immigrant from a horrible situation that comes to the US, becomes successful, and then pays it forward through massive charitable work and using the skills and resources they've acquired to help others. From Andrew Carnegie to Thomas Peterffy (penniless, unable to speak English, taught himself to program and built Interactive Brokers) to Jan Kuom (WhatsApp founder born in Kiev who lived in public housing when coming to the US), they have taken their disadvantages and built gigantic fortunes and helped others because of the poverty they came from.

Wendy's Hamburger's Founder Dave Thomas was adopted, and because of that created the Foundation for adoption that bears his name. In 2019 alone over 1,400 kids were adopted through its efforts. The softest hearts have the hardest shells to protect them.

Action item: what is the most difficult thing you've gone through this year so far? What is the treasure guarded by that dragon?

09 SEPTEMBER

"When you see how fragile and delicate life can be, all else fades into the background."

Jenna Morasca

There is nothing as resilient and simultaneously fragile as life. I have seen people that were sold into sex slavery as teenagers escape and become powerful and wonderful human beings, and others that have been given everything be empty and devour the world like Ungoliath devouring all the light of Valinor. I have friends that should be dead. Were dead and somehow came back against the odds and live each day like it is their last and they need to maximize every moment. And I buried my best friend in our early forties and miss him every day.

My oldest friend wanted an entire brood of kids, and would be a great mother. Fate made it so she couldn't have a biological child, but she carried a donated egg and gave birth and has a wonderful daughter she loves fiercely. She pours the love she would have given to a half dozen to the one. We all know someone that had an injury and became addicted to pain killers. There but for the grace of God go I, because we are all one car accident or slip from being tested to our limits by the randomness of the world. Instead of placing total blame on the addict, we should place some on the people that make the drugs and those that restrict alternative pain remedies, but most of all we should show empathy and love the sinner/hate the sin. Life (and people) are too fragile to just cast blame when a little time and appreciation and understanding could actually correct or mitigate a not good situation.

"The wound is where the light enters you." Rumi. It is also where your light pours out to others who need it. We have all seen the news story of the high potential high schooler accidentally killed in a random car accident or the victim of gang violence. Of the soldier or Marine killed on their last day of their last tour of duty. Of the baby in the NECU that fights and grows and eventually plays professional sports or becomes a doctor and saves thousands of lives. The chance encounter that blossoms into a life-long love.

"Many that live deserve death. And some that die deserve life." Gandalf

We are mere mortals, specks in the cosmos. Flickering flames that can slowly burn or flash, an explosion of light or as nothing in the Void. Our time on this globe is not determined by us, but what we do with that time is.

As Dr. Manhattan says: You are life. Rarer than a quark and unpredictable beyond the dreams of Heisenberg. Do the best with what time you have. That is all that can be asked of anyone handed the ultimate gift of life.

Action item: maximize today. Burn your candle bright before it fades into the Void or is snuffed out.

10 SEPTEMBER
"Life is strong and fragile. It's a paradox."

Joan Jett

My friend Boozer (yes, that really is his last name) reminded me last week that I am a badass and most men wish they could be me. I have lived a half dozen lives and achieved things few others have. I am essentially unique.

I am also weaker than anyone will ever know and I struggle with it all the time, facing those fears daily and trying to defeat and harness them. I often succeed, but on some days they are too strong and I struggle the entire day no matter how great I appear or what I accomplish.

Welcome to the dichotomy of life.

David Goggins was and probably is one of the baddest men to walk the planet in the past few decades. He talked about how he wanted to be tough and intimidating because he was so weak and scared inside that he created an image. I bet you have someone in your life that has created an image, a false persona to cover their Voids. Maybe even you.

But in the process of becoming a Navy SEAL Goggins had to start addressing the Voids in him, and why they were there. When he started ultrarunning (like ten levels above what I do), it forced him to address these issues all the way down to his core and he evolved to a higher level.

And then his body failed. He literally could not get out of bed, let alone run the 135 miles of Badwater (the toughest race on the planet). Strong and fragile, Goggins evolved again. And again.

The professional athlete that is killed in a car accident. The women dying in childbirth. The cancer survivor saving other people's lives. The person donating an organ to a stranger and saving their life. The survivor of abuse who becomes excellent in their profession and quietly an activist and rescues those in a similar situation. The near-death experience that makes someone appreciate and truly live life.

"Life is what happens to you while you are busy making other plans". John Lennon

Action item: we don't know what we would do in horrible circumstances. Some of us get crushed, some step up and fight with inhuman resolve. Remember that everyone you see is fighting some form of battle, and we all do the best we can. Be kind to yourself today when you need it and hard when called for.

11 SEPTEMBER

"The great lesson my mother and father gave me was almost invisible. It was a strong sense of being rooted."

Dan Rather

One thing we can never choose is our parents and family. But if you have been blessed in this respect, you probably have been given a feeling of belonging, of a home that is there even when you are away and can always return. There is something about coming home and your mother being there with her cup of coffee and cigarette. Even though my mom is gone, her cleaned out ash tray remains and the coffee my dad makes is still the same brand, filling the kitchen with the same aroma and carrying me back to being a little kid or teenager or recent college grad when I would actually drink that coffee with her. This sense of nostalgia, of being able to return home and find peace in a chaotic world, is a true gift.

Where are your roots? Have you returned to your family home and even though it's changed (as have you), enough is still the same to give you that sense of security and a connection to your past to neutralize the chaos of the present? Gone down the street you grew up on and remember Old Mrs. So-and-So and her pies, and the time crazy Mr. Smith yelled at you for going over his fence to get your ball? Those random memories that flash back into your head and fill your heart are precious mementos from your past that are as personalized as the scribbles on your wall, and mean something to you. The feeling of home changes as we age, as we lose our loved ones and the brightness of the future clouds over with time. But the emotions and the energy are still there for us to tap into, and the lessons of love and the other positive attributes our parents modeled and we bear to this day. It is the foundation that we build our current relationships off of, it is the blueprint we attempt to parent from, and will always be the benchmark for what we try and do for our own kids. We always feel like we come up short but here is the secret: our parents tried to shield us from the not great parts, and our brains are wired to remember the better parts anyway so the two factors create a huge bias when we look back.

Be like your parents and just do the best you can, and hopefully your kids will feel rooted in the same way that you do. Deep roots allow the tree to grow tall and strong and bear fruit. As I write this passage I think about my mom, who was there as my father traveled to give me that sense of rooting. September 11th was her birthday, and this vignette is partially to honor her and the lessons she taught me. From the flat spot on the back of my head from getting smacked (always deserved) to the love of the land and the belief that all are welcome and no one leaves your house hungry (except you because others come first), my mom rooted me.

When I open my mouth to say something to my hooligans, and my mom comes out of my mouth? Yeah, that's deep roots making the family tree strong.

Action item: what are some of your best memories from being a kid? Replay them in your head. Share them with your kids.

12 SEPTEMBER

"At the end of the day, the most overwhelming key to a child's success is the positive involvement of parents."

Jane D. Hull

There are numerous studies that show that parents who read to their kids produce better outcomes, from grades and graduation rates to starting salaries and lower rates of arrest and incarceration. We can debate all the factors around why there is such a strong correlation but one thing has been shown over and over: kids with parents that invest time and participate in their lives turn out better on average.

What are some of the best things that your parents did for you? You probably don't remember the toys (even if you got the awesome Millennium Falcon Legos set) but you do remember the road trip or the birthday party where something weird happened (like the cops showing up for my son's first birthday because of the noise) or the times they were there for you emotionally. These memories show "presence" more than "presents," and become touchstones we go back to and build from in our own lives.

If you are a parent (or aunt or uncle), how involved are you? Like really. Do you sit there with your face in your phone while the kids are playing, or do you get down on your hands and knees and build with them or have a tea party? Are you a bit player in their story or are you center stage with them, dressing up and laughing and a key component of the tale? The more deeply involved, the stronger the bonds and the more likely the kid is to be a well adjusted adult.

Do you help with homework and show how it can relate to real world situations? Talk with them about your work and how it ties back to some of the things in their day to day activities so they can start piecing it all together? Blur the line between work and school so that they build an understanding in a low key manner of what you do and what it takes to be a success because they have a role model from the earliest remembrances?

It's not wasting time with your kids, even if you are trying to find the shoes they literally just had so you can get out the door. It's not spending time, because the time is valuable and will bear dividends: it is investing time with the kids so that they have the social and emotional capital to succeed and grow in the future. Being actively involved with them is the best guarantee of success for them, and for you as their parent.

NB: 9/12 is my parents' anniversary, and my brothers and sisters still celebrate it even though my mom has been gone for a while. Until I die I will honor my parents and their legacy of love.

Action item: read to your kid today. Even if they are 17.

13 SEPTEMBER
"Ohana means family, and family means no one gets left behind or forgotten."
Lilo and Stitch

Your family may not look (or be) "normal". It doesn't matter. Family is the people that choose to be together as much as those that are genetically linked.

There is a reason why people who have been in combat refer to each other as "Brother". "For he who sheds his blood with me, he is my brother" Shakespeare's *Henry V.*

You might not literally shed blood, but go through experiences that are traumatic and lead to a bonding and an adoption into the group, the family that you chose. We all have that "Uncle Shash" or "Aunt Diem" who is closer to our parents than their own blood, that BFF who you call your Sister From Another Mister and would do anything for. That kid who maybe broke your nose when you were seven and ends up at your kitchen table all the time and calls your mother "Ma". Yes, I'm pointing at you Vinny Sadowski.

After my best friend Rich died of cancer my then five year old declared "I miss Uncle Rich. He was my favorite uncle." To this day his favorite trip is to go to Boston to see his cousins (several of whom are 6'4"+ with flaming red hair) and we are an eclectic group but like the hodge-podge pack in Ice Age (a mastodon, a saber tooth tiger, a giant sloth and a human baby. Don't ask which I am...) we are there for each other no matter what. My nephews have a bizarre group of uncles looking out for them, but no matter what weird thing they need at any point in their life one of us is there to help fill the gap. Rich can not be forgotten or replaced, but we do the best we can in his stead because that is what family does.

Who are the members of your tribe, your weird pack that comes together more often than your blood and who have each others' backs? The ones who are precious to you and you would do anything for, from fighting at their side to fighting them when they are making self destructive decisions?

Ohana.

Action item: no one gets left behind or forgotten. Dust off the scrapbook (or digital photos) and look at those that you have loved and lost physically. Do not forget the good times and lessons.

14 SEPTEMBER
"Friends are the siblings God never gave us."

Mencius

We all have that Uncle Robert or Aunt Swapna that we have to explain "well, they're not really my aunt/uncle but they are part of my family." This is so common that it shouldn't even need to be explained why you have "cousins" that are of the entire rainbow of ethnicities and religions, because they are family even if they don't share the same last name or genetics.

"Brother From Another Mother" my favorite brother describes it. He's not blood but he's family and closer to me in personality and mindset than my biological brothers, and I love them equally. His sister is my BFF and is in my phonebook as "My Favorite Sister" because my mom always said she liked her more than me. But that's ok because her dad always loved me best! You more likely than not are nodding at this and thinking of your couple of friends that make up your inner circle and you'd do anything for, no question asked.

We have the family we are born with, and the family we chose. The latter have bonds just as strong if not of blood, and last for lifetimes in the same way, even passing down for generations. As my nieces asked when they were young: are they a blood relative or a love relative? Out of the mouth of babes...

Veterans refer to their "brothers in arms" for the risks they did and would take for those that always had their back in the most dangerous of situations, a bonding that supersedes genetics. John 15:13 declares it "Greater love hath no man than this, that a man lay down his life for his friends." That willingness to make the ultimate sacrifice for another earns the title and privilege of family status. Those that are there for you when you need them, whether they share the same name or not, are the most important people in your world.

Action item: who is that sibling of choice, that person who is part of you but not technically family. Reach out to them today and talk with them.

15 SEPTEMBER

"Because when I look at you, I can feel it.
And I look at you and I'm home."

Dory, in *Finding Nemo*

Sometimes, oftentimes, words fail. We can't express the emotions that another brings out from our soul, how they make us feel. They are just "right".

As a writer I struggle to try and express this feeling, where a particular person just feels like a warm hug even if you aren't touching. Where there is a comfort with them that is older than your relationship, a natural fit like two pieces of a jigsaw puzzle. They are home, because home is where the heart is, and they live in yours.

This feeling is strengthening, and scary. It makes us vulnerable, but in that vulnerability is immense power. I don't need to try and explain because you feel me.

This feeling that certain people bring up from the well of our soul is predictable (our parents, maybe our best friend for decades) and random: you come across someone and it clicks. Dolly Parton and Kenny Rogers sang that you can't make old friends, but sometimes it feels like this person you met relatively recently has been there with you forever. They have been part of you and you didn't know it, and you can't describe it. It isn't love in the traditional sense or biochemical, it isn't a soul mate or anything supernatural. It just is, and it's right.

Embrace it and accept it. Treasure this.

Action item: that person (or people) that give rise to this in your heart are important. Tell them so.

16 SEPTEMBER
"Where we love is home – home that our feet may leave, but not our hearts."
Oliver Wendell Holmes, Sr.

There is a particular place in the Catskill Mountains that is my Happy Place. For generations my family has gone there, we have fought to keep the sanctity of the environment, and it recharges me mentally, physically, and emotionally even if it takes a ton of work to keep up the old building and care for the property. The rock walls that I built when my older two were babies after the Flood of the Century (and then the next FOTC a few years later) are called Little Guy's Wall and Wee One's Wall and should still be there for my grandchildren. This is home.

In the middle of winter when the cabin is closed and I need a mental escape I am either on the beach someplace nameless that is completely fictional, or I am there at the cabin, picking blueberries or swimming in the lake on a blazing summer day after running for an hour on the brutal mountain slopes. This is where fantasy and memory mix.

If I am not writing (which I do a lot of at the cabin because of the relaxed pace of being on the mountain) or at a race, there is basically nothing else I would rather be doing than chopping trees and maintaining the place that holds my heart.

And yes, you can read that as an analogy for relationships in your life or for your career.

Where is that psychic home that your mind wanders to? Is it that one particular town that your family has gone to over and over, with that beach you played on as a kid and you now take your kids there? Is it that one hike that you just find yourself drawn to repeating over and over? Your gym, whether a shiny modern place or the basement dungeon that we trained martial arts in for decades that still holds the chi of a thousand students in its walls? That one place on the river that your grandfather took you to so you could fish together? Wherever it is, treasure it and go there whenever you can, in mind or body.

Remember with your heart, even if not physically there.

Action item: find a picture of your happy place, your emotional home. Put it on your laptop home screen or on your phone.

17 SEPTEMBER
"Not all who wander are lost."

JRR Tolkein

He dropped out of college but hung around, attending whatever class caught his fancy. He traveled to India to learn, and founded multiple companies on his journey before returning home years later to Apple. Of course I'm talking about about Steve Jobs.

Sometimes, life is filled with side quests that we need to go on to acquire knowledge, friends, and resources to complete our main objective.

When you are off the beaten path, who can say that you are not learning what you need for a later challenge, whether it is bookkeeping skills you'll require for your startup venture or the cooking skills that impress your crush and help make them your partner?

The actor Matthew McConaughey spent years as the most bankable Romantic Comedy actor in Hollywood. He made a conscious decision to stop doing them, and for almost two years did not have a single project. Was he lost? Or was he walking with purpose, because then the floodgates opened with challenging projects including Dallas Buyers Club which earned him The Academy Award for Best Actor.

Omar Kayyam, Copernicus, and Ben Franklin all wandered in their interests yet took lessons from all areas and have left legacies that stretch a thousand years. Leonardo da Vinci might be the greatest example of this.

"If I knew what I was doing, it wouldn't be called research" is the signature line of one of the most brilliant experimental physicists I know.

The overflowing wastebasket of the writer, scrunched up pieces of paper rejected and thrown aside like an ex-lover, is the classic image of someone who knows where they are going but not quite the right way to get there.

Dating is an attempt to find the right way, or at least companion, on the road of life.

Sometimes the people that seem on the straight and narrow are actually lost, and those that appear to wander are actually working towards a very specific goal.

Sometimes you have to get lost to find yourself, in the woods or a book or your thoughts.

Action item: look at your life and your path. Are you on your main quest, a side quest, or just fumbling around? Where are you trying to reach?

18 SEPTEMBER
"Knowledge is an unending adventure on the edge of uncertainty."

Jacob Bronowski

"Madness and genius are one step apart. I'm just not sure which foot to lead with." JRRT

"There are things known and there are things unknown, and in between there are the doors of perception." Aldous Huxley

On the threshold of the doorway is the greatest uncertainty but also the greatest opportunity, the edge of the knife between the known and the unknown. It is here that the heart and mind race, discovering the secrets of the world around us. Here is where children live, and no one is more alive in the moment, enjoying the adventure than a kid.

Think about doing an escape room: solving problems as the clock counts down, the heart pounding as the stakes get higher as time shortens. Admit it, it is pretty awesome. Now instead of solving a problem that is purely for amusement or entertainment, add some real stakes to it. Financial rewards for solving the problems of building a business, or a rescue mission with a life on the line. The attorney before the jury, or the salesperson trying to close the deal. One foot firmly planted in their area of expertise and knowledge, the other beyond the pale in the uncontrollable and barely knowable. There is a reason why competitive individuals are drawn into these areas.

Our knowledge set as individuals and a society is built off of fundamentals that we hopefully master but continuously add to, expanding upward and outward with the occasional deconstruction of what was built previously when revolutionary ideas shift the foundation of our edifice. The unending improvement and expansion is ingrained in us not from childhood but from the dawn of our species, the need to explore the undiscovered country and learn about our world being one of the most human characteristics.

Look to the borders of your knowledge, for just like the maps of old just beyond the edge there be monsters. Great unknowns, scary concepts, dragons that could devour us or yield their treasure hoards of wealth and innovation. This edge of the unexplained is dangerous like the frontier but where adventure and riches and stories are to be had.

Action item: walk the border of uncertainty today. Go right to the edge of your knowledge and stare into the abyss. Discover things you don't yet know,

INTERNATIONAL TALK LIKE A PIRATE DAY!

"There is more treasure in books than in all the pirate's loot on Treasure Island."

Walt Disney

Yes, as kids we all dreamt of gold and emeralds and overflowing treasure chests. We knew if we followed the directions and solved the problems, kept our wits about us and were brave we could have adventure and riches.

Sounds like the dreams of all startup entrepreneurs actually. A little less cutlass play, but probably seas just as stormy and cramped working conditions with often ill tempered and bad smelling coworkers. But a lot less rum too.

Treasure Island is the promised land, the Easy Street we all ultimately wanted. Post-IPO to those of us that came of professional age in the dot com era. To nerds today it is becoming a unicorn (company valued at a billion dollars or more) and being acquired by one of the tech giants.

Or maybe you fantasize of hitting the Mega Millions for mega bucks, same result: fabulous wealth for a great risk and maybe a limited time of soul crushing effort. And then retire to the countryside, take on a new identity, and live like a landed squire and buy respect. The classic pirate fairy tale of "happily ever after."

Yet the old gold of the Pirates of the Caribbean ilk is as nothing compared with what can be mined in cyberspace (and I am not talking just Bitcoin). True wealth goes beyond mere financial power (which is never a bad thing) but extends even further into other realms.

Even without a treasure chest of loot you can read (books or now the interwebz) and find all the information you need to live a healthy lifestyle, from food to webMD to hiring a personal trainer that will yell at you over Zoom so you can maintain that mid-20's figure even into your 50's.

With diet (maybe hiring a private chef because pirates only make barrrrbeque) and preventative medical care (no scurvy so you'll keep your teeth), you will have better health than even the Royal Governors could imagine.

You can travel to new lands (and even worlds) without ever boarding a ship.

You can learn any craft from navigator to cooper or even Quartermaster. Remote learning, attending classes, just seeking information the way pirates sought treasure is easier than swabbing a deck now.

Education is expensive, but ignorance even more so. Literally all the knowledge of humankind is available with a library card (cost: zero pieces of eight) getting you access to the scrolls and tomes and computers and the maps to all the wealth in the world, as well as discussions with mermaids and face to face encounters with giant squids and great white whales and indigenous peoples. The insights of Blackbeard and Sir Francis Drake and Madame Cheng for those that would hear the tales and harken to their wisdom.

All the clues are there for you to pursue, if ye be of stout heart and open mind.

Action item: the treasure map does not have an X marking the spot of the treasure, but the clues are all there for fabulous, epic wealth. Go to the library and plot your course.

20 SEPTEMBER
"A room without books is like a body without a soul."

Marcus Tullius Cicero

I needed some insight, so I consulted the Emperor, Marcus Aurelius. He is a living influence, sharing his wisdom to me through Meditations, his personal journal. Teddy Roosevelt chimes in through his autobiography, as do Ben Franklin and Jimmy Carter and General Jim Matthis. Jim Thorpe, Leonardo da Vinci, and Herb Kelleher speak up from the table where they are playing cards with Patrick Bet David and are interrupted by Marie Curie. All are alive through books.

Before the internet, one of the best ways to determine the future success of a person was to look at their personal library and what they had checked out from the public one. Access to information and the experiences of others are critical for informed decision making, and the more complex the world becomes the more knowledge and wisdom we must seek or else we fall behind and are in danger.

As Matthis was telling Kelleher over cards, if you haven't read hundreds of books you are functionally illiterate. Merely a shell of a person or a leader. "Not all readers are leaders, but all leaders are readers." President Harry S Truman. Books expose us to the wisdom of the ages and the insight of other mere mortals like ourselves. Reading the accounts of The Revolutionary War or the Civil War or Vietnam from the point of view of a private in the field, hungry and scared, is very different from the perspective of a Washington or Grant or Westmoreland, and in many ways more useful for those of us not in full command of the organization. Having access to both rank and file and elite leaders rounds out our perspective and makes the situation come to life in a way that we can glean more understanding from, understanding we can apply in our own daily battles. The poets from Yeats or Frost back through antiquity like Virgil and Li Bai or Al Mutanabbi poured their souls onto pages for us today to feel and experience.

Confucius, Plato, Diogenes, Schopenhauer, and even Winnie the Pooh expose us to philosophy. Milton Berle and Jerry Seinfeld and Tina Fey make us laugh while Sylvia Plath and Kafka and Camus make us cry. Both emotions dwell in our soul and need expression.

CS Lewis and Hemingway inspire us while Thomas Sowell debates Malcolm Gladwell, making us think. Then Dave Barry puts a completely different spin on things, as do Douglas Adams and Scott Adams and Gary Larson through their own media. If you felt your soul dance and shimmy in a dozen different directions reading this passage, you probably have many rooms with books because your body holds an erudite spirit. If not, you might want to go apply for a library card.

Action item: you can never have too many books. Go get some more.

21 September

"To acquire knowledge, one must study; But to acquire wisdom, one must observe."
Marilyn vos Savant

Yes, filling your head with facts and figures is important. But I have seen too many people who think they are wise because they

Can write a washing bill in Babylonic cuneiform
And tell you ev'ry detail of Caractacus's uniform
In short, in matters vegetable, animal, and mineral
I am the very model of a modern Major-General

Gilbert and Sullivan, from the *Pirates of Penzance*

We all know that guy who can tell you the stats of every baseball player for the St. Louis Cardinals in the 1980's. That guy in my office also locked himself in the file room and put a metal pie plate in the microwave and I believe was terminated for ethical violations. Not exactly the Wisdom of Solomon there.

"Theoretically it should work." In a massless, frictionless world. With no wind or losses of energy. There is a big difference between the textbook and real life. But out of the lab, non-controlled situations are quite different from the perfect fake conditions, and we see this in every interaction we have with other humans.

We have two eyes, two ears, and one mouth and are meant to use them in that proportion. Louis XIV of France, The Sun King, was one of the most powerful monarchs of Europe and also highly effective. Unlike many of the others that lead countries, Louis was known for his ability to listen and observe, to hear all sides of a story from multiple sources before coming to conclusions and issuing his edicts.

Sir Richard Branson states: listen more than you talk.

The tv show "Undercover Boss" was pretty entertaining, but the premise of putting the leader among the workers in a stealth manner so that they could understand more than what was in the reports on their desks was brilliant. It not only humanized the employees but let the boss experience the hardships and triumphs that their people dealt with, and exposed problems in a manner that made them truly real to the person that could make change via fiat. Every boss that did this ended up much wiser for their direct observations.

Action item: keep your mouth closed and your eyes open more today.

22 SEPTEMBER

"Do not seek to follow in the footsteps of the wise. Seek what they sought."

Matsuo Basho

Not many of us are going to be walking around carrying a katana sword today. But we can understand the principles that the samurai lived with under bushido (their code), and how they trained their mind to be indifferent to risk so as to be able to function better in the chaotic world we dwell in. The lessons of the warrior, even if our methodologies and weapons have evolved.

I have read hundreds of case studies from a variety of sources, and in discussing them with others I am always amazed by the people who say "well, we'll just do exactly what they did and get similar results." What this cloning approach ignores is the fact that situations change, the people involved have different experiences and motivations, and the market catches up to first movers and innovators. In short, the only way to get the same results is to have the EXACT same inputs and same external situations, which is impossible. But if we understand the concepts that were applied and look at the uniqueness of this particular scenario, we can make a superior play because we are applying ideas instead of techniques, and as such can adapt the appropriate components.

Instead of following the exact workout of a professional athlete, look at the core exercises and why they are doing them, then look at others within your sport and meld the concepts into something appropriate for you and your body. Instead of following the latest celebrity diet craze, read up on the concept behind it and why it works. Understand a little more of the science and use the parts of it (like volumetric eating, fat burning enhancements, whatever makes sense) and use them instead of thinking you'll look like Chris Helmsworth or J Lo just because you go on their radical diet for a month.

Meet with your mentor, but instead of just doing what they did 15 years ago to be successful, brainstorm with them on what you should do based on the current technology, investment/tax landscape, regulations, and your personal constraints (kids, financial, physical limitations or gifts). Don't do what they did, do what they would do today if they were you. Big difference, and better results probably. Instead of doing what your parents did with you growing up (even if you turned out really well), remember that the world your kids will grow up in is very different from the one you grew up in. Take the core values your parents taught you, and look at how you can still have your kids adopt them but in a faster more technology driven world. Teach them the lessons but evolve the delivery.

Action item: take three minutes and write down "Success as a XX looks like:" Could be as a parent, partner, friend, or at work. Now find someone who meets that definition and ask them "If you were to do it again in today's world, what should we do?"

23 SEPTEMBER
"The two most powerful warriors are patience and time."

Leo Tolstoy

Is time your ally, or your enemy? Is compound interest working for, or against you (investments versus debt)? Sometimes, it takes time for the vine of truth to bear its fruit. If you can wait and let it grow, you might feast while those who sowed lies ultimately starve.

Patience is what allows time to work. Those of us with a bias for action must fight our tendency to do something, anything, to move the process along. Waiting like a farmer for the rhythms of the seasons and the natural cycle of things does not sit well with those of us who try to make things happen. But for the men and women of action that can learn patience, like a warrior meditating on a rock, true power arises.

Patience prevents us from plucking the fruit of the vine too early, before it is ripe and fully grown. Patience is the internally developed virtue that allows time to gather its power and perform its miracles.

Develop your patience, and you develop your power. Ways to become more patient (from the least patient person I know):

Count to five. Twice if need be.
Put the phone on "do not disturb" and then put it in the drawer or other room.
Set a timer for an hour before responding to that email or text.
Hand write out the points you want to address. Then type it after you think.
Close your eyes and picture yourself on a beach in Tahiti with a drink in hand. Or rampaging with a horde and destroying everything. Both work to take the edge off.
Take a walk around the block or office.
Go get a coffee.
Take four deep, long breaths.
Ask a question. And not "Why haven't you won the Darwin Award yet?"

Keep track daily of the number of times you lose your patience.

Patience is a special type of discipline, and discipline takes practice to improve as well as tools to make it easier. You won't have the patience of Job if you start with the temper of Jobs, but if you work on it like it's your job you will improve and allow time to work for you.

Action item: chose two techniques to apply today.

23 SEPTEMBER
"The two most powerful warriors are patience and time."

Leo Tolstoy

Is time your ally, or your enemy? Is compound interest working for, or against you (investments versus debt)? Sometimes, it takes time for the vine of truth to bear its fruit. If you can wait and let it grow, you might feast while those who sowed lies ultimately starve.

Patience is what allows time to work. Those of us with a bias for action must fight our tendency to do something, anything, to move the process along. Waiting like a farmer for the rhythms of the seasons and the natural cycle of things does not sit well with those of us who try to make things happen. But for the men and women of action that can learn patience, like a warrior meditating on a rock, true power arises.

Patience prevents us from plucking the fruit of the vine too early, before it is ripe and fully grown. Patience is the internally developed virtue that allows time to gather its power and perform its miracles.

Develop your patience, and you develop your power. Ways to become more patient (from the least patient person I know):

Count to five. Twice if need be.
Put the phone on "do not disturb" and then put it in the drawer or other room.
Set a timer for an hour before responding to that email or text.
Hand write out the points you want to address. Then type it after you think.
Close your eyes and picture yourself on a beach in Tahiti with a drink in hand. Or rampaging with a horde and destroying everything. Both work to take the edge off.
Take a walk around the block or office.
Go get a coffee.
Take four deep, long breaths.
Ask a question. And not "Why haven't you won the Darwin Award yet?"

Keep track daily of the number of times you lose your patience.

Patience is a special type of discipline, and discipline takes practice to improve as well as tools to make it easier. You won't have the patience of Job if you start with the temper of Jobs, but if you work on it like it's your job you will improve and allow time to work for you.

Action item: chose two techniques to apply today.

24 SEPTEMBER
"The measure of a man is what he does with power."

Plato

Money and alcohol are exactly the same as power. The old saying is that power corrupts, but there are numerous examples ranging from Marcus Aurelius to Herb Kelleher (former CEO of Southwest Airlines) to Representative Chris Gibson (retired Colonel US Army, PhD, and now President of Siena College, who used to fly from Washington DC on Southwest Airlines and stood in line like all of us normal people, and still does) of it not changing the person other than allowing them to do more good at a higher level.

Power is an enhancer. It shows how bad a bad person can be (Nero, Detroit Mayor Kilpatrick, NY Governor Andrew Cuomo), or how a good person can leverage capabilities for a greater positive impact on the world around them. Examples you might not know of include George Michael giving tens of millions away to charity on the condition it be kept secret, Tony Robbins donating money and meals since being on the receiving end of a Thanksgiving food donation as an underfed kid, and Dietmer Hopp (SAP co-Founder) and Pierre Omidyar (eBay co-Founder) who have given over a sixth of their wealth away to assist others while planning to give away even more over time.

People that are comfortable wielding power can do so to great or terrible effect, it all depends on how they have developed. We have all seen the tyranny of a boss who is like that because they are a jerk all the way through, and maybe got into their position by getting results but also by burning people along the climb up the ladder.

Contrast this with the martial artist that as a white belt saw the senior students sweep the floors, that saw the Instructors remain humble and restrain their power even when they could blast a student, who watched their Master choose the simple paths and avoid bragging or showing their abilities outside of the training hall, will probably model this restraint when they are a deadly weapon themselves. If this martial artist were not trained in the proper use of power they would be a danger to society, as much as the narcissistic jerk of a boss that runs a large company and their ego drives them beyond the pale and leads to a company implosion (Enron, WorldCom, Tyco, etc.).

Keanu Reeves is famous for what he does quietly when the camera is off. Giving millions to hospitals. Helping random homeless people. Pushing a broken-down car (and thus influencing future Hollywood stars as to how to act), supporting the unseen support crew of his movies. He could act like a diva and develop a drug habit like all too frequently happens to actors that have early success, but Neo uses his power for good. Would you have the restraint if you had it all at your fingertips like he does?

Restraint is the measure of a man or a woman. Just because you can do something doesn't mean you should. The freedom of the freshman in college away from home for the first time can be telling: do they drink their way out of school or do they take advantage of the opportunities to learn inside and outside the classroom?

Do they use their freedom to revel in hedonism or do they use it to explore themselves and apply discipline to improve themselves? Without the governor of the parents and in a new place where they can create a new self, which path they choose reflects who they are deep inside.

Same with the recently divorced or retired. I have seen too many people unable to handle the sudden freedom and spiral out of control because internally they don't measure up, and only the externally imposed standards kept them in check.

When you have the power to do anything that you want, what do you do?

Action item: look at how you apply your power over other people, whether in a relationship, with kids, or in the office. Do your choices indicate that you measure up well, or should you change yourself to be more worthy of power?

25 SEPTEMBER
"Our deepest fear is that we are powerful beyond measure."

Marianne Williamson

In the movies, it is not until the hero is comfortable wielding their power do they realize how truly powerful they are and can then complete their journey and face their nemesis. Their internal battle is more difficult than the ultimate external one, if not so graphic and entertaining.

I have seen athletes hold themselves back because they are afraid to truly let go, be it on the slopes or in the ring. When they finally do accept their ability and fully unleash it, they are faster and stronger than they ever comprehended. The lover with immense passion that finally shows it, both to themselves and to their beloved. The artist that removes the constraints on themselves and lets their true ability shine like Jackson Pollock or any of the surrealists (Andre Breton, Leonora Carrington, Dali) without filter.

The salesperson who finally faces their internal doubts, overcomes them, and suddenly is in a totally different sphere of production because they are the best version of themselves instead of a poor copy of another.

You are powerful, the only governor on your speed and capability is the one you put there. The more often you push yourself to that self-imposed limit, the further the limit pushes out. And you are capable of going well beyond that limit if you can achieve the state of Flow, of harmony and "no mind". You can suddenly realize your potential and apply it.

As Yoda instructs young Skywalker: do, or do not. There is no try.

Just do it.

"Let it go!" Elsa the Ice Queen in *Frozen*.

We fear success, maybe because we have no model for what it looks like or we have Imposter Syndrome, or we have unmet psychological/emotional needs on Maslow's Hierarchy. Some people fear love for the same reason others fear success because it is intensely powerful and we might not know if we can handle it, so we sabotage ourselves and prevent our own greatness by subconsciously doing stupid things and making ourselves trip up. Success, love, physical excellence all have unconscious as well as conscious components, and to unlock the full potential they must be in harmony and allow the power to flow through us unhindered. When we restrict ourselves via self imposed limits, we lessen the world.

Action item: let it rip. Go for broke. Today, just today, be the ultimate version of you.

26 SEPTEMBER
"Knowing what must be done does away with fear."

Rosa Parks

Many fears, especially the paralyzing variety, are because we are overwhelmed and have no clue what to do. But action overcomes anxiety: motivation is literally rooted in the word "move". One small step when afraid breaks the terror and moves us forward, a tiny positive movement and the start of a feedback loop of progress and bravery.

Are you terrified of leaving your job? But know that you should because the writing is on the wall? You know what must be done: improve your LinkedIn profile, polish your resume, start quietly communicating with friends in the same field outside of your current company. Knowing what to do, breaking the overwhelming task into small doable chunks and then starting to do them makes it a plan and eliminates the panic. You might not have to execute the plan, but you know you can if need be and the fear subsides.

Your marriage is a dumpster fire? The first step is to work on yourself. If you haven't or won't, you will stay stuck in Hell. If you do start working on yourself (honestly assessing yourself and your partner is the start, looking after your physical and mental health is the next, etc.) and you are on the right path. If you're going through Hell, keep on moving.

Giving up smoking or another physical addiction is one of the most terrifying things, but not seeing your grandkids graduate or your child walk down the aisle is even more so. You know what you need to do. If the idea of totally walking away from the old you (smoker, addict, whatever description you use) is overwhelming, take the small steps. They are usually 12 step programs for a reason, not one giant leap.

Afraid of that test? You know what needs to be done. Start studying.

One of the things about martial arts training is that we repeat the actions thousands of times. It eliminates fear through training that becomes automatic action.

Pilots are the same way in a much bigger situation. Remember Captain Sully Sullenberg landing in the Hudson River?

Special Forces and SWAT Teams, firefighters, EMTs. Doing overcoming fear. Face your fears. You'll see them shrink when you look directly at them and start walking in their direction.

Action item: what is one thing you are afraid of in your life? Walk towards it.

27 SEPTEMBER
"It is easy to forgive a child who is afraid of the dark; the real tragedy of life is when men are afraid of the light."
Plato

We all know people that don't want to be confused with the facts. That is a tragedy, especially if their willful ignorance leads to the deaths of others as opposed to winning the Darwin Award. The Light of Truth will eventually shine bright enough for facts to come out and let things be seen as they really are.

We all know people that are afraid of success because they don't believe they deserve it. So they will sabotage themselves in a variety of ways to keep themselves at the level they subconsciously believe that they deserve. Some of us still work like we are afraid that "They" will figure out we are in over our head and don't deserve to be here so we bust our ass twice as hard all the time. Some of us... being me. Maybe you.

Sunlight scares away the monsters and makes vampires disappear in a puff of smoke. But some people are so used to having those monsters there that they are afraid of not having them around to use as an excuse. They fear the light because they are comfortable not becoming better because it is less scary than dealing with the monsters in their head and the changes they need to make to be what they could become.

Some people want "plausible deniability" so they don't have to confront brutal reality, whether nefarious things going on in their company (think Enron and the organizations that helped them to lie, cheat, and essentially steal), or the person denying their partner's infidelity that is in plain sight because they are not nearly as discrete as they claim, or the parent denying their teen's drug use. The abused spouse (mentally or physically) that covers up for the monster that hurts them. These are all people afraid of the light.

It's not always easy to do the right thing, there can be significant negative financial and reputational consequences. But when lives are on the line, when the mental health of the innocent (like your kids) is at stake, when the darkness that is so dangerous and will claim more lives is such that you can stop it and save others, it is time to walk into the light even if it is painfully bright and makes you tear up.

Action item: what Truth are you afraid to face? What light makes you shield your eyes and turn away? Face them.

28 SEPTEMBER

"If you are lucky enough to find a way of life you love, you have to find the courage to live it."

John Irving

Not everyone is cut out to be an entrepreneur, the uncertainty and massive effort and risks. For those of us with the temperament and work ethic though it is the most glorious adventure, even if it is crazy and exhausting and frustrating and sometimes we want to abandon the quest because it is so difficult, especially when others bark in our ear about getting a "normal job."

Many of my friends are engineers (probably because I went to an engineering school, funny how that works), and they want to solve problems and not have to make critical decisions about people or money because of the unpredictability. These people might become tech leads or even Chief Engineers, but they would never want to move into the sales or executive function components of their businesses for a ton of reasons, the least of which is they don't want to wear a tie. They just don't like the components of those roles. As one friend said: I don't people well. And that's ok, and why she isn't in sales or leadership and that is totally ok.

Some people aren't cut out to be parents. Instead of forcing them or shaming them, let them just have their fur babies and peace.

Some people are better off single, others desperately need someone so they aren't alone. As long as they have explored the other option enough to know that it is not for them then it is their choice for what is best for them is what is best for them. Love the life you live but do it by choice not because of fear of the other unknown.

If you can find a career that aligns with your god given talent and compensates you fairly for what you do, that is awesome.

Some people love differently. That's ok. If you're not loving them, or asking them to love you, butt out and let them be happy.

Some people are city folk because it fits with them. Not me, but that's ok. I'll go visit the Big Apple and catch a Yankees game or work for a few days and come back to my trees and the small town vibe I love with my bunnies frolicking in the yard. Country boys can survive.

Work how you want to work, play how you want to play and as long as it doesn't hurt anyone you be you. If others don't like it, that's a "them problem" not a "you problem".

Action item: what is something you want to do but just haven't had the courage to do? If it doesn't hurt others, take a deep breath and start doing it.

29 SEPTEMBER
"If you want to be an anomaly, you need to act like one."

Gary Vaynerchuk

To get different results from everyone else, you need to act differently.

I used to start my business day earlier than any of my peers and keep working when they went to the bar at five because I didn't want to be average but exceptional. Are you willing to work exceptionally hard to get exceptional results?

Andre the Giant was unlike anyone to ever come before in the wrestling world. So he (and Vince McMahon) promoted him very differently. If you were 7'2" and 500 pounds you'd be different and act it too.

Richard Feynman acted differently (and not just talking about the bongo drums) because he thought differently and was essentially unique, like some of the greatest theoretical physicists. His foibles were legendary but contributed in many ways to his exploration of the universe and ultimately a Nobel Prize in Physics.

If all your friends are partying until late o'clock and you do too, what do you think your results will be?

Dennis Rodman was a definite oddball. But he loved rebounding and defense more than anything and built his Hall of Fame career around something few others even wanted to do. Sure his fashion sense was outlandish to say the least, but his work ethic and defensive mindset was only equaled by a handful of players and none did it his way. Seven All-Defense Teams, five Championships and two Defensive Player of the Year awards are the results of digging deep as The Worm did.

There was only one Frank Sinatra. As he said, he did it his way.

Picasso too.

If you are going to be unique, be unique as opposed to trying to be a cookie cutter clone of others. Be the best you you can be, not by trying to be just like others but a unique combination of inspirations from others, filtered through your own belief system, to create something unlike anybody else because it is the differences that are remembered, not the similarities with every other sheep on the planet.

Action item: to truly unlock your individual god given gifts, what should you do today?

30 SEPTEMBER

"Dare to be stupid!"

'Weird' Al Yankovic

I do stupid things all the time. Sometimes they are so dumb that they are brilliant.

Sometimes I am much more of an idiot than a savant. Helps keep the ego in check.

As Thor proclaimed "I make grave mistakes all the time."

Because here is the thing: if you don't make mistakes, you'll never have successes. You can't grow and learn and innovate if you don't try things that have never been tried, or look at things from a totally different perspective.

Post It Notes were a mistake. When they were commercially rolled out in 1980 they did over $2,000,000 in profits that year. Today over 50 BILLION individual Post IT Notes pages are sold annually.

The Slinky was a mistake too. As was penicillin.

The microwave oven came about because someone stupidly walked in front of the radar and melted a candy bar.

Whomever decided to try salt and caramel together created a craze equal to chocolate and peanut butter or peanut butter and jelly. In fact the first humans that decided to plant seeds were probably considered stupid by their friends.

Mixing rock and rap was considered stupid. Then Run DMC re-ignited Aerosmith's career and sold over three million albums and changed pop music forever. Sending cupcakes to your crush might be stupid but hey it might work, because cupcakes equal love.

Sometimes I even ask myself "what is the most idiotic, foolhardy thing I could do here?" Helps me be better grounded and have a stronger understanding. There is a reason why there are some pretty weird warning labels on products because they need to be from people actually doing things we would never think of. That's also how the Code Talkers stumped the Germans in WWII.

"That's so stupid it could actually work." I've heard that more than a few times. If you don't try, you'll never know.

Action item: what is something really dumb you can do today that won't endanger anyone?

OCTOBER IS CRISP DAYS AND COOL NIGHTS,
A TIME TO CURL UP AROUND THE DANCING
FLAMES, AND SINK INTO A GOOD BOOK

John Sinor

01 OCTOBER

"Fear is stupid. So are regrets."

Marilyn Monroe

"Oh, I can't do that!" Why not? A baby will fall down over and over and over, with no fear, to be able to walk or climb up and get a cookie. As an adult, don't you want that cookie, be it the date with your crush or the promotion or the chance to go to Paris? Don't be afraid to try, or you'll have that regret watching others get what you gave up on.

The saber tooth tiger isn't going to disembowel you if you try something new. Someone might laugh at you, but is it someone whose opinion you care about? Then say "screw it", put on your big boy or girl panties, and try it. You might like it, you might hate it. But you won't know either way unless you overcome your fear and do it. No regret.

One of the greatest fears people have is speaking in public. More than they fear sharks or fire. Yet how important is it to be able to stand in front of a group and persuade them, whether you are convincing your boss for the raise or the auditorium full of parents and get them to see that investing in kids' education will help your town and everyone in it? If you are afraid like most people you won't get up there and convince them, and five years later you'll regret not stepping up when your kid's programs are cut.

Speak up.

Stand in front of the mirror and convince yourself, then present to a dozen teddy bears, then some friends, then step up to the podium and do what you used to fear. No regrets for giving it your best shot, and the skills you develop you can use in other areas and improve your personal outcomes, because you faced that great fear.

"Oh, I can't take the risk to start a business!" Why? You don't have to drop your life savings into it, sit at your kitchen table and figure out how to try it as an experiment in a low risk manner. Overcome that initial fear. Start, and see if you can make a go at a small level before risking more once you are comfortable with the small risk and ready for more. Overcome fear with micro-actions. Or else have regrets for not taking that teeny tiny little step, to see if you could do it.

The regrets of failure will always be much less than the regret of giving into fear and always having to ask "what if?".

Action item: what is that one big but irrational fear holding you back? Grab a piece of paper and right down all the little things that you could do, the micro-actions to overcome it. Choose one and do it!

02 OCTOBER
"I'd rather regret the things I've done than regret the things I haven't done."

Lucille Ball

If it weren't for Lucille Ball, we wouldn't have Star Trek. No Spock, no "Beam me up", no "He's dead Jim" memes. No Picard, Klingons, or Uhuru. No George Takei "Oh my!!!" Think about that. No final frontier without risking action.

And be glad Lucy took the risks that led her to be able to bring us that entire version of the future. What if Columbus gave up and didn't try to find a different trade route?

If Lincoln hadn't taken the risk of politics, or Elon Musk risking his Paypal payout on an electric car? What if Kerry Underwood hadn't risked going on American Idol, or if I never risked writing this?

What if you hadn't asked that person out that is sharing your bed tonight, that has brought those cute little humans into the world with you? Even if you are fighting with them, or even not sharing a bed anymore, do you regret those kids? I should think not.

A guy named Milton failed in business several times, but learned from each attempt and then got it right. You've probably had a Hershey Bar, and are glad that he didn't regret his failures before the success that bears his name.

We create more risks in our mind than actually exist in the world for almost everything we can choose to do.

The meek will inherit the earth because those that dared, that were bold and took action and would rather make an error of commission than omission will have already enjoyed the lion's share of benefits. Scraps go to the fearful, the banquet to the fearless.

If it's not fatal, you can recover.

No guts, no glory.

Action item: what is that one thing you'd love to do but are afraid of that carries a low level of risk? Just get off your butt, stop questioning and do it. Even if you fail, it won't be fatal!

03 OCTOBER

"What would life be if we had no courage to attempt anything?"

Vincent van Gogh

This is a question that is often asked in some variation. And one that people rarely sit down and actually think about, instead of throwing out some off the cuff ideas that are surface actions but not reflective of their deep beliefs and needs.

Many people say they would ask for a raise or attempt a marathon, which are not bad things. But they are primarily reflections of what is easily attracting their attention and distracting from the real issues instead of the fundamental want. Instead of saying "make more money", is the REAL goal to be financially free? Instead of being able to be a slightly better wage slave with some nicer stuff, is the goal to be truly wealthy? To be in charge, so that you can have a greater impact?

Instead of looking at the incremental improvement in your situation, really delve into WHAT you want and WHY so that you truly do have the courage to attempt something significant.

Action item: grab some paper and a pen, and go somewhere you can really think. Eliminate all distractions (pets, kids, work, devices, everything possible). Sit there for a half hour with yourself thinking about the question "What would I attempt if I couldn't fail?" and write it down. Don't be afraid to go deep.

04 OCTOBER

"It is not the size of a man but the size of his heart that matters."

Evander Holyfield

Olympic Medalist who would win titles in three different weight divisions spanning three different decades, Holyfield took down Iron Mike Tyson as well as other monsters and truly was the Real Deal in the ring.

"Not the glittering weapon fights the fight, but rather the hero's heart." Proverb

If your heart is in the right place and big enough, your mind and body become nigh on unbreakable. You can bear any beating or burden, withstand any temptation, for what you believe in so deeply that the hell you have to experience to achieve the heart's desire can not dissuade you. Punch above your weight by unleashing the power of your heart.

David versus Goliath.

Little town versus Corporate Conglomerate.

The underdog who won't give up and keeps fighting when there is no logical reason for them to still be standing.

The mother who pulled a double shift and is cooking for the kids.

The dad who coaches and works and goes to school to better himself and his family, no matter how exhausted he is and everyone says give up.

The plucky entrepreneur working their job then burning the midnight oil until early o'clock night after night.

The three-year-old with the rare brain cancer, and their family that refuses to give up.

The hearts of champions that are bigger than their bodies or circumstances, that inspire and amaze us. Thank you. Thank you for making us believe in the impossible, because you live it.

Action item: go watch a video of a disabled kid or athlete overcoming the odds. Now emulate their courage and will in all you do today.

05 OCTOBER
"When the heart is full, the eyes overflow."

Sholom Aleichem

Beauty is in the eye of the beholder, but when you see everything through the eyes of love, everything becomes beautiful.

Flowers smell sweeter, the colors of the sky are more vibrant, the music more moving when love is flowing through your veins. Everything is enhanced, sharpened and clearer because of the internal boost that love gives. The neurochemical cocktail supercharges your senses while buoying your spirits and actually enhancing your cognitive capabilities.

Love is the ultimate high, lighting up the dopamine and serotonin receptors in the brain like the most addictive of drugs.

Think about when you were newly in love. Did you have more spring in your step? Did you feel like dancing in your giddiness, a euphoria that lasted for days and weeks and made the sun shine even if it was raining? Did that feeling pour over into all other relationships, making you a little nicer to people and happier even with the most boring work or cleaning task?

When your love was green like the early shoots of Spring, how wonderful was everything? As wonderful as Louis Armstrong's "What a Wonderful World", with everything aligning for you and nothing able to shake your positivity?

"Love bears all things", and the early stages of love give us stamina and other resources we normally don't tap into. Everyone becomes a poet when in love, channeling their inner Cyrano de Bergerac because of their Muse.

In love, beauty is everywhere. It dominates our vision, and our thoughts. It is Fiddler's Green and the Elysian Fields on earth, a piece of heaven. Enjoy every moment of it.

Action item: take a moment, and think of the person that loves you the most. Close your eyes, and picture their face. Take a deep breath, and hear their voice. Spend a moment with them, and let the feelings surround you like a hug. Open your eyes and carry this feeling into your day.

06 OCTOBER

"Poetry is when an emotion has found its thought and the thought has found words."

Robert Frost

Poetry is the most concentrated form of writing, succinctly conveying more than the words. It is a distilled spirit of 100+ proof compared to the wine of plays or the beer of essays that must fill volumes to give the same shudder of emotion a poem quickly conveys, a shot of feeling.

Great poetry will make you feel in the same manner as music can, but with a deeper connection and less abstraction, a direct emotional blast to the body that can leave you ready to cry in seconds or fill your heart in moments. Often both, as poetry captures the essence of life and life itself is complex beyond words.

Whether it is sonnets (Shall I compare Thee To a Summer's Day?), haiku (I cry in the rain...), or the free verse favored by Walt Whitman and Langston Hughes, poetry of all forms conveys the experience from head to gut of the poet, the moment of pure being in all of its glory and terror. Poems capture life in lines, and the art of the poet is to not say everything so that the reader can think and feel...

Action item: google poetry, and either read or listen to some today.

07 OCTOBER

"We should always remember that sensitiveness and emotion constitute the real content of a work of art."

Maurice Ravel

The Impressionists were outcasts of Paris' painting scene because the establishment that controlled the art world (literal licenses for painters just like attorneys and doctors) rejected them for being unconventional and not adhering to the prescribed code of painting. Yet who can argue with the feel of Monet's (or Manet's) works? Van Gogh's The Starry Night, one of the most recognized paintings in history, would not have made it into the exhibits because it violated all the rules and yet is on coffee mugs everywhere.

Art is about capturing in some medium (stone, paint, words, etc.) emotions, feelings, and messages by the artist and transferring them to the observer. The ephemeral is made material.

Art has at times been constrained and overly constrained: the iron clad structure of the haiku is both guide and guard, the classical style of sculpture ennobled and enslaved simultaneously. The best works seem to transcend their limitations, the worst remain pale chained prisoners in a line of miserable replicas of what was once great. Breaking these chains is left to innovative geniuses that too often suffer for being different.

"The principle of true art is not to portray, but to evoke." Jerzy Kosinski

Art should not be intellectual, requiring intense mental effort to understand and decode. It may take thought to fully comprehend and unravel the mysteries in a piece, but the raw emotion should be an instant impression impacting the observer. An instant should convey an eternity and a timeless moment between the ticks of the clock in the same heartbeat.

Great art merely is, the way a sunset or the moon over a snowy landscape is.

Action item: open up your computer or grab your phone, and search "art". Find something you like, and just appreciate it.

08 OCTOBER

"Unexpressed emotions will never die. They are buried alive and will come forth later in uglier ways."

Sigmund Freud

That which you seek to bury will sprout and multiply, bearing bitter fruit and spreading its seed. Those who claim to have never had trauma are burying it, and it will burst forth at some point and overwhelm them and those around them.

Those who do not express their love risk having it slowly turn to hate, festering in their heart like a poisoned wound.

Let it out. Let it all out.

Tell your crush that you feel for them. Better to know they don't feel the same way and build a lasting friendship than to have the cancer of jealousy and doubt eat away at you. They might realize they feel the same way, or develop it over time, or you might realize it was based on an illusion and move forward. All are better than purgatory slowly declining to hell.

Find a way to confront the trauma of being bullied or the rage from losing a parent. Not doing so will cause the pressure to build like a volcano and eventually explode, destroying things all around. Unresolved trauma not only harms the individual but their children and those that love the person who is still harboring the hidden harms in their heart.

Look for an emotional pressure valve, a way to release some of the steam in a controlled manner before an uncontrolled rupture tears you apart and sends emotional shrapnel everywhere, causing collateral damage to the innocent people in your life. Reduce the pressure, open yourself slowly and let yourself heal.

Action item: choose any or all that work for you:
Grab a piece of paper and start writing what you need to express. You don't have to share it with anyone, but you need to get it out of your soul.
Talk to a professional about what you need to get off your chest.
Talk to the person in your life you need to talk with.
Take a piece of paper and draw or paint what you are feeling. Or use another media.
Go someplace alone and talk out loud to yourself.

09 OCTOBER

"Stoicism is the domestication, not the elimination, of emotions."
Nassim Nicholas Taleb

When most people think of stoicism they think of the unfeeling grey rock of a person that experiences neither anger nor joy, that feels nothing and just glides through life in an unemotional and unconnected manner. This is far from the truth and the original intent of the philosophy.

Stoicism is about controlling the negative emotions and finding joy in the everyday, without allowing passions (positive or negative) to overtake you. Think of the baseball player that has a 162 game season stretching over six months (plus pre- and post- season so potentially 180+ meaningful games over basically eight months). A loss hurts but unless it ends your season there is another one tomorrow so save the emotional energy and maintain an even keel, and even a walk off win is (hopefully) less than 1% of the victories you will experience throughout the year and tomorrow is another game. Enjoy the moment but turn the page and do the best you can with each game, at bat, and pitch.

Stoicism is about using reason to restrain emotion, not destroy it. It is about control of yourself and how you choose to respond to external stimuli, ranging from being chosen Emperor (like Marcus Aurelius) or having your leg broken by a wicked human (Epictetus), a flat tire or your kid spilling the milk. Stoicism is about empathy for others but strictness with yourself.

Take as an example my autistic son. For his benefit I need to be comforting and understanding if something doesn't go exactly as he foresees it happening, and to assist him I must be gentle and guide him without becoming overly negative or upset even when he spills his medicine or makes a huge mess or does something unknowingly dangerous. At the same time I need to be positive, model good and rational decisions, and be the master of my negative feelings and temper even in the worst situations.

This is what Stoicism (as opposed to stoicism) is in real life: the daily grind of tiny decisions that could have massive negative outcomes being controlled, the self-discipline to act with empathy but firmly for a better outcome, and putting duty to others (family, business, country, etc.) before our own temporary personal desires, to subsume ego to overall excellence and a greater good.

Do Stoics feel joy? Absolutely. It might not be the wild, unrestrained ecstasy of others but rather the joy in the process of doing the steps towards a goal (like a good five mile training run, or writing a page a day for your book, or weeding the garden), the simple pleasures of good conversation and food with friends, or celebrating the triumph of a friend and their good fortune. Understanding that fate is fickle and no situation (good or bad) is permanent leads to being more intrinsically driven and rewarded than externally focused. It is more sustainable and allows moments of joy consistently in everything from a beautiful flower to a sunset to a joke or meme. Knowing that all things end lets Stoics enjoy the moment with less anxiousness and greater appreciation.

Not unfeeling, but not out of control feelings so that they can be embraced and enjoyed within reason.

Stoics know they can't control most of the universe (and especially other people), so they focus on controlling themselves and what they can control (thoughts and decisions that lead to actions and the cascading effects) and what they can influence (like how we react to how others act).

Stoics are actually joyful because they reduce their expectations of themselves and others, premeditating the negatives (memento malorum) and enjoying pleasure as they find it without becoming addicted to it or having hedonic adaptation. They learn to love the grind of becoming better as its own reward, not the external validation too many people seek today via social media or instant dating sites.

A stoic accepts. They deal with it.

C'est la vie.

Action item: today, don't overreact to the stupidity or anger of others.

10 OCTOBER

"You cannot control what happens to you, but you can control your attitude towards what happens to you."

Brian Tracy

Your crush decides they no longer adore you and starts dating someone else. You can still care for them and want the best for the person that you liked so much, or you can be bitter and hateful and burn it down. Probably hate yourself too.

You lost your job in a downsizing. Do you wallow in misery or do you decide to start your own gig? You spill coffee all over your suit. Do you make a joke or do you start dropping F Bombs?

Traffic is bad, like being stuck for hours. Do you call your clients and try to make the time productive or do you scream and hit the steering wheel?

You lose your kid at the amusement park because they wander off. Do you freak out or calmly go find a security guard, give them a picture from your phone and a good description, then start searching on your own too?

You lose a game. Do you blame your opponent and the weather, or do you say "we need to get better" and alter your training and strategies to win next time?

Kids having a bad morning? Do you melt down too or try to model calmness and use humor to get them to do what you have to and change their attitude too?

Clients say no all the time. Don't take it personally, but learn to be better each time and keep the opportunity open.

Action item: even when things don't go your way, adapt and make the best of it.

11 OCTOBER
"You can't control what you can't measure."

Tom DeMarco

The mere-measurement effect is a psychological phenomenon where a group will change their performance based on the idea that they are being observed. We see this with teenagers acting stupid when members of the opposite sex that they want to impress are around, and we see it in business when it comes to measuring activity or productivity efforts.

Even better than the illusion of paying attention is actually tracking things. Imagine if they didn't keep score in professional sports? Do you think that there would be the same effort?

In the business world we track everything that we can in an attempt to gain more insight that can improve outcomes and profitability. From how many times someone picks up the phone to the number of appointments they get and on through to the number of sales, each step in the process is tracked and ratios determined. If someone has below average ratios it indicates more coaching/training is needed, and someone outperforming may have a new best practice that should be captured and taught to others. Business is a game like baseball, and stats for advanced metrics allow the team to win by having better insights.

Calories are something that individuals try to count. Without portion control (no, unfortunately the entire package of Oreos is NOT a single serving), the consumption is way too high and so too becomes the weight. One thing I read that is more effective than measuring is taking a picture and looking at it, as a picture is worth a thousand words and effectively communicates "this is too much!"

Fitness trackers have come into vogue in a major way in the past decade, and have helped those that use them to increase their fitness levels by measuring and presenting information, so if I am in need of only another .2 miles to hit my daily goal the onus is on me, I can't claim willful ignorance and use it to be lazy.

One of the things about weight loss is that even something poorly measured (like weight as opposed to fat, or minutes exercising per day, or glasses of water consumed) is better than nothing and if consistently applied will contribute to improvements.

Mindfulness comes from measuring.

Action item: download a step counting app on your phone and start using it.

12 OCTOBER
"If you can not measure it, you can not improve it."

Lord Kelvin

Tim Ferriss is infamous for how he has tracked every workout since he was a teenager, an OCD level of documentation that allowed him to turn himself into a human lab rat.

My first week as an intern in financial services I was introduced to "activity tracking" and became nigh on psychotic about recording and understanding my numbers. For a guy with ADHD, this structure was exactly what I needed to have success, especially given my lack of sales acumen. All I had to do was measure, increase the appropriate inputs, and work on skills that evidenced weakness from the ratios. A formulaic approach to improvement that led me to success.

Baseball has evolved into a game that tracks literally everything (spin rates on a curve ball, exit velocity of a batted ball and launch angle, foot speed on the bases, everything) so that players (and teams) can gain insight, find areas for improvement (or note declines and warning signs), and develop a true picture of capability even with small sample sizes. The feedback loops are focused and very short, yielding improvements and performances that would amaze players from two generations ago.

Why do you think teachers give homework and quizzes? Not because they enjoy grading them, but because they provide a feedback mechanism for the students, so that they can see "oh, I don't really know this material" and use that insight to improve on those topics. That's why in the real world licensing exams have study guides and practice tests and ways to measure performance so that there can be focused effort and improvement to reach the passing thresholds.

Younger members of the Millennial Generation and Gen Z have grown up in a hyper-scheduled, track everything environment. The question is, how are they taking this mindset that they were raised in and applying it to their personal and professional development? Most of us have some form of fitness watch or step counter on the phone, yet how many actually use them as a consistent feedback mechanism to improve their lives? When it is this convenient to see how many miles a day you move or keep an eye on your blood pressure, what logical reason is there to not pay attention to the couple of important indicators of your health that can also be drivers of fitness and growth for the future?

Action item: choose one personal thing (steps, sleep, time studying, etc) to track today and one work related thing. You'll see results within two weeks, just from paying attention to the numbers.

13 OCTOBER
"The measure of intelligence is the ability to change."

Albert Einstein

I am not the person I was three years ago, and neither are you.

I have a close friend whom I value dearly, and I screwed up many things in our friendship because of my arrogance, because of my stress levels with other crap going on in my life, and I became judgmental because I could see that their choices were out of alignment and had a very high probability of causing harm. But I wasn't smart enough to communicate this properly. So I compounded the issues instead of helping to alleviate them.

And once I wised up to the extent of the damage to our relationship because of my biases and actions and failures I did everything I could to repair it, to act more empathetically and supportively instead of from my jaded perspective that had evolved over a few years. I'm still trying my damnedest. I don't know yet if we will salvage this, but I'm smart enough to know how important this relationship is and that it is up to me to change the things I need to change or else there is no chance of long-term companionship and closeness. Because I did not understand and make the micro-changes before massive reversals were needed.

I was dumb.

Are you intelligent enough to say "umm, this is not where I want to be" and make different decisions for your future, or are you going to stay in your bad place or on your path to an even worse place?

"Everyone thinks of changing the world, but no one thinks of changing himself." Leo Tolstoy

There are too many people who hate where they work, a majority of Americans actually. In a country where you can decide to leave your employer at any time (or be terminated) and go get a different job relatively easily, in a world with the internet where you can learn essentially anything with some effort, and a connected society where you are only a few degrees of separation from the decision maker that can completely change your economic future, there is little logical reason to hold you back. Are you smart enough to look at this situation and start doing the little things so that three years from now you aren't still stuck in a job that you hate even more with extra psychological baggage and less time on your side?

Jack Welch was famous for getting organizations and people to change before they needed to, so that they were not forced into sub-optimal decisions because of lack of time or capability. If you can see that things are not great at your job (or in your relationships, or with your health), are you smart enough to start making micro-adjustments so that when you are at a critical decision point you have the skills and the resources and the will to make the best choice, not for the short term but for your long-range health and happiness?

Can you see the road ahead and pre-plan and prepare so that you are not flying by the seat of your pants and making short term emotional decisions that feel good in the second but are counterproductive in your grand scheme of things and lead to much worse outcomes, because of not being intelligent enough to make tiny changes that alter your trajectory and ultimate landing point in life?

Action item: it is time to intelligently alter your future. If you keep doing what you are doing in the most important relationship you have (with yourself or someone else), are you going to like where it goes? What are three tiny changes you can make today to end up with a better outcome?

14 OCTOBER
"Open your arms to change, but don't let go of your values."

HH The Dalai Lama

"We hold these truths to be self-evident" Thomas Jefferson in The Declaration of Independence. Values form the bedrock that we build our lives off of, and if the bedrock is broken or shifts the structure will collapse.

Most of our values we discover by the time we are adults, and solidify them in the early stages of our professional lives. By the time we are in our mid to late 20's we generally know who we are and what we stand for, and those who don't position their lives on a solid substrate spend years (or even the rest of their lives) in instability because they have not built from a firm foundation. That friend of yours foundering emotionally or bouncing around relationally or with work? It could be that they are trying to find people and situations that align with their value system, or that they lack a value system and as such are blown aside as easily as the little pig whose house is made of straw. It is pretty evident which they are after a little bit.

What are your values? If we look from a psychology point of view we can talk about the Big Five Personality Traits (Extraversion, Agreeableness, Openness, Conscientiousness, and Neuroticism) and this leads to predispositions and natural biases, but values are even stronger and deeper than this layer of your mental makeup.

Values per dictionary.com is a "quality desirable as a means or as an end in itself."

A strong work ethic (as a value close to my heart) is reflected in Conscientiousness from the Big Five, but is broader and deeper in that a conscientious worker often has limits around a task whereas a strong work ethic goes until the job is done, not until the clock says stop. This is not saying that the person that values hard work does not know how to relax, nor looks for work for work's sake and ignores innovation that could make life easier, it is just that getting the job done and done right is so ingrained in them that 9:00 on a Thursday night working at their desk (or in the field because it's still light and the job isn't done) is just the way they are.

Valuing truth, even to the point of personal sacrifice, is why many whistleblowers do what they do. Fighting bullies, whether the corporate type or excessive control in the hands of the President of a college or the guy mugging little old ladies is an external action of a particular value. The value of protecting the weak. Even if the bully is seemingly unstoppable, someone who deeply holds this value will change their tactics to fight City Hall but won't give up the fight if they truly believe the little guy is being harmed.

Change is inevitable, but the fundamental rules of physics or personal ethics are not malleable. They may be clarified over time (think how Quantum Physics has enhanced not replaced Newtonian Physics, or psychology has enhanced empathy instead of destroying it), but in the end the rules we govern ourselves by are near constants in our lives and guide and light our journeys, even when the road is rough or the world is dark and stormy around us.

Values keep us in alignment like the magnetic North allows us to navigate even when we can't see in the chaos around us, and keeps us firmly supported even when the ever changing weather turns our path to mud.

Action item: what are your core values? Are you living them or lipping them?

15 OCTOBER

"Values are like fingerprints. Nobody's are the same, but you leave 'em all over everything you do."

Elvis Presley

I had a former work partner tell me once "I'm not you Joe. I don't want to work that hard." Yes, I was a bit shocked and had some choice words for someone that wanted to have equal participation in the rewards but was unwilling to do even 10% of the tasks needed to generate the revenue. My work ethic value was critical to the success of the firm, and after we agreed to separate I was able to generate even more revenue and not share it with someone who did not want to get his hands dirty. I had no problem leaving fingerprints every place I ever worked.

What is your mark that is always left on what you do? Do you insist on mentoring and teaching newer people in the organization so that they understand the vision, and inspire them to consistently do their best work because that is a closely held personal value? Leaving fingerprints that remain decades after you leave.

Do you always tell your kid you love them, even when they are being a punk, because exhibiting that caring attitude and making sure in no uncertain terms that they understand is part of who you are at your deepest level? Leaving a mark such that when they hang up the phone they tell you they love you before you can say it to them?

Do you always call everyone older than you sir or ma'am because your parents would have smacked you in the back of the head for being disrespectful?

Does everyone you interact with know that when things get tough you are going to crack a joke to lighten the mood, even if under fire (literally or figuratively) because that making people relaxes and better able to perform via humor is who you are and the smiles and laughter, even in a graveyard humor situation, is who you are?

Will you never take something you didn't earn and are entitled to even if you could get away with it?

How would someone, a disinterested independent third party observer, characterize your value system just from watching you work?

If your grandfather shadowed you for a week, would they be proud of what you exhibit?

Action item: look at the last project you did at work and at home. What would your mom say about it?

16 OCTOBER
"Only loss teaches us the value of things."

Arthur Schopenhauer

Youth is wasted on the young. They will never know the value of it until it is gone, and their muscles ache when the cold rains come.

Same with love. That which flamed hot and then fades or is snuffed out leaves a burn and the scent of scorch and maybe a wistful smile once they are no longer part of your life.

If you have been rich and lost everything you long for the old days. And if you can rebuild your fortunes, you appreciate every material good thing as you never could without suffering that loss to teach you gratitude.

If you have ever had a back or knee injury, you know how wonderful it is to just be able to walk across a room. Savor that feeling, and take care of yourself so you don't return to the immobility and pain you lived through before.

We can't save time in a bottle like Jim Croce sang.

Loss is inevitable as we live. Friends leave our life due to transfer or cancer. Parents inevitably pass on, often slowly losing their memories and fading before our eyes before the light fades from theirs. Our neighborhoods change, those places that were important to us disappear. Children grow and leave the nest, and the relationships we had with them sometimes are irrevocably shattered. This is the nature of life.

The truly wise enjoy the moments before they become memories.

Action item: tell the people you love that you love them, and capture a fleeting moment of joy with them.

17 OCTOBER
"We knew nothing of loss. Nobody has taught us pain."

Francesca Marciano

Pain is universal. We all experience different types. And they are all valid. As my friend Athena reminded me, I can never truly know the loss of a miscarriage, nor her the feeling of a full on kick to the testicles. They are both valid and part of our learning experience.

My godson lost his father to cancer, watching him wither away and had his entire universe disrupted before turning thirteen and then buried the person that they were depending upon in the most critical parts of his life. It took five years for Ryan to come to grips with this loss.

Losing a pet dog at five is an early indicator of what is to come in our lives. We will lose everything and everyone eventually, fading into the darkness from whence we came and facing our fate based upon our choices while we were here. But does that make it any less glorious while we are here on this former Eden of Earth?

Just as salt slices the tongue and enhances all other flavors, so too does pain enhance the joy in our lives.

The Gods of Olympus envied the mortals for their short lifespans of intense feeling and pain.

If you have never lost the person you love to the depths of your soul, you can't comprehend the heights of love and ecstasy that another can bring. But someday you probably will.

Until you have been physically broken, you can't appreciate comfort.

If you have never been truly ravenous, food is not ambrosia.

Memento Mori the Stoics teach us. Remember Death. So that you can truly be alive.

When we walk out of the shadows of a house into the sunlight, our eyes water with the brilliance and we are overcome momentarily. Walking out of the pain we experienced in the mini-Hells we must traverse allows us to regard even Purgatory as a small Heaven.

Pain can be weakness leaving the body as the Marines say. It could also be what David Goggins claims: the callusing of the mind so that we become immune to the pain because we are accustomed to it. This however has the potential to numb us. I prefer to look at pain as the tempering fire that removes our impurities and strengthens the steel that will support us in difficult times in the future. Without pain we are still filled with voids and flaws that weaken us and could make us crack under pressure later.

Too many people chose to repeatedly avoid pain, and take the easy route. They don't realize how fragile this makes them emotionally for the inevitable. When their relationship goes to hell because they were unwilling to have the little tough talks and the underlying cracks developed into chasms that can't be crossed. When they avoided "the talk" with their kids about the ups and downs of life and how emotions and hormones run wild, and now their kid is pregnant or attempts to kill themselves because they never learned to cope because they had no strong model in the parent.

Small amounts of pain are preventive and preemptive. Those who can not take the small pains will have great traumas.

Action item: what is your most painful experience? Face it, embrace it, and contrast it to feel the pleasures more powerfully.

18 OCTOBER

"Life is pain, Highness.
Anyone who tells you differently is selling something."
William Golding, in *The Princess Bride*

Princesses (and Princes) growing up in their secluded and protected castles are isolated from the real world in many ways, and as such miss critical perspectives that we peasants and farm boys know: life ain't easy. It is harsh, and unfair, and even true love is no guarantee of happiness.

Salespeople in the 1990's were taught to find the pain and squeeze until the buyer felt immense discomfort, then offer a way to release the agony (usually through the purchase of their product). This method is outdated but is based upon a psychological fact: we all have pain, and anyone that denies it is burying something that will inevitably grow and burst forth. Pain is part of life, and anyone denying it is selling something, either to themselves or others.

Think of pain as pressure building up in a vessel. As heat is applied from the outside, the molecules inside (often steam) absorb the energy and move about quicker, hitting the internal walls faster and harder. As the pressure builds, one of two things can happen ultimately: either there is a controlled release through a pressure valve (literally blowing off some steam), or if this does not happen the pressure builds until there is a sudden and epic rapid failure and deconstruction. An explosion, sending shrapnel all over and causing collateral damage. Keeping all the pain bottled up eventually leads to a catastrophic event. So too with people.

We all have trauma in our life. Anyone that denies it really is a protected Princess (and is in for a painful, potentially deadly fall from her tower), or has walled it off in part of their mind. And we all know what happens in the stories when you hide a dark secret: it becomes a monster and comes back a hundred-fold stronger and destroys the kingdom.

Dumbrowski analyzed growth through trauma, of pain becoming power. Maya Angelou said she wrote over her scars. Mark Manson explored his pain and it led to his best seller The Subtle Art of Not Giving a F*ck. Michael Jordan used the chip on his shoulder to become the best in his field. Same with Tom Brady, and Mike Tyson. I used it to push my training for years. Maybe you have too.

Pain pushes people to greatness. Past our normal limits because we use the physical pain to numb or cover the emotional ones, and over time we address the root cause and hopefully heal these psychic wounds but have traded them for various physical ones. We use pain to produce skill and strength and become our shield and diversion. But it is better than wallowing in freakish misery, alone with our fears and emptiness.

Action item: what hurts you, to your very soul? Don't fly from it but sit with that pain, explore it and understand it. Use it, or it will use and break you.

19 OCTOBER

"There is a thin line that separates laughter and pain, comedy and tragedy, humor and hurt."

Erma Bombeck

There is a reason why the Janus masks representing plays are both laughing and crying, capturing the spectrum of emotions, the dichotomy of feelings. Love and hate are so close as to be inseparable at times. A tragedy is if it happens to me, a comedy if it happens to you.

"The line dividing good and evil cuts through the heart of every human being." Aleksandr Solzhenitsyn in The Gulag Archipelago. One of the beautiful things about an Irish wake is the amount of laughter. The stories, bringing forth the entire range of emotions. Yes, we cry and often during it but the mirth and humor is woven through the entire event in such a way as to bring out the richness in the fabric of the deceased's life, to cathartically surfacing all the feelings so that we can address them and move forward. A celebration of them that lets their memory remain but with minimal pain. At these wakes there are tons of anecdotes and jokes, and the danger is more about affronting the living than the dead. There is something called "Irish Alzheimer's" where the only thing that people remember are the grudges. In emotional situations, where humor is being used, it is easy to cross the line and hurt someone's feelings. And when you have thirty plus cousins in a variety of situations, someone is always getting offended by something....

The entire world is really a balancing act, a dynamic equilibrium of constantly changing variables that we do our best to try and recognize and accommodate. Someone that you adore might have had a bad night's sleep because of an issue with their kid which is compounded by their boss having marital issues and an innocuous word from you could be the spark for an explosion that any other day would not have been a big deal. Sometimes these explosions are relationship ending, sometimes the pieces can be picked up. It depends a lot on the mindsets of the individuals involved as someone holding a grudge, even if unfounded, can not extend a hand in friendship if it is clasped in a fist.

Other times, that one word from you might be enough to pull someone back from the edge of disaster. One bad day can force someone over the edge, yet a single word or action can tether them and draw them back to safety, pull them back from their temporary madness and self-destructive plans. We never know about these crucial interactions, but if you see someone on that path a true friend would make sure they reach their hand out, even if the other person's is still a fist of rage. Life is dichotomies separated by the thinnest of walls and choices. It is fragile and funny and fierce and forgiving, so if you cross that thin line, don't be too arrogant to apologize and try to restore the balance. We are all the most devilish angels God has made.

Action item: if you have crossed the line, make amends.

20 OCTOBER
"There is a thin line between our hopes and dreams."

Rani Mukerji

I hope to win the Mega Millions, then I dream of getting a pirate ship.

The main thing about hope is the external basis of it. There is little in it under our control (other than buying the lottery ticket). The results are in the hands of probability or providence. Nothing you or I can do to influence the outcome (at least without breaking the law or buying $100,000 worth of tickets).

Dreams are basically what our hopes can become once the first impossible threshold has been overcome, when the doors of possibility have flung open. Of buying an island and throwing lavish pirate themed parties, or building that charity to help autistic kids get the life skills they need to navigate our world, or taking your crush to Paris for a week and proposing at the base of the Eiffel Tower while minstrels serenade you. Dreams are what you can do after the "What if…" has happened. They are the "then".

Dreams can be what we work towards, that powers us through the tough parts of the journey where hope may seem lost. Dreams of the IPO are what power the young entrepreneurs through another long night of coding or talking to yet another VC to secure funding while being exhausted and barely making ends meet. Hope is getting the VC meetings.

Hope is sustaining in the short run but uncontrollable. And ultimately it can fade, as the POWs in Vietnam found out if they had too high hopes of when they would be returned home as James Stockdale pointed out. Hope is a good short-term kick, a spiritual espresso shot but rarely is kept up for extended periods.

Dreams can be sustained for years. The Founder tries to get the VC to buyin to their dream, literally. The dream of the parent struggling with childhood cancer of their kid getting through the treatments over the next year and being able to play outside in a few years, eventually driving and going to the prom. These are dreams that can give something to fight for day in day out, even the rough days when we want to give up and scream about how unfair the universe can be.

Hopes and dreams are intricately linked and depend upon each other, like the two partners in a marriage that each bring something and support the other. Let the line blur.

Action item: grab a piece of paper. On one side write all the things you hope for this year. On the other, write your dreams for the future. Mail this to yourself.

21 OCTOBER
"Who looks outside, dreams; who looks inside, awakes."

Carl Jung

Externalities, be it fancy clothes or the flashy BMW, are merely trappings of success, yet too many people value these show pieces instead of the internal abilities that have given the capability to purchase these toys. All too often we see the guy that spends a disproportionate amount of his salary to get the really nice car to attract the beautiful woman that sees the vehicle and the watch and clothes and thinks this is a man of value, only to find out that they are morally or emotionally bankrupt and lack the skill and will to truly be a success.

Being seduced by the pretty face or slamming body or mansion and other adornments that give the illusion of wealth and beauty is common, with people buying into the "Lifestyles of the Rich and Famous" view of what happiness is and lusting over the champagne dreams. Chasing these accoutrements has brought many a person down as they rush headlong into situations and relationships with wild ideas of stardom and dot com (or crypto) riches with little or no work. Because they are looking for external validation and chasing the elusive butterfly of happiness that always flutters off.

Contrast this with the people that have decided that what Society has endorsed as "making it" is merely the clanging of cymbals and distractive noise. Keanu Reeves truly embodies Ted from "Bill and Ted's Excellent Adventure" in many ways because the wealth and accolades mean little to him. He's cool to them beyond an initial "whoa". He gave away his paycheck from one of the Matrix movies, has funded hospitals, helps the crew on his film in ways that few stars could even think about, and by all accounts is just a pretty normal, thoughtful, and helpful human being. It could be because of the tragedies in his life that have moved him along a classical Stoic path, it could be that he has invested the energy for self-reflection and decided that above a certain level of wealth or attention it doesn't matter and so uses it for others, or maybe he took the red pill, who knows. But in a world of fake Hollywood illusions and dreams, Keanu has his eyes open. He's awake and unplugged.

I have a friend who started his tech company focused on the outside world, on what they could do from a cool visual or skill perspective, and who could buy their products and ultimately their company so he could follow the same path of other outwardly successful entrepreneurs. But as this person moved along the development path, small changes and out of synch feelings with the successes caused him to question and slowly shake off the cloudiness of his dream and he awoke to the greater potential of what he was doing and what he personally could become, the non-financial implications of what his team was creating and how they had an opportunity to fundamentally impact at risk citizens and the authorities that interacted with them.

His dream has morphed into a vision that he holds himself and the team to, a mission that while it may have some good economic perks for them is more focused on delivering change in these communities and saving lives while giving not just hope but a plan for improvement. D awoke and is out of bed and working, because he looked inside.

I don't care about a trophy within a day of winning it. It is the process of becoming a champion that is more important than something that is going to collect dust. The only real opponent is myself and my self imposed limits, not the guy across the ring trying to hit me. Defeat the enemy inside to have everything you need to defeat any enemy outside.

Action item: don't be enticed by the dreams of others, the flash and excitement. Look inside yourself, for the challenges that will make you better and by default yield externally visible results.

22 OCTOBER

"The world needs dreamers and the world needs doers. But above all, the world needs dreamers who do."

Sarah Ban Breathnach

I can't tell you how many students I have met with a great idea for a business. They even get together with a few buddies, put together a basic business plan and start working. And then they stop, because inevitably they realize that to bring this dream to reality is going to take brutal hard work, sacrifices of time and fun and friends that they are unwilling to make, and they can't do it.

The world needs tradesmen and women. Welders, electricians, machinists and operators: people who work with their hands and build things. If not for the back breaking work of these people over generations we would not have the infrastructure to build and ship products, the resources to develop technologies, nor the societal wealth to explore the boundaries of our knowledge.

These are balanced by the mental creators and knowledge workers, the poets and painters and coders and teachers that make minds and raise spirits and lift our eyes to the heavens. These people are critical for innovation and evolving an economy in a way that makes life easier and better for others, be it from improved drugs to better farming methods or the soundtracks we play while we work in our offices or on the road.

Sometimes these two areas overlap, a Venn diagram that leads to radical improvements because of the application of technology to physical problems that directly translate into increased lifestyles, whether it is an improvement in energy that can bring a society forward a hundred years in a single one, or an innovation for stronger glass that saves lives. Usually these come from a large organization with a couple of dreamers and a slew of doers. Yet look what happens when these two strengths are combined in a single human.

The coder with an idea that busts hump around school or their regular job. Instagram was built in two months like this, a dream with massive hard work. The person who starts a soup kitchen and over time helps hundreds of people claw their way out of poverty.

The person given the opportunity for a sales job and uses it to build a life they never dreamt off by working fifteen hour days for years as they lay a foundation for success unlike anyone in their family.

The single parent getting their degree while working full-time in a dead end job, following their dream and inspiring their kids simultaneously while modeling hard work and faith.

Action item: dreams are built by action. Work a little harder on building the future you dream of today.

23 OCTOBER

"Start by doing what's necessary; then do what's possible; and suddenly you are doing the impossible."

Francis of Assisi

Maybe you have struggled with an injury, physical illness, or depression, and all you could do was get out of bed to go to the bathroom. If that is all you could do, and you did it, that is good. The next step might be getting some nourishment. That is sorta important for healing. If that's all you can do, just do that.

If you can do a little more, like maybe take a shower, that's a good possibility. Get to that point when you can.

Then keep doing a little more. Eventually....

This goes for recovering from heartbreak, or doing a marathon, or mastering an instrument or any other skill. Do what you can, then do a little more when you can.

If you have suffered a heart-rending loss, even breathing may seem impossible but it is necessary. Take that first breath, no matter how ragged or your desire to scream to the heavens.

As Dr. Martin Luther King Jr said: If you can't fly then run. If you can't run then walk. If you can't walk then crawl, but do whatever you do. You have to keep moving forward.

Staying in Hell is a guarantee that the pain does not diminish. Only moving forward and through the torment can make it ever stop.

Do the minimum necessary. Then you can do more when you are mentally and physically ready. It might be today, it might be next week. But eventually you will do what you think is impossible now.

Action item: what is paralyzing you, that you are so afraid of doing that you literally can't? Do the smallest possible part of it. Because that first step is all that is necessary.

24 OCTOBER
"A man should so live that his happiness shall depend as little as possible on external things."
Epictetus

If you need to chase and capture butterflies to be happy, you will get worn out and never catch what you seek. So it is when external validation and rewards become your reason for living; even if you catch the object of your desire it will die or fade. The BMW will start to wear out, the promotion will no longer excite, the trophy will lose its shine. All things tarnish and diminish, other than the fire inside that you light and feed from your soul.

A child will spend hours or days playing with an old refrigerator box.

A notebook and pencils will amuse an artist or writer for weeks, maybe months until the pages are all covered with their work. The act of creation is internally driven and depends little upon external approval to make the creator pleased with their works.

Runners run. They don't necessarily need races to feel good about putting one foot in front of the other. My team did a slew of crazy virtual races during the Covid Pandemic (ranging from a Beer Mile to a Backyard Ultramarathon) and not one of us got a medal or any other accolades other than "you're crazy". The effort and accomplishment was its own reward, and the happiness did not depend upon yet another race t-shirt.

Even if you love someone dearly, your happiness can not depend upon them and be sustainable. People change. Their relationship with you will alter (especially if they depend upon external things for happiness so will be mercurial). My widowed friends still love their now deceased husbands and miss them, but they can still find happiness in their children and careers and their physical activity and self-development, all the things that made them happy independently of their husbands. Some have even found new relationships (they do not replace the love of their lost one obviously).

Look inside for the things that make you happy, truly happy. A new hair cut will grow out and need to be done again, but planting your garden (even if it needs to be redone annually) is not just making something but garnering skills (knowledge, patience, discipline) that make the simplest rewards disproportionately sweet, like those early tomatoes that you grew yourself. The pride in the accomplishment is not dependent upon nameless people on social media giving you a thumbs up or even your kid saying they like the dish you made with your harvest. Just as the plants grow and blossom and produce fruits of their own, so too should be your happiness.

Action item: pretend you have no internet, can't shop, and there is no social media. You can't talk to other people. What are you going to do today to be happy?

25 OCTOBER

"It is not easy to find happiness in ourselves, and it is not possible to find it elsewhere."

Agnes Reppier

Depending upon others for your happiness is a fool's errand, because people are fickle, ever changing and more complex than all the weather patterns in the world combined with an infinite number of butterflies flapping their wings.

The constant search for external validation, for happiness in things or dependent upon the approval of others is not even a zero-sum game but a temporary one of diminishing results doomed to destruction. You become trapped in the hedonic adaption, the ever-increasing need for dopamine hits like an addict until there is no joy left as you have sucked it all in and burnt your brain out. Like all extractive systems, it runs out over time because as Margaret Thatcher said about Socialism: eventually you run out of other people's money. Eventually, there is nothing left to feed your ever-growing hunger/addiction, then your happiness collapses and consumes itself like a black hole consuming itself.

Looking internally is much more difficult to begin with. Instead of getting a relatively easy social media "like", you need to do something that makes you personally give it a thumbs up. No filter, no retakes, just actually living and doing something that makes you say inside "that's cool" or "good job". This is more difficult and not publicly visible, plus not scalable the way a pretty woman on Instagram or a funny meme is. You aren't getting ten thousand likes from yourself for doing things like having a good breakfast or solving that math problem or helping someone. You aren't going to burn out your brain either though which is ultimately better.

One definition of happiness is making consistent progress towards a meaningful goal. This is mainly internally driven, involves overcoming obstacles, and is not short term in nature. Someone starting as a white belt and enjoying their martial art and progressing up the ranks is an example of this, or someone building a business or learning an instrument or language are good representatives of this internally driven happiness. There are inevitable frustrations along the path, but there is no big shiny castle at the end with treasure chests and bags of happiness with butterflies fluttering all over. It is a never ending quest where the journey is the reward.

Learning to bake and making beautiful cakes is as internally driven mastery and development as it is externally rewarded when someone loves the product. So too writing. These hybrid type endeavors are wonderful, especially as they can be shared with others and the experience of shared savoring is another documented component to happiness. It is not really about winning blue ribbons or making some best sellers list, it is about creating something and then sharing it with others that can have joy from our creation and having a mutual experience. It is inclusive, and can happen over and over again in variations.

Again not scalable to a thousand likes, but having your friend say "thank you, I really enjoyed this" is not dependent upon uncontrollable and disconnected external validation but an outside individual that you like and respect and spend time reinforcing and appreciating the already strong internal drive. This is the sweet spot of happiness, because happiness is like lighting other people's candles. It brightens the world without diminishing your light nor causing you to burnout from searching or jealousy.

Action item: what do you do that is internally focused that makes you happy? Do more of it today.

26 OCTOBER
"The idea is to die young as late as possible."

Ashley Montagu

No, it's not about looking young with the botox and the lip injections and plastic surgery. It is to BE young as opposed to looking young, which are often directly opposed.

Being young involves maybe falling off your bike in your seventies. Yeah, you will get some scrapes and maybe bust something, but you will have a good story and the fact that you are still out there pumping and pedaling instead of sitting on your duff and physically deteriorating into someone that can't even walk to the bathroom on their own.

There was a movie my mom loved called *Second Hand Lions*, where these two brothers had adventures ranging from joining the French Foreign Legion in their teens to fighting punks in their seventies to ultimately crashing their biplane in their late nineties, going out with their boots on, hooting and hollering all the way. They had scars and bumps and bruises and most of all stories, epic stories of their adventures that even their greatest rival told his grandchildren about and this young prince came to pay his respects to the legends. That is dying young as late as possible.

I know martial artists still training hard into their eighties, able to destroy men a quarter of their age. Even at an advanced age they are flexible and youthful and still learning about the world around them like they were novices. There is a guy who still runs Ragnars in his late eighties. He is an inspiration to us all, and he always has a huge smile on his face because he is as happy as a little kid doing something he loves at a point where most people are either buried or in wheelchairs.

My goal is to win my age division in a race, in the age 100+ division. That is being young even when old. Picasso painted into his nineties, still trying new things. Pablo Casalles was practicing into his nineties, thinking he was still improving. My friend Rita Block went blind in her mid-eighties and still was a killer bridge player. She also fished even though she couldn't see, and her wit would slice you to ribbons.

It is not the length of life but the quality of it. I know people who are just grumpy old men in their forties, ready to shuffle off to a rocking chair yelling "get off my lawn" and in serious emotional and cognitive decline. And I knew people pushing 100 who would get up and dance and tell jokes and play board games and wanted to hear about the latest band you saw.

Age is just a number. Stay young in your spirit, and you will never truly grow old.

Action item: what makes you feel like a kid? Do it. And more often.

27 OCTOBER

"You can only be young once.
But you can always be immature."

Dave Barry

Just because you are getting older doesn't mean you have to feel or act your age. When someone has a grandkid they instantly become younger. It's a medical fact, I saw it on the interwebz!

After being 39 I became 30-10, then 30-11, then....

Yes, I still wear a Looney Toons tie every once in a while. Because I can, nyah nyah nyah (sticks out tongue).

When was the last time you acted like a kid? Played a prank in the office (not on April Fool's Day)? Had a pajama party or built a blanket fort? Why? Do you think you are too old for such shenanigans? If you think you are too old, then you're older than you think and approaching curmudgeon (termagant if you are female) status.

At least get some crazy socks! Tacos, maybe robots or dinosaurs. Something not argyle and boring, I can literally feel the fun draining from my body just talking to you, you old fuddy duddy stick in the mud. "Fun" is a three letter word, not a four letter one.

Look, life is serious business, I get it. No one is getting out of here alive.

But does that mean we need to be so serious all the time? Do we have to look at everything like it's a life or death situation? Deployed troops understand the importance of lightening the mood and getting laughs where they can, and I guarantee that nothing is going to explode at your work if someone laughs. Probably not. Hopefully not.

Goof around a little, especially if people are under stress.

Play a joke on the boss. If they are a good one they'll laugh. If they aren't, then they fire you and you collect unemployment while plotting your next move, hopefully to another company that doesn't have the Anti-Fun Police in charge of everything.

Sometimes, the most logical choice (per Spock) is to act irrationally. Get someone to laugh, it actually makes for a better work environment and increases people's cognitive functions. So being immature is actually a productivity enhancement tool and advanced leadership. So there!

Action item: do something immature but not dangerous today.

28 OCTOBER
"I am too childlike to be immature."

Lee Siegel

Children run around naked, tell you exactly what they feel, get hangry or overly tired, crash and wake up as angels all over again. They truly live at full speed, and because of their limited exposure and framework of experience that they are building out can not really be said to act immature in the same way that a hurricane cannot be said to be immature. It merely is, and that is part of the wonderful experience and frustration with children.

Children are stimuli sponges, soaking up everything they see, hear, touch, and taste. And they need to build out a framework for all of this information on the fly, with little basis to draw from beyond what they have already experienced and codified. That is why a three year old can think that chocolate milk comes from brown cows with absolute sincerity.

Children are completely amoral to begin. As Pirsig says in Zen and the Art of Motorcycle Maintenance: "and what is good Phaedrus, and what is not, and who is to tell us the difference?" Young kids are a blank slate in this respect, and as such exhibit just the natural human tendencies to be simultaneously selfish and selfless, to need companionship but demand independence in a bundle of ever shifting emotions and feelings trying to figure out the overwhelming world and do the best they can. For the first five years or so they are just completely overwhelmed, growing in body and mind in all directions and starting to have influence and control over themselves and their world. They are starting to learn the mores of their society and they learn by watching and playing. This lays the foundation for their personalities and moral frameworks.

So in a world where the child is still figuring out the rules that they are supposed to live and grow under, they have a pass for not holding to the standards of grown ups. A two year old that says "I'm tired" and sits down in the middle of the hallway is funny and merely expressing their reality, a forty-five year old that does the same thing is looked at askew. Same if the four year old decides they are hot and strips off their clothes, and the grown up gets even weirder looks for doing this than the one admitting they are tired.

Not knowing any better is an acceptable excuse for a little kid, because they have short memories and little experience and low capability to harm others with most of their actions. But once someone is physically mature the rules are obviously different, because of the experiences and the potential to harm someone. Example: a four year old says they don't love you anymore over something stupid, and the next day they are back to loving you. An adult saying the same thing does not return to loving the next day, maybe not ever and then there is divorce proceedings and nastiness and...

The child is developing themselves and evolving into a mature form. Part of the joy of play (be it recreational or creational like in art or music or writing) is not knowing the normal rules and limits, the exploration of what is and could be that we see in artists pushing their boundaries like when Picasso explored cubism or Dr. Seuss creating new words and worlds. Just like a white belt in martial arts or a rookie in the big leagues, they can be like a kid in attitude and are forgiven for rookie mistakes or errors in following unwritten rules that they are trying to understand like the kid on the first day of kindergarten.

Their wild eyed enthusiasm gives them a pass too, but over time they are expected to figure out and follow the codes of the organization the same way that even Picasso matured in each phase of his artistic expression.

Action item: if it has no negative consequences to others, be immature like a four year old today to recapture that wonder at the world around you.

29 OCTOBER
"Never lose the childlike wonder."

Prof. Randy Pausch

One thing that I hope when I am an old man is that I am as enthusiastic as I am today, and can talk to kids about their favorite dinosaur (mine is stegosaurus) and comic book character (Thor) and cartoon character (still Daffy Duck, because I'm dith-pickable!). To be able to literally get down on the floor, eye level with a toddler and dramatically play dress-up or look for bugs and check out the really cool new rock that they found.

The Nobel Prize winner in Physics Ivar Gaiver was one of my professors, for a class called "Creativity and Invention". I talked to him frequently, even for years after I took the class and into his late 70's he was snowboarding and pursuing interesting ideas in research that caught his fancy. In many ways he was a big kid, and other professors doing research in the department were similar in their enthusiasm and attitude. It was fairly infectious, and was one of the most motivating things about being a scientist: seeing these old men and women still coming into the office to chase ideas and play with numbers just like they did when they were teenagers. My other advisor Dr. Block in Nuclear Engineering refused to retire. Ever. They will carry him out at 100 years old and he'll be saying "but wait I have an idea!"

Do you have that level of dedication and interest in what you are doing, where you lose track of the time because it doesn't feel like you are working? Where sometimes you are amazed that they are paying you for something that you'd do for free, like many pro athletes express with their game? Are you a wide-eyed rookie even a decade in, approaching each day like it's your first and you want to go make new friends and do something awesome?! Why not?

I still try to learn something new every day, even if it is a totally random thing that I would never think useful in a professional capacity. Because the random facts are interesting and mind broadening and sometimes lead to another idea, and then another, and all of a sudden you have equations written all over the board and are asking colleagues to come in and discuss and then you have a paper and then....

Isn't that the very essence of childlike wonder, whether it is chasing butterflies and catching lightning bugs or playing with blocks for hours or just watching the rain stream down. The capacity of the younglings to observe and learn is the essence of good science and art, and keeps the spirit green and growing long after our hair is grey or going.

Action item: carve out some time, go to Youtube, and watch The Last Lecture.

30 OCTOBER
"Halloween is an opportunity to be really creative."

Judy Gold

One year for Halloween I dressed up as General George Custer. Another year I dressed up as a tooth. In college I put on a viking helmet, brown sweater, and carried a dowel spear and walked around channeling Elmer Fudd singing "kill da wabbit! Kill da wabbit! Wif my speah and magic helmet!" I went trick or treating in the dorm and I got some interesting loot that year.

Not everyone in the office has to draw whiskers on their face and wear a headband with ears and be a cat, or dress up like a psychopath "because they look like everyone else." Have some fun with it (within the constraints of your office handbook if need be).

My friend Kerry sewed stuffed kittens to her clothes and was "The Crazy Cat Lady", a perfect costume for her. Robin had fake insects all over her jeans. She was Ants in My Pants.

A postal worker friend dressed like a zombie and put a fake bullethole on his forehead. He actually got in trouble (and suspended) for his "Dead Postal Worker", so know that there are some limits and in our society today where everyone is offended by something it is better to err on the side of caution on things that are of minimal importance. Save your capital for the big deals.

I make a great nerd, complete with pocket protector. Someone pointed out that it was my own clothes and bow tie I was wearing, I just went a little extreme. A guy in my office had a Superman S shirt and kept his dress shirt partially unbuttoned. Subtle and funny.

These were all costumes costing less than a lunch out but with some decent thought and execution, that got others around them laughing. Each one of these outfits the wearer had thought about for a few weeks or longer and figured out a way to pull it off. When was the last time you brought that level of creativity to a problem at work or home? Why?

Creativity is a skill like writing or public speaking in that the more you use it the stronger it becomes. You might not necessarily write a brilliant line of copy on demand or compose the next #1 hit, but relaxing and goofing around and playing with concepts with very little constraint can be practiced and lead to better overall ideas. These could mean a lot of money to your company, a lot of fun for your office, or stories that you and your friends will tell for decades. These are all good things.

Action item: tomorrow is Halloween. Figure out your costume today, then immediately turn to a problem you've been struggling with since your creative juices are flowing.

31 OCTOBER - HALLOWEEN!

"I love the spirit of Halloween and the energy that comes with it."

Katharine McPhee

A chance to become someone else for a day and request things you never would, an opportunity to channel fantasy and live the illusion for a night. What is not to love?

As kids we all played dress up, becoming superheroes and princesses and fairies and firefighters. To be dragons and cats and robots. Who said we had to stop playing dress up all the time when we turned ten or eleven? Halloween lets us relive that aspect of our childhood in a socially acceptable manner.

In Celtic tradition, Halloween (Samhain) is the night when the barriers between the worlds fade and the spirits can walk the earth. It is a night of frivolity, a chance to suspend the normal rules of doing homework and chores and bedtime to go out and have fun.

Why did we stop doing it?

I personally love to dress up for Halloween, typically as The Joker so that I am still in a suit for work (even if it looks like I stole it from Steve Harvey), complete with green hair and makeup and wicked laugh. Why not inject a little humor and chaos into the stuffy office? My clients love it, my old manager hated it. Clients laughed, joked, bought more products, and introduced more clients with the story of "you should have seen what Joe did…" Results speak, and a shot of fun in the arm to an organization occasionally is good for morale and the bottom line.

Halloween is an excuse to be a kid.

Sometime after everyone starts thinking about pumpkin spice everything, it is time for skeletons and spider webs and black cats. It is not channeling the supernatural, it is channeling childhood and confronting things that scare you and are a bit out of your comfort zone.

Halloween lets you face your fears in a playful way, be they tarantulas or monsters under the bed. It is this confronting our demons (internal and external) that leads to long term growth, the very thing that we used to be encouraged to do. So why are you avoiding it now?

Are you afraid of the dark?

Action item: be a kid today. Dress up, and ask coworkers and friends for candy. Because you can.

FEAR NOT NOVEMBER'S CHALLENGE BOLD -
WE'VE BOOKS AND FRIENDS,
AND HEARTHS THAT CAN NEVER GROW COLD:
THESE MAKE AMENDS!

Alexander Louis Fraser

01 NOVEMBER

"What is a superhero? They're supposed to represent hope, opportunity, and strength for everybody."

Aldis Hodge

As children, many of us dreamed of becoming superheroes, of going from scrawny nerd to wise-cracking defender of the little guy or being a fierce and unstoppable Amazon, with a clearly defined code separating right from wrong that we enforced to save the world while still preserving our secret identity and keeping a fairly normal life beyond the chaos of stopping bad guys.

Some superheroes became embodiments of ideals (Superman's Truth, Justice, and the American Way, Captain America as the flag made flesh, Black Panther the proud, wise and noble leader), others represented what we could become (Iron Man as the engineer become billionaire playboy genius philanthropist or Batman, the World's Greatest Detective who was born out of unspeakable tragedy). All are more than what we could reasonably be, but gave us something to strive for. They inspire us, modern day myths and morality plays in one spread across the pages and screen for children of all ages.

These superhuman symbols are put on shirts you see in the gym, on posters in schools, and on a bazillion YouTube clips analyzing everything from psychosis to confidence. Window washers dress up outside of children's hospitals to embolden the kids who are literally fighting for their lives. Even adults are influenced by their early heroes, subconsciously (or not so subconsciously) modeling the better aspects of their early archetypes. Not everyone will look at The Punisher or Guy Gardner or Spawn in a positive light, but being human includes drawing emotional strength and morality from our heroes, even when they are as flawed as we are.

As our world becomes ever more fractured and chaotic, as the old institutions that illustrated right from wrong and reinforced the moral lessons we grew up with continue to decline, we need the symbols of hope more than ever. We need heroes, even if they are not as perfect as they once were.

Action item: who was your favorite hero? Why? What did they teach you that you should remember?

02 NOVEMBER
"You're not free unless you can show the good and bad."

Chadwich Boseman

The truth is like a pancake: no matter how thin, there are two sides.

People (and thus relationships and history) are complex, dynamic swirls of black and white that paint complex and ever evolving pictures about a situation. Based on that point in time, a person can be a hero or villain depending upon the scenario and the perspective that they are viewed from.

We are all this mixture of darkness and light, of base drives and higher ideals. As Jung says we carry our Shadow, and having it integrated into our being is critical for our personal evolution and emotional freedom. Understanding our darker parts contrasts to our light and lets it shine more brightly, and drawing strength from the fears we have faced unchains our potential for greater achievement because we understand what we are afraid of.

As people we need to be free to express our entire range of feelings and emotions to be whole. To tell someone we love "No, that isn't good for you" without fearing that they will walk out the door, to set boundaries with the boss (no I won't do an extra 20 hours, but I can give you five), to show our kids that sometimes we struggle with anger but we don't let it explode. Freedom is not hiding from your faults but acknowledging them and working on them as appropriate.

We all strive for an ideal, to be perfect. It is innate in the human condition to strive for better, but part of excellence is acceptance of the limitations. Understanding the not great parts that come with someone (like Marilyn Monroe saying that if you can't handle her at her worst you didn't deserve her at her best, or Brett Favre being a gunslinger of a quarterback who could make the huge throw or toss a gut-wrenching interception) allows us to not put someone in a tiny box that hides half of who they are.

Diamonds are beautiful for their multiple facets, just like people.

We have two eyes to give us perspective on things we look at. Use both eyes when looking at people and events too.

Action item: choose one person you are close to. Write a list of bad things about them, and one of good things about them. Your perspective might shift, but you will see them as a more complete person instead of an idealized caricature.

03 NOVEMBER

"There is nothing either good or bad but thinking makes it so."

William Shakespeare

Something happens, you make a choice of how to react, and there is a consequence (Ellis' ABC Model). What you chose to do is based upon your belief system and how you perceive the world, the event, and the people involved. Are you looking for the good in a situation or focusing on the negative?

Lose your job? It could be the worst thing in the world, or as Jocko Willink would say "Good." Good, now you have a chance to pause, reflect, spend a few days with those you love, and launch that thing you've been thinking about.

Cancer scare? Does it push you into a hedonistic bender where you break all of your internal rules, or does it force you to re-evaluate and eliminate things that waste your time and make you focus on taking care of your health and the important relationships in your life, that you now realize are more precious than ever? For me, it was the latter.

Child diagnosed with autism? Do you curse the sky and the world or do you look for your child's innate differences that can be strengths, that make them unique and to be appreciated?

What direction does your thinking push you towards, the glass being half empty, or half full?

For the most part, the world merely is. A snowstorm is neither good nor bad. It is a natural event, like that injury that could make you give up physical activity or force you to change your approach and improve. Your perception of the event, your thinking, your choice of future outcome.

Seneca said that a sword is neither evil nor good, it is merely a tool in the hands of a man. Same with a gun, or a keyboard. It is the choice of the individual, based upon their belief system, as to whether it is for good or ill.

Every day we have millions of interactions with our environment, millions of micro-choices as to how we perceive the world and act upon it and keying off future interactions. Think about how you look at the world and choose to react.

Action item: look back at yesterday. Choose an external event, and reflect on how you evaluated it and what you did. Was your thinking good or bad?

04 NOVEMBER

"And what is good, Phaedrus, and what is not good? Need we ask anyone to tell us these things?"

Robert M. Persig, Zen and the Art of Motorcycle Maintenace

We live in a world of judgement, of social mores established to create relatively peaceful societies and minimize the potential to upend the structure, be it from established politicians and political parties to religious institutions to education designed primarily for the post agrarian industrialized world. We have been told that we should go to the best college we can, study something we like, graduate and build a career while after a few years getting married, having kids, and becoming good members of our community that don't ask too many questions and perpetuate the cycle for the next generation.

Is that good for YOU though?

We have over a million trade jobs unfilled in the US that pay really well and can lead to a great career and opportunity to own a business.

With the internet, we can build a business from almost anywhere. A house in the suburbs with a white picket fence and minivan could be the right thing for many people, but is it right or good for you?

Maybe you don't want kids, can't have kids, or shouldn't have kids. Why follow societal norms on this?

Maybe you love working and look at retirement as a waste of your potential, and want to die at your desk at 88 working on a really cool project. Is that not good?

"Rules are for the obedience of fools and the guidance of wise men" Harry Day observed. Some laws (like gravity) are inviolable. Some (Thou Shalt Not Kill) are really good ideas. Others are like Barbosa says the Pirate Code is: more like guidelines. It is up to us to know the differences.

Action item: look at the rules (written or unwritten) you follow. Which one should be broken?

05 NOVEMBER

"When the wolf is trying to get in, you gotta stand in the doorway."

B.B. King

As Kenny Rogers said at the end of *The Coward of the County*: sometimes you've got to fight to prove you're a man.

Take a stand against what you believe is wrong, whether that's Mega Corporation trying to move in and destroy your small town, or your friend making horrible choices that will destroy their life. Erin Brokovich showed what one person ready to fight could do. So did Rosa Parks and Gandhi. Fight for what you believe is right.

JRR Tolkien through Gandalf proclaimed "I have found that it is the small everyday deeds of ordinary folk that keep the darkness at bay." The little things like saying "No" to a small thing that could be the slippery slope (like bending a rule at work, or taking advantage of someone, or overstating charitable deductions). The little acts of pure intentions, of not taking advantage of others and the situation and causing micro-harms, is the sign of diligence against the creeping darkness, the entropy of evil that naturally exists in the world.

Fight the fights.

If you see something wrong, say something. Or better yet, DO something.

"If you don't stand for something, you'll fall for anything." Malcom X.

Make your stand.

Fight for what you believe in, and defend your house (your family, your profession, your mind).

Plant your feet in the doorway and fight.

Action item: what is the one thing you will fight for, no matter the cost or consequences?

06 NOVEMBER
"If you fell down yesterday, stand up today."

H.G. Wells

If you can breathe, you can fight.

Doesn't matter if yesterday beat you into the ground and you feel like you lost everything from your business to your best friend to your dog. Get up and fight.

If it's not fatal, it's not final.

There are bad days, Bad weeks. Long rough patches. You can lay down and die, or stand up. Even if you are bloodied and shaky like Rocky ten rounds in, getting back up in defiance of the odds, refusing to stay down will give you the chance to win today and inspire those watching you, be it a three-year-old or a 23 year old. Never throw in the towel.

You lost yesterday? Rip that page off the calendar and throw it in the garbage, and stand up and fight today.

One of the things about building a successful business is "the grind", where you have to do essentially the same things over and over and over and over again to get traction and make progress. It could be making a hundred (or more) calls in a day, or banging on the keyboard for five hours before lunch and then again after it. The grind seems like it has no end in sight at times, but if you then look back over the weeks or months (even years), you can see progress and little victories every day, no matter how beaten down you were.

If you don't stop in a marathon, you eventually finish.

Those of us who are special needs parents (autism like my kids, diabetes like some of my friends, childhood cancer or congenital issues like other friends), know that there are some days where we fall, that are horrible and crush our souls. And the next day we get out of bed and do what we need to do, because our kids need us. There are no days off in the fight for your child's life. They don't quit, how can we?

Action item: you got out of bed today, you can stand up and not give in. What do you have to fight today?

07 NOVEMBER

"In matters of style, swim with the current; in matters of principle, stand like a rock."

Thomas Jefferson

In the 1980's I never had parachute pants, but I did have a rad mullet. In the 1990's I rocked sideburns. I keep my hair short now because a certain someone prefers it that way. I could grow it out and look like a pirate if I re-pierce my ear (something that made my mother cry at 18 "you'll ruin your life!"), but quite frankly I don't care about surface appearance. It is all just a temporary illusion or show for others. Pirates can wear whatever we want. In fact it used to be basically only pirates that had tattoos, now everyone does other than me. Styles change, fundamentals don't.

I wear a tie for work because I believe that it is my uniform. I will appear in at least a tie and jacket (preferably suit and tie), because it is a matter of professional principle to me. Doesn't matter what the current trend or style is: a man in a suit carries more respect and authority in business. A woman in a dark pantsuit carries a similar gravitas. That is a psychological principle. I refused to give in and grow an Apocalypse Beard. Or do video calls while wearing shorts. Sorry not sorry, I drew a line and I was not crossing it. My principles are inviolable.

Other people that you know let their standards slip. Don't you let yours slip, even when there are plenty of reasons to do so, because those "reasons" are really glorified excuses to violate the little rules, which can and does lead to the breaking of vows and crossing lines that shouldn't be crossed. As my mom reminded me: you know right from wrong. Make the right choice. Make me proud.

Styles change, fundamental principles don't. "Do Not Kill. Do Not Rape. Do Not Steal. These are principles, which every man of every faith can embrace. These are not polite suggestions, these are codes of behavior and those of you that ignore them will pay the dearest cost." The Boondock Saints

You know what is right. It doesn't matter what it says on tv or in a paper or someone on the street: you know what is fundamentally right, and what is just surface appearance window dressing for bad behavior. Stand properly, as Steve Rogers declared: Doesn't matter what the press says. Doesn't matter what the politicians or the mob says. Doesn't matter if the whole country decides that something wrong is something right. This Nation was founded on one principle above all else: the requirement that we stand up for what we believe in, no matter the odds or the consequences. When the mob and the press and the whole world tell you to move, your job is to plant yourself like a tree next to the river of Truth and tell the whole world "No, YOU move." Captain America might be an ideal, but it is ideals that principles direct us towards becoming. Know your truths, understand what your fundamental principles are and what is mere makeup.

Action item: what principles are you unwavering about? Live them today.

06 NOVEMBER
"Being happy never goes out of style."

Lilly Pulitzer

As they sang in Annie: you're never fully dressed without a smile. It takes a good looking person and makes them beautiful. It is an accessory that goes with everything from the little black dress to blue jeans, and can be shared easily. Marilyn Monroe called it: a smile is the best makeup any girl can wear.

"Because of your smile, you make life more beautiful." Thich Nhat Hanh

If someone sees a smile, it fires up the mirror neurons in their brain and they are more likely to smile too. When someone smiles, their body releases dopamine, serotonin, and endorphins that act as stress reducers and antidepressants. Your smiling at someone is literally the best medicine for stress and the homeopathic counter to a crappy day. Your happiness is contagious, and you should spread it around as much as possible.

Happiness unfortunately is not a consistent state of "upness" with no variation. It is not a constant sugar rush of perfect sweetness like Unakitty in The Lego Movie, where everything is awesome and Minions bring you cupcakes and backrubs while the Oompa Loompas do all of your work. We all have not great moments and days, sometimes weeks of negative funk. There are inevitable ebbs and flows like the tides, and when you are low someone else might pick you up so we have an obligation when we are riding high or cresting to spill over our happiness into others that need it. The cycles of nature apply to our human emotions, but through our interactions with others we can mitigate and shorten the downs, and this is part of our obligations to our loved ones and communities.

"Everyone smiles in the same language." George Carlin

Happiness is global. Every human being has the capacity to smile, and essentially every single one of us has the capacity to be happy, even in some of the worst circumstances. Viktor Frankl in "Man's Search for Meaning" talks about seeing rainbows while in the Nazi concentration camp, of men pausing for the beauty of a sunset and smiles spreading across their faces in moments of pure bliss amid the horror.

If someone nearly dead, suffering from soul sickening atrocities can be happy for a moment, can you do anything less?

Action item: smile at 10 people today.

09 NOVEMBER
"Forget about style; worry about results."

Bobby Orr

Kevin Youkilis was known as "The Greek God of Walks" in Boston. His swing was as ugly as his goatee. But he got results: 3 All Star Games, 2 World Series Rings and a Hank Aaron Award.

Tim Ferriss won a Chinese Kick Boxing title by dropping like 30 pounds, then super hydrating to normal weight and literally pushing people off the platform. Zero style points, but still Champion. My cooking will never win any awards for the plating and presentation. But it's healthy and tastes good.

There are rarely style points in life. Outcomes matter. Did you finish the marathon? Everyone other than the elite runners get the same medal and t-shirt, even if you look like a shuffling lumbering wreck at the end like I do instead of a fleet footed gazelle. People still ask "You ran a marathon?!" Even if you brute force the work and your methods completely lack elegance, the outcome is what matters. The firebombing of Tokyo in WWII was brutal, merciless, inelegant (especially by comparison to the attempts at precision bombing that failed). But it got the results, and Gen. Curtis LeMay was later awarded the First Order of Merit with the Grand Cordon of The Rising Sun by the Japanese because his savage attacks showed the Japanese people (with the atomic bombs) what he was willing to do to end the war quickly. Millions of Japanese and Allied Forces lives were spared because LeMay ignored style for a massive flame tsunami of intimidation.

Engineers often do back of the envelope calculations. They aren't exact or even pretty, but they let us know if what we are planning is going to fail and collapse. Quick and dirty and effective.

Sometimes, I am as subtle as a brick to the head. It gets the job done most of the time. But it always gets the message across. I have zero style, but....

Action item: instead of trying to be suave and perfect, just tell them!

10 NOVEMBER

"You don't get any medal for trying something, you get medals for results."

Bill Parcells

For some reason in the mid-1990's we started awarding everyone prizes in all competitions. Before then the only place you would get a participation medal was a marathon (or Ragnar) because 26+ miles is a major achievement no matter how quickly you complete it. But now everyone gets a trophy in every contest even if they don't finish. There is no incentive to bust your butt, improve, and finish in the top five of a hundred-person event if there is no difference between succeeding and failing.

If everyone that shows up gets the same ribbon, is it worth anything?

Trying hard carries rewards, it teaches discipline and the value of sacrifice over time for deferred pleasure, good things that directly translate into life-long success and riches (financial and otherwise). But trying is only part of the equation.

There are millions of singers that try hard and never hit the charts.

There are millions of actors that have never hit the big screen, let alone starred.

Teaching people that trying hard is good enough is dangerous because it leads to entitlement as the standards decline and people get the T Shirt and medal for just signing up for the race and paying the money. They get the same outward rewards for staying in a comfy bed as the lady that gets up at five am and does her miles in the cold and snow and muck. Doesn't seem fair.

Being treated equally is not being treated fairly.

If one business partner does 90% of the work, should they get the lion's share of the proceeds or should it be split equally with the other two that contributed little? When you had a group project, if you had the (inevitable) slacker on your team, did they deserve the same grade as those who burnt the midnight oil over and over again, that didn't go out while the slacker partied?

I had an eight-year-old tell me: only winners deserve trophies. Sounds harsh, but that kid has champion material inside and will succeed because he hates to fail enough to accept only the best and isn't jealous of others being rewarded for their work and wins. He deserves a medal, when he wins it.

Action item: where can you exert more effort and actually get a win, instead of just showing up?

11 NOVEMBER

"I hated every minute of training, but I said : don't quit. Suffer now and live the rest of your life as a champion."

Muhammad Ali

Pain is forgotten. Broken bones heal. Even scars fade. But glory is eternal. Achilles is remembered through history, as are the other great heroes and champions down the ages. Immortality through achievement.

Ahnold Schwarzennegger asked Ali how many sit ups he did. Ali responded with: I don't know, I don't start counting until it hurts. That is the mindset of a champion. Suffer, and justify the suffering with victory later as Jordan Peterson says.

In the early stages of your career, you should suffer. Live below your means. Train extra. Study, and practice, and do more than you should. Work harder than anyone else does, on yourself and in your work. Push yourself hard, because that suffering will give you power your peers won't understand. You can win in the work arena, because you put in the work to do so.

What do you want to be the champion of? Your relationship? Then do the hard work. Open yourself up to the painful conversation with your partner. Be vulnerable, and do the little things that you might hate (like the dishes) because those little pains make the relationship stronger and champion caliber. Your passion? Get up and get out of bed early to practice and train, whether it is reading other poets and writing every morning, or hitting the gym and the road to build your body for your athletic endeavor.

Feed your mind properly, study the greats in your field, expose yourself to the motivational materials that make sense. Lay out a training plan, whether it is increasing miles or practicing art. Train like a champion, think like a champion, and ultimately perform like the champ.

Push yourself to the edge of your capabilities (red lining, as in pushing your car so hard that it is on the edge of the danger zone) over and over again to expand the envelope of possibility. It hurts going to the edge, mentally exhausting and physically painful. This danger zone is where champions are made, whether it is as an intellectual professional or in the ring. Once you have been here, it can't be taken away from you.

I wear my blackbelt on my soul, not around my waist; it can never be taken away from me because of the suffering I went through to earn it. This is what being a champion takes, and creates.

Action item: how can you push yourself to excellence in one area, to suffer and become better and better and eventually the best? Start suffering, but for a reason: to be The Champion of Your World.

12 NOVEMBER

"It is up to us to live up to the legacy that was left for us, and to leave a legacy that is worthy of our children and of future generations." Christine Gregoire

What were your grandparent's names? What did they do to lay the foundation for your parents? And what have your parents accomplished, and sacrificed for you?

If given those gifts, are you making their sacrifices meaningful? Or are you wasting your legacy? We all are handed gifts from the previous generations, Could be looks, intelligence, athletic ability, wealth. Maybe my writing ability (as opposed to me). The question is, are you using your talents or not?

My grandfather was a trumpet player, and I certainly didn't inherit his musical abilities. He gave that up to build trucks and provide for his children. My father was the first of his family to go to college, on an ROTC scholarship. I have been given love of family and a willingness to work, a drive to go to the next level because that is what Templins do. My son thinks the best compliment possible is "to work like a Templin." He will probably live up to the legacy of my forefathers.

My mother's family were farmers. The love of the earth runs deep with us. I can't raise a beautiful flower garden but I can grow my own food, and my kids help with the garden. Learning what helped teach that side of my family our work ethic that I am instilling as was instilled into me on the farm as a kid (and I have the barbed wire scars to remind me).

What have your parents taught you that goes beyond tying your shoes or being a fan of a particular team? How to cook family recipes? A love for traditional songs? A tradition of public service or volunteerism? These are more valuable than gold in many ways.

Did your family members serve in our military, protecting our country? My kids know their maternal great-grandfather was the Sargent portrayed in the movie Patton, who later was a liberator of one of the concentration camps. That is a tremendous legacy, but ones the younger generations understand and try to emulate in other capacities.

Make your ancestors proud. A thousand generations lived, sacrificed, and died for you to be you.

Action item: look back at your family history and find inspiration.

13 NOVEMBER

"May the happiest days of your past be the saddest days of your future."

Irish Proverb

We Irish are a weird bunch: completely pessimistic yet brimming with optimism. Could be the reason why Sigmund Freud declared: this is one race of people for whom psychoanalysis is of no use whatsoever. We hope and love and fight and cry and sing and laugh, the full gamut of human passions all wrapped up in a bright-eyed Gaelic package.

Our hospitality is legendary and ancient, a deep part of the culture. But even more than that is the one thing that we seem to have more of than any other people: hope. Hope not necessarily for ourselves, but for our children and our friends and others. The Stockdale Paradox was almost written for the people of the Emerald Island, because we can be up to our eyeballs in a situation and crack a joke and talk about going to the pub when it is all over.

"The sun will come out, tomorrow" sang little orphan Annie. That hope for a brighter day to get through the current darkness is as Irish as it comes, especially when you look at the desperate situation (living in an orphanage with a horrible overseer in the midst of the Great Depression) and hope is literally the only thing she had. And when good fortune came upon her, what did she try to do? Share it with others, and her joy.

Happiness is one thing that the more you give it to others, the more of it you have.

If you are a parent, you might be holding on to the American Dream, that your children will have a better and happier life than what you experienced. Herein though lies the issue: by trying to give the next generation everything and having them not experience the difficulties that crafted us, we are actually raising the bar of their expectations to unreasonable levels. When I was a kid we had one thing to play with: outside. We had to learn to amuse ourselves and be happy with little. This means that today I don't need much to find joy. Contrast that with my kids who didn't have to get up at early o'clock to take care of the animals or use their imagination for amusement thanks to technology; they have built up a tolerance for happiness and so it takes more to make them happy than it does those of us who struggled early. We don't want our kids to have all the difficulties that we had as kids, but having enough hardship can set the threshold of enjoyment and appreciation lower so that they don't need ever increasing stimulation like a dopamine addict to be happy.

To appreciate the little things, you need to have little things.

Look back to when you were in college (or grad school if you did this) or just getting started: crappy apartment. Old and busted car, or if new it was probably cheap and tiny. Tight budget and working your butt off. Lots of Ramen. That occasional splurge for a better beer as opposed to the normal pisswater we drank because we couldn't afford anything better. Remember that level? Contrast it with what you have now. Your worst days now are probably better than anything you dreamt of at 22.

The question is though: are you happy? Or have you stepped on the hedonic treadmill where you need to constantly up your dopamine surges, where what you once dreamt of is so commonplace in your life that you no longer appreciate it or derive joy from what would have once made you ecstatic. That car, the house, the dream job all fade in terms of the enjoyment we get from them because we adapt to that level if we don't force ourselves to appreciate it.

One way to help make your todays happier than all the days that came before is to steal an exercise from the Stoics, specifically the voluntary discomfort of Seneca: set aside a certain number of days, during which you shall be content with the scantiest and cheapest fare, with coarse and rough dress. If you have ever gone camping for a few days, you know how wonderful that shower and your own bed and a good meal are.

The best cheeseburger I ever had was after not being able to eat for five days from mouth surgery. Force yourself to experience poverty again to appreciate your wealth. This will enhance your happiness.

And so this is one of the secrets of the Irish culture: we know life sucks. We know that good times don't last, be it with work or our loved ones. There is always a storm around the corner so we can enjoy the moments of sunshine and calm before it, and after we bask in the rainbow of having survived the hardship.

Never forget how hard it was and you can truly be happy in the current relative ease.

Action item: chose voluntary discomfort today. Don't turn on the heat (or air conditioner) in your car, or do an intermittent fast so that when you do have the comfort, you truly experience it and the happiness is contrasted against the past.

14 NOVEMBER
"I believe that the future can be bright for us."

John F. Kennedy, Jr.

Americans have been optimistic since our first settlers arrived from Europe, and even before that with the natural positive attitude of the First Americans. Wars, recessions, pandemics, political and societal unrest have all been just blips along the curve of prosperity, growth, and generally improving life in the United States and most of the Western world.

It's not all sunshine and unicorns. Every person, every family has issues. Every town has problems, every job has setbacks. It's called life, and it is not perfect but on the whole it is pretty good and looks better over time.

One out of three kids today is predicted to live to 100. And with medicinal and nutritional improvements, a sixty year old today will live on average another three decades and be healthier, wealthier, and more educated and entertained than previous generations.

We all carry smart phones so we have unlimited access to all the world's knowledge if we choose to tap into it. We can learn any language, communicate with a friend or expert anywhere on the planet, and create exquisite works of music and art. Or Tiktok dances, which can be a nice amusement and distraction but the boredom of wealth and productivity, combined with jealousy (from others showing their best and people assuming that is "normal") is a major threat to happiness and relationships in this hyperconnected world.

"The future's so bright, I've got to wear shades" Timbuk 3

It's not that the road ahead is easy: it never is. This little thing called "life" is there to mess up your well planned path. People will get sick (maybe you), the economy is going to be a roller coaster, politics is not going away. But what lies ahead is still better than what is behind, if we chose to make it that way.

Your job is going to change radically over the next two decades, maybe even be eliminated. But if you know this, you can be prepared. Make sure your Linkedin profile is up to snuff, expand your network so that you have the contacts to be able to draw from when appropriate, and keep developing yourself as a person and a professional. Use that smartphone in your pocket to learn something every day and your future can be bright because you will cast your own light on the path ahead.

Your health is going to deteriorate at some point, that is the way organic life works. But you can stave it off by allocating some time each day for your physical and mental health by doing some calisthenics and making good food choices because they are relatively easy to make (as are bad ones). You can make your physical future brighter with some good personal responsibility choices. One of the things that leads to mental well being is having deep meaningful connections.

Use social media for more than posting pictures of food and cat memes, use it to truly connect with a few people in your life that are important to you so that you can build very strong emotional bonds that can carry forward for decades. When the dark times inevitably come, these connections will brighten your day and help you through the rough patches.

The future is bright, but how brilliant is greatly influenced by your personal choices. You can choose to do things that will dampen your light, leading to a darker future. Or you can choose to fuel your fire and burn brightly, lightening the way for yourself and others.

Action item: go invest fifteen minutes to polish your Linkedin profile or resume, and find one thing to learn that will help you at some point. This will make the path ahead a little better lit for you.

15 NOVEMBER

"Thus a focus on the future motivates people to change in the present."
David Howe

"Begin with the end in mind" as Covey says. "A people without a vision will perish." Book of Proverbs What is the goal you are working towards? Is it to fit into that outfit for a reunion, or to pass an exam? Focusing on what you want in the end (or a particular point in the future) makes it easier to make the little choices along the way like not having the cupcake or turning the tv off to study. Having no target to aim for means you will definitely miss the goal.

The future is not under our control, but definitely under our influence through our decisions on a day to day and hour to hour basis. If you are told by the doctor that you won't see your kid graduate from high school in a decade unless you stop smoking or drop a hundred pounds, that future is important enough to alter the actions of today. But until the doctor smacks you upside the head with some blunt truth you might not realize it (or rationalize the inevitable outcome away) and your regular consistent choices of present pleasure destroy the future you desire. Truth can hurt, as do the small sacrifices but they all hurt less than the massive future poor outcome.

An addict can not focus on the future because the desire for their fix is overwhelming in the moment. Whether it is the bottle or on their phone, they need that hit and will do anything for it UNLESS there is something down the road that is so overwhelmingly important that it restricts them from the current pleasurable action. Constantly putting this important future (of getting their baby back when they are clean, or of the trip to Paris when they no longer smoke, or financial freedom from breaking a spending habit) reinforces that vision of a future and makes it more real than the current need for instant gratification or escape. As friends and family of people in these situations we have a duty to create an environment that reminds them of the positive future they want rather than the negative past they are avoiding or the current pleasure they hunger for.

What are you focusing on for the future? Running a race? Earning that degree? Buying a home of your own? Create an environment for yourself that reinforces the microdecisions that will get you there. Don't have junk food in the house if it is a weight issue. You can't eat it if it's not there. Remove the apps on your phone that waste your time or lead you into situations that are negative for you. Take your study materials with you to someplace where all you can do is study (or write) and work towards that future you want.

Put up pictures, whether of the degree you are working towards or that car you are saving for or of the trip you want to take. Hang that dress up outside the closet so you see it every day.

Action item: change your phone lock screen to reinforce the future you want.

16 NOVEMBER

"Focus is a matter of deciding what things you're not going to do."

John Carmack

No. Such a little word, and yet so powerful.

No, I am not going to come in late again boss, I am going to spend time with my family and mentally recharge so I am more productive.

No honey, I am not going to spend money on that even though it makes you short term happy because it is contrary to our long term goals.

Marcus Aurelius: Most of what we say and do is not essential. If you can eliminate it, you'll have more time, and more tranquility. Ask yourself at every moment "is this necessary?"

No kiddo, I am not going to let you go to X because I don't approve of the other people there and think they will be a bad influence on you. I don't want to be up late worrying about you.

No, I am not going to volunteer and take time away from my kids.

Seneca: No person hands out their money to passers-by, but how many of us hand out our lives!

No, I am not going to take on that project in the house, I'll hire someone else to do it so I don't lose the next month of weekends and exhaust myself and become a meanie to those close to me because I have no time to relax and spend time with the kids while they are young.

Lin-Manuel Miranda: You will have to say no to things to say yes to your work. It will be worth it. No, I'm not going to sign up for another marathon because all the training time and physical exhaustion will take away from other things that are more important to me right now.

No, I'm not going to take on another hobby so I can invest the time to get even better at the one I'm currently pursuing.

Focus makes even a low powered bulb brighter by concentrating its output onto a small area, increasing the intensity and the energy density. This allows a kid with a magnifying glass to start a fire by concentrating weak sunlight and pinpointing more energy.

Focus is what unlocks greatness, by being able to say no to being ok at many things simultaneously.

Action item: say NO five times today to things that could steal your time.

17 NOVEMBER

"The ability to simplify means to eliminate the unnecessary so that the necessary may speak."

Hans Hofman

Michaelangelo said that his David was already in the block of marble, he merely removed what was covering the statue to reveal it to the world.

Bruce Lee talked about subtracting the extraneous, the extra movements and thoughts that were unneeded, stripping his martial arts down to the critical essence.

Early stage public speakers are taught to eliminate the "like", "um" and my personal demon "you know". These clog up the spaces between the words where the power resides.

In science we are taught to find the signal in the noise, the information hidden among the variability and background "stuff" wherein the messages lay. HP (Hewlett Packard) was built off of devices designed to find the signal amidst the noise.

Monks and meditators of all forms are taught to sit and eliminate the random thoughts popping into their head, to listen to their heart and the world around them to find peace and insight.

Writers are taught to eliminate the flowery superfluous verbiage, the unnecessary adornments, allowing the succinct truth to stand on its own. Hemingway is still read, his purple prose dime store novel contemporaries have been replaced by the current generation of bodice rippers that will cycle into the trash where they belong. The Old Man endures for his simplicity.

"I'm sorry, I was wrong" is worth more than you can ever imagine, because it is simple and speaks the needed truth.

As Abe Lincoln apologized: I would have written you a shorter letter if I had more time. To distill something to the essence takes effort, effort that is rewarded by being remembered. We all learned "Four score and seven years ago" because it was spot on and simple. It still speaks to us today.

Action item: choose one thing you do often. Study it. How can it be simplified?

18 NOVEMBER

"Where you see wrong or inequality or injustice, speak out, because this is your country."

Justice Thurgood Marshall

"I have found that it is the small everyday deed of ordinary folk that keep the darkness at bay." JRR Tolkien speaking through Gandalf.

It is not through the Great Powers that change comes, that the innocent are protected. It is through the actions of the common man and woman, who see inequity or abuse and say "no".

It is the child standing up to the bully, or the assistant standing up to the boss that is crossing the line and saying "thou shalt not!", even if they put themselves at risk in doing so.

"Since it is so likely that children will meet cruel enemies, let them at least have heard of brave Knights and heroic courage." CS Lewis

Rosa Parks refusing to move.

Bobby Sands and the rest of the Hunger Strikers.

The Rev. William J Barber II.

That nameless teenager on the train who tells her friends "That's not cool, knock it off."

Not all heroes wear capes, most are just average people who see a little thing wrong and make a small choice, a tiny act of defiance against tyranny or oppression by saying quietly but firmly "no." Not on my watch. I will not let someone make a disparaging remark about Asian Americans.

No. That's not cool, making a derogatory comment about someone's religious garb.

No sir, Mr. Politician. I won't let you bend the rule because laws apply to all of us equally, even if you have a modicum of power.

Give that kid the same chance as the others, regardless of where they came from. Don't stay silent in the face of the little attacks on freedom and dignity and opportunity and fairness that present themselves constantly. Little lies become Big Lies if the truth remains quiet.

Stand up and speak up, before you can't.

Action item: just today, don't let things slide. Confront the small injustices before they become accepted and institutionalized.

19 NOVEMBER

"Insults are the arguments employed by those who are in the wrong."

Jean-Jacques Rousseau

We have all tried to have a reasonable discussion with someone that then turns it into invective and attack, often ad hominem because the points we are making are valid and indisputable. So they emote and redirect or attack.

Often we see the other person go DARVO on us. Deflect, Attack, Reverse Victim and Oppressor. A classic technique of narcissists when faced with facts that they don't want to face because these facts disprove their gaslighting and other lies. DARVO is like an aikido move for those who have no rational basis in an argument so they redirect away from themselves.

We all get angry sometimes when we are having a discussion with a contrary party. Anyone that has gone through a divorce or a bad breakup is nodding their head reading this, maybe even feeling the tightening in the gut or clenching in the jaw just remembering the vitriol and negativity of it. We were not perfect in our friendships, but when things got heated we probably drifted into the wrong too and maybe said something that we shouldn't have, that was over the line in multiple ways. Emotions, especially anger, make us stupid and say stupid things. Cool heads don't insult other people. "Stand by a rock and insult it, and what have you accomplished? If someone responds to insults like a rock, what has the abuser gained with his invective?" Epictetus

Being the "grey rock" is an approach for dealing with narcissists and other abusive types that try to get a rise out of you for their own benefit. They are trying to goad you into an emotional (and often dumb) response so they can move the conversation from facts and logic to emotions and feelings where they can dominate or at least not be dissected with objective reason. Define and stick to the rules of engagement. Stay with logic and facts, if you are right the truth is your ally in this because it is powerful and can only be overcome by emotion.

Inside us we have three people: a Child, an Adult, and a Parental figure. The Adult is our logical and reasonable persona, with plenty of patience. The Child is exactly that, and throws temper tantrums and insults. The Parent is the finger wagging "I know best because I'm in charge and that's that". Arguments that deteriorate into insults involve both parties either acting as an emotional Child, an overbearing Parent, or one of each. An Adult though can mellow the other persona out by staying rock steady and unemotional, bringing the other individual to their level and allowing a reasonable discourse even if they disagree. Maintaining this position, this centrist but emotionless center of logic, is the best way to eliminate the insults and be able to have a mutually beneficial interaction.

Action item: stay in the middle, as a logical grey rock when others become emotional.

20 NOVEMBER
"An injury is much sooner forgotten than an insult."

Philip Stanhope

I've taken more than my share of physical hits. I don't even remember most of the ones that have led to broken bones. But the emotional strikes? Some of those can still smart decades later, because bruises fade but a cut to your soul can bleed forever.

We remember the teacher who insulted us in second grade, saying we were foolish or stupid. That insult can damage a kid and make them believe it, decreasing their capability and confidence for their entire life. We don't remember the dozens of times that we fell on the playground.

That person who we asked out in high school who played that cruel trick on us, embarrassing us in front of the entire school and setting back our emotional development by a decade. That hurt more than any physical injuries we sustained during gym class.

That boss, screaming at us about our incompetence in our first week, making us feel small and worthless. For the entire tenure on that job, less than 100% will be given.

That bully who day after day intimidated us and made us cry on the inside.

That random stranger with the hurtful comment that turned a great day sour.

They say "adding insult to injury" because it is more painful that way.

Words are powerful and can harm even when not intended. I have made my kids cry unintentionally. And yes, I feel like a monster and try to repair the damage but a crinkled piece of paper will always carry the creases.

I have insulted people that I care for deeply without meaning to, and it has taken weeks or more to try and smooth over the breaks in the relationship if we were lucky. Some have never been repaired and might not ever be. And that is on me for saying hurtful things that I never should have uttered or typed.

Action item: think before you speak today. And if you insulted anyone recently, make amends.

20 NOVEMBER
"An injury is much sooner forgotten than an insult."

Philip Stanhope

I've taken more than my share of physical hits. I don't even remember most of the ones that have led to broken bones. But the emotional strikes? Some of those can still smart decades later, because bruises fade but a cut to your soul can bleed forever.

We remember the teacher who insulted us in second grade, saying we were foolish or stupid. That insult can damage a kid and make them believe it, decreasing their capability and confidence for their entire life. We don't remember the dozens of times that we fell on the playground.

That person who we asked out in high school who played that cruel trick on us, embarrassing us in front of the entire school and setting back our emotional development by a decade. That hurt more than any physical injuries we sustained during gym class.

That boss, screaming at us about our incompetence in our first week, making us feel small and worthless. For the entire tenure on that job, less than 100% will be given.

That bully who day after day intimidated us and made us cry on the inside.

That random stranger with the hurtful comment that turned a great day sour.

They say "adding insult to injury" because it is more painful that way.

Words are powerful and can harm even when not intended. I have made my kids cry unintentionally. And yes, I feel like a monster and try to repair the damage but a crinkled piece of paper will always carry the creases.

I have insulted people that I care for deeply without meaning to, and it has taken weeks or more to try and smooth over the breaks in the relationship if we were lucky. Some have never been repaired and might not ever be. And that is on me for saying hurtful things that I never should have uttered or typed.

Action item: think before you speak today. And if you insulted anyone recently, make amends.

21 NOVEMBER
"Envy is an insult to oneself."

Yevgeny Yevtushenko

Know your worth. You are the product of almost four billion years of life on this planet. Of millions of years of hairy semi-upright creatures getting less hairy and more upright, learning to use tools and eventually (hopefully) a turn signal when they drive. You are the current peak of evolution on the planet. You live in the most successful time in history with the longest life expectancy, more calories per day than ever, and the knowledge of the entire planet at your fingertips. You probably live in the First World, which makes you top 10% of the current humans, who are in the top few percent of those ever to have lived. Not too shabby.

You have it pretty good, even if your car is old and you have a ton of student loan debt and no significant other to cuddle with. So what if someone else has a nicer car? Does yours function and get you where you need to go? Why be envious of someone's Ferrari (which they can't drive on ice or in snow by the way), or someone else having a sunroof (again, rain. And if you have skin as pale as mine, you couldn't open said sunroof without SPF5000. Plus it will mess up your hair with the wind). Why insult all your forebears and the miracle that is you being jealous of someone else's set of four wheels, especially when in two decades we will have self-driving vehicles and eventually flying cars? Why?

Who cares if someone else has the latest and greatest technology? I remember when the Apple 2e was the bomb, with those awesome floppy disks. And a 256? Man that was cool and I wanted one. A baby toy has that much computing power now, so why be jealous of what someone else has today, when in a few years it will be an antiquated paperweight?

Student loan debt? First, how much fun did you have in college? Did you maximize your educational opportunity, both in the classroom and outside it? And did you learn how to learn, so that post college your knowledge and skill base continue to expand so that you can increase your earnings and look at those loans as what they were: the price of admission to a great future? Or are you going to waste your time and energy being jealous of someone else? That is wasting energy in addition to wasting money. Envy is an emotional reaction to a scarcity mentality. It can be neutralized by letting that awesome neocortex that has evolved since we started standing upright to rationally understand that life is pretty good and probably getting better in a world of increasing abundance. So why be envious of someone or something that in a few years will be outmoded and relegated to the scrap heap of history?

Action item: when you feel yourself becoming jealous or envious of what another person has, engage your brain and find five reasons why it really won't matter in a few years.

22 NOVEMBER

"As iron is eaten away by rust, so the envious are consumed by their own passion."

Antisthenes

Desire is the root of all suffering per Buddhism. Suspend desire, and jealousy, and envy, and you will achieve enlightenment. Much easier said than done.

A little jealousy is a good thing. It makes us strive to do better if we see a nice car that we want and could achieve in a few years, or someone getting promoted at work, or a friend doing something physical that we can't quite do yet. Envy is a next level of this though, and instead of firing us up and inspiring us to do and be better, it causes us to excessively want something, often something we can't have (someone, a limited item, an experience that is well beyond our capabilities, a position we don't deserve, etc.).

Instead of entreating us to be better, envy ends up eating us and turning us bitter. I have struggled with envy in the past, I am not going to lie. When I thought I deserved something at work because I had checked all the boxes (many times over as it were), and the position was given to someone else. Or when the beautiful woman with whom I had the seemingly deep connection, who said I was the most caring and thoughtful man she ever met, chose the apparently inferior person to date because of convenience. Or someone who lied and cut corners and hurt others and then through no effort of their own was literally handed the bag of money. All of these got under my skin and deeply bothered me, eating at me and keeping me awake at night. And that is a "me" problem, because I let my ego be affected by other's decisions and luck.

"But why?" can and will destroy you. It almost destroyed me, and sometimes it still pops into my head and heart and starts gnawing away at my internal structure and makes me doubt myself and others.

Envy is a deep poison that can re-enter the well of your soul even years after you think you have drawn it out and discarded it. It is insidious, a mist of darkness that enters even the smallest cracks in your being and contaminates you slowly, a cancer of mind and belief that is darker than any other force because of how it sneaks in and spreads through you. It must be constantly guarded against and expunged before it gains a hold inside. And when you discover it, you must turn the full power of your mind and heart and spirit against it to burn it away. Use other people and resources to help destroy this internal evil before it consumes your soul.

Action item: what (or who) makes you jealous? Why? Is it a healthy desire that can make you better, or is it envy that will make you bitter? Look directly, unflinchingly at it. What do you need to do to expel it from you, like the poison it is?

23 NOVEMBER
"The way you think, the way you behave, the way you eat, can influence your life by 30 to 50 years."
Deepak Chopra

Our continuous daily choices compound and determine our long term health. We all know the effect of smoking cigarettes or vaping: drastically reduced lifespans with some pretty nasty side effects like popcorn lung, emphysema, and cancer. This health choice is pretty apparent. But what about some of the not as graphic choices?

Boxes of donuts don't come with a skull and crossbones on them. Sodas aren't labelled "POISON", and tv programs and social media don't come with warnings about the potential harmful side effects like prescriptions do.

Yet all of these things could potentially seriously negatively affect your health and shorten your lifespan. And yes, I am still going to keep eating donuts but not like I did as a 19 year old.

Cigarettes don't take 7 minutes off your life for each one you smoke as I was told growing up, but actually closer to 11 minutes each. Pack a day? 220 minutes, over three and a half hours per pack. You can do the math. Single best thing to do for your health is to stop smoking, and it will save you a ton of money too.

If you do smoke and need help stopping, there are resources online or talk to your doctor. And get an accountability buddy to help you break the patterns that make you want to smoke.

A single soda can reduce "healthy life" (the quantity and quality of it) by as much as a cigarette. When was the last time (outside of New York City) you heard of a large campaign to cut down on soda consumption?

I'm not saying you can never have a rum and coke (I would be a total hypocrite to do so), but maybe not have a six pack a day nor the super jumbo (even if diet) with lunch. Between the calories (12 per ounce), the sugar, and the other stuff (carbonic acid, preservatives, etc) it really is not in the top five of things you should be drinking. Just saying.

The founder of Dunkin' Donuts Bill Rosenberg believed they were healthy and had one every day. But he had one a day (not a half dozen) and did multiple other things that offset the sugar and calorie consumption (he had lung cancer but kicked it and lived about thirty more years) so his moderation and balance neutralized much of the negative effects.

On the flip side, thirty minutes a day of sweat-inducing activity has been shown to have a large positive effect on quality and quantity of life. Like, increasing your lifespan by close to a third. And no, running a marathon a day won't make you immortal but will allow you to have more donuts. Social connections are another life enhancer. A strong social network (not the movie, but in real life honest to goodness friends and family that you regularly interact with) is worth multiple years to you.

Social connections are another life enhancer. A strong social network (not the movie, but in real life honest to goodness friends and family that you regularly interact with) is worth multiple years to you.

So eat healthy, don't smoke, exercise regularly, and see your friends. That leads to a pretty good life and a longer one too.

Action item: are you getting enough social contact and exercise? Go for a walk today with a friend (or call one while walking).

24 NOVEMBER

"We're learning things every decade we grow through, and ultimately, you do end up with a different way of looking at things."
Florence Pugh

Think about the you of ten years ago. You probably look back and say "I was such an idiot! If I only knew then what I know now." And a decade from now you will say the same thing. That's called growth.

Our first decade we are learning how our bodies work, how society works, and important things like our favorite color (blue) and dinosaur (stegosaurus). Our personality is developed from our family, environment, and genetic factors. This is our base we build the rest of our lives off of.

In our teens we develop most of the core of our personalities, we develop the base habits of our lives (eating, activity, learning, work ethic, etc.) and our general thought patterns (heuristics) that act as the chassis for the rest of our mental development (assuming no traumatic changes).

After about twenty or so, we are just using what we had built in those first two decades, but it doesn't mean that we aren't evolving. The life experiences you have in high school, college, and your first couple of years in "the real world" are the basis of how you continue to grow mentally, but not an absolute determinant of the future.

As an example, in my early twenties I left the lab and entered the business world, doing financial consulting. The analytical approach from my days as a researcher formed the basis of my approach, and the majority of the clients I went after were enginerds like me, but over time (from experience) I broadened my skill set and learned to deal with "normal" people. To understand them I started studying psychology, and after two dozen years I actually have a decent idea why most people do what they do. Most people, as there are some that will always be an enigma. So how I interact with people has evolved tremendously from arrogant hard core math focused wonk to more emotionally and psych driven teacher and collaborator. Even if at my core I'm still a dinosaur loving nerd that tries to solve all the world's problems.

Having kids forces growth and change of how you think and act, especially if you have a special needs kid like I do. That teaches you more patience, and makes you try to develop more empathy.

Not a bad thing.

Look at your own relationship. If you have been married for over a decade, I guarantee your spouse is not the same as when you were married, and neither are you. Hopefully you both have grown instead of deteriorated, but you are not the same people you were.

How you perceive the world in your forties should be different than in your twenties because of your experiences and responsibilities, even if you have the same sort of rose-tinted glasses from your early experiences. They are probably just darker now, and maybe even bifocals.

Humans evolve (not like Pokemon in terms of appearance and powers but mental processes and social awareness), and the continuous improvement and expansion of our views is what helps keep us mentally stimulated and young in attitude.

Action item: look back at you of a decade ago. What has changed with your family? With your job? Now, look forward ten years and ask yourself who you need to become to have that person come into being.

25 NOVEMBER

"Empathy begins with understanding life from another's perspective."

Sterling K. Brown

Walking a mile in another's shoes is a good thing, because you can understand where they are on their journey and why their feet hurt. The ability to look out through their eyes is even better, to truly understand their perspective on the world.

Empathy is all about trying to understand the why behind people, and then the what. Why do they think and act and react the way that they do? What experiences did they have to shape their outlook, their framework for decision making, and their overall and current emotional states? What are they thinking and feeling now, and if I do a particular thing how are they going to interpret it and act? It is about their experiences and outlooks so that we can understand what we would do in the same situation, not from our knowledge and mindset but from theirs.

Empathy is the goal of talking with a child that has done something (like maybe taken a toy from another) and getting them to swap places with the other party, to understand and express "what would you feel like if Juan did that to you?"

Empathy is picking up some of the work of your coworker who is taking care of a parent with cancer, because you know how tired they are.

Instead of getting angry with your friend, empathy is thinking about what it was like to grow up in their situation and how losing a parent young could leave a mark on their psyche so that they are always afraid of being abandoned. Then her decisions seem not so erratic, if you can operate from her mindset of losing loved ones and lack of trust.

Most of us that have had kids had a baby up all night at some point and have gone to work looking like a zombie. When you see a new mom or dad like this, bring them a coffee and provide a sympathetic ear.

Empathy does not mean endorsing bad behavior, nor does it mean that you have to let standards slide into chaos. But it does make your heart an equal party to decisions with your head, and where there can be some flex in the rules or processes (knowing when an exemption or some additional tolerance is appropriate), will go a long way to strengthen relationships.

Action item: before you get upset, pause and ask yourself "why would they do that?". Then think about how this person has gotten to where they are in life today, and then make your decision as to how you will react.

26 NOVEMBER

"Distance not only gives nostalgia, but perspective, and maybe objectivity."
Robert Morgan

Maybe they say hindsight is 20/20 because it allows us to have a bit more perspective, not the rose-tinted glasses or the dark clouds that we usually see the world through.

Yes, we might have a little haze around the image as we gaze at something well removed from where we stand, the slight fuzziness of memory tinged with faded but still felt emotions. But being out of the moment, no longer having the visceral reaction, allows us to see things a bit clearer and to understand what we couldn't when we were too close to the situation. It lets us more truly see what was as opposed to what we wanted.

"Looking back is a way to sharpen the focus on the things you want to change in your life." Sarah Paulson

My military friends always have an After Action Brief, where they review what happened away from the fog of war. Pro athletes watch the game tape, even of their most devastating losses. I review my business meetings to see where I came up short (or actually succeeded), and do the same with my relationships to be a better friend in the future. Yes, it sucks looking at how I messed up but hopefully I mess up less in the future.

This can be difficult looking back at a failed relationship or business gone sour will potentially re-open some old wounds and refresh the pain. But it will be dulled from the initial experience, and not making the same mistake a third time is a sign of maturity and growth. Who knows, you might even find a way back into one of those situations and correct it (not in a Quantum Leap style but from the current point forward).

"Looking back, my life seems like one long obstacle race, with me as the chief obstacle." Jack Parr
Instead of waiting until we are old and grey to look back, what if we looked back weekly to have enough time to not be in the moment but have the actions and emotions still be fresh enough and relevant to the near future? We could maybe be somewhat objective and have enough distance from the objects to see the big picture.

Action item: Look back at last week and last month to see where you messed up, and what you can learn from the situations. Start incorporating this reflection action into your day regularly so you can learn more lessons without having to wait years or until it is too late to alter your future actions.

27 NOVEMBER
"Laughter is the closest distance between two people."

Victor Borge

Laughter bridges the gap between minds and souls faster than anything else.

Former FBI hostage negotiator Chris Voss points out that if you can get somebody to laugh, you start establishing the rapport needed to communicate, and your chance of a successful negotiation is significantly higher.

Want better productivity? Laugh more. Harvard Business Review says so. And hey, it's Hahvahd. They ah wicked smaht.

Reduce stress between you and another person? Get them to crack a smile. You can see how important this is in a personal relationship or a sales situation, but remember that almost everything in life is a form of sales situation and all interactions are personal on some level.

There are few things as awful as a really bad dad joke. Just reading about one you are probably grimacing or rolling your eyes, hoping that I don't write something horrible. Sorry, I'm not that punny.

If you groaned in appreciation, we are now bonded and you actually will be slightly smarter for the next few minutes, plus make better decisions. This is one of the reasons humor in our daily lives is critical to well grounded relationships, beyond the fact that we live in a stressful world and laughter reduces the stress hormones in your system and can heal your body and mind. This is not metaphysical mumbo jumbo (although laughter is the best medicine), but actual biochemistry. So as Han Solo tells Chewie: laugh it up fuzzball!

One observation of mine that could be completely false but sounds good: the closer someone is to your heart, the more you can make each other laugh. Call it Templin's Law of Love:

$C = 1/(L2)$
Where C is Closeness
L is Laughter

Laugh more with the people you care for and you will draw closer together, no matter how far the distance between you physically.

Action item: focus on making yourself and others laugh today. The more, the better!

28 NOVEMBER

"The distance between insanity and genius is measured only by success."

Bruce Fierstein

"People said I was crazy until I actually did it". This could have been said by any great entrepreneur, artist, underdog politician, or anyone with big dreams that brings their fantasy to reality when the world doubts them.

One component of genius and insanity is the ability to see something that isn't there. Disney flying over the Florida orange groves and seeing the theme park, Tesla seeing a world of wireless transmission. The kid playing guitar in their basement and imagining crowds. The little girl watching the US National Team in the Olympics that someday plays for them. Seeing what could be but is not yet is part of the vision of the crazy, the creative, and the creators of this world.

Everything looks insane at one point. "You want to bury those stones from the fruit and expect to get more fruit?! Are you crazy Thag?!" "So you want all people to have an equal say in government, and no king Thomas? That be madness!" "So you think men and women should all be equal? Insane!" "So you say you can send lasers down these light pipes and people can eventually request movies sent over them to their house whenever they want? Are you damaged in the head, son?" That last one I actually heard when I was doing research and made a presentation to the brass. Netflix anyone?!

Crazy is as crazy does, and some things are just so crazy that they actually work and end up changing the world. As Steve Jobs said, those who are crazy enough to think they can change the world just might do so. Mozart was considered a nutcase.

The Surrealists were called crazy. So were the Expressionists. Even the Baroque back in the day were thought to be too "out there," before becoming the establishment. Rock and Roll was once called the Devil's Music and now is mainstream. Actually it's pretty lame stream by comparison to the craziness of Led Zeppelin and Black Sabbath and the 1980's hair metal scene, but maybe it is because we don't have Keith Moon or Ozzy Osbourne to mix it up and show some genius insanity to the music world. Mad geniuses.

We used to have brilliant scientists that looked like Einstein. Michio Kaku is one of the few rock star scientists we have today (sorry Neil de Grasse Tyson). Maybe we need more weirdos and crazy hair. I mean, look at Dr. Sir Bryan May of Queen! Crazy leads to innovation because it challenges the status quo by thinking differently. Same with genius. The difference between the two is literally a quantum of acceptance.

Action item: What is the craziest idea that you've had? Dust it off and explore it like a scientist and see if it is insane or genius.

29 NOVEMBER

"I tell you, in this world, being a little crazy helps to keep you sane."

Zsa Zsa Gabor

Or as Jimmy Buffett says, if we weren't all crazy we'd all go insane.

Douglas Adams insightfully proclaimed: Would it save you a lot of time if I just gave up and went mad now?

The world is completely random and irrational, no matter how much we want to believe otherwise. No matter how great your faith, no matter how wonderful your plan ("the best laid plans of mice and men…"), no matter how good or smart or dedicated you are, life is going to happen and it is a crazy ride.

"Life is what happens when you are busy making other plans." John Lennon
There is a country song whose chorus sums up the world pretty well. Billy Currington croons about an experience with an old man he meets in a bar and spends an afternoon drinking and philosophizing with:

> God is great
> Beer is good
> And people are crazy.

If you accept this thesis then life is better.

Madness is really the modus operandi of the world around us. Not five-year plans from a centralized state, not the carefully constructed road map for our kids to be popular and athletic and get good grades then attend the same college we did and find a wonderful spouse and give us grandbabies, not even your idea of how this morning is going to go. The sooner you realize that having a framework for how you hope things go but contingency plans (like for the rain on the way to the amusement park, or what to do if your vehicle decides to fry the battery on your way to an important work meeting, etc. etc. etc.) and flexibility in your attitude to roll with the ever threatened and all too often sucker punches from life, the better off you will be.

Relax. "We're all mad here." The Cheshire Cat from Alice in Wonderland

Action item: we know the world is nuts and getting worse. Accept it. Revel in the madness. Do something (not dangerous) that causes someone to ask you if you are crazy. Then look them in the eye and say "no, are you?" and continue on with your day.

30 NOVEMBER
"Every man has a sane spot somewhere."

Robert Louis Stevenson

Even the person with the most dysfunctional belief system has some rationality behind it, a method to their madness that can be understood and used to have a discussion with them with relatively decent outcomes.

Even the Internal Revenue Code has a form of logic behind it. Convoluted and byzantine and at times just plain weird, but at least there is a kernel of consistency, if you can think like a tax attorney that has spent too much time painting in a small, enclosed area.

If your partner is acting irrationally, set aside your belief system and biases for a moment. Try to look out through their eyes and back over their past, as to why they are doing it. Maybe they have trauma from their teenage years that they haven't resolved. Maybe someone cheated on them and so they have little experience trusting someone. Maybe they are going through a hormonal change, or are struggling with something at work that they haven't yet shared. Being empathic, really trying to understand and look out through their eyes, will allow you to interact with them in the way that they need right now to help preserve and strengthen your relationship.

Find the eye of their storm of madness, where there is calm and clarity.

Have you ever gotten down on a knee to be eye to eye with a little kid, and looked at the world from that perspective? Being tiny, weak, not allowed to make decisions outside a very narrow area, lacking understanding of most of what is going on and few people taking the time to interact with you and help you get a hold of the chaos? Do you think that the random outbursts now make a little more sense? Could you act to give them some agency and control with responsibilities that might help them focus and control their outbursts?

Even the most psychopathic of people have some internal rules and logic they follow. No one is purely an agent of chaos and destruction, and even if they were you could understand their seeming randomness if you can filter the world as they do, and be able to predict what they would do next. This is how profilers and spies and white hat hackers work: thinking like the bad guys so they can stop them. Isn't understanding your boss (or employees) and loved ones that important?

Action item: look for the why behind people's what, the reason that gives rise to their action.

DECEMBER, BEING THE LAST MONTH OF THE YEAR, CANNOT HELP BUT MAKE US THINK OF WHAT IS TO COME.

Fennel Hudson

01 DECEMBER

"Fantasy is hardly an escape from reality.
It's a way of understanding it."

Lloyd Alexander

Some people use fantasy to escape from the world. Others use it as inspiration, a way of asking "what if?" and then working to make that possibility an actuality. Taking fantasy and making it reality.

Science fiction becomes science fact, and it is not limited to this space.

We have all day-dreamed, but have you used it to start focused meditation and visualization? Countless athletes pre-play the game in their head, seeing themselves hitting the winning shot. Psychologists have repeatedly shown that positive visualization of skills and outcome are as good or better than physical practice for those that are above average talent.

Do you see yourself winning that deal?

Do you fantasize about what it will feel like walking across that stage to receive your degree, or that award? David Goggins talks about the feeling of becoming a Navy SEAL, the forward projection of him wearing the dress whites for those few moments of indescribable ecstasy as what carried him through eighteen months of training and THREE Hell Weeks. That fantasy created his reality. Ever fantasize about asking your crush out? Play it over in your mind a bunch, then do it? Why not? Einstein fantasized about riding a beam of light and it led to incredible advances in physics.

Jules Verne fantasized about going to the depths of the ocean in 20,000 Leagues Under the Sea and to the moon in From the Earth to the Moon. 100 years later the Nautilus was prowling the world for the US Navy and we were about to put a man on the moon.

In Harry Potter the Mirror of Eristed traps people by showing them their deepest desire, but you can look into that mirror and instead of counting on magic or dreams to make it come true, you can then get to work figuring out how to make that fantasy reality and bring it into being with hard work and creativity. Inspiration, instead of escapism.

Action item: get a piece of paper. In five years, if everything went right, what could your world look like (work, home, physical, educational, etc)? Now make it not a possibility but an actuality, fantasy becoming reality.

02 DECEMBER

"We don't create a fantasy world to escape reality. We create it to be able to stay."

Lynda Berry

James Nesmeth was a decent golfer who hoped to win some championships, but his dreams were delayed for a few years. Major Nesmeth spent seven years in a prisoner of war camp in Vietnam, but played golf every day in his head. Emaciated and weak upon his return, one of his goals was to play his favorite course which he did soon after returning home after his ordeal. He took 20 strokes off his previous average, even with his damaged body. His mental game was on point.

Natan Sharansky spent 9 years in a Soviet prison, half of it in solitary confinement. To maintain his sanity he said to himself "I might as well use the opportunity to become the world champion" and played chess against himself. A decade later he beat Garry Kasparov, reigning champ.

Viktor Frankl re-wrote the manuscript taken from him when the Germans put him in the concentration camp. Children of abuse often create alternate worlds that they slip into to survive. Sometimes, creating a better illusion or distraction will let us make it through horrible situations. Maybe you could apply this without going through the soul crushing experiences just discussed.

Ever do a multi-minute plank and think about being on a beach someplace?

Ever imagine defenestrating your boss instead of actually saying something you'd regret later as you cleared out your desk? Better to create the fantasy than the negative reality here.

What about imagining what it would feel like to land that deal, thus creating a fantasy of confidence that actually helps you in your job?

Every little kid that has played baseball has pictured themselves hitting the game winning home run in the World Series. Some of those little kids are in the big leagues now and have a shot at it. They use fantasy to create reality. Many authors use their writing as a way to deal with their demons or past. The semi-real nature of their creation allows them to use lies to tell the truth and process their experiences. Maybe that explains some of what you've read so far...

Reality isn't always cupcakes and butterflies and singing birds. Sometimes we need to create our own rainbows to make it through the storms.

Action item: what is the toughest thing you face regularly? Create a fantasy around how to overcome or escape it. Work on making that fantasy your reality.

03 DECEMBER

"A poor man with nothing in his belly needs hope, illusion, more than bread."

Georges Bernanos

One of the reasons that terrorist organizations are successful is because they offer a version of hope to their people. During the height of the Afghan War, an engineer could make a few hundred dollars a month in Afghanistan if they could find a job, but the Taliban could pay them several times that as a fighter. Many young fathers signed up because it was the only way to feed their family, the only hope that they had in a war-torn land. Many did not truly believe in the aims of the Taliban, in the same way that many Germans did not believe in what the Nazis promised in the 1930's or Chinese in the 1940's under Mao. They looked for whatever hope they could in that situation.

A loaf of bread will power a man for a few days, maybe a week. Hope can power them for years.

A human being is capable of tremendous suffering and resourcefulness, if they believe. The single mother of four kids that somehow works multiple jobs, feeds them, gets them to do homework and to school and keeps them on the straight and narrow when she is near the end of her rope all the time. This superwoman is powered not by the sun but by hope.

The startup entrepreneur working hundred hour weeks and sleeping on the nasty office couch to take their dream from their sleep into reality, totally underfunded and over their head but filled with the fortitude of hope. This story has played out hundreds if not thousands of times.

The POW who withstands torture and degradation is sustained by hope even as their body is tormented and broken.

The guy who struggles in the minor leagues to make it to the Big Show.

The band that fills their van and tours relentlessly and couch surfs while building a following for years.

All of these people stay on their path not because of anything in their belly other than fire. Because of belief and a desire that lets them work longer and harder than normal people, and keep at it long after those without their optimism and expectation of eventual success have given up and pursued something easier but less momentous.

Action item: what sustains you more than food? What makes you rise early and work late?

04 DECEMBER
"If we choose, we can live in a world of comforting illusion."

Noam Chomsky

It is so easy today to be willfully ignorant of the world around us. Instead of seeking differing ideas and opinions that force us to open our mind, we can easily enter an echo chamber where our own thoughts are amplified and reflected back at us, reinforcing our belief systems and assumptions until every other idea is drowned out. It is the tale of Narcissus brought into the cyber realm, because we become enamored with ourselves and ultimately perish.

We can use Snapchat and filter everything we show to others.

We can create a profile on a dozen different dating sites, each different and casting a false image, a mirage to other thirsty people who are projecting their own phantasms for us to appreciate. Lies interacting with lies as the Scottish psychologist Laird would say. How true will these relationships be?

We can use the internet to find others that reinforce our beliefs instead of challenging them, tribes building walls to keep differing ideas out instead of welcoming them in to help strengthen us.

We can live on credit and promises, believing politicians will make the world a better place instead of rolling up our sleeves and doing the hard work in our neighborhoods to actually create change and instill hope. We look externally instead of internally, and ignore the facts that don't jibe with our illusion. It's so easy.

We can hit the snooze button, rationalize away bad behavior or poor choices that make us feel good in the moment but damage our futures. That cigarette or donut or drink won't harm us... Things will be better when So and So gets elected...

It's not my fault the boss chose otherwise...

Maybe they'll outgrow it...

Just one more episode and then I'll go to sleep...

Our greatest seducer is ourselves. Stop deceiving yourself.

Action item: look in the mirror. Look yourself right in the eye and tell yourself a truth you don't want to hear.

05 DECEMBER

"Great achievement is usually born of great sacrifice, and is never the result of selfishness."

Napoleon Hill

Make of yourself a sacrifice to yourself, and you shall be remembered for eternity in song.

When I was a competitive martial artist I worked about sixty hours a week building my business, plus studied an additional dozen to fifteen hours a week for my professional designations. I would train Tae Kwon Do every morning from 5:00 to roughly 6:15 on my own, seven days a week. Two nights a week plus Saturday morning I would go teach on campus, getting there forty-five minutes before anyone else to train.

After an hour or so long class I would train for another fifteen minutes. Twice a week I drove forty-five minutes each way to see Master Grant and did an hour of teaching and then an hour of wicked hard training before discussing philosophy for an hour and driving home, to be up by 5:00 and repeat the cycle.

I had no social life, but what I was trying to achieve was worth more than hanging out in a loud crowd at a bar where you'd have to scream to be heard. I made a sacrifice to my future self, and it was worth it.

My Fraternity (Pi Kappa Phi) raised thousands of dollars a year locally and contributed thousands of hours to community service every single year. Getting college students out of bed at the crack of dawn to go raise money for people that they will never meet, to help people that will never help them, is a sacrifice that great men and women have made over and over again across the Fraternity and Sorority system for decades. Not out of selfish motivation or to check a box on a resume, but because it is the right thing for our communities.

Getting a college degree is not easy. It requires sacrificing time and money, sitting there studying when you'd rather be socializing or partying. It is a case study in delayed gratification. But the achievement is worth the offering of time and effort.

Few startups succeed without the founders dealing with the opportunity cost of going and accepting a "real job", then dedicating a hundred hours a week and burning the midnight oil, sacrificing youth, friendships, and often health to build something worthwhile that could be great.

The band that practices late at night because everyone is working and then has to take unpaid time to go play gigs in crappy little bars and sleep in the van and sell their crap to be able to record a demo.

The writer, writing and deleting and re-writing and banging their head in frustration for weeks and months and years to craft a masterpiece.

The parent with the special needs kid who gives up everything for them, to eventually see them graduate.

The young Marine who sacrifices themselves to save civilians.

That dyslexic kid, determined to be able to read.

The coach who buys equipment so her players can compete.

These are the sacrifices needed for greatness, either in ourselves or someone we love.

Action item: the difference between Good and Great is the price you pay with time and effort, with blood and sweat and tears. Give the extra today to be great.

06 DECEMBER

"Great achievement is usually born of great sacrifice, and is never the result of selfishness."

Sadhu Vaswani

No matter what.

The mother who throws herself in front of a car to protect her child.

The five year old boy who fights the dog to protect his kid sister, becoming horribly scarred but saving her life.

The soldier that rushes into fire to save others, ready to lay down his life for his brothers.

Love is an action word as Mr. Rogers said, and we see how powerful it is over and over when someone does something dangerous for others.

The firefighters on 9/11: they ran up when others ran down.

My Fraternity Brother Anthony gave a kidney to a complete stranger. He inspired all of us with this action, and when another Brother needed a kidney we all lined up to see who would be a match and donate (JP was the winner). These were the selfless actions of love.

We often think of these large, often visible sacrifices as the real sign of love, and these are the actions that show the best of us. And they occur more often than the media would let you know. But it is often the small actions that get overlooked that compound to show love.

The hockey mom getting up at four am to get the kid to the rink for practice. The attorney working pro bono to help people become citizens, or to give legal aid to the poor. The parent who feeds their child through the tube.

The person who sticks with their addict friend and takes the abuse and helps them into rehab and goes to meetings and if they get the text "I need you" is there, even at two am.

True love is giving of itself without conscious thought, a reaction that is so much deeper. It is putting the other before the self because that other means as much to you as your own happiness or well being. True love, in acts grand or miniscule, is how we keep the darkness at bay with tiny candles and grand flames that show the fire inside and the light of our love.

Action item: do something little but selfless for three people today to show love.

07 DECEMBER
"Sometimes you have to be selfish to be selfless."

Edward Albert

"You are no good to anyone else if you are broken." My friend Athena reminded me of this when I was up to my eyeballs working on this book and had multiple other high stress situations simultaneously and couldn't (or wouldn't) take time for myself. I was literally breaking and a friend will tell you "Stop!" when you are doing that, even if we refuse to listen.

A great friend will force you to stop, maybe by showing up with a bottle of wine or cupcakes, maybe by calling your assistant and booking an appointment with you where you are forced to not work, maybe by just holding a mirror up and saying "I am worried you are not taking care of you."

Special needs parents, single parents, the hyper driven. Those taking care of an aging parent or a family member battling cancer. Startup company. Student in a high-pressure environment. Returned Vet. These are all the superhumans carrying the weight of the world that like Atlas sometimes need a break before they break.

Sometimes our body says "enough" and forces a shutdown to prevent a full-on breakdown. Hopefully it is just a weekend where you don't have the alarm on and grab an extra hour or two of sleep so you can heal physically and mentally. Other times it might be our entire body locking up, or our mind just completely shutting down because it needs to rest and recharge. If you see the signs of stress overwhelming you, you MUST heed them and take a break to deal with the issues or at least gather your strength.

There is a physical training issue called rhabdomyolysis (rhabdo) where the body has been overused to the extent that it breaks down. It happens when you overtrain so much that your muscle cells burst and leak into your bloodstream, potentially causing kidney damage and a host of other issues. Rhabdo is basically two steps beyond overtraining and often comes from pushing the body to the limit repeatedly to the point of almost (or actual) failure without sufficient rest and recovery. Are you chancing rhabdo of your soul? Your mind and emotions?

Rest. Recover. Sometimes, the best thing you can do for others is to say "no", and take care of yourself for a little bit.

Pause.

Action item: get your calendar. Schedule some "you time" in the next week. Something that the only focus is your physical/mental/emotional rest and recovery.

08 DECEMBER

"Create the kind of self that you will be happy to live with all your life."

Golda Meir

For it isn't your Father, or Mother, or Wife,
Whose judgement you must pass.
The feller whose verdict counts most in your life
Is the guy staring back from the glass.
- Dale Wimbrow

At the end of the day, you must look yourself in the eye. When the tie is off, the makeup removed, all the external surface trappings gone and you look into the mirror and stare at your own soul, do you like what you see?

Most people don't like themselves. They say they do, but how many can stare into The Accountability Mirror (as David Goggins calls it) and look right into their own soul? To unflinchingly assess themselves, their choices, their actions, and their shortcomings? Too few, because it is uncomfortable dealing with the guy/gal in the glass.

None of the lies that you tell your spouse.
None of the half truths you tell the kids.
None of the misdirections you use with the boss.
None of the covering of holes you use with your acquaintances.
You, naked in front of yourself. Looking into yourself and all the bad bits that we hide from everyone else. Not physically, but inside where no one else can see.

Alone with you.

Most people can't do it because facing our Shadow, embracing our demons, accepting our faults and fears is the most difficult yet powerful thing we can do as a human and yet to become what we are capable of is necessary pain.

And yet if you are willing to do this, to hold yourself accountable to the person in the mirror, you could become the person you could be and should be more like. Our better self. The angel within that we all have but ignore because it is easier or more enjoyable to follow the devil on our shoulder. The angel that reminds us that the harder path has more and better rewards, even if it is lonelier and rougher. The angel that shines its light into our soul and helps us face that internal darkness we all struggle with, that you might be seeing in the eyes of the mirror.

Action item: go look in the mirror. Talk to the guy/gal in the glass. Set a timer on your phone and spend five minutes looking at you.

09 DECEMBER

> ## "Loneliness is the poverty of self;
> ## solitude is the richness of self."
>
> May Sarton

Do you know anyone that is so afraid of being alone that they will do anything to avoid it? Spending hours a day on social media, playing online games, working extra hours to avoid silence with self, putting up multiple dating profiles so they can talk to dozens of people daily so that they don't have to have a serious talk with themselves? This person is so afraid of being alone because they don't like to be with just themselves since it is bad company for whatever reason, so they do whatever they can to not sit down 1:1 with the person in the mirror. Contrast this with the individual that has no need of others to complete themselves. You can call them a Sigma personality, or as I personally identify with: Ronin. Masterless samurai who look within and find essentially all they need, who do not need the external validation of the world to continue their training for life and pursue their purpose.

Sun Tzu said "he who knows his enemy and himself will ever be victorious." Instead of looking at this from the point of view of battle, look at it in terms of understanding your own psyche. If you know yourself, have reflected and studied yourself, you should be comfortable in your own skin and not need the flashy car or lip treatments or clothes or external prizes to be good with yourself. This self-explored and self-supporting person is ok being alone with themselves because they are good company.

For the individual that knows themselves and is good with that person, being on their own is not scary. It allows them time to contemplate and have internal discussions, to clarify their belief systems and motivations. Instead of being a punishment, "time out" to this person is a chance to get to work on their magnum opus: themselves. They are rich inside. Contrast this with the person with the poverty of self, the voids inside that they refuse to face and fill. Being alone means no one else is there to distract them from the holes inside, and they can easily fall into these gaps. There is no external direction and no internal compass and so they get lost in their journey and wander in the darkness and this terrifies them so they will do anything to avoid it. If forced to be alone they can break easily, and so solitude is torture because they torment themselves.

Eventually, the external glitz and glitter, the shiny distractions will either never be enough or will disappear. Someday the lonely person will have to turn inside to start coming to grips with themselves if they don't want to have an incomplete and ultimately empty (but maybe externally pretty) life. The sooner that they can start sitting with themselves, even on a limited basis, the sooner they can become ok with the individual in the mirror.

Action item: sit with yourself for fifteen minutes. No phone, no music, no other people or distractions. Ask yourself "what am I doing?" and really face your internal truths.

10 DECEMBER

"There are people who have money and people who are rich."

Coco Chanel

I have a client who is worth tens of millions of dollars. He is diabetic, his kids hate him, he is grumpy all the time, and he for the most part is miserable to be around because for all his money he is poor for the rest of his life. I know a lot of people with barely a pot to piss in who are joyful, have great relationships and health, and are moving in the right direction with their lives. Although they will probably never be wealthy, their current financial status does not bother them because they are working towards success and have their family and a future.

Who is rich? My first few years out of grad school I had the richest life. I worked my keister off and had enough to pay my bills, even though I didn't have a ton extra. I still had my crappy grad school apartment with the T Rex roaring phone and no tv (because I was never there except to sleep). I was doing meaningful work and consistently growing. I was training Tae Kwon Do daily so physically was good, and I had an amazing network of friends that I interacted with. I started to get involved more deeply in community service, and I saw my parents every couple of weeks but talked to them regularly. I was rich!

Material wealth is a good thing in that it allows you to have stability and security and to do things. Maslow's Hierarchy of needs reminds us that without shelter and food and safety we can't really take care of higher, more complex needs but the difference between a four hundred square foot apartment and an eighteen hundred square foot house and a five thousand square foot McMansion isn't that great when it comes to the function it serves. Once the physical needs are met, the emotional ones come into play and this is where we separate the haves from the have nots, the people that are emotionally bankrupt from those that are rich.

The times that I have felt the most broke were not when I had the least money. Usually the opposite: financially doing well but missing more important things in my life. Not seeing my kids during my divorce drained my emotions more than my bank account. Money is easy to acquire if you have figured out the rules to the game and are ready to work hard and smart. But physical separation from your kids, having a devastating injury or illness, or losing a loved one too soon, or not having a direction/purpose so no focus while aimlessly wandering and squandering friendships, those are losses much worse than a stock market crash or bankruptcy.

Choose to be wealthy. Choose to invest in relationships and community even more than the financial markets. Opt for the deferred gratification that comes from doing the difficult but meaningful things that build lasting wealth instead of temporary financial security.

Action item: invest in your relationships today. Spend time on people that matter instead of material things.

11 DECEMBER

"The greatest good you can do for another is not just to share your riches, but to reveal to him his own."

Benjamin Disraeli

Give a man a fish and he will eat for a day. Teach a man to fish and he will never go hungry.

Ever know the salesperson that is cold calling lists and sometimes getting leads handed to them by their supervisor, literally throwing the dog a bone? If that supervisor taught the salesperson how to find their own leads (whether through research, or asking for introductions from current clients, or doing seminars, building a YouTube channel, whatever methods are appropriate) that salesperson could produce more than ten times what they currently are and probably make a ton of money for the supervisor. Maybe the supervisor doesn't do it because they don't know how, or is afraid of the salesperson outselling them and getting promoted, or leaving for a better organization. Whatever, but if the supervisor really cared about success and growth and the greatest good, they would develop their people to be able to sustainably produce instead of being dependent.

Telling someone they have a beautiful soul is one thing. Helping them to see them the way that you do (with more than eyes) so that they can see how wonderful you think they are and understand their beauty is a whole other level. Once they comprehend their inner beauty they won't need the external validation of others and will actually become even more beautiful.

Teaching someone the concepts around why something is done, is better than just how it is to be done. Because they will buy into the safety ideas behind the checklists, or they will understand the rationale for doing a process and might be able to innovate it so that there is a time or material savings for the organization. This understanding is worth a lot more than the time it takes to show the other person.

Comprehension is better than memorization.

Understanding is better than regurgitating.

Helping someone mine themselves and uncover their inner riches is better than handing someone a bag of gold or money, because the money will run out but the inner talents will allow them to make money over and over again, even if the world around them changes as it inevitably does.

Action item: help someone else understand their potential and capacity today. Help them learn to find and use their internal riches.

12 DECEMBER

**"Share your smile with the world.
It's a symbol of friendship and peace."**

Christie Brinkley

There is literally nothing more beautiful than the smile of someone you love. It lets their soul shine out for all the world to see.

When you see your friend smile, the years fade away and distances disappear.

When you smile, your relatives see your parents and grandparents in you, brought forth again in happiness.

A smile is the universal language. Tribes that have barely had contact with the world share it as much as someone in Beijing or nowhere Minnesota. A smile is part of the human condition and vestige of our oldest communications before we learned to speak.

"Peace begins with a smile." Mother Teresa

"A simple smile. That's the start of opening your heart and being compassionate to others." Dalai Lama

Look at a baby smile, and try not to do so yourself. Even knowing it might be just gas, those chubby little cheeks and cherubic grin are contagious. Share the smile.

Because of mirror neurons in the brain, when we see someone smile we automatically react and smile ourselves.

When we smile, the amount of stress hormones in our body decrease. We literally feel more at peace when we return a smile that someone has given us.

When we smile, our body produces happiness hormones too. These have been tied to increased relationship bonds i. e. friendship. Smiling at someone that smiles at you increases friendship and connectivity, keys to happiness and health.

Smile, and the world smiles with you.

Action item: pay attention to when other people smile today, and return the favor and the smile. Spread joy faster than any virus by sharing your smile.

13 DECEMBER

"Do not lose your inner peace for anything whatsoever, even if your whole world seems upset."

St. François de Sales

"Any person capable of angering you becomes your master." Epictetus

"Calm is a super power." Bruce Lee

When the world rages around you, remain calm.

When the emotions sweep over you, find your center and placate your soul.

When chaos reigns without, calm within.

The world is insane, people are crazy, there is nothing outside that you can control, no matter how much financial, business, or military power one wields.

All we can control is how we react to it.

Be like the grey rock, unperturbed by the rains or winds.

Instead of the surface of the sea whipped to a frenzy by the storm, be the depths of the ocean, unmoved and unchanged by what goes on in the shallows.

Panic runs like a fire through the grassland.

Calm is contagious.

Deep. Breath.

Deep. Breath.

Deep.

Breath.

Action item: close your eyes and take a breath. Again. As many times as it takes for the passion to ease in you.

14 DECEMBER

**"Then stirs the feeling infinite, so felt
In solitude, where we are least alone."**

Lord Byron

Contemplative psychotherapy is a mix of Eastern and Western concepts, Buddhism and Brain balanced. A key component of it is to expose ourselves to the grandest works of nature and sit in awe thereof. To allow our smallness but simultaneously our unique place in all of the greatness of the universe to fill us. To embrace how we are tiny sparks in creation that soon fade but in that little burst we are also part of and influence everything that there is.

Have you ever stood at the edge of the Grand Canyon and gazed out in quiet wonder?

Stood on the deck of a ship in the middle of the ocean, the horizon at the edge of your view? Closed your eyes and felt the gentle swell of the unending sea rock you while the breeze teases your hair with promises, ancient and future?

Gazed up into the cosmos, in the dark and silent night, seeing billions of years ago in the flickering stars that may not even exist now? Calming yourself and letting your eyes adjust to see the Milky Way that we live in spread across the sky and seep into your soul, connecting with what was and is and shall be?

Some fear being alone because they can't stand being with themselves. Some realize how tiny we are in the cosmos and shrink further from that. Yet if you sit in the small stillness long enough, you can remember the connections with the infinite that surrounds us. This is where the unseen hand touches our soul and we remember the limitlessness that gave us birth and we will return to it at some point.

Action item: go where you can expose yourself to nature unspoilt, and see the greatness of the world. Look into the night sky until you can feel the unending universe tug at your soul.

15 DECEMBER

"The best and most beautiful things in the world cannot be seen or even touched – they must be felt with the heart."

Helen Keller

A blind woman could see clearer than most of us. Not distracted by illusion and surface, Keller saw the truth.

I loved a woman of great physical beauty, and one thing she never comprehended was that I told her half her beauty was inside and that I could see it because I looked with more than my eyes. I don't think she will ever understand, but hopefully you do.

The unconditional love of a child. When they fall asleep in the car and you carry them in to put the little one into their bed, and as you are walking in they unconsciously put their arms around your neck in a hug. This is one of the most beautiful things a parent can experience, and makes up for an entire day of them being a little terrorist.

A cup of coffee left at your desk with a note that says "thank you." The coffee is wonderful and always appreciated, but it is the sentiment behind it that is moving and memorable.

That feeling when they first take your hand and look into your eyes.

Winning the big one. Not for the trophy or any prize money, but just the exhilaration of victory.

That last hug from your best friend that you will never see again.

We all have a lot of physical stuff; medals and plaques and awards, material objects of beauty and worth. But think about them. Would you trade them for an hour with your lost love? To sit in your grandparent's kitchen baking again? To talk to your favorite aunt or uncle and just enjoy being with them? To feel free and alive like you did with that one person that is gone?

Stuff happens. And stuff fills our life. But stuff is just that: objects and things that take up space but don't fill our heart and soul. That comes from experiences, from time with the people we treasure. Those moments are more beautiful and precious than all the gems on earth.

Action item: what is the most beautiful memory you have? Close your eyes and relive that precious moment.

16 DECEMBER

"I haven't understood a bar of music in my life, but I have felt it."

Igor Stravinsky

Some things can't be explained, can't be understood and merely need to be experienced and felt.

How do you describe a sunset that can capture the colors and textures, the rose light shimmering all around as the trees stand out in stark relief? Even the greatest physicist would fail to explain this, but merely enjoy and experience it with the wonder of a child.

How do you take the feeling of love lost, the shattered soul where every breath is pain, and put parameters around it for another person to comprehend the breadth and depth of loss and longing with the slightest sliver of hope that is beyond foolish? There is no way for someone else to understand the years and individual moments of this, unless they have been through their own version thereof.

A Veteran does not understand war, even if he wears four stars and was involved in many of the decisions of it. But he can still feel it decades later.

I can explain the biomechanics behind throwing a reverse punch, rotating the hip and driving the center of mass forward as you push with the back leg into the front stance and convert potential energy into kinetic energy to break the board. But not until you have done so can you comprehend.

A picture is worth a thousand words. Not even a thousand pictures can capture a feeling.

Action item: instead of trying to explain something to another person, show them. Have them feel what you do.

17 DECEMBER

**"Chains of habit are too light to be felt
until they are too heavy to be broken."**

Warren Buffet

It's just once.

Then a second time.

A third.

And then you can't stop.

So don't start doing something that you know you shouldn't be doing, and it can never become an unbreakable habit.

Smoking.

Lying.

Cheating.

Don't start and then you don't have to worry about trying to stop.

Don't cross the line and you will never have to worry about trying to get back across the border.

With that being said, I'm not foolish or arrogant enough to think we don't slip up. I have made more than my share of mistakes and I will probably continue to do so. The question is how do you recognize that something is starting to become a habit that is not good for you and put a stop to it while you still can, before the chain is too heavy to break?

Ignoring obvious danger signs (drug use, law breaking, gambling with anything more than you can afford to lose and not blink an eye over, having a dating app (or multiple) while insisting you are married, etc), it can be very difficult for us to recognize that we are drifting into the danger zone of building a bad habit. I'm just hitting the snooze button. I'm just having drinks with the guys in the middle of the week. I just kissed my tennis partner...

If you say "just", you are starting to rationalize a behavior and that is a red flag for you.

If you ever say "what am I doing?" that is a definite sign you are at or over a line.

But unless you have that sudden insight, you probably won't notice that you are going down the slippery slope until it's too late. Unless someone else sees and grabs you before you fall off the cliff. Ask someone who knows you well and likes you well enough to tell you hard truths to give you feedback.

Not your too nice friend as they will sugar coat stuff. Look to your friend that's a bit of a jerk and too honest, because quite frankly if you are asking these questions you need tough love. Questions they should ask you:

Do you do this when you are stressed? As a coping mechanism/avoidance technique?

Would you be cool with explaining exactly what you are doing to your mom or grandfather?

Are you spending more time/money in this activity than you were three months ago? How far will you go?

If you of last year was sitting here with me looking at what you are doing today, what would they say?

If you keep on this track, where will you be in six months? What could you see yourself doing at that point?

Can you go one day without it? Three days?

Is this now, or could this soon, hurt you or those you care about (physically, monetarily, or emotionally)?

Are other people that know you well noticing changes in your actions or appearance?

As you read those questions, maybe your gut clenched in self-realization. If that happens, you have an issue that is becoming a bad habit. Realization and acceptance are the first steps. Get help and stop before the chain is too heavy to break.

Action item: call that jerk friend and have them really talk to you to help hold up the mirror so you can see if you are developing a bad habit. If you are, ask them to help you break the chain and stop what you are doing.

18 DECEMBER
"Quality is not an act, it is a habit."

Aristotle

Hopefully, roughly 350 days through this book, you have come to an understanding that individual actions add up and that instead of being surface decoration, they eventually sink into your very Being and become part of who you are to your core. Excellence is not a mask but who you are under it all.

Quality is the essence, not the surface.

Habits make us or break us.

We are all slaves to habit, the question is are we mastered by good habits or poor ones, routines that improve us like exercise and reading and continuous mental/emotional growth, or are we following routines that will lead to bad outcomes like smoking or being mentally/physically lazy? The continuous daily choices will determine our outcomes in either a virtuous or vicious cycle, and it is all in your head.

"Well-being is realized by small steps, but is truly no small thing." Zeno of Citium

How long a habit takes to be fully adopted depends upon not just how much of a change it is, but how we set it up. If like me you roll out of bed, grab the cup of coffee that is ready to go and immediately read, it won't take long to get into this (or other habits you add to them using James Clear's Habit Stacking from his book Atomic Habits), and then add other good actions like a five minute walk or few minutes of meditation. Habits that aren't piggy backed on existing routines are more difficult to adopt simply because you don't have the structure in place to reinforce the positive choices to the point that they become automatic, which is the goal.

Set yourself up for success instead of failure. Eliminate the negative stimuli that inevitably lead to bad decisions. This is why alcoholics remove all alcohol from their residence: it's a lot more difficult to slip if there is nothing to slip on. Making it so that a poor choice requires a difficult action makes that choice harder. This is why people with addictions need to cut certain people out of their lives because those people inevitably lead to bad choices. This is why companies automatically enroll people in their retirement plans, setting the default towards success instead of failure to make the good habit (saving for retirement) easy and the bad one (grabbing a bag of chips) tough. Use your environment to reinforce the actions towards your goals.

Action item: insist on excellence for yourself. Look around you. What is one change in your environment that will lead to easier, better decisions? Make it happen.

19 DECEMBER
"Excellence is not an exception, it is a prevailing attitude."

Gen. Colin Powell

Attitude is everything.

My children have been taught that I don't care about the outcomes with their grades or their sports or music because that is not within their power. I care about two things that they can completely control though: attitude and effort. These are the internal drivers of success and 100% under their influence.

Attitude is what determines if you have resilience to deal with the adversity that you will encounter, and the greater your mission the greater the adversity you will face. If you look at the challenges as opportunities for improvement and growth instead of barriers, you will look for ways to overcome them and become better instead of being stopped in your tracks as others might be. Ryan Holiday named one of his books The Obstacle is the Way for this reason.

Failure is the result of attitude as much as success is.

Excellence is an external reflection of internal standards. Those standards are an extension of your attitudes.

Successful organizations have a culture of excellence. It is an attitude of showing up, doing your job to the best of your ability, and assisting your teammates when they need it. A good attitude is part of the DNA of the group and is what separates a flash in the pan lucky group from the continuously performing one because the successful one has an attitude of improvement so their excellence is internally motivated and sustainable. Alabama Football focuses on moment by moment excellence, knowing that championships and victories are built off of winning the individual plays, of each man doing what they need to do moment by moment. That is a victorious attitude.

Attitude means showing up ready to work, even if you aren't feeling it. Attitude is practicing harder than others play, so that when the time comes you can exhibit your excellence. Attitude is willingness to try new things, to be told you can be better, to be held accountable and to hold those around you to those standards of greatness. Attitude is smiling through the pain of improving, knowing it is worth it to become better and ultimately the best.

Attitude is everything, and gives rise to excellence.

Action item: check your attitude. Is it at the right level to make you excellent? Fix it.

20 DECEMBER
"Excellence is not a skill, it's an attitude."

Ralph Marston

When Bill and Ted declared "Be excellent to one another!" they were not talking about any ceremonies or ritualistic ways of greeting (although air guitar is not a bad way to say hi), but rather the mindset and overall interaction of how humans should treat each other.

Are you excellent toward your work, giving it your full attention and pouring yourself into even the crappiest tasks so that in the end it is excellent, even if you hated doing whatever it was? That is the sign of a true professional: an attitude of excellence.

Are you excellent to your relationships? When even if you want to scream at someone because of their poor choices (a reflection of not being excellent to themselves), you will go out of your way to help them whether it is jumping their car or picking them up from jail or sitting there as they cry something out? This reflects a caring and loving attitude, even if you fumble for the right words to say beyond "I'm here for you."

Are you excellent to yourself? You don't need to measure your foods down to the gram or master the mandolin nor develop the skill of perfect bow tie tying, but do you look in the mirror and know the person looking back is trying hard and making progress even if there is a long way to go? Are you hard enough on yourself to unlock your potential, but easy enough to know that you aren't where you want to be yet? That is a positive self attitude that leads to improvement instead of false perfectionism.

Saying "I don't know, let's figure it out" reflects an attitude that will lead to more knowledge and skills. Everyone starts not knowing things, and the Master has failed more times than the beginner has even tried. But the Master has skill because they have the attitude of an open-minded beginner even as their capabilities grow.

Teaching your kids that they can have the attitude of excellence without being all the way there yet leads to conscientiousness, one of the best indicators of success. Almost all of my friends that are in position to hire someone will take attitude over skill because skills can be taught or honed, but an attitude adjustment is more difficult.

Be excellent to people today. Especially yourself.

Action item: insist on excellence for yourself. Look around you. What is one change in your environment that will lead to easier, better decisions? Make it happen.

21 DECEMBER

"To err is human; to forgive, divine."

Alexander Pope

We all mess up. Admit it. You make errors. I make mistakes all the time. I try to learn from them and not make the same type of mistake again, but the only person that never makes mistakes is the person that isn't doing anything and will accomplish nothing. That's not me, and probably not you. Just saying.

"Let he who is without sin cast the first stone." John 8:7

So now that we are in agreement that we aren't perfect, that we just do dumb things or succumb to the devil side of our nature at times, we need to look to our lighter and better aspects. We would expect to be forgiven if (when) we erred. So we therefore must forgive others, even if their actions (or inaction) has harmed us.

The person that messed up at work and caused you to have to work the weekend. Forgive them.

The teenager making chips that caught the stove on fire. Hug them after. I did.

The teammate that cost you the game. Console them.

The lover that cheated. More difficult, but love them and forgive them.

The drunk who hurt your child. They need forgiveness, and your child would do so. Can you do any less?

Forgiveness is not easy. In fact, personally pardoning someone that took something valuable from you that you will never get back is the greatest act of love and the highest minded, noblest thing a human can do.

Nelson Mandela forgave those who imprisoned him for decades.

Forgiving others takes strength, and the greater the wrong done to you the greater the strength of character it takes to forgive someone. Be strong. Be an example.

Don't just turn the other cheek, but embrace the other person. Forgive.

Action item: who are you angry with, holding a grudge against. Let it go. Forgive them, and heal yourself.

22 DECEMBER

"To forgive is to set a prisoner free and discover that the prisoner was you."

Lewis B. Smedes

"He who is devoid of the power to forgive is devoid of the power to love." Dr. Martin Luther King Jr.

"The weak can never forgive. Forgiveness is an attribute of the strong." Mahatma Gandhi

It takes a big person to forgive another, especially when they have harmed you. The greater the damage, the stronger we must be to forgive them.

This does not mean that you forget, nor leave yourself vulnerable to the same type of harm, especially if it was inflected for ill intent (like a business partner stealing a quarter million dollars from your company after defrauding you because they were a con man and should have been in jail for decades but cut a deal to save their own skin). We must learn from our previous mistakes and being a little wary in the future is not a bad thing (especially if you see similar patterns and flags in the future so you can run away), but don't become jaded because that is remaining a prisoner of the previous harm.

We all make mistakes, whether of omission or commission.

Sometimes we don't know any better, and sometimes we are just weak or lazy. We must forgive ourselves, even when it is difficult because we will carry that pain around inside our hearts and it will seep out and infect our other actions, making us less than we should be and harming others. Even if the loathing we carry is for another and what they have done, the poison is still there and turns our hearts. Forgive them and you will heal, helping others around you.

"Forgive others not because they deserve forgiveness, but because you deserve peace." Jonathan Huie

"Forgiveness is a gift that you give to yourself." Tony Robbins

You deserve that gift. You deserve to be set free. You deserve to let your spirit fly again, unchained by the weight of hate.

Action item: forgive someone today so that you can forgive yourself.

23 DECEMBER
"You cannot shake hands with a clenched fist."

Indira Gandhi

Open your hand and you can begin to open your heart.

You can not try to make peace while preparing to strike the other party. It is hypocritical and two faced. It puts you at war with yourself as well as the other person.

Anger will continue to breed in your heart, and overtures of peace or friendship will be as false as a mask and as apparent.

Open your hand. Let go of the hate you hold.

Don't hug while holding a knife.

"Those with open hearts always have open hands." Rumi

"There is more power in the open hand than in the clenched fist." Herbert Newton Casson

If there can be no trust there can be no peace. If there is no peace, it is an eye for an eye until everyone is blind. Let there be trust so there can be peace, whether in a relationship or between companies and countries.

"This aggression will not stand, man." The Dude in *The Big Lebowski*

"Hug it out." Almost every mother, ever.

As Elsa sings: let it go. Let go of the anger and the hate that is clenching your fist and jaw.

Action item: take out a piece of paper and write the name of the person at whom you are angry. Now write every reason you are angry with them, every little and big thing. Start crossing them off one by one as you say "I forgive you for…."

24 DECEMBER
"When the power of love overcomes the love of power the world will know peace."
Jimi Hendrix

I am definitely not some crunchy granola hippie. I am clearly a capitalist and like to be compensated when I create value, which I strive to do in all things. But that doesn't make me greedy, and certainly not power hungry.

I have been offered the chance to helm multimillion dollar firms, and I probably would have had a blast doing it. I turned them all down because they actually had excessive concentrations of power in the hands of the #1, and having been on the receiving end of what that can be like I declined. Even if I thought I would use that power for good, to be a benevolent dictator, it is still against my moral principles.

When offered The One Ring, Gandalf cried as his eyes flashed "Do not tempt me! For I do not wish to become like The Dark Lord himself. Yet the way of the Ring to my heart is pity, pity for weakness and the desire of strength to do good. Do not tempt me! I dare not..."

Many in this world seek power, believing that it will allow them to meet their aims. Some desire power and wealth. Others start with noble goals of protecting the weak, and end up with blood on their hands. Look at the repeated revolutions in South America, and Asia, and Africa where a belief in doing good combined with excessive power and no restraints lead to new forms of imbalances and terror. Better to disperse the power broadly (as in a constitutional republic) so that there is less chance for hate to have unchecked strength and be able to do great harm. Instead of being the face of the Revolution and the Leader, better to get broad results and be relatively unknown but unspoiled.

Power in itself is not evil. Marcus Aurelius wielded the full might of the Empire in Rome. And even the prototypical philosopher king fell short.

Even in something as mundane as a small Cub Scout pack, power can corrupt. I might be the Packmaster (because someone has to be willing to get in trouble with the powers that be or talk in front of groups), but my leadership team makes all decisions with me and we implement them together. I get to see the kids smile, and the parents bring awesome ideas to the group, and things get done well, and there is laughter and accomplishment and the Scouts love coming to meetings, seeing their friends, and learning. This is worth so much more than an ego boost or a chance to lord power over others.

In the book *Why Nations Fail*, economists Daron Acemoglu and James A Robinson introduce the idea of "Inclusive" and "Extractive" organizations as one of the long-range primary determinants of economic growth to a society. Extractive ones exist to accumulate power and wealth into the hands of a few, and as such hamper total growth and destroy prosperity over time. Inclusive ones disperse the decision making and results/rewards across a broad swath that allows many (even a majority) to participate in both decisions and outcomes.

This is superior overall, creating much richer societies, a greater success for the lowest economic tiers, and sustainability because of less entrenchment. It allows people to pursue what they love to do (like become a scientist or write books) as opposed to what their parents and other forebears always did (work the land) or the government tells them they have to do. This ability to pursue their hearts and dreams, this choosing of an avocation, yields better outcomes for citizens and societies as a whole.

Love over power.

Give power to others to have greater growth and richer experiences.

Give more and get more.

Action item: do you obsess over and try to hoard power? How can you empower others, and this garner more rewards for everyone?

25 DECEMBER

"Still, as Christmas-tide comes round, they remember it again - Echo still the sound 'Peace on earth, good-will to men!"
Lewis Carroll

I don't care what Higher Power you worship, from Allah to Jehovah to Vishnu or The Flying Spaghetti Monster or the loving God of the New Testament, this is the time of year for all hostilities to cease and welcome all people as our brothers and sisters.

Garth Brooks in the song *Belleau Wood* tells the tale of The Christmas Truce during the trench warfare of WW1. During The War To End All Wars (a misnomer if ever there was one), the brutal fighting completely stopped on a Christmas Eve as the soldiers on both sides sung hymns such as Silent Night, and instead of shooting a soccer game broke out under the moon and stars in a brief interlude of sport and humanity along the front lines. If men literally trying to kill each other can suspend a war and trade cigarettes and handshakes on a battlefield, I think we can find it in our hearts to forgive the meaningless slights of others and mend relationships.

Peace on earth.

Good will to all.

This is the way of almost all the great religions on our planet, so why do we use differences in opinion on the powers behind it all as an excuse to hate and hurt? Is that what the Birthday Boy preached?

Bury the hatchet, and not in someone.

Make amends, extend the olive branch. Now is a time for forgiveness, whether it is your friend that took your crush or your kid brother that did something dumb a decade ago. Forgive and make peace with all those who have offended you or you have offended, and you will finish off the balance of this year much lighter in spirit.

"Let there be peace on earth, and let it begin with me" was always one of my father's favorite lines in a hymn at church (even though he sings even worse than I do), and it is something that has stuck with me since I was a little kid. I'm certainly not perfect but I try to forgive, try to make peace with others and within my own heart. It isn't easy, but just committing to the struggle makes me more aware and hopefully have better thoughts and actions that lead to more peace.

Pax vobiscum.

Action item: peace be with you. Go forth and share signs of peace.

26 DECEMBER

"We need joy as we need air."

Maya Angelou

Plants need air and sunlight to grow. Joy is the light for people and lets our spirits grow.

"There is no path to happiness. Happiness is the path." The Buddha

The world can be a nasty place. Humans do horrible things to each other, as evidenced by the atrocities of the concentration camps. Yet even there, the prisoners would pause and stare at a beautiful rainbow. Viktor Frankl describes the sheer joy in his heart at the sight, starving prisoners gaining sustenance and strength from the colors in the air. Joy amid the darkness kept them going. Look at a kid with a new box, and how they can play for hours, happier than a parent that won a million dollars in the lottery. And their joy is contagious, it is nearly impossible to hear a kid going from a submarine to SpaceMan Spiff to driving a tank to pretending to be a kitty cat without feeling the glee. A few minutes around them and we breathe easier (once we are done laughing at them).

A meal with close friends, filled with laughter. This is food for the soul.

A morning walk, as the sun paints the world gold and the birds warble and discuss overhead, no cars or people disturbing the commune with creation.

That warm soup after a cold wet day, the steam rising and the scent filling your nostrils.

A hug after being apart for far too long.

These are the moments of joy that build a life, that make us appreciate the world.

These are not expensive moments, but they are precious and are treasured in the later dark days.

These memories are a breath of fresh air, invigorating our spirits in tough times.

They make our soul smile, even more than our face.

Joy, the purest emotion a person can feel. Like pure sunlight for our heart.

Action item: what brings you joy, makes you smile from the inside out? Experience it and share it.

27 DECEMBER
"The present moment is filled with joy and happiness."

Thich Nhat Hanh

At this moment, you are alive.

In this moment, the past merely was. It can not impinge upon you, it can not harm you. In this moment, the future is but a potential, a dream of what could be and will unfold as is right.

Now.

Now exists.

Breathe. You can, and that is good.

Feel the fabric on your skin. Enjoy its touch. The blood courses through your veins, carrying your breath and life throughout your body.

Breathe.

Feel.

Breathe.

This is life. This is happiness, in the moment.

This.

Breathe.

Feel.

Joy.

Breathe.

Breathe.

Action item: at some point today, just stop. Stop, close your eyes, and breathe. Feel. Enjoy.

28 DECEMBER
"Today is a gift. That's why we call it the present."

Eleanor Roosevelt

Did you wake up this morning? Good, you have been gifted another day here on earth. Something denied to too many other people. Don't waste it.

Every day we have is a gift, an opportunity and an obligation. We get to open that present of another day and do something with it, a unique and unrepeatable chance to learn and grow and have an impact on the world.

"Today is a gift I honor by fully living it." Mary Anne Radmacher

How do you properly show someone appreciation for a gift? By using it. If Grandma gave you an ugly Christmas sweater you would wear it, at least once. Maybe to a whole bunch of Christmas parties because it is so ugly you want to show it off, and it was made with love. That is how you honor the donor.

If someone gave me a cookbook, I would make a few dishes from it and at least show them, but more likely share the food. That is how to honor this gift.

My parents gave me a great example of a loving and caring relationship until (and even after) my mom died. I honor that gift by trying to model that in my relationships, and sharing that love with others.

If you have been given an opportunity (such as a job), seize it and make the most of it. Pour yourself into that work and do the best job possible. This is how you honor the gift of the opportunity.

Someone has given you their heart? Don't break it. Protect it, nurture it. Help them be the best they can be and you become the best you can be for yourself and them. That is honoring the gift of the relationship.

Play with your kids, and enjoy their presence in your life because their youth and wonder is a fading gift, like a sunset.

Do not waste the time you have been given, that is the best way to honor the gift and your life itself. Live today, because there are millions that would have done almost anything for one more day.

Action item: open your present. Enjoy the gift of today, and share it!

29 DECEMBER

"I'm looking forward to the future, and feeling grateful for the past."

Mike Rowe

The past does not determine our future, but lays the groundwork for it like the foundation of a building. Most foundations required clearing the land, digging out roots and rocks and earth, and then either pouring concrete or building off of bare bedrock. None of it is easy work, but the foundation is critical for a structure to rise.

The hard work of laying that foundation, even if it was a very dirty job, is something that you should look back on and be thankful for the opportunity. It might have been one of the hardest things you ever had to do (maybe going to school while working, or overcoming trauma or injuries as part of your finding bedrock), but in addition to having something solid to build off of, you have what Malcom Gladwell called "desired difficulties", obstacles in your way that helped become the way by making you better and giving you experiences and skills that will allow you to build to impressive heights. Because you had to dig down deep.

And now that the foundation has been laid, and it is strong and supportive? Now you can rise to the sky, as high as you wish. And that is something to look forward to.

To lay a new layer of bricks every single day, with your best, most conscientious efforts to lay them straight and true. To have your plan and check it regularly to make sure you are building what you want (instead of what someone else says, or something easier but not as important). To know that what you are constructing will resist the winds and the rains and even the earthquakes that will come, because the base was built strong through adversity so the higher levels will not collapse when the weather or world changes.

You are both architect and construction crew on this job. You get to determine when to call for lunch break or quitting time. You get to supervise the quality of the materials and the workmanship. You determine if you are more concerned with form (looking pretty to bystanders) or function (meeting the purpose it was designed for). All of this is in your power.

Build something you will be proud of, a legacy that a hundred years from now people will still admire. Because it was solidly built from the bottom up.

Action item: dig down a little deeper today. Look at the adversities you have overcome to get to your present, and see how you can use them to build a better today and tomorrow.

30 DECEMBER

"The way we experience the world around us is a direct reflection of the world within us."

Gabrielle Bernstein

We project ourselves on the world and see it not as it is, but as we are. Someone who doesn't trust others because they lie will assume everyone else is a liar because that is their internal bias that they project on everyone else. Same too with the Polly Anna who sees nothing but good in everyone and as such becomes vulnerable to lies because they can't comprehend that there is bad in people.

Your Reticular Activation System (RAS) is how you have programmed your mind to interpret the signal in the noise of the world around us. Ever wonder how one person repeatedly finds business opportunities that no one else sees? It is because they have developed themselves to notice the tiny openings of potential that others miss because they are not subconsciously looking for these chances.

So how is your mind set up to see the world? What are your internal biases and tendencies that you then see everywhere?

Do you look for beauty in everything from the sunset to a flower to just the way a little kid laughs with joy while trying to ride a bike? This is not the world being beautiful, this is you being in a mental and awareness state to be predisposed to notice those things as opposed to the dead frog or the storm clouds and bees in the same situation that a negatively biased person would fixate on. Do you see a fight with the person you love as a weakening of your bonds, or an opportunity to work on your relationship and strengthen it? A chance to exercise resilience, or an excuse to fly away? The two people in the relationship can look at the same facts in totally different ways because they are different people inside. To understand the other we need to understand the world within them and try to share ours so there is understanding and hopefully healing and growth.

To a criminal defense attorney, everyone is guilty. To a social justice warrior, everyone is oppressed. To me, everyone has potential they haven't tapped. We project ourselves onto others, and see in them the aspects of ourselves and our mindsets that we want to see.

How are you looking at the world? Is it through rose tinted glasses? Dark goth shades? How you see it does not change the way it IS, but how you see it lets you find the parts that resonate with what is in you, a harmonizing of infinite strings that pick up on vibrations outside of us and reinforce them in our mind to hear the tones and music we want to listen to.

Action item: what are your tendencies of looking at the world? How does that shade your perception? For today, explore this filter you observe the world through and try to shift your perspective a little.

31 DECEMBER
"Without reflection, we go blindly on our way."

Margaret J. Wheatley

Well, you completed another revolution around the sun. I guarantee that some things went right this past year better than you could have hoped, some things went wayyy worse than you could have conceived, and stuff came out of the blue that you never thought of. That my friend is called life. Before you get into the celebratory mode, it is always good to look back and assess what came before so that the lessons are not lost. I always take about an hour on my own to look at what went on with my businesses, my writing, my physical health, and my relationships. I look through my camera roll, I see what I've saved in various social media. I look at who I've lost, and who is new to me and becoming important. I basically do an inventory of my life, because no matter what crap happens, it is pretty darn good to be me.

Hopefully you can say the same thing after spending a year or so reading this book and developing yourself into a more excellent version of you. And just like one year rolls into the next as we turn the calendar from December to January, you can go back to the beginning and go through this book again to build an even better you based off of your previous growth.

Things that went well:
1.
2.
3.

Things that went poorly
1.
2.
3.

Unexpected things:
1.
2.
3.

Lessons Learned:
1.
2.
3.

Ideas for Next Year:
1.
2.
3.

AFTERWORD

All my life's a circle;
But I can't tell you why;
Season's rolling round again;
The years keep rollin' by.
Harry Chapin

"It's the circle of life, and it moves us all, through despair and hope, through faith and love, 'till we find our place, on the path unwinding." Elton John

And so we turn the page on the calendar as we complete another trip around the sun, returning to where we were a year ago but different and hopefully better.

Every Day Excellence was designed to not be a cute cat calendar that you flip to the next month and don't think about the previous image, but a reusable tool that you go through again and again with a slightly different perspective at each use. I hope your first pass through it helped you grow, helped you fill in voids and heal, and maybe broadened your perspective in some relevant ways. Repeating the exercises again over another cycle will undoubtedly be redundant in some ways but refreshing like watching a favorite movie or hearing that song you loved a decade ago. Yet it will also be new in many ways as the person you are today is not the person you were a year ago, and that evolution has hopefully been aided in some small way by this work.

If you can look back at the previous version of yourself and have found this helpful to your growth, I ask that you share your experiences to help others. Post on social media if that is your thing. Or discuss a quote with a coworker. Give a copy of the book to a friend or family member. The beautiful thing about ideas is that when shared, they multiply instead of being exhausted like other resources.

You can be the catalytic event in helping someone beyond your circle, a ripple that affects others in a positive way you can never know. I hope that this work is like the wings of a butterfly that creates a nurturing storm somewhere for you, one that leads to beautiful flowers and fruits in your life.

Thank you for taking a piece of me with you on your journey. May the road rise to meet you, and the wind be at your back until we meet again.

Joe

FURTHER READING

"Not all readers are leaders, but all leaders are readers."

Harry S. Truman

Here are some books that I would definitely suggest. And as General James Mathis says: if you haven't read hundreds of books you are functionally illiterate. These are a decent start.

12 Rules for Life
 Dr. Jordan Peterson

The Art of War
 Sun Tzu

The Holy Bible

The Chronicles of Narnia
 CS Lewis

The Lord of the Rings
 JRR Tolkien

The Daily Stoic
 Ryan Holiday

*The Subtle Art of Not Giving a F*ck*
 Mark Manson

48 Laws of Power
 Robert Greene

The Complete Works of William Shakespeare

Your Next 5 Moves
 Patrick Bet-David

Mythology
 Edith Hamilton

The Tao Te Ching